ENTREPRENEURIAL MARKETING:
GLOBAL PERSPECTIVES

ENTREPRENEURIAL MARKETING: GLOBAL PERSPECTIVES

EDITED BY

ZUBIN SETHNA
University of Bedfordshire, UK

ROSALIND JONES
University of Birmingham, UK

PAUL HARRIGAN
University of Western Australia, Australia

United Kingdom – North America – Japan
India – Malaysia – China

Emerald Group Publishing Limited
Howard House, Wagon Lane, Bingley BD16 1WA, UK

First edition 2013

British Library Cataloguing in Publication Data
A catalogue record for this book is available from the British Library

ISBN: 978-1-78190-786-3

ISOQAR certified
Management System,
awarded to Emerald
for adherence to
Environmental
standard
ISO 14001:2004.

Certificate Number 1985
ISO 14001

INVESTOR IN PEOPLE

To Navaz, Mahya, Kai and Kaus, Here's my 'story'!
Nigel Bradley, inspiration personified

To my family who always help me along the path;
Glenys and John Pearce, husband Vern, daughter Liz,
sisters Sian and Ruth

To my brother, Niall

Contents

Part B: Approaches to Entrepreneurial Marketing

List of Contributors

Pierre Berthon	Bentley University, Waltham, MA, USA
Björn Bjerke	Linnaeus University, Kalmar, Sweden
David Carson	University of Ulster, Newtownabbey, Northern Ireland, UK
Amitava Chattopadhyay	INSEAD, Singapore
Jenny Darroch	Claremont Graduate University, Claremont, CA, USA
Blakley Davis	Oklahoma State University, Stillwater, OK, USA
Jonathan H. Deacon	University of South Wales, Newport, Wales, UK
Peter Fraser	University of Hertfordshire, Hertfordshire, UK
Damian Gallagher	University of Ulster, Newtownabbey, Northern Ireland, UK
Audrey Gilmore	University of Ulster, Newtownabbey, Northern Ireland, UK
Paul Harrigan	University of Western Australia, Crawley, WA, Australia
Jacqueline Harris	University of South Wales, Newport, Wales, UK
Gerald E. Hills	Bradley University, Peoria, IL, USA
Claes M. Hultman	Örebro University, Sweden
Rosalind Jones	University of Birmingham, UK
Chickery J. Kasouf	Worcester Polytechnic Institute, Worcester, MA, USA
Olivia F. Lee	Rutgers College, Piscataway, NJ, USA
Andrew McAuley	Southern Cross University, Lismore, NSW, Australia
Morgan P. Miles	University of Tasmania, Launceston, Australia
Adam Mills	Simon Fraser University, Vancouver, British Columbia, Canada

Michael H. Morris	Oklahoma State University, Oklahoma, USA
Sussie C. Morrish	University of Canterbury, Christchurch, New Zealand
Chloë H. Nelson	Nelson's Eye Patch, Norfolk, UK
Michele O'Dwyer	Kemmy Business School, University of Limerick, Limerick, Ireland
Leyland F. Pitt	Simon Fraser University, Vancouver, British Columbia, Canada
Zubin Sethna	University of Bedfordshire, Luton, Bedfordshire, UK
Eleanor Shaw	University of Strathclyde, Glasgow, Scotland, UK
David Stokes	University of Kingston, Kingston Upon Thames, Surrey, UK
Daniel Sun	University of British Columbia, Vancouver, Canada
Mari Suoranta	University of Jyvaskyla, School of Business and Economics, Finland
Can Uslay	Rutgers College, Piscataway, NJ, USA
Fang Wan	University of Manitoba, Winnipeg, Canada
Sengun Yeniyurt	Rutgers College, Piscataway, NJ, USA

Cover photo provided by David Smith from Outdoor Active

I am a determined individual who likes a challenge; be it physical or mental, or preferably a combination of the two! My particular passions are climbing and triathlon. Climbing and its inherent risks quickly galvanise an individual's self reliance, ability to judge risk, and help develop the fortitude needed to complete a task during times of stress. It is this stepping out of one's "comfort zones," by taking risks that promotes self learning, and given a successful outcome, ones confidence to undertake more challenges.

Triathlon on the other hand, for me, is all about training and the ability to plan. Whether that's your time, balancing different areas of your life such as family, or even goal setting, having the ability to motivate yourself when there is no immediate threat is an excellent skill to have. The depth of character this skill requires, and consequently develops, is different, yet and very complimentary to the reactive skills climbing promotes.

I personally believe the combined ability to plan, and be reactive, means you have the best chances of successfully meeting the challenge ahead, whatever their nature and context.

David Smith (M.Sc.)

A little about the company:

The company was first founded in 2007. The focus of Outdoor Active is to help people explore, get fit, and learn through outdoor activities. This is done by delivering high quality courses and activity sessions. At Outdoor Active we are an institutional member of the Institute for Outdoor Learning (IOL) and fully licensed to offer outdoor activities to under 18's by the Adventure Activities Licensing Service (AALS), which is controlled by the Health & Safety Executive (HSE). Further to this we are a Duke of Edinburgh Approved Activity Provider.

About the Editors

Zubin Sethna's Ph.D. thesis examines the entrepreneurial marketing activities within ethnic firms in the United Kingdom, and his research interests lie at the marketing and entrepreneurship interface. As Principal Lecturer (Associate Professor) in Marketing at the University of Bedfordshire's Business School, Zubin oversees the postgraduate portfolio. Zubin has successfully launched five businesses (one of which won a National Award) and in his capacity as Managing Consultant at Baresman Consulting (www.baresman.com), Zubin has integrated marketing strategy/communications with management consultancy and training for numerous organizations both in the United Kingdom and internationally, and across a variety of industry sectors (including Health Care, Professional Services, Music, Travel, Manufacturing, Retail, IT, Education, and "cottage" industries). These 22 years of industry experience allow him to take a practice-based approach to teaching whenever he is in the classroom. Zubin previously taught Innovation and Entrepreneurship on the AMBA accredited MBA program at the University of Westminster, and prior to that ran an immensely popular and successful "Business Start-up" program for creative industry graduates from the University of the Arts London. Zubin is currently Co-Chair of the Academy of Marketing's Special Interest Group on "Entrepreneurial and Small Business Marketing" (with Roz Jones) and has been invited to conduct keynote lectures at HE institutions in the United Kingdom, EU, China, and India, and regularly speaks at South East Asia's leading Business School, the Indian Institute of Management Ahmedabad (IIMA). Zubin also serves as an Editorial Board member for two respected international journals: *Journal of Research in Marketing and Entrepreneurship*, and *Journal of Urban Regeneration and Renewal*. In addition to this, Zubin has also previously been instrumental in attracting funding in excess of £350k for academic projects from leading public and private bodies such as Department for Education and Skills (DfES), Learning and Skills Council UK, and Harrods!

Rosalind Jones is a Lecturer in Marketing at the University of Birmingham, UK, and a Fellow of the Higher Education Academy (FHEA). Previously she was Lecturer at Bangor Business School, Wales and Visiting Professor at Jyvaskyla University, Finland. She teaches entrepreneurship at SIM, the Singapore Institute of Management. She is an active member of ISBE, the Institute of Small Business and Enterprise, a founder member of GIKA the Global Innovation and Knowledge Academy, and on the steering committee of the University of Illinois Chicago (UIC)/American Marketing Association (AMA) Marketing and Entrepreneurship Interface Group, USA. Rosalind is also a Member of the Academy of Marketing (AM), UK and she co-chairs the Academy of Marketing Special Interest Group in Small Business and Entrepreneurial Marketing with Zubin Sethna. She is a member of the "Senior Levitt Group" at the Chartered Institute of Marketing (CIM), and a "Chartered Marketer." She is the CIM SME Ambassador for North Wales. Her research interests include entrepreneurship and small business, entrepreneurial marketing, and more specifically, marketing in SMEs. Her current research focus is on technology and hospitality industries, innovation, e-marketing in SMEs, internationalization strategies, and the strategic orientation of SMEs. She has published in leading marketing and small business journals including the *Journal of Research in Marketing and Entrepreneurship*, *International Journal of Marketing Research*, *Journal of Marketing Management*, *International Small Business Journal*, *Journal of Small Business and Enterprise Development*, *The Services Industries Journal*, and the *International Journal of Entrepreneurial Behaviour and Research*. Rosalind serves on the Editorial Advisory boards of Management Decision and the *Journal of Research in Marketing and Entrepreneurship*. She is a reviewer for several other international journals and conferences in this field. In 2012 she received the Emerald Outstanding Reviewer of the Year and her paper (Jones & Rowley) published in the *International Small Business Journal* was a top "most read" paper in 2012.

Paul Harrigan is an Assistant Professor of Marketing at the University of Western Australia. He received his Ph.D. on the topic of CRM from the University of Ulster in the United Kingdom in 2008. His research interests span Customer Relationship Management (CRM), Social Media Marketing, and Small Business Marketing. He has published in these areas in journals such as the *Journal of Marketing Management* and the *International Journal of Electronic Commerce*. He also teaches in these areas and broader marketing areas at his home institution in Australia and as a Visiting Professor at the University of Southampton in the United Kingdom and IESEG School of Management in France. He is a member of a range of academic bodies, such as the Australian and New Zealand Marketing Association, the Institute of Direct and Digital Marketing, and the UK Academy of Marketing holding several committee positions that are responsible for conference management, and directions in research and education.

A Foreword: Qualitative Recollections

The Early Past

The year was 1982. A research conference had just been held and the term "entrepreneurial marketing" (EM) had been used without definition or fanfare. It was a by-invitation meeting, approximately 25 attended and a book was to be published with 15 papers. It was the first time that academia had convened a meeting on this topic and the discussions reflected a fragile domain with debate over the most fundamental issues. The term "small business" was used but some warned the scholars that this attached a negative connotation, going back to previous critiques of education in U.S. business colleges and demands to eliminate overly applied coursework and to instead be more analytic and quantitative.

Although professors in attendance deemed this meeting a "success," there was little momentum at its conclusion. The organizer later concluded that it was a "meeting ahead of its time" and history had shown that the academy at that time was not accepting of this topical realm. Yet a small core group of faculty continued to engage in discussions at conferences and the ember from the first meeting was not completely extinguished. One conclusion was that, above all else, scholarly efforts should focus on the marketing/entrepreneurship interface.

The timing was good as entrepreneurial behavior at this time became more policy relevant in many countries around the world and the research in this new interface had potential to yield contributions and fertilize two academic disciplines; marketing as well as the fast growing academic field of entrepreneurship. In hindsight it is interesting to notice that aspects of what was discussed in the early 80s in this symposium have become main-stream in the contemporary marketing discourse of the 21st century. The most important contribution of this early pioneer effort however, was probably to lay the foundation for the future developments in the marketing/entrepreneurship interface.

Fast Forward to 1986

It was decided to once again "test the water" and three research meetings were held in conjunction with the annual conference of the American Marketing Association (AMA), the United States. Association of Small Business and Entrepreneurship

(USASBE), and the International Council for Small Business (ICSB). In each case, three or four hours were devoted to discussions among 15–20 faculty researchers on what came to be called "the interface" — of marketing and entrepreneurship. Unlike the conference in 1982, a measure of entrepreneurial passion began to emerge, and it was decided to once again host a scholarly meeting called the Research Symposium on Marketing and Entrepreneurship. This was held at the University of Illinois at Chicago campus in 1986, with a published proceedings (to become known as the "blue books") in 1987. Three highly regarded scholars were invited to add credibility and address this new subject area: Jagdish Sheth (University of Southern California), Hans Thorelli (Indiana University), and Merle Crawford (University of Michigan).

Two years later (1988) a second Symposium was held with a "Blue book" published in 1989 and a Research Symposium has been held every year since. In some years two meetings were held to encourage engagement of researchers around the world. Two symposia were held in Sweden, two were cosponsored by the highly regarded INSEAD, and one each in Melbourne and Hong Kong.

Fast forward to Milestones

There have been several important research milestones over the past three decades including:

1984	First empirical study of the marketing and entrepreneurship interface in Babson College's Frontiers of Entrepreneurship Research;
1989	Created American Marketing Association Task Force on Marketing and Entrepreneurship;
1990	First Session Track in AMA Summer Marketing Educators' Conference;
1995	First annual UK Academy of Marketing Symposium. Also first academic book, Marketing and Entrepreneurship in SMEs by David Carson and coauthors at Ulster;
1999	Founded *Journal of Research in Marketing and Entrepreneurship*;
2002	Publication of Entrepreneurial Marketing: The Growth of Small Firms in the New Economic Era;
2008	Publication of Rethinking Marketing;
2013	THIS new book! – *Entrepreneurial Marketing: Global Perspectives*

Other major milestones included developing a very important longitudinal research database, originally called the Entrepreneurship Research Consortium (now PSED); and a large database sponsored by the U.S. National Federation of Independent Business. Also, the quality and number of related Journals increased dramatically, and the annual Research Symposium on Marketing and Entrepreneurship added a Kauffman Foundation Doctoral Student Consortium component. The growing number of young scholars bodes well for the future of the M/E interface.

Research in recent years has offered a combination of qualitative and quantitative methodologies, and higher levels of understanding using more advanced methods (e.g., structural equation modelling). Based on an increased flow of new research over several years, we offered a definition of "EM." As debatable as it may be, this definition highlights findings provided by several researchers:

> EM is a spirit, an orientation as well as a process of passionately pursuing opportunities and launching and growing ventures that create perceived customer value through relationships by employing innovativeness, creativity, selling, market immersion, networking and flexibility.

Research as well as anecdotal observations of hundreds of entrepreneurs yields frequent references to the role of "passion." EM is not an analytical, dispassionate concept, but instead a rich, exciting, qualitative process. Research has also confirmed that a marketing orientation and an entrepreneurial orientation are linked by EM, and a day-to-day focus on opportunity recognition is central to the nature of entrepreneurship. So it is no surprise that market opportunities are inherently within EM. Launching ventures in new and mature firms to create value for customers is also a critical part of EM, supported by numerous studies. Qualitative immersion in a marketplace is often far more important than formal market research. And EM places special weight on building networking relationships, being creative and innovative, and being flexible with special attention to effectuation. Perhaps more important than any element is selling. As the expression goes, "nothing happens until there is a sale."

Conclusion

We propose that by combining all of these EM elements, we have a new "school of marketing thought" that is fundamentally different from other schools identified by marketing scholars. There is a great opportunity for marketing professors to fully embrace this new school, to the advantage of their students and the rapidly changing society in which we live. THIS new book is excellent in moving EM knowledge forward, to the benefit of us all. We congratulate Zubin, Roz and Paul for creating such a valuable volume! It will undoubtedly become another benchmark in development of the EM domain.

Professor Gerald E. Hills
Bradley University

Professor Claes M. Hultman
Orebro University

An Introduction to Entrepreneurial Marketing: Global Perspectives

Marketing and entrepreneurship have, until quite recently, remained two quite independent scholarly domains. In 2002, Morris, Schindehutte, and La Forge provided a definition of entrepreneurial marketing as, *an integrative construct for conceptualising marketing in an era of change, complexity, chaos, contradiction, and diminishing resources, and one that will manifest itself differently as companies age and grow. It fuses key aspects of recent developments in marketing thought and practice with those in the entrepreneurship area into one comprehensive construct.*

Since then, research in this field has grown in significance across the globe. Hence, this book presents important theoretical developments with regard to research at the entrepreneurship and marketing interface. The editors have invited acknowledged authors working in this exciting discipline, from around the world, to divulge and present in a comprehensive format, a book which addresses critical issues for businesses, both small and large, from global perspectives. This cutting-edge research is drawn from empirical research and the study of the following topics in diverse country contexts: new venture creation; marketing in small-to-medium-sized enterprises (SMEs); renewal of existing businesses facing market challenges; internationalization; innovative cost-effective marketing strategies and practices, along with recent exploration of entrepreneurship theory and entrepreneurial behavior of individuals and, in organizations.

This book addresses a significant gap in the reporting of scholastic research at the interface of marketing and entrepreneurship. Research in this area is very much driven from the practical experiences of researchers working closely with entrepreneurs both in large organizations and small businesses, who are frequently challenged by the increasing diversity and competitiveness of markets. There are a variety of definitions of entrepreneurial marketing. For this publication, we are informed by the viewpoint of Hills and Hultman (2006) in construction of the book chapters. As such, entrepreneurial marketing can be described as an umbrella strategy which acknowledges three broad areas of research: marketing that takes place in new ventures or SMEs; entrepreneurship activities within larger organizations; and innovative and cost-effective marketing strategies that provoke market change.

Academics researching in this field total over 600 globally. This includes membership of the dedicated special interest groups of the UK Academy of Marketing (cochaired by Zubin Sethna & Rosalind Jones), the American Marketing

Association (chaired by Vince Pascal — Eastern Washington University), and the Australian and New Zealand Marketing Academy (chaired by Sussie C. Morrish). There are tracks dedicated to research on entrepreneurial marketing at every major academic conference in the world, including those run by the above organizations and also the European Marketing Academy. These conferences attract between 500 and 1000 participants. Focusing specifically on the entrepreneurial marketing part of these conferences, they attract academics from the range of marketing subdisciplines, where researchers with expertise in areas such as branding, digital marketing, services marketing, marketing analytics, arts marketing can all apply their topic to the context of entrepreneurial marketing.

This representation of entrepreneurial marketing in academia goes some way to reflect its dominance in practice where, globally, SMEs constitute 95% of all business organizations, and therefore the vast proportion of most countries' GDP and employment. Thus, how they *do marketing* is of major concern. Even in larger organizations, the entrepreneurial nature of marketing is important, and this book also focuses on marketers working in these environments. A topic such as entrepreneurial marketing is vitally important in the current climate where it is creative and innovative marketing approaches in small and also larger businesses that will help lead to economic upturns.

The book is deliberately split into two parts: "Part A — Perspectives of Entrepreneurial Marketing" which sets the theoretical scene and "Part B — Approaches to Entrepreneurial Marketing" which provides some more practical approaches.

Part A: Perspectives of Entrepreneurial Marketing

The first contribution to our book comes from Gilmore, McAuley, Gallagher, and Carson who really set the scene with a piece on the interface between entrepreneurship and marketing, presenting different international perspectives on how these two fields can and should link, the research methodologies and teaching approaches driving this relationship and future directions for an established yet dynamic entrepreneurial marketing discipline. The next contribution by Kasouf, Morrish, and Miles builds on this foundation by exploring the interrelationships between entrepreneurial experience, explanatory style, and effectuation logic in an attempt to better understand the antecedents of entrepreneurial self-efficacy for policy and practice. Thus, contributions to knowledge are made to both the entrepreneurship cognition literature and to policy and practice around facilitating business creation. At this stage the book takes a step back to discuss the language and the associated meaning of words that are used in the highly socialized setting of a small firm. Deacon and Harris wade through the plurality of research views and the historical bases to explore the influence of the spoken word on the meaning and practice of marketing in a small firm context. This stream of enquiry has been pursued based on the observation that small firms are a social construct and exist in contextual suspension. With this new found understanding of Contextual Marketing, we move back to the business creation theme, where Bjerke and Hultman examine the role that marketing plays in various business start-ups, distinguishing between rational and natural business start-ups and today's narrow and broad views of the field of entrepreneurship. Across this matrix of contexts, the ultimate conclusion is that the outcome of all marketing and entrepreneurship processes is to interpret environmental information and transform these interpretations into perceived opportunities. Jones & Suoranta's contribution follows, and presents how SMEs can be innovative or rather entrepreneurial. However, the way in which smaller firms and entrepreneurial new ventures take products and services to market is often very different from large organisations. SMEs face a number of internal and external business challenges which they overcome by implicitly using an entrepreneurial marketing orientation (EMO) which is particularly visible in knowledge intensive high-technology sectors. The research findings used to make the point that not all SMEs are entrepreneurial show that firm focus on marketing is different in each region and that firm orientation is often different, which inevitably impacts on firm development and growth. In the next chapter, Uslay, Yeniyurt, and Lee discuss how SMEs can use entrepreneurial marketing to internationalise into developing economies. They maintain that SMEs should strive to provide customization at levels that global players are unable or unwilling to provide. This should lead to niche-customer loyalty and allow for the emergence of global specialists. Second, where small firms may have less to lose from experimentation in their international efforts, they should be the ones to take risks (and grasp opportunities) with social media, viral/buzz marketing, and other evolving marketing media. So, having ascertained that all businesses, large and small, begin with an opportunity, it is this premise on which Morris, Davis, Mills, Pitt, and Berthon build their discussion around the need to better understand opportunity. Marketing has tended to define opportunity around customers, while entrepreneurship has tended to focus on opportunity recognition as a personal orientation or skill. The gap that their chapter fills is a richer sense of the underlying nature of opportunities, their associated properties, their sources and how they come about, and the roles marketers and entrepreneurs play in defining an opportunity as it emerges. Part and parcel of the personal orientation is a key business strategy which we know as networking. In her chapter, Shaw, looks at how SMEs proactively utilize a complex web of networks to access the resources necessary for their creation, development, growth and sustainability. The chapter opens by briefly considering the entrepreneurial process before exploring, in some detail, the different types of resources needed to support the entrepreneurship process. Following this, the chapter considers in more detail the role and contribution of entrepreneurial networks in providing access to these resources and so supporting the process of entrepreneurship. In this way, SMEs are able to work to overcome their principal limitations of limited resources, expertise and impact. In this final chapter of Part A, we discover that there are more dimensions to entrepreneurial marketing than just large and small firms. Sethna discusses the roles of ethnicity and culture in the creation and management of SMEs. This chapter reviews the past literature from a cultural, global perspective to presents a thought piece and a new perspective on the relationship between "modern-day" networks and SMEs. Vast and varied viewpoints are touched upon including historical globalization, ethnicity as a conceptual culture emulsifier, cultural values, absorption, and "multi-local" identities not to mention the issues related to diasporic meaning and its relevance to contemporary SMEs. Sethna introduces the key notion of trust and its role as a binding agent of diaspora and networking activity and proposes that despite the fact that interrelated factors such as market conditions, selective migration, culture, social networks, and group strategy (i.e., the relationship between opportunity and ethnic characteristic) have developed over a long period of time, the resulting conceptual patterns drawn in the field of entrepreneurial networks by the diasporic SME is very similar to the patterns being drawn by SMEs in 2013, a suggestion that we are "going around in circles."

Part B: Approaches to Entrepreneurial Marketing

Part B starts by doffing its cap to corporate or large firm marketing with Darroch, Morrish, Deacon, and Miles discussing how entrepreneurial marketing is very much alive in large firms. They present three alternative means to create competitive advantage, summarized as cost reduction, superior quality or leveraging a shift in consumer behavior, and/or radical, disruptive, proactive innovation to develop a competitive advantage based upon the creation of a new product market space. It is this third strategy on which they focus and through which entrepreneurial marketing becomes vital. To follow this, O'Dwyer and Gilmore look at the specific ways in which SMEs can innovate in their marketing activities, adapting the theoretical TAPE framework (Transformation, Assimilation, Prediction, and Exceptionality) to categorize SME Innovative Marketing constructs like marketing variables, modification, integrated marketing, customer focus, market focus, and unique proposition. They conclude on the importance of maintaining a profit-based vision and marketing being driven by customers. And it is "customers" that we stay with for the next chapter. Harrigan focuses on how SMEs manage one component of their network; their customers! He presents research showing how SMEs carry out customer relationship management (CRM), and use new social media technologies as part of "social CRM." It is clear that marketing in SMEs is different from marketing in larger organizations, but many of the strategies and subsequent terminologies that are often related to marketing in large organizations actually originated in small business. CRM is one such means of marketing. The next chapter, by Stokes and Nelson, is the second to examine social media use in SMEs. They begin by recognizing the historical mismatch between marketing theory and SME marketing practice, particularly at the level of marketing tactics in, for example, marketing communications. Here, marketers rely heavily on recommendations that involve direct customer contact and word of mouth communications. However, the point they ultimately make is that social media may be the marketing tool that is leading to a convergence between corporate marketing and entrepreneurial marketing. From word of mouth to brand, the next contribution by Wan, Chattopadhyay, and Sun starts off with the statement that a few small businesses take branding seriously. However, with a clear and sharp brand identity, a start-up company can have a successful brand foundation that can mould and shape the company, as it grows from a small business to becoming an established corporation through the creation of a sharply differentiated brand image. Conversely, without a solid brand foundation, a start-up can get lost in its routine business functions and never fully evolve to become a significant player in its industry and target segment. Brand strategy, they argue, is therefore as important as business strategy. The final contribution to our book comes from Fraser, and comes right back to the soloist in entrepreneurial marketing, or the sole trader. Fraser highlights the trend that all businesses are streamlining, from the largest to the smallest. However, it is true that the number of employees surviving the changes in large corporations is declining and the number surviving in small organisations is increasing. More than that, there are more and more individuals who are going out into business on their own. The extent to which many in the arts, crafts, trades and professions earn their living working "on their own" is often overlooked. However, the local and the small scale efforts of the soloist can also be viewed collectively and globally. From this perspective, individual enterprise whether full time or part time, even on the smallest scale can be seen as significant in the context of identity, economic and personal development, and the creative potential emerging from relating. This chapter looks at how these soloists, technically the solo self-employed, operate and survive in the United Kingdom today.

History has shown us that in nearly every previous global economic downturn, it is the new, entrepreneurial or growth businesses that have pulled the economy out of a recession. Jim Spanfeller, former president and CEO of Forbes alluded to this in a 2009 interview with bigthink.com. In December 2010, David Cairncross of the CBI's Economics and Enterprise Directorate recommended in an SME Council Paper that the UK government should *Focus on growing businesses. Policymakers must shift their focus towards understanding how to maximize growth in the relatively small pool of fast expanding companies.* Robin Bew, the editorial director and chief economist for The Economist Intelligence Unit said to a group of Harvard Business School Executive Education participants in March 2011 *The entrepreneurial process is very important in driving America out of this recession.* Jonathan H. Deacon further ratified this perspective in an editorial in the *Journal of Research in Marketing and Entrepreneurship* in July 2011.

Gerald E. Hills recently commented that "As markets and technologies change, so changes marketing. The evolution of EM and acceptance around the world will lead to more successful strategies for entrepreneurs." Thus, this book delves into some of the leading components of entrepreneurial marketing; the perspectives and approaches which are enabling EM to fast become an established school of thought.

Zubin Sethna, Rosalind Jones, and Paul Harrigan
Editors

References

Hills, G. E., & Hultman, C. M. (2006). Entrepreneurial marketing. In S. Lagrosen & G. Svensson (Eds.), *Marketing, broadening the horizons*. Denmark: Studentlitteratur.

Morris, M., Schindehutte, M., & La Forge, R. W. (2002). Entrepreneurial marketing: A construct for integrating emerging entrepreneurship and marketing perspectives. *Journal of Marketing Theory and Practice, 10*(4), 1–18.

Part A — Perspectives of Entrepreneurial Marketing

Chapter 1

Entrepreneurship and Marketing Interface Research – A Synopsis and Evaluation

Abstract

Within the realms of academic research, it is appropriate to reflect on the genesis of a research stream; assess its achievements, and postulate future research directions. Such is the intent of this chapter that provides an overview of research at the marketing and entrepreneurship interface (MEI). A number of perspectives have been discussed in the literature and these are reflected here. Notwithstanding this debate, and on a more practical level, the skills and competencies that an understanding of the MEI can embed in our graduates through teaching are highlighted. On an equally practical note, the range of research methodologies utilized by MEI researchers are discussed before considering international research trends at the MEI. The chapter concludes with an overview of the work published in the *Journal of Research in Marketing and Entrepreneurship* as a means of illustrating the scope of research conducted at the MEI before considering future directions.

1.1. Introduction

Academic interest in the commonalities, differences, and interface between marketing and entrepreneurship has evolved and developed over the past 30 years. Research at the marketing and entrepreneurship interface (MEI) has built upon the two main constituent disciplines of marketing and entrepreneurship. Although the two disciplines share much in common, many authors have highlighted that entrepreneurship and marketing have largely developed as distinct disciplines (Carson, 2010; Webb, Ireland, Hitt, Kistruck, & Tihanyi, 2011). To some extent, this is evident in the textbook literature, but it is less evident in practice. Both fields have a common managerial foundation and are heavily influenced by management disciplines such as finance and accounting, human resource management and operations management. Both incorporate themes such as innovation and creativity, the importance of being opportunistic, flexible and change oriented, and are essentially process based and market driven (Carson, 2010).

The recognition of these commonalities between the two disciplines has led to the formation of Special Interest Groups, one in the UK (Academy of Marketing, Small Business and Entrepreneurship SIG) and one in the USA (AMA/UIC Marketing and Entrepreneurship Interface SIG) during the 1980s, where researchers and academics have focused their research on the nature of the MEI. As a result, a range of researchers from a multitude of disciplines have become interested in marketing, entrepreneurship, and their interface. In addition, it is notable that another group of researchers have over the years held a succession of meetings focused on international entrepreneurship under the auspices of the McGill International Entrepreneurship Series. Many of the themes explored by this group are familiar to the marketing/entrepreneurship researchers and indeed some researchers participated in both groups but the McGill group was probably distinguished by providing a more "management" focus.

The marketing/entrepreneurship researchers have traditionally come from a variety of background disciplines such as business, economics, psychology, and sociology, and they have brought a range of different research methods and techniques with which they are familiar and applied them to the interface context. A multiplicity of theories and paradigms are now reflected and diversely illustrated in research at the MEI. Historically, there have been researchers in both marketing and entrepreneurship seeking single general theories for marketing and entrepreneurship, respectively, particularly those whose research is based within a positivist paradigm. It appears unlikely, and indeed unnecessary, that any one single theory or research paradigm will ever assert its dominance over the others or gain a universal acceptance. Consequently, there is a growing acceptance that a diverse range of methods are useful for investigating marketing and entrepreneurship phenomena (Anderson, 1983; Arndt, 1983; Brown, 2003; Carson, Gilmore, Perry, & Gronhaug, 2001; Deshpande, 1983; Hunt, 1991; Smith, 2003; Tashakkori & Teddlie, 1998). This is reflected in the work published in the *Journal of Research in Marketing and Entrepreneurship* (JRME), the journal most closely associated with the Academy of Marketing, Small Business and Entrepreneurship SIG and the AMA/UIC Marketing and Entrepreneurship Interface SIG.

In the absence of universally agreed theories, researchers at the MEI have been able to develop research around paradigms that serve to crystallize and reinforce scholarly thought in specific areas within each discipline. In short, while the MEI can be seen as a specific area, it has not yet become a significant paradigm in its own right. However, there has been a considerable growth in the literature pertaining to entrepreneurial, entrepreneurship, and intrapreneurship constructs and a range of subareas involving typologies of the entrepreneur, entrepreneurial development, entrepreneurial management, and SME start-up, growth and development.

The study of small businesses is and should be vitally important in this domain. Today just as ten, twenty or even 30 years ago, most enterprises in any developed or developing economy are predominantly SMEs (Carson, 2010).Depending on how they are defined, anything from 80% to 98% of all enterprises in any developed or developing economy are small, with limited resources, limited expertise and limited impact on the market sector where they operate. With so many enterprises under-served by academic research and learning, the MEI domain has sought to take account of the nature of SMEs and the impact their characteristics will have on how they do business and especially in relation to marketing.

Over the years, studies of SME start-up owners and small growing firms have illustrated that they are not "typical" business men/women. In starting up their businesses, they are often inherently entrepreneurial in terms of looking for an innovative solution to a market-related problem (Gilmore, 2011). The focus of much of the early research in this domain was on the entrepreneur or owner/manager, rather than the firm and so the research methods were designed to encapsulate the individual's characteristics and decision-making behaviors. The "process" behind the decision and actions, that is, how and why decisions are made was fundamental to understanding the nature of marketing at the interface (Carson et al., 2001; Hill, 2001), in the early days.

In this chapter, we will present an overview of research at the MEI. This is not necessarily an agreed domain and so the next section will consider different perspectives that have been put forward within the research. The importance of teaching at the MEI and its relevance in today's post-Global Financial Crisis world economy will highlight the skills and competencies that both entrepreneurship and marketing can bring to the higher order thinking of our graduates. A core element of this chapter is to review the methodologies utilized by MEI researchers and to review the work dedicated to international perspectives on the MEI. To illustrate the range and scope of research at the MEI, all of the papers published in JRME (the journal that in itself was a product of the activity of researchers working at the Interface) from 2000 to 2011 were analyzed, and the research themes of these papers are discussed in the last section of the chapter.

1.2. Differing Perspectives at the Interface

There have been considerable attempts to conceptualize and organize research relating to marketing and entrepreneurship in order to emphasize and acknowledge the theoretical perspectives and build on the collective theory generated from over 30 years of research.

The historical starting point of much of the research at the interface was to consider the commonalities between marketing and entrepreneurship. Given that all businesses, whether start-ups or well-established companies need to provide a product/service offering for a market, with a suitable price and promotional message, they need to carry out some fundamental marketing activities.

Research at the interface illustrated that some researchers and practitioners view marketing through an entrepreneurial lens, that is, they plan and execute marketing activities by applying an entrepreneurial focus. Studies of entrepreneurs and small businesses illustrated that although marketing was carried out; it was not in the formal, organized and planned manner described in marketing textbooks and was different to how marketing was carried out in larger organizations. Instead marketing activity and decision making was very much led by the entrepreneur and influenced by his or her characteristics and requirements.

Other researchers coming from a nonmarketing background have approached interface research with an entrepreneurship framework, taking account of the characteristics of entrepreneurs and the challenges of working in a dynamic environment. They have viewed marketing issues through an entrepreneurship lens.

Still other researchers have studied marketing and entrepreneurship and, instead of looking at the commonalities between the two domains, have focused on the unique aspects of the MEI. Such studies have tried to illustrate that the combination of marketing and entrepreneurship creates something that is distinctive that evolves from both marketing and entrepreneurship concepts and practices (Hansen & Eggers, 2010).

1.3. Overview of Research Methodologies at the Interface

As studies of marketing and entrepreneurship have progressed, the unit of analysis has varied depending on the research problems to be investigated, but has included the business unit, the firm, its market, or industry. Studies have been carried out in relation to specific projects, within regional contexts, different countries, and comparative cross-country analysis (Gilmore, McAuley, Gallagher, Massiera, & Gamble, 2013).

Over the past 30 years MEI research has developed beyond reliance upon positivist-based quantitative methodologies and recognized the value of qualitative methodologies; there are now many widely accepted methods used to study entrepreneurship and small business marketing. Qualitative data collection techniques, particularly case research and in-depth interviews have been widely used along with direct and participant observation, focus groups, and use of public databases to help expand knowledge of MEI. Mixed methods that combine quantitative and qualitative techniques have also been used.

In the early days of MEI research a large proportion of studies involved causal empirical research. Traditionally in the entrepreneurial field, surveys were used extensively in researching the nature and characteristics of entrepreneurs, and they have become more widely used in the MEI field. They are useful for focusing on a number of marketing or entrepreneurial issues in the study of Entrepreneurs/ Owner–managers (EOMs) and the markets where they operate. For example, surveys can be aimed at EOMs as they are the "key informants" in a study of MEI decision making. Many surveys have been carried out to ascertain EOMs perceptions of the importance of marketing to their businesses, to gather information on how entrepreneurial they think they are, and many other marketing and entrepreneurial-related phenomena. Operationally it can be challenging to carry out a large survey in this field. Response rates are difficult to achieve as often EOMs do not respond because their focus is primarily on their own firm and on day-to-day priorities. Researchers at the interface (Schwartz, Birch, & Teach, 2007) caution that comparing survey results from different studies that utilize different data sets collected under different conditions at different times may only lead to confusion regarding our understanding of MEI phenomenon. They argue that similar firms ought to be analyzed longitudinally and results compared over time. For example, entrepreneurial firms ought to be compared with similarly entrepreneurial firms.

Studies of entrepreneurs and SMEs that seek more in-depth understanding require more than straight forward testing of variables or the use of testing techniques, as isolating and manipulating variables may create an artificial environment and will remove the opportunity to understand the change processes inherently involved in human action and behavior within a business context. Research within the business context is important since small firms should not be stripped of their context (Aldrich, 1992; Borch & Arthur, 1995; Brown & Butler, 1995). Understanding phenomena is unlikely to stem from research administered from a distance. Bygrave (1989) contends that entrepreneurship is not a smooth, continuous linear process, and therefore should not be studied using methods that were designed for such processes. Similarly SME marketing and management is not a simple, linear process. Some research has tried to mirror entrepreneurial and small owner/manager's decision-making processes, even if they are unstructured, to gain an in-depth understanding of the influences upon decision-making and activity. Such investigations benefit from a research approach that allow the phenomenon to be studied closely (Gilmore & Carson, 1996).

1.4. Research Methods and Gathering Information at the Interface

The closer the research and researcher get to the actual decision-making process, the greater the richness of findings in providing a genuine understanding of the MEI. Often EOMs gather information intuitively. They may use a variety of apparently unconnected approaches to piece together a picture of market information that serves as a foundation for decision-making and action (Carson et al., 2001).

Observation studies in MEI research have been useful as a stand-alone method and used as an additional method in the study of EOMs activities, how they act and react in specific situations, and the impacts of their behavior. Observations have been used to delve beyond opinions and what EOMs say they do and focus on actual behavior. Data from observation studies can reveal insights into the behaviors surrounding the implementation of marketing activity and any related entrepreneurial activities in different situations, especially in dynamic or turbulent environments.

Research at the MEI has also borrowed from ethnographic research frameworks. Some studies involving a researcher "living" in firms for an extended period of time have been useful in gaining understanding of MEI phenomena. Being a participant in a company's day to day activities, attending meetings and observing how decisions are made and executed can be very useful. For example, it may provide insight into how company priorities are decided, the importance and priorities given to some areas and not to others, the criteria used to differentiate between important and less important issues, different managers' positions, opinions and recommendations in relation to each current issue and who has the final say in decision making.

Content analysis of company materials has been useful in MEI research for determining the history and development of a company or departments within a company and other marketing and entrepreneurial-related information. For example, the development of a product and service range, distribution and services-related activity, the promotional activity of the company and how it has changed over time.

Conversational analysis can be a useful technique for research at the MEI and for EOMs. For example, this technique can be used with different levels of staff involved in the delivery of a specific product or service; regarding frontline staff and supervisors' perceptions of their roles in a product/services delivery situation, dealing with customers and handling customers' complaints. This can help researchers and EOMs understand the feelings and reactions of staff and lead to insights in relation to improving service delivery.

Some studies have encouraged EOMs to record their daily activities in a diary (Ottesen, Gronhaug, Lorentzen, Bendiksen, & Gilmore, 2007). This has been used for companies faced with a new competitor or a significant change in their business environment. For example, EOMs in the fishing industry in Norway were asked to complete dairies during a time when competition from a company in another country was severely threatening their business and the whole community's way of life. The study highlighted the complexity of the problem and the interrelated nature of the small and entrepreneurial businesses with the sustainability of the community and environment in a relatively isolated coastal region.

Action research has also been used by MEI researchers. Action research is essentially about a group of people who work together to improve their way of doing things in an organization. In relation to research at the MEI it is useful where small teams or task forces can work together to improve their work processes. For example, a small team working with a consultant to run new computer software and incorporate it into their daily processes. This kind of activity often occurs in business but it only becomes action research when it is studied and evaluated in some way. This is usually carried out by an outsider who tries to facilitate a change or improvement in activities in some way.

Focus groups have been widely used by MEI researchers. They are an extremely useful and often cost-effective method of gathering insightful aspects about a research topic; for example, focus groups can be used to identify a range of opinions regarding a business issue, and a manager may bring a team together to brainstorm ways of solving a problem.

There is evidence of researchers using other qualitative approaches such as writing historical case analysis of specific entrepreneurial companies and using storytelling (recommended by McAuley, 2007) to help illustrate the in-depth MEI phenomena within its historic, industry and/or company context. For example, some studies of retailing EOMs have illustrated how a business has evolved throughout two or three generations of people from the same family, other "stories" have illustrated the development of entrepreneurial activity and SME business enterprise in the context of social and economic change.

The use of a combination of techniques can help achieve a wider and more in-depth understanding of the complex, often vague processes and outcomes of managerial decision making in the context of wider business activities and the business environment. They permit the study of the interactive and performance dimensions of decision-making activities studied within a natural setting and can be used over a longitudinal time period, and reflect a dynamic or "change" environment. A combination of methods can be chosen to suit the purpose of the research, and to build and develop understanding as the research time progresses (Bryman & Bell, 2007; Easterby-Smith, Thorpe, & Lowe, 2002; Gilmore & Coviello, 1999; Tashakkori & Teddlie, 1998). There are many advantages of using a combination of research methods to understand EOMs and how they do business (Gilmore & Carson, 1996; Gilmore & Coviello, 1999). It allows the researcher to take account of the specific characteristics of the firm and decision makers in question; and enables research to be carried out within a relatively dynamic business environment. Thus, a combination of methods will provide a useful means of studying the complex, interactive, and personal nature of entrepreneurial decision making. Some of the most commonly used methods used in tandem with each other include focus groups discussions, small surveys, observations studies, ethnographies, content analysis and in-depth interviews. The use of a combination of two of more of these allows a variety of data to be gathered, for example, verbal reports, observed occurrences, written reports, historical documentation, and data involving researcher experience within a specific context.

Research that increases flexibility and variety by using a "pot-pourri of interpretative techniques" (Das, 1983, p.301), and accommodates the study of phenomena from different perspectives is vital for research at the MEI. Variability and flexibility will allow techniques to be adapted for business and managerial situations. In particular methods can be adapted for research in entrepreneurial and marketing situations to take account of specific industry and business contexts, individual owner–managers' viewpoints and idiosyncrasies and organizational circumstances.

Clearly, the choice of methods is important whereby each one contributes some understanding about specific aspects of decision making and behaviors of EOMs, and allows later research stages to build and develop on previous learning and understanding. In this way a rich portrait of the phenomena under study can be achieved. This permits the researcher to learn about the "inputs and outcomes but also gain an understanding of the texture, activities and processes" (Belk, Wallendorf, & Sherry1988, p.449) occurring in the day to day operations and activities and the impact of these occurrences on enterprise activity.

1.5. Pedagogy and Teaching at the Interface

Teaching and researching at the interface requires some careful consideration of the common characteristics or aspects of marketing and entrepreneurship. As an independent discipline and academic subject, marketing came to prominence in

North America in the mid twentieth century based on what is now known as the Marketing Mix or the Marketing Management paradigm, also commonly known as the 4 P's approach. This was an approach developed for and particularly suited to the highly competitive distribution systems, mass media and transaction-based mass consumer goods market and micro-economic conditions of North America and it became the dominant and undisputed paradigm of that time. This dominance can still be seen today in many standard introductory marketing text books that illustrate the tools and techniques of marketing, for example, the four "P's" (7's or other extra-polations of the marketing mix) and management decision-making frameworks such as segmentation, target marketing and market positioning (Borden, 1960, 1964; Little & Marandi, 2003; McCarthy, 1960; Palmer, Lindgreen, & Vanhamme, 2005).

Toward the end of the 1970s and the 1980s, many academics began to question the value of this transactional marketing management/mix approach to marketing – especially in Northern Europe. They queried its value and relevance in an increasingly "hyper" competitive, fragmented and globalized marketplace that was subject to rapidly changing and advancing technological, economic, social and political/legal environmental complexities; and where customers were becoming increasingly sophisticated and savvy (Aijo, 1996; Bitner, 1995; Buttle, 1996; Egan, 2008; Gronroos, 1994a, 1994b, 1996, 2003; Kandampully & Duddy, 1999, 2001; Little & Marandi, 2003; Palmer, 2002).

The Marketing Mix itself (the 4 P's) was increasingly being questioned as a narrow set of variables that overlooked other key variables by focusing upon functions and limiting marketing to short-term "transaction-based" exchanges at the expense of long-term prosperity (Christopher, Payne, & Ballantyne, 1991; Gronroos, 2003). It was even viewed as a straitjacket for toolbox management thinking where "customers become numbers" (Gronroos, 1997, p. 325). Some authors even claimed that it was an easy way to teach students by emphasizing the functional aspects of marketing for those accustomed to this environment; and had led to a pedagogic style whereby students everywhere were learning *how* to market rather the *why* of marketing (Gronroos, 1997; Hooley, Lynch, & Shepherd, 1990; Gordon, 1998; Harker & Egan, 2006; Palmer et al., 2005; Varey, 2002).

By the 1990s it was apparent that this traditional approach to marketing was no longer relevant to the increasingly complex and modern marketing reality of a global post-industrial era and the technological advances in mass communication and distribution of the twentieth century (Bliemel, Eggert, Fassott, & Ballantyne, 2004; Palmer et al., 2005; Sheth & Parvatiyar, 1995). In teaching marketing today it is still important to note the importance and relevance of its underlying concepts, but that it now must go beyond this and requires an awareness, knowledge and understanding that it is also about focus and attitudes.

Similarly, teaching entrepreneurship is about concepts, focus, and attitudes, but these are based on the characteristics of entrepreneurs and emphasizing the common traits of how they operate in a competitive environment. Therefore, teaching at the MEI involves considering marketing decision-making issues from the perspective of common themes (not marketing tools and techniques) and investigation and consideration of new ways of doing and adapting marketing to suit entrepreneurial activity. It is also about asking students to consider the influence a marketing perspective has on entrepreneurship and vice versa. This enables a skills and competencies-based approach to be taken in the teaching that in turn takes the students into an appreciation of the practicalities of "being an entrepreneur." Case-based material, guest speakers and action learning approaches have significant contributions to make in this regard.

There has also been an increasing trend in marketing/entrepreneurship education to expose students, beyond those undertaking business degrees, to the ideas and concepts of what basic entrepreneurship entails. So the creative arts students, engineers or those taking general studies are engaged in basic ideas of business creation and business start-up. This can be beneficial in opening up the minds of graduates to other possibilities beyond "being employed" on graduation while at the same time improving their employability. In a global job market faced with uncertainty the ability to be fluid in working patterns and numbers of jobs undertaken will for some be an important survival skill. An appreciation of MEI will assist in this.

Two broad approaches to teaching entrepreneurship have been used with some success. First, one based on conveying the fundamentals of entrepreneurship and the key concepts delivered in a traditional lecture mode and building toward the development of a business plan. The second approach involves a more hands-on experience-based approach where the students engage in entrepreneurship through the lived experience of starting and running a business.

The importance of marketing and entrepreneurship teaching has probably never been more relevant to the global economy. A recent blue ribbon Kauffman Panel on Entrepreneurship Curriculum in Higher Education (2007), although focused on the USA but has a global resonance, found that entrepreneurship education was critical to a modern business curriculum by stating that:

> First, entrepreneurship is critical to understanding and succeeding in the contemporary global economy. Second, entrepreneurship is already an expanding area of American college learning. Third, entrepreneurship is becoming a basic part of what university themselves do. Fourth, entrepreneurship meets many of the goals of a quality American undergraduate education. To neglect entrepreneurship or relegate it to the educational side-lines makes undergraduate learning orthogonal to the world it is supposed to help students learn to understand.

The importance of marketing in driving innovation, productivity and growth has been recognized ever since Levitt (1960) made the connection between market orientation and business survival. Marketing has become a key driver within many organizations and in terms of the MEI teaching offers students a significant compe-tency that coupled with entrepreneurial awareness is a distinctive advantage. There has been enough research in the marketing domain to support the argument that companies using certain marketing practices achieve a better performance – profits, market share and return-on-investment when compared with their competitors.

The key to this is formal marketing planning, comprehensive situational analysis, looking to the future, undertaking frequent market research, setting aggressive marketing objectives, being innovative in offerings or processes, offering superior products or services at comparable or higher prices than competitors, using market intelligence to understand customers, competitor and general trends.

These simple entrepreneurship and marketing traits or competencies are the essence of what graduates can benefit from exposure to teaching and learning in this area. It can also give them an understanding of the rapidly changing environment that entrepreneurs must face. Following Bjerke and Hultman (2002):

- change is inevitable and some change will be drastic and some unpredictable
- growing uncertainty undermines traditional attempts to plan
- the best strategic resources are insightful and visionary change agents
- soft capital counts – networks, processes, learning
- competition is intense
- being fast is important; and
- technology is rapidly changing.

Set against these challenges is the desire to instil entrepreneurial marketing excellence in our graduates. For Bjerke and Hultman (2002) this entails:

- mastering the value-creation process and finding resources to structure the value constellation
- implementing a value-creating vision and getting feedback
- changing the rules of the market
- leading and managing
- exceeding customer expectations; and
- balancing transactional, relational, tangible, and intangible in the marketing strategy.

All of this thinking, 10 years on, is still very relevant to our teaching today. Researchers and educators at the MEI have a responsibility to prepare students for the world they will work in. The thinking at the MEI has a crucial role to play in this in helping develop the enterprising people of the future.

1.6. International Perspectives

There has been some difficulty in seeking to compare studies of EOM in different locations and with different economic and social environments. To start with, the definition of the SME is by no means uniform across geographical boundaries. Variation in definitions of size and other basic characteristics leads to enormous variation in the unit of study ranging across micro, small, and medium firms. Thus, the transferability of the findings and replication of studies is difficult to achieve as is the creation of foundations on which to build theory.

There has been a general assumption that literature on internationalization had failed to address the particular experience and context of the smaller firm. This is partly explained because much of the early work in international marketing focused on activities of multinational enterprises (MNEs). Many articles have commented on this; it is evident in the international literature that follows the evolution of internationalization from economic trade theory through the influence of pre-export studies and the long-lived stages model.

Despite this, internationalization has been an enduring topic of interest for the research community and it is possible to trace development in theory over time, as it has been applied and adapted in relation to entrepreneurial and SME characteristics and activities. Some researchers at the MEI have attempted to evaluate the topic and state of play in the context of SMEs and entrepreneurs who have expanded internationally (Bell, 1995; Fillis, 2004; McAuley, 1999).

Mapping the historical development of research into the internationalization process and isolating the start of a body of literature is partly like trying to find the source of the Nile; not always easy. In terms of the UK-based literature many authors identify a work by Simmonds and Smith (1968) that focused on the first export order as a marketing innovation. This was published in the *British Journal of Marketing* that later evolved into the *European Journal of Marketing*. By the early 1970s work was emerging that focused on successful exporting (Cunningham & Spiegel, 1971). By the mid-1970s the focus was very much on what became known as the Stages Approach to Internationalization (Bilkey & Tesar, 1977; Bilkey, 1978; Johanson & Wiedersheim-Paul, 1975; Johanson & Vahlne, 1977).

By the 1980s the volume of research in this area was growing as were the themes explored in the research that included strategy, a myriad of performance indicators and exporting behavior. Such was the nature of the enquiry to the various topics that by the end of the 1990s the field reflected a kaleidoscope of contributions that in and of themselves were interesting but the bigger pattern was not being identified in the work. In a review paper at the time, McAuley (1999) suggested some future directions for research, namely:

- increased global coverage, that is, a greater diversity in the countries where studies were conducted
- multiple sector studies to go beyond a concentration on manufacturing and in particular to involve the service sector
- cross-cultural studies to improve the insights gained across international boundaries
- multiple methods of approach to allow different insights to be gained from using a greater range of methods
- increased relevance to policy makers; not losing sight of the fact that part of the outcomes of this work should be relevance to stakeholders beyond the academic domain; and
- interdisciplinary work to be made a priority in order to strengthen overall insights.

An evaluation of the research in international marketing conducted up to 2010 showed that there had been an increase in the global coverage of studies as Thailand, Vietnam, India, Brazil, and Canada appeared in research (McAuley, 2010). There was also a growth in the number of inter-continental studies as Table 1.1 illustrates. In addition multiple sector and cross-cultural studies have increased as a proportion of the total, as has the number of studies using multiple methods. On the down side, there was a decrease in the proportion of studies using a longitudinal research methodology and very little focus on outcomes that might be of relevance to practitioners. In addition Africa as a location for studies was still invisible.

Conceptually no one model has emerged to completely "explain" international phenomena but there is probably general agreement that a holistic view is the best way of understanding the behavior observed in SMEs. While much of the early work focused on the establishment chain (stage) models, economic models or the network perspective (Coviello & McAuley, 1999), none have totally encapsulated the nature of SME and entrepreneurial international processes and activities. As Etemad and Wright (2003) have observed: "… while parts of each theory can help explain parts of the SME internationalization phenomenon, none can adequately explain all aspects of the process." This, at least in part has led to the growth of interest and use of multiple methods that has allowed a rich and deep understanding to be attained. So while a general theory of SME behavior may be lacking it does not mean there are not significant insights in the body of research. Of course it may be that a general theory is in fact an illusion and the sheer diversity of behavior makes a single unified theory impossible. Perhaps our thinking should be altered to focus on a suite of linked theories feeding off a common foundation instead?

Table 1.1: SME research trends.

	1989–1998	1999–2009
Increased global coverage	11 Europe; 5 Australasia	13 Europe; 4 Australasia; Americas 1
Intracontinent cross-cultural study	2 within Europe	3 within Europe
Intercontinent cross-cultural study	None	6 (2 Europe-Americas; 4 Europe-Australasia)
Multiple sector studies	6/16	11/24
Cross-cultural studies	2/16	9/24
Multiple methods	3/16	9/24
Increased relevance to policy makers	Minimal	Minimal
Cross-sectional/ longitudinal	14 cross-sectional/ 2 longitudinal	22 cross-sectional/2 longitudinal

Source: McAuley, 2010, p. 37.

It is possible that in the post-global financial crisis (GFC) world there will be an upsurge of interest once again in the internationalization process of SMEs. Much of the global response to the GFC is based on how do countries make it possible for their entrepreneurs to innovate and create new businesses. Can we now take this potential opportunity and widen the conversation across interested researchers globally and focus more collectively on themes, shaping our conceptual, empirical methodologies used to build a unified perspective on the international behavior of SMEs with regard to marketing and entrepreneurship?

1.7. Illustration of Research at the Interface: 12 Years of JRME Publications

The JRME was launched in the late 1990s to publish research that focused on phenomena studied at the MEI and is associated with the both the UK's Academy of Marketing Entrepreneurial and Small Business Marketing Interest Group and the American Marketing Association's Marketing and Entrepreneurship Interface Special Interest Group. This journal has become an important outlet for studies pertaining to the interface between marketing and entrepreneurship. To illustrate the range and scope of research at the MEI, all of the papers published in JRME from 2000 to 2011 were analyzed and the research themes of these papers are summarized below.

During this 12 year period, 94 papers were published and covered a wide variety of topics. These ranged from those that were set in the context of the SME marketing/entrepreneurial *interface*; some focusing on specific aspects of either *marketing* as applied to specific *companies* or *entrepreneurship* applied to *specific aspects of* managing and *running* business; and some concerned with *research methodology* issues or specifically of use in an *educational and pedagogic* setting. The research focus of the papers is illustrated in Figure 1.1.

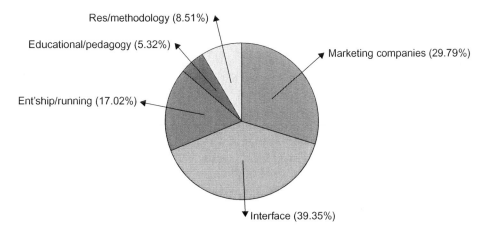

Figure 1.1: Research Focus of JRME Papers 2000–2011.

Some earlier papers discussed the nature of SMEs and the nature of entre-preneurial marketing. For example, recurring themes included SME and entre-preneurial marketing activities, entrepreneurial traits, especially those of successful entrepreneurs and the importance of personal contact networks.

1.7.1. SME Marketing/Entrepreneurship Interface

These papers illustrated a wide variety of topics such as studies of different entrepreneurial firms, the use of networking to improve sales performance, opportunity recognition, life experiences and cultural influences on entrepreneurial activity, entrepreneurial partnerships in franchising, creative thinking, innovation capabilities and technology for competitive advantage.

While most of these papers were conceptual in nature, the remainder used the full range of methodologies with a fairly even split between qualitative and quantitative methods; mixed methods was used in two papers. They also covered a wide geographic area with most being concerned with USA, UK, Australia or were cross-country; in some papers the geography was not relevant as they were conceptual in nature.

Studies covered a wide range of different sectors with many concerned with cross-sector analyses or the technology andmanufacturing sectors; for other papers the sector was not relevant as they were focused on conceptual academic research.

1.7.2. Specific Aspects of Marketing Applied to Specific Companies

These studies focused solely on specific aspects of marketing *as applied to specific companies* and while the value and use of knowledge and experience of marketing, as well as being marketing orientated, were regular recurrent themes, they included a wide range of topics such as competitive activity for SMEs; cooperation between firms; relationship marketing versus sales driven activity; cost driven firms; how exporting SMEs overcome hurdles; CRM for SMEs; branding for SMES; adoption of e-marketing by SMEs; as well as a number of papers based on how to improve the dissemination of knowledge.

Many of the papers focusing on specific companies marketing used a predominantly qualitative method. A small number of papers used a quantitative method or mixed methods. While they did cover a wide geographic area, many studies were carried out in the UK; the remainder were either cross-country or based in a range of countries.

Studies covered a wide range of different sectors with most concerned with either cross-sector analyses or the technology sectors.

1.7.3. Entrepreneurship Applied to Specific Aspects of Managing and Running Business

Some studies focused on a wide range of aspects such as the difficulties and challenges of running a business over time; entrepreneurial/managerial characteristics and types; business strategies and the importance of entrepreneurial and organizational leadership. In addition, there were papers reporting on studies about how to improve business; how to improve business performance; identifying the characteristics of high growth organizations; dealing with the high risk nature of business especially for micro businesses; and how to deal with business failure. There were also papers on the nature of marketing orientation and how it can be defined and is different or similar to entrepreneurial orientation. While in more recent years there appears to be a growth of interest in social entrepreneurship as a subject area and how this can be used to benefit different communities; this was not noticeably reflected in the JRME between 2000 and 2011 with only one paper (out of the 94) overtly focused on it (Smith & Nemetz, 2009).

While a small number of these papers were conceptual in nature, the remainder used predominantly a quantitative method. A qualitative method was used in only three papers and mixed methods were not used at all. While they did cover a wide geographic area they were predominantly concerned with UK or USA; the remainder were either cross-country or based in a range of countries.

Many studies were concerned with cross-sector analyses and the remainder covered a wide range of different sectors; for only three papers the sector was not relevant as they were focused on academic research concepts.

1.7.4. Research Methodology Issues

Some papers were predominantly conceptual in nature covering theoretical debates, justifications and opinions on the range and use of methodologies including the role of science and statistical theory, as well as indications or pointers on future research direction and priorities. A small number of papers were quantitative in their focus and were concerned with either employing a factor analysis in the technology sector (in the USA) or the development of scale measurement in a cross-sector study in China.

1.7.5. Educational and Pedagogic Issues

Some papers were predominantly conceptual in nature, some were written as case studies for use in a class room setting and others on encouraging student reflection and the use of Web 2.0 in entrepreneurship education. There was also a paper that examined how amendments should be made to the UK higher education teaching curriculum in light of a qualitative study (Resnick, Cheng, Brindley, & Foster, 2011).

1.8. Conclusion

In this chapter, we have outlined the development of research at the entrepreneurship and marketing interface. The discussion has summarized the differing perspectives of researchers in this area. Over the years, some researchers have viewed marketing through an "entrepreneurial lens"; others have viewed entrepreneurship through a "marketing lens"; some have studied phenomena by examining the commonalities between both marketing and entrepreneurship; and others have focused on the unique aspects of the entrepreneurship and marketing interface to identify the distinct nature of the MEI.

Research methodologies at the MEI have been diverse and wide ranging depending upon the research problem to be investigated. In this chapter, the different methodologies were discussed and illustrated in the context of MEI research to highlight the value and scope of research over the years. An examination of pedagogy identified that there are different approaches to teaching at the MEI, ranging from presenting the fundamental key concepts in a traditional lecture setting to a more hands-on experiential approach, with students engaged in a more "live" experience of starting and running a business. Internationalization at the MEI has been an enduring topic of interest for this research community and this chapter has traced the development of theory as it has been applied to entrepreneurial and SME characteristics and activities.

An illustration of research at the MEI was presented by examining the research focus of papers published over the past 12 years in the JRME, the journal most closely associated with the Academy of Marketing, Small Business and Entrepreneurship SIG, and the AMA/UIC Marketing and Entrepreneurship Interface SIG. Based on this overview, it is evident that SME/entrepreneurial marketing researchers are interested in a very wide range of topics, with many different themes in a very complex arena of national and international business.

Looking to the future and possible research work in this area, it should be noted that there are many opportunities for further research at the MEI. In addition to specific studies relating to entrepreneurs and entrepreneurship, there is still a strong need for research into SMEs and how they operate. Given the large number of SMEs that are still underserved by academic research and learning in mainstream marketing, strategy, finance, and other business disciplines, the study of SMEs is vital to the understanding of start-up and growing businesses, which as we have noted, are vital to most developed as well as developing economies.

It is likely that the need for research at the MEI is going to increase in the post-GFC economic climate. SMEs and their smaller micro cousins are going to play a pivotal part in rejuvenating communities and assist them to find a sustainable future, at least in part based on a different economic mantra than the one followed by global business until the GFC. This will include an increased focus on social enterprise that, as has been observed here, has to date played a minute part in the literature.

Much can be learnt from the MEI from both a research and a teaching perspective. Much is known and much has been shared by the researchers interested in the MEI. Arguably more could have been achieved in establishing the field in the mainstream marketing and entrepreneurship academies, but that should not detract from what has been achieved. The field is attracting many good early career researchers and that will ensure the vigor of the field for years to come. This book reflects what has been achieved but more is to be written and yet more to be understood about the true impact of the MEI in our economic life.

References

Aijo, T. S. (1996). The theoretical and philosophical underpinnings of relationship marketing: Environmental factors behind the changing paradigm. *European Journal of Marketing, 30*(2), 8–18.

Aldrich, H. E. (1992). Methods in our madness? Trends in entrepreneurship research. In D. L. Sexton & J. D. Kasards (Eds.), *The state of the art of entrepreneurship research* (pp. 191–213). Boston, MA: Kent PWS.

Anderson, P. F. (1983). Marketing, scientific progress, and scientific methods. *Journal of Marketing, 47*(4), 18–31.

Arndt, J. (1983). The political economy paradigm: Foundation for theory building in marketing. *Journal of Marketing, 47*(4), 44–54.

Belk, R., Wallendorf, M., & Sherry, J. (1988). A naturalistic enquiry into buyer behaviour at a swap meet. *Journal of Consumer Research, 14*(4), 449–471.

Bell, J. (1995). The internationalisation of small computer software firms; a further challenge to the stage theories. *European Journal of Marketing, 29*(8), 60–75.

Bilkey, W. J. (1978). An attempted integration of the literature on the export behavior of firms. *Journal of International Business Studies, 9*(1), 33–46.

Bilkey, W. J., & Tesar, G. (1977). The export behaviour of smaller-sized wisconsin manufacturing firms. *Journal of International Business Studies, 8*(1), 93–98.

Bitner, M. J. (1995). Building service relationships: It's all about promises. *Journal of the Academy of Marketing Science, 23*(4), 246–251.

Bjerke, B., & Hultman, C. M. (2002). *Entrepreneurial marketing: The growth of small firms in the new economic era*. Cheltenham: Edward Elgar.

Bliemel, F., Eggert, A., Fassott, G., & Ballantyne, D. (2004). The evolution of relationship marketing and the international colloquia: Guest editors commentary. *Journal of Relationship Marketing, 3*(4), 1–5.

Borch, O. J., & Arthur, M. B. (1995). Strategic networks among small firms: Implications for strategy research methodology. *Journal of Management Studies, 32*(4), 419–441.

Borden, N. H. (1960). The concept of the marketing mix. *Journal of Advertising Research, 4*(June), 2–7.

Borden, N. H. (1964). The concept of the marketing mix. *Journal of Advertising Research, 4*, 2–7.

Brown, B., & Butler, J. E. (1995). Competitors as allies: A study of entrepreneurial networks in the US wine industry. *Journal of Small Business Management, 33*(3), 57–65.

Brown, S. (2003). Crisis, what crisis? Marketing, midas and the croesus of representation. *Qualitative Market Research: An International Journal, 6*(3), 194–205.

Bryman, A., & Bell, E. (2007). *Business research methods* (2nd ed.). Oxford: Oxford University Press.

Buttle, F. (1996). *Relationship marketing: Theory & practice*. London: Chapman.

Bygrave, W. D. (1989). The entrepreneurship paradigm (I): A philosophical look at its research methodologies. *Entrepreneurship: Theory and Practice, 14*(1), 7–26.

Carson, D. (2010). Interface research: A commentary on a commentary – Ten years on. *Journal of Research in Marketing and Entrepreneurship, 12*(1), 8–10.

Carson, D., Gilmore, A., Perry, C., & Gronhaug, K. (2001). *Qualitative marketing research*. London: Sage.

Christopher, M., Payne, A., & Ballantyne, D. (1991). *Relationship marketing: Bringing quality, customer service and marketing together*. London: Butterworth Heinemann Ltd.

Coviello, N. E., & McAuley, A. (1999). Internationalisation and the smaller firm: A review of contemporary empirical research. *Management International Review, 39*(3), 223–256.

Cunningham, M. T., & Spiegel, R. I. (1971). A study in successful exporting. *European Journal of Marketing, 5*(1), 2–12.

Das, H. T. (1983). Qualitative research in organisational behaviour. *Journal of Management Studies, 20*(3), 301–314.

Deshpande, R. (1983). Paradigm lost: On theory and method in research in marketing. *Journal of Marketing, 47*(Fall), 101–110.

Easterby-Smith, M., Thorpe, R., & Lowe, A. (2002). *Management research: An introduction* (2nd ed.). London: Sage.

Egan, J. (2008). *Relationship marketing: Exploring relational strategies in marketing* (3rd ed.). Essex: Pearson Education Ltd, Harlow.

Entrepreneurship Curriculum in Higher Education. (2007). *Entrepreneurship in American higher education a report from the kauffman panel.* The Kauffman Foundation.

Etemad, H., & Wright, R. (2003). Globalization and entrepreneurship. In Etemad, H. & Wright, R. (Eds.), *Globalization and entrepreneurship: policy and strategy perspectives* (pp. 3–14). Northampton, MA: Edward Elgar Publishing.

Fillis, I. (2004). The internationalizing smaller craft firm: Insights from the marketing/ entrepreneurship interface. *International Small Business Journal, 22*(1), 57–82.

Gilmore, A. (2011). Entrepreneurial and SME marketing. *Journal of Research in Marketing and Entrepreneurship, 13*(2), 137–145.

Gilmore, A., & Carson, D. (1996). 'Integrative' qualitative methods in a services context. *Marketing Intelligence & Planning, 14*(6), 21–26.

Gilmore, A., & Coviello, N. (1999). Methodologies for research at the marketing/entrepreneurship interface. *Journal of Research in Marketing and Entrepreneurship, 1*(1), 41–53.

Gilmore, A., McAuley, A., Gallagher, D., Massiera, P., & Gamble, J. (2013). Researching SME/entrepreneurial research: A study of journal of research in marketing and entrepreneurship (JRME) 2000–2011. *Journal of Research in Marketing and Entrepreneurship*, forthcoming.

Gordon, I. H. (1998). *Relationship marketing.* Ontario: Wiley.

Gronroos, C. (1994a). From marketing mix to relationship marketing – Towards a paradigm shift in marketing. *Asia-Australia Marketing Journal, 2*(1), 31–45.

Gronroos, C. (1994b). Quo vadis, marketing? Toward a relationship marketing paradigm. *Journal of Marketing Management, 10,* 347–360.

Gronroos, C. (1996). Relationship marketing: Strategic & tactical implications. *Management Decision, 34*(3), 5–15.

Gronroos, C. (1997). From marketing mix to relationship marketing-towards a paradigm shift in marketing. *Management Decision, 35*(4), 322–339.

Gronroos, C. (2003). Taking a customer focus back into the boardroom: Can relationship marketing do it? *Marketing Theory, 3*(1), 171–173.

Hansen, D. J., & Eggers, F. (2010). The marketing/entrepreneurship interface: A report on the 'Charlestown summit'. *Journal of Research in Marketing and Entrepreneurship, 12*(1), 42–53.

Harker, M. J., & Egan, J. (2006). The past, present and future of relationship marketing. *Journal of Marketing Management, 22,* 215–242.

Hill, J. (2001). A multidimensional study of the key determinants of effective SME marketing activity: Part one. *International Journal of Entrepreneurial Behaviour & Research, 7*(5), 171–204.

Hooley, G. J., Lynch, J. E., & Shepherd, J. (1990). The marketing concept: Putting theory into practice. *European Journal of Marketing, 24*(9), 7–24.

Hunt, S. D. (1991). *Modern marketing theory: Critical issues in the philosophy of marketing science.* Cincinnati, OH: South-Western Publishing Company.

Johanson, J., & Vahlne, J-E. (1977). The internationalisation process of the firm – a model of knowledge development and increasing foreign market commitments. *Journal of International Business Studies, 8*(1), 23–32.

Johanson, J., & Wiedersheim-Paul, F. (1975). The internationalisation of the firm – Four swedish cases. *Journal of Management Studies, 12*(3), 305–322.

Kandampully, J., & Duddy, R. (1999). Relationship marketing: A concept beyond the primary relationship. *Marketing Intelligence & Planning, 17*(7), 315–323.

Kandampully, J., & Duddy, R. (2001). Service system: A strategic approach to gain a competitive advantage in the hospitality and tourism industry. *International Journal of Hospitality and Tourism Administration, 2*(1), 27–47.

Levitt, T. (1960). Marketing myopia. *Harvard Business Review, 38*(July–August), 24–47.

Little, E., & Marandi, E. (2003). *Relationship marketing management*. London: Thomson Learning.

McAuley, A. (1999). Research into the internationalisation process: Advice to an alien. *Journal of Research in Marketing and Entrepreneurship, 1*(1), 11–17.

McAuley, A. (2007). 'If a picture paints a thousand words' – Reaching beyond the traditional for alternative insights. In D. Hines & D. Carson (Eds.), *Innovative methodologies in enterprise research*. Cheltenham: Edward Elgar.

McAuley, A. (2010). Looking back, going forward: Reflecting on research into the SME internationalisation process. *Journal of Research in Marketing and Entrepreneurship, 12*(1), 21–41.

McCarthy, E. J. (1960). *Basic marketing*. Homewood, IL: Richard D. Irwin.

Ottesen, G., Gronhaug, K., Lorentzen, T., Bendiksen, B.-I., & Gilmore, A. (2007). Responding to eroding competitive advantage. *The Marketing Review, 7*(3), 235–246.

Palmer, A. (2002). The evolution of an idea: An environmental explanation of relationship marketing. *Journal of Relationship Marketing, 1*(1), 79–94.

Palmer, R., Lindgreen, A., & Vanhamme, J. (2005). Relatinship marketing: Schools of thought and future research directions. *Marketing Intelligence & Planning, 23*(3), 313–330.

Resnick, S., Cheng, R., Brindley, C., & Foster, C. (2011). Aligning teaching and practice: A study of SME marketing. *Journal of Research in Marketing and Entrepreneurship, 13*(1), 37–46.

Schwartz, R. G., Birch, N. J., & Teach, R. D. (2007). Quantitative methodological considerations. In D. Hines & D. Carson (Eds.), *Innovative methodologies in enterprise research*. Cheltenham: Edward Elgar.

Sheth, J. N., & Parvatiyar, A. (1995). The evolution of relationship marketing. *International Business Review, 4*(4), 397–418.

Simmonds, K., & Smith, H. (1968). The first export order: A marketing innovation. *European Journal of Marketing, 2*(2), 93–100.

Smith, M. (2003). *Social science in question*. London: Sage.

Smith, T. C., & Nemetz, P. L. (2009). Social entrepreneurship compared to government foreign aid. *Journal of Research in Marketing and Entrepreneurship, 11*(1), 49–65.

Tashakkori, A., & Teddlie, C. (1998). *Mixed methodology: Combining qualitative and quantitative approaches, applied social research methods series (Vol. 46)*. London: Sage.

Varey, R. (2002). *Relationship marketing: Dialogue & networks in the E-commerce Era*. Chicester: Wiley.

Webb, J. W., Ireland, R. D., Hitt, M. A., Kistruck, G. M., & Tihanyi, L. (2011). Where is the opportunity without the customer? An integration of marketing activities, the entrepreneurship process, and institutional theory. *Journal of the Academy of Marketing Science, 39*(August), 537–554.

Chapter 2

The Interrelationships Between Entrepreneurial Experience, Explanatory Style, Effectuation, and Entrepreneurial Self-Efficacy

Abstract

The present study explores the interrelationships between entrepreneurial experience, explanatory style, and effectuation logic in an attempt to better understand the antecedents of entrepreneurial self-efficacy for policy and practice. This chapter contributes to the entrepreneurship cognition literature by explicitly framing the interrelationship between entrepreneurial experience-creating of human/social capital, the two dimensions of explanatory style (optimism vs. pessimism), effectuation, and entrepreneurial self-efficacy. In addition, this chapter enhances our understanding of the cognitive conditions that facilitate business creation by proposing a theoretical framework and propositions to advance theory development in entrepreneurial cognition and self-efficacy.

2.1. Introduction

The process of entrepreneurship involves choices, and the actual choice to start a business is only made by a subset of people interested in entrepreneurship – those who positively assess opportunities, accept risk, and ultimately initiate entrepreneurial action, while so many others simply choose not to act (see Casson, 1982; Kickul, Gundry, Barbosa, & Whitcanack, 2009; Shane, Locke, & Collins, 2003). Business creation involves not only the discovery and assessment of the match between capabilities and opportunities but also the willingness and confidence to risk the resources needed to create the venture and thereby potentially exploit the entrepreneurial opportunity (Kreuger, 1998). Moreover, many new ventures are started despite high failure rates, implying that some people perceive attractive opportunities in circumstances where others do not (Simon, Houghton, & Acquino, 1999).

Opportunity recognition has long been a central theme in the entrepreneurship literature. While the concept has been defined in several ways, perception of the opportunity is at the center of most definitions (Hansen, Shrader, & Monllor, 2011). As Krueger (2000) noted, one has to identify an opportunity before acting on it. Thus, the question of why some people identify and act on opportunities while others do not has emerged as a central question in entrepreneurship research (Blanchflower & Oswald, 1998; DeCarolis, Litzky, & Eddleston, 2009; Gatewood, Shaver, & Gartner, 1995; Markman, Balkin, & Baron, 2002; Shane & Venkatraman, 2000). In a rapidly changing global environment, it is critical to understand what drives the job creating, wealth generating phenomenon of entrepreneurship as large corporations, public agencies, and financial institutions flounder. Moreover, while this chapter addresses new independent ventures, this discussion might apply equally as well to corporate entrepreneurship as companies facing rapid change need to continuously renew to compete effectively, and social entrepreneurship where resource constraints combined with increased demand have dramatically altered the business models of many not-for-profit organizations.

The question of who actually will exploit the entrepreneurial opportunity puts the potential entrepreneur at the center of venture formation. Carland, Hoy, and Carland (1988) argued that understanding the entrepreneur is a critical dimension of understanding entrepreneurship. However, previous work has identified significant problems in studying the traits of entrepreneurs, since many characteristics of successful entrepreneurs did not distinguish them from effective executives or other leaders (e.g., DeCarolis & Saparito, 2006; Gartner, 1988; Shaver & Scott, 1991). Gartner (1988) argued that researchers should study the behavior and activities of entrepreneurs, rather than traits. He later suggested that researchers address the characteristics of entrepreneurship that might predict future entrepreneurial outcomes (Gartner, 1989).

The emergence of research focusing on cognitive factors began to address this issue (e.g., Baron & Ward, 2004; Farmer, Yao, & Kung-McIntyre, 2011; Krueger, 2000, 2005). Cognitive factors are a critical element of opportunity recognition, since the discovery of opportunities depends on the possession of information, and the cognitive processes necessary to value it (Shane & Venkatraman, 2000). As Krueger (2005) noted, increasingly cognitive research puts the entrepreneur back into entrepreneurship. The thrust of this stream of scholarship is to understand how entrepreneurs interpret information, construct the perception of their environment, and develop a sense of who they are. While traits such as need for achievement or tolerance for ambiguity may not differentiate those who pursue an opportunity, differences in the perceptions of resources relative to opportunity may impact entrepreneurial intention. Although there is a large and growing body of literature on the importance of entrepreneurial self-efficacy (ESE) (e.g., Chen, Greene, & Crick, 1998; Krueger & Dickson, 1994; McGee, Peterson, Mueller, & Sequeira, 2009), the emergence of effectuation logic as a driver of entrepreneurship makes the interpretation of resources and capabilities critical issues in entrepreneurial action, since these decisions are influenced by the individual's attributes – who they are, who they know, and what they know (Sarasvathy, 2001). These factors or "means" are driven by perceptions of one's abilities and resources. In this light, an appropriate starting point is to look at the central actor in the processes and the antecedents of ESE that can propel an individual to start a business and become an entrepreneur.

The present study develops a conceptual framework that describes the interplay among cognitive factors at the fuzzy front end of entrepreneurial actions. The model is developed in the next section of this chapter and assumes that experience is a critical driver of one's perception of capabilities and intention, but that experience is interpreted through a lens of cognitive bias, impacting perceptions of self-efficacy, and the consequent effectual planning.

A cognitive bias, how entrepreneurs think, reason, and make decisions is a powerful dimension in the explanation of entrepreneurial behavior since decisions to act are driven by perceptions of situations (Baron & Ward, 2004; DeCarolis, Litzky, & Eddleston, 2009; Simon et al., 1999). In our framework, we explicitly incorporate explanatory style as a measure of cognitive bias, and argue that it drives the interpretation of experience (measured by social and human capital), affecting the development of ESE. Likewise, effectuation logic impacts ESE as the entrepreneur attempts to leverage their human/social capital "means" in the pursuit of some entrepreneurial outcome.

The contributions of this study are twofold. First, we propose an explanation of the antecedents of ESE by using explanatory style to moderate the relationship between experience, measured as social and human capital, and ESE. Gregoire, Corbett, and McMullen (2011) concluded that while there is an impressive and growing body of literature addressing cognitive issues, critical shortcomings are (1) the lack of attention to the origins of cognitive variables and (2) the reciprocal interrelationships among cognitive variables and their impact on cognitive action. Likewise, in their meta-analysis of the relationship between human capital and entrepreneurial success, Unger, Rauch, Frese, and Rosenbusch (2011) found that although there is a relationship between human capital and entrepreneurial success, research needs to consider the impact of moderating variables. This study develops a framework that explicitly addresses these issues and attempts to clarify the interrelationships between cognitive (1) resources, (2) variables, and (3) entrepreneurial processes.

Second, effectuation has received significant attention in the entrepreneurship literature since Sarasvathy's (2001) article. It offers a powerful explanation of entrepreneurial planning and action, focusing on available resources rather than end goals. Effectuation logic is dynamic, opportunity driven, and entrepreneur centric. Understanding the interrelationship between cognitive resources (social and human capital), cognitive variables (explanatory style and ESE), and effectuation adds a significant dimension to advance our understanding of entrepreneurial decisions.

Although ESE has been well defined (see, for example, McGee et al., 2009), the antecedents of ESE and its interrelationships with entrepreneurial experience, explanatory style, and the role of effectuation logic are much less understood. Defining the relationship between ESE and effectuation is critical since effectuation is driven by the perception of resources and capabilities. In this model, we propose that

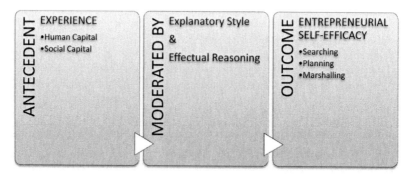

Figure 2.1: Relationship between experience and entrepreneurial self-efficacy.

those perceptions are related to ESE. The effectual self-assessment of the entrepreneur's "means" will change both relevant entrepreneurial experience and their subsequent impact on ESE.

Moreover, a richer understanding of the antecedents of ESE has significant implications for public policy, curriculum development, and scholarship. We incorporate explanatory style as a measure of cognitive bias. Explanatory style is a variable that has been related to success in sales representatives, athletes, and cancer patients (e.g., Fu, Richards, Hughes, & Jones, 2010; Seigman & Schulman, 1986; Seligman, 1991) as the interpretive lens that drives how people perceive their capabilities. In turn, ESE impacts the calculus of effectuation that in turn results in either entrepreneurial action or inaction. Linking ESE to an interpretive dimension is consistent with recent research that suggests that the process through which one acquires information affects how that information is used in assessing opportunities (Corbett, 2007). This research builds on the concepts of experiential learning (Kolb, 1984) and creative cognition (Ward, 2004) that argues learning is the integration of experiences and existing knowledge. Our framework proposes that human/social capital generates different levels of ESE depending on one's explanatory style and adoption of effectual logic. These relationships are illustrated in Figure 2.1.

The proposed framework provides a glimpse inside the entrepreneur's "black-box" heuristic model, and therefore makes a contribution toward a more complete understanding of entrepreneurial intention and action (see Krueger, 2007). The following sections will discuss the elements of the model, concluding with a set of research propositions derived from the conceptual framework. We begin with self-efficacy and entrepreneurship, the center of the model. We then discuss the proposed antecedents of self-efficacy and the impacts of explanatory style and effectuation logic on ESE.

2.2. Self-Efficacy and Entrepreneurship

The essence of self-efficacy is manifested in the confidence to execute a specific course of action (Bandura, 1986, 1997), thus self-efficacy affects the perception that the individual can achieve his or her goals. Boyd and Vozikis (1994) augmented Bird's (1988) model on entrepreneurial intentionality to propose that a task-specific measure of self-efficacy, "entrepreneurial-self-efficacy," is an antecedent of entrepreneurial intentions and goal setting. Shane and Venkatraman (2000) argued that entrepreneurial opportunities exist because different members of society have different beliefs about the relative value of sets of heterogeneous resources and their capabilities to exploit these resources and capabilities into wealth creating assets.

Jackson and Dutton (1988) and Brockner and James (2008) found that the relationship between perceived control and intentionality shifts decision maker uncertainty about future outcomes into positive opportunities (e.g., situations with potential gain, likely resolution, and the means to resolve the issue), and threats (e.g., issues with potential loss and an inability to control the situation). This perspective was supported by Krueger and Dickson (1994), who found that changes in perceived self-efficacy resulted in changes in opportunity perception (for positive change) or threat perception (for negative change), and is consistent with Bandura (1994) who suggested that a strong sense of self-efficacy makes it more likely that people will approach difficult situations as opportunities rather than threats. Recent work by Fu et al. (2010) also found strong and positive relationships between sales-specific self-efficacy and both intentions to sell and sales performance. In addition, self-efficacy seems to elicit a perception of greater control and may explain why entrepreneurs are willing to engage in courses of action that seem risky to others (e.g., Markman, Baron, & Balkin, 2005).

Self-efficacy can be a general concept describing an individual's perception that they have the capabilities to be successful in life, or a task-specific variable that addresses only the domain of interest. Some argue that entrepreneurship is too broad a construct and requires too many diverse skills to have a specific measure, and prefer general self-efficacy (Chen, Gulley, & Eden, 2004; Judge, Erez, & Bono, 1998). On the other hand, many agree with Bandura (1997) that the explanatory value of self-efficacy is enhanced by its specificity. Stajkovic and Luthans (1998) noted that more empirical work has been done with task-specific self-efficacy, and they provided support for Bandura by finding a strong and positive relationship between task-specific self-efficacy metrics and workplace performance in their meta-analysis.

Chen et al. (1998) found a positive relationship between self-efficacy and the likelihood of becoming an entrepreneur and suggested that the critical factors that differentiated venture founders from nonfounders were the respondents' self-efficacy of innovation and risk-taking. Given this, there is evidence that lead entrepreneurs to score higher on self-efficacy measures than team members (Ensley, Carland, & Carland, 2000). In a study of entrepreneurship students on five US campuses, Zhao, Seibert, and Hills (2005) found that ESE fully mediated the relationship between a number of entrepreneurial skills and entrepreneurial intention, suggesting that entrepreneurial efficacy is grounded in developed entrepreneurial skills, and, that ESE drives entrepreneurial intentions.

Whether intentions result in venture formation is another issue. Markman et al. (2005) suggested that starting a venture is a challenging undertaking that requires a high level of confidence, and proposed that self-efficacy drives career choice (since people make decisions based on perceived abilities) and that stronger self-efficacy will result in better performance in the difficult circumstances that entrepreneurs face. In addition, using a general measure of self-efficacy (e.g., the perceived ability to handle difficult situations), they found that entrepreneurs reported higher levels of self-efficacy than nonentrepreneurs. This is consistent with previous literature reporting a strong relationship between self-efficacy and career choice, since self-efficacy drives the selection of a course of action such as one's willingness to persist in the face of difficulties and setbacks (e.g., Bandura, 1988; Betz, 2001).

Restricting the model to task-specific ESE, there are still questions about the behavior domains that are most appropriate to include in it. Some studies have used one-dimensional measures of ESE, asking subjects to self report their confidence for success in a single question (e.g., Arenius & Minniti, 2005), or a single factor (e.g., Baum, Locke, & Smith, 2001; Baum & Locke, 2004). Ensley et al. (2000) suggested three domains of entrepreneurial skills (1) technical, (2) human, and (3) conceptual. This framework expanded on the Chen, et al. (1998) measure of ESE (later refined by Forbes, 2005) that assessed the respondents' level of self confidence in five functional areas including (1) marketing, (2) innovation, (3) management, (4) risk-taking, and (5) financial control. In a subsequent study of nascent entrepreneurs McGee et al. (2009) further refined and developed the multidimensional ESE model to include the following dimensions that assess the ability to (1) identify venture ideas, (2) strategically plan, (3) marshal resources, and (4) manage.

2.3. Experience: Entrepreneurial Outcomes and the Creation of Human and Social Capital

Experience that builds skills, resources and capabilities and that creates social and human capital is valuable in venture formation and performance (see, for example, Diochon, Menzies, & Gasse, 2008; Gimmon & Levie, 2010; Terjesen, 2005; Ucbasaran, Westhead, & Wright, 2009). While it is tempting to focus on start-up experience, a more fine grained view of experience may be valuable in understanding entrepreneurs (Ucbasaran, Westhead, Wright, & Flores, 2010). A prospective entrepreneur typically approaches a new venture opportunity with a bundle of attributes that she expects to increase the likelihood of success. Some of this is direct entrepreneurial experience, while she may also learn through a variety of modes, both in formal education, learning relevant skills in other venues, and, often, having a network of contacts and relationships that will be valuable in running the business or securing support.

A more inclusive multidimensional perspective of entrepreneurial experience that takes into account other forms of experience is useful in understanding the link with ESE. Entrepreneurial experiences that create human/social capital should explicitly include learning (formal and informal education), work and volunteer activities, family background, social networks, and other pursuits that impact a prospective nascent entrepreneur's desire and capability to found a business (see, for example, Diochon et al., 2008; Gimmon & Levie, 2010; Terjesen, 2005; Ucbasaran et al., 2009).

While experience is a driver of self-efficacy not all people with the same experience or stock of human capital demonstrate similar levels of self-efficacy for an activity such as business start-up.

Whether one sees entrepreneurial action as the result of a causal, sequential process (identifying an opportunity and strategically gathering resources) or an effectual process (identifying means and establishing the parameters of action), human/social capital are a critical foundation of opportunity assessment. Davidsson and Honig (2003) measured human capital formation through formal education, informal training such as workshops, and work or start-up experience and found that education and experience were related to nascent entrepreneurial activities such as writing a business plan, but not related to venture success. DeCarolis et al. (2009) assessed the relationship between venture creation and two types of social capital: social networks (professional affiliations) and relational capital (information generated by social networks). They found that social capital was related to venture formation through an illusion by the nascent entrepreneur of control (based on social networks) and risk propensity (based on relational capital). Experience impacts ESE by increasing human/social capital, providing a richer resource base for a person assessing an attractive entrepreneurial opportunity.

2.4. Explanatory Style as the Moderator of Experience and Entrepreneurial Self-Efficacy

In addition to confidence, cognitive styles may also affect ESE. For example, Kickul et al. (2009, p. 439) found that subjects with a more intuitive style "were more confident in their ability to identify and recognize opportunities," while those with a more analytic cognitive style "were more confident in their abilities to assess, evaluate, plan, and marshal resources…" Erez and Isen (2002) found that a positive mood was associated with greater task persistence and higher motivation than a neutral mood, and concluded that positive mood influences the cognitive processes that underlie motivation. They suggested that positive mood may affect goal commitment and goal setting, certainly two elements of successful entrepreneurship and opportunity recognition. In their discussion, they noted that positive affect (an optimistic explanatory style) influenced the perceived link between effort, performance, and outcomes.

Our framework proposes that both prior entrepreneurial outcomes and personal factors affect ESE, as moderated by an individual's explanatory style, the mechanism of how someone explains stimuli in their lives through the lens of an optimistic or pessimistic perspective (Seligman, 1991). Krueger (2007) argued that a research focus on deeply held beliefs is critical to better explain and predict entrepreneurship. In a similar vein, Baron (2008) concluded that there is a pervasive link between affect (feelings and emotions) and cognition. Further, he suggested that this relationship is especially relevant to entrepreneurship for two reasons. First, entrepreneurs often operate in environments that are unpredictable and uncertain, and standard procedures may not be effective. In these circumstances, affect may drive decisions.

Second, entrepreneurial tasks often involve activities that are related to affect, including creativity, making judgments, and forming productive working relationships. An alternative perspective is offered by Hmieleski and Baron (2009, p. 473) finding "a negative relationship between entrepreneurs' optimism and the performance (revenue and employment growth) of their new ventures." Hmieleski and Baron (2009) discussed several reasons why this relationship may have been found including (1) the sample population was very highly optimistic and (2) that previous studies suggest that optimism and task performance are typically curvilinear. In addition, a plausible but speculative explanation could be that optimism tends to be positively related to the new venture behaviors of opportunity creation, assessment, and exploitation, while negatively related to the subsequent task of venture management.

Seligman (1991) provides a very useful description of optimism and pessimism, and measures it via explanatory style – the interpretation that people give to events in their lives. In essence, it is how people attribute the positive and negative experiences in their lives. Optimism is a potentially powerful factor in the explanation of entrepreneurship. Jensen and Luthans (2006) found that authentic entrepreneurial leadership, which they defined as a leader who is able to motivate associates to be future oriented and committed to the organization, is positively and significantly related to optimism. Arakawa and Greenberg (2007) found that manager optimism was linked to employee engagement and performance. While these are indirect associations with opportunity recognition, each of these studies link positive affect, sometimes in the form of optimism to entrepreneurial success. Optimism has been related to sales force performance, where agents' sales volume and tenure with the agency were related to optimistic explanatory style (Seligman & Schulman, 1986), performance after athletic setbacks, where the performance of Olympic caliber swimmers after receiving disappointing feedback was related to optimism (Seligman, Nolen-Hocksema, Thornton, & Thornton, 1990); and illness, where pessimistic explanatory style was related to mortality (Peterson & Seligman, 1987).

The development of substantial self-confidence is dependent on the interpretation of events and the development of a confidence that setbacks can be learning experiences and leveraged to create subsequent success. As Gillham and Seligman (1999) argue, self-esteem produces a fragile self-confidence that does not sustain under pressure and setbacks. True self-efficacy is developed under conditions in which one deals with accomplishments and setbacks.

Explanatory style is measured on a continuum from pessimistic to optimistic, using the attributional style questionnaire (ASQ) for self-reporting (Peterson, Semmel, von Baeyer, Metalsky, & Seligman, 1982; Peterson & Villanova, 1988) or the content analysis of verbatim explanations (CAVE) for the analysis of archival data such as newspaper articles, speeches, or interviews (Schulman, Castellon, & Seligman, 1989). The foundation of these instruments is based on three dimensions of explanatory style:

> **Permanence**: "Is this forever?" In the case of a setback, is the negative event permanent or transient? If the person perceives the setback to be permanent, s/he is left with less confidence that it can be overcome.

Pervasiveness: "Does this affect everything?" If the setback is perceived as something that affects many elements of his/her life, the person will have less confidence that s/he can deal with a setback. Negative events are interpreted in light of a generalized incompetence.

Personal: "Is it my fault?" If setbacks are perceived as being caused by transient external factors, the person will be less likely to interpret negative events as his/her "fault." Thus, confidence is more likely to develop.

For example, a salesperson with an optimistic explanatory style might explain a sales rejection by seeing the event as a temporary setback that was confined to that situation and the result of the prospect simply not seeing the proposal as a solution to that particular problem. That rejection would have little impact on the salesperson levels of optimism and self-efficacy in subsequent sales calls. On the other hand, if the event was interpreted as a general inability to sell then the event would be a rejection of the person, not the product, and not seen as situational, the now sadly pessimistic sales representative would probably investigate other occupations. Considering Baron's (2008) argument this variable is a potentially valuable element to explain the development of ESE. When operating in uncertain environments, there is a high likelihood of setbacks, and how these are negotiated could affect entrepreneurial success. These linkages are summarized in Table 2.1 that adapts McGee et al. (2009) conceptualization of ESE into an effectuation logic framework with examples.

2.5. Experience and Entrepreneurial Self-Efficacy

One of the most appealing elements of exploring self-efficacy is that it is malleable and can be developed in individuals, either as an individual or public policy initiative. Thus, if we would like to increase entrepreneurial behavior in a region, we can develop mechanisms to increase the self-efficacy of the region's nascent entrepreneurs with programs targeted to help nascent entrepreneurs develop ESE. But what are these experience based factors that can enhance ESE? Bandura (1982, 1997) identified four factors that influence self-efficacy:

Enactive mastery: Repeated performance of the task specific skill is the most powerful driver of self-efficacy because the person becomes convinced that s/he has the ability to succeed and becomes resilient in the face of failure and setbacks.

Vicarious experience: When observing another person perceived to be similar to oneself performing/demonstrating a skill, one's own self-efficacy can increase. This process, also called modeling is not as effective as enactive mastery, but may be beneficial when enactive mastery is not possible (Gist, 1987), or as a supplement to enactive mastery.

Table 2.1: Entrepreneurial self-efficacy from an effectuation logic perspective.

Effectuation Logic Questions[a] (The interpretation of ESE)	Link To Explanatiory Style (The lens through which the nascent entrepreneur perceive themselves and the environment)	Dimensions of ESE[b] (The self-perception of selected entrepreneurial skills)
What do I have (what are my means)? Who am I? Who do I know? What do I know? What resources do I control?	OPTIMISTS: Recognizes attractive opportunities that are exploitable with the "means" that they control. PESSIMISTS: Searches the environment; perceives that there are NO attractive opportunities that are "exploitable" with the means that they control, even if there are.	SEARCHING
Where I am now in terms of venture creation & what can I do with it?	OPTIMISTS: Perceives that they have the means to successfully exploit the opportunity and DO NOT FORMALLY ENGAGE IN PLANNING. PESSIMISTS: Perceive that investing in planning may offer a reason to NOT pursue the entrepreneurial opportunity.	PLANNING
How can I combine who I am with what I know, with who I know, and what I control most effectively and efficiently?	OPTIMISTS: Attempt to SYMBIOTICALLY combine and leverage their set of "means" to EXPLOIT the entrepreneurial opportunity and create new wealth. PESSIMISTS: Fret over the organization of resources to the extent that they never actually combine resources to create new wealth.	MARSHALLING

Table 2.1: (*Continued*)

Effectuation Logic Questions[a] (The interpretation of ESE)	Link To Explanatiory Style (The lens through which the nascent entrepreneur perceive themselves and the environment)	Dimensions of ESE[b] (The self-perception of selected entrepreneurial skills)
What do I need to do to exploit these "means?" Where do I go from here?	OPTIMISTS: Failure and adversity is seen as a normal part of business and a learning experience. New entrepreneurial initiatives are developed from the ashes of failed efforts by reallocating their resources to better opportunities. PESSIMISTS: If they start a venture and there is any adversity then they "retreat."	IMPLEMENTION

[a]Adapted from Sarasvathy (2001).
[b]Adapted from McGee et al. (2009).

Verbal persuasion: This is the process that tries to convince a person that s/he is capable of performing the behavior. This may be the strategy of an effective mentor.

Physiological arousal: When an individual is in an aroused and anxious state, self-efficacy may be activated or inhibited if the physiological reaction is positive or negative respectively. Thus a positive arousal (e.g., excitement with the task) encourages the individual to engage whereas a negative arousal (e.g., anxiety over the task) inhibits self-efficacy.

These four dimensions that Bandura (1982, 1997) found of experience can be developed and managed to create a viable entrepreneurial ecosystem. For example, the SPARK Entrepreneurial Challenge program for students at the University of Auckland builds on all four factors to develop in interested students (of all levels and from all areas of study) a high level of ESE (see www.spark.auckland.ac.nz) through their entrepreneurial eco-system including (1) creating a level of *enactive mastery* in students by facilitating student business venturing and start-ups with formal university courses in entrepreneurship, workshops in entrepreneurship, competitive funding, angel investments, management assistance, and a top ranked venture incubator; (2) providing the opportunity to *vicariously experience* entrepreneurship through speakers and workshop presenters who were former SPARK participants; (3) creating a supportive climate for entrepreneurship with *positive verbal persuasion* and support; and (4) generating tremendous *physiological arousal* by hosting high stakes venture funding competitions for the students where the winners of the contest are awarded seed funding to develop their business – and building the human/social capital of the SPARK program participants.

Likewise, enactive mastery can be developed through youth development and business leadership programs such as Junior Achievement, Distributive Education Clubs of America (DECA), or Collegiate Entrepreneurs' Organization (CEO). In addition, formal university entrepreneurial education, short-term management development programs, and on-the-job training (OJT) experiences such as working in a family business or other entrepreneurial venture can provide a nascent entrepreneur with both the capabilities and confidence to be willing to engage in proactive, risky, and innovative initiatives. Vicarious experiences can be provided by the media highlighting successful entrepreneurs, social networking with entrepreneurs, national awards given to successful entrepreneurs, or any other program that promotes capitalism and entrepreneurship as paths to enhanced social welfare. Verbal persuasion can be offered by any form of entrepreneurial development training, such as mentoring or management and organizational development consulting. Physiological arousal can be encouraged by entrepreneurial community projects that create social benefits through competitive grants for developing innovations or entrepreneurial businesses. Table 2.2 illustrates selected experiences that can enhance ESE with supporting anecdotal evidence.

2.6. Effectuation Logic

Sarasvathy's (2001) work on effectuation logic was disruptive to decades of entrepreneurship scholarship that assumed a more causal and sequential approach to entrepreneurial decision making. Her work offered an entirely different perspective to understand the logic of the decision-making processes that entrepreneurs use, adding a dimension to the traditional perspective of entrepreneurship that had previously included three consistent components: the propensity to be innovative, proactive, and risk accepting (see, Covin & Slevin, 1989; Lumpkin & Dess, 1996; Miller, 1983).

Effectuation logic suggests that entrepreneurship starts with the entrepreneur's (or entrepreneurial team's) recognition of their ability to leverage experience into a set of capabilities and means that they might exploit in venture formation. Terjesen (2005) implicitly links experience with the dimensions of effectuation logic when she categorized experience-derived human/social capital into (1) "knowing how," (2) "knowing whom," and (3) "knowing why." Terjesen's (2005) dimensions maps on Sarasvathy's (2001) means such that "knowing how" relates to "what I know"; "knowing whom" to "who I know"; and "knowing why" relates to "who I am."

Table 2.2: Correlates of entrepreneurial experience.

Correlate of Entrepreneurial Experience[a]	Selected Examples That Can Develop the Dimension
ENACTIVE MASTERY (Management capabilities development)	Education: Student Clubs such as DECA, Jr. Achievement, or CEO Secondary and post-secondary formal education in entrepreneurship and small business management Management training and development, Small business management workshops Work/volunteer: Family business experience, general business experience, entrepreneurial experiences creating new organizations
VICARIOUS EXPERIENCE (Role modeling)	Role models & networking: Entrepreneur in family or social network, business angel in family or social network Society & Cultural: Culture values entrepreneurs, culture values capitalism, low social cost of business failure, government support of entrepreneurship
VERBAL PERSUASION (Coaching)	Entrepreneurial mentoring and coaching, management assistance and consulting advice
PHYSIOLOGICAL AROUSAL (Joy & Fear)	The joy of creation, arousal from entrepreneurial success and failures, stimulation from working with and helping others[b]. Fear of the uncertainty of venturing

[a]Adapted from Bandura (1982, 1997).
[b]Dayan and Di Benedetto (2011).

Effectuation logic is embodied by its three core principles: affordable loss, rather than expected gains, cooperative rather than competitive analyses and leveraging contingencies rather than avoiding them. How entrepreneurs effectuate was demonstrated in Sarasvathy (2001) and compared with managers (Read, Dew, Sarasvathy, Song, & Wiltbank, 2009). Morrish (2009, p. 46) found additional support for these principles in a study of portfolio entrepreneurs and concludes "that portfolio entrepreneurs do employ effectuation processes at the preliminary and early stages of venture and portfolio development... [where] portfolio entrepreneurs start out as effectuators and manifest this through the three basic principles of affordable loss, leveraging contingencies and in taking on strategic partners." In her study, she found that while success has not always come easy, many of the successful ventures eventuated through the entrepreneur's determination to forge ahead using different contingencies despite early setbacks. These portfolio entrepreneurs were using effectual reasoning to draw on their life and work experience in pursuing entrepreneurial opportunities, thus demonstrating a higher self-efficacy than those that do not act on perceived opportunities.

2.7. Propositions

The model illustrated in Figure 2.1 proposes that the development of self-efficacy is the result of external events and individual capabilities that are moderated by explanatory style and interrelated to the logic of effectuation in nascent entrepreneurs. Different people may see the same environmental factors, and/or have the same experiences, but exhibit differences in self-efficacy depending on how they explain the events in their environment and their skills. Confidence is more likely to be developed in those who interpret events optimistically. Explanatory style is proposed as a moderator rather than a mediator given the model suggests that explanatory style affects the magnitude of the relationship between the independent variables and efficacy. It is proposed that the independent variables work through explanatory style, increasing the magnitude of explanatory style as an intervening variable. This is consistent with the Baron and Kenny (1986) distinction between mediation and moderation.

Not all potential entrepreneurs have similar capabilities in all dimensions of ESE. Moreover, the categorization of perceived skills into the dimensions of ESE has implications for the manner in which an entrepreneur moves forward to exploit an opportunity. Ucbasaran et al. (2009) note the relationship between entrepreneurial specific human/social capital and ESE. Individuals no doubt vary in their capabilities, thus no two individuals are the same. For example, some people may be well-trained engineers or "grow up" working in a family business such as a retail store, a small manufacturing plant, a farm, or a restaurant, yet have little confidence in their ability to successfully start a new venture despite a wealth of relevant experience. Likewise, the technical elements of running a business are sometimes sophisticated and require significant engineering or science expertise. In others the operations may be less complex but require expertise in performing the many tasks associated with a successful enterprise.

Again, we argue that the interpretation of one's background is affected by explanatory style and one's self-efficacy perception can vary despite encouragement from mentors or family, or despite seeing colleagues of equal ability succeed. Bandura and Locke (2003) found that people can demonstrate different levels of efficacy despite similar levels of achievement. A student may receive the same grades in courses and demonstrate the same level of knowledge as another student, yet not have the confidence to exploit that knowledge.

Related conclusions were drawn in recent studies of entrepreneurial education. In investigating the antecedents of entrepreneurial drive (the propensity to pursue opportunities) Floin, Karri, and Rossiter (2007) concluded that there was not a clear relationship between entrepreneurial drive and specific courses or experiences during the undergraduate education of their subjects. They suggested that other factors such as maturation could account for that development.

Experience may indeed account for self-efficacy among entrepreneurs and mitigate the impact of failure in some ventures. Morrish (2009) found that many portfolio entrepreneurs have a positive view on failure arguing that that it does not matter if one fails as long as they learn from the experience and apply the lesson to the next venture. Yamakawa, Peng, and Deeds (2010) also concluded that entrepreneurs who learn from failure by internalizing the causes of the setback are more likely to succeed in subsequent ventures. While the focus on internal causes of failure may appear to contradict the foundations of explanatory style, they suggested that these entrepreneurs considered what had gone wrong and what they can do to be more successful next time. This is consistent with the feeling that the setback is not permanent, or pervasive.

Three of the possible foundations of self-efficacy identified by Bandura (1997) are based on experience. Enactive mastery (the successful performance of the task-specific skill), vicarious experience (observing another person with similar capabilities mastering the skill), and verbal persuasion (being convinced by another that one is capable of the behavior) are all part of an individual's experience. Human and social capital are effective indicators of the sometimes diffused concept of "experience." However, we propose that the interpretation of experience drives whether experience is converted to self-efficacy. People with the same level of skill may differ in their perceived self-efficacy (Bandura & Locke, 2003). We propose that ESE is developed by experience interpreted by explanatory style. We suggest that an individual's explanatory style moderates the relationship between experience and ESE. Thus:

P1: The relationship between entrepreneurial experience and ESE is positive and moderated by explanatory style.

P1a: The relationship between human capital and ESE is positive and moderated by explanatory style.

P1b: The relationship between social capital and ESE is positive and moderated by explanatory style.

McGee et al. (2009, p. 970) suggest that the dimensions of ESE should be considered as "they indicate that the various types of self-efficacy or underlying dimensions may have individual and unequal relationships to multiple dependent variables…" The first dimension of ESE is confidence in the ability to search for entrepreneurial opportunities. This ability results in the perception of opportunity before others, and drives the entrepreneur to use her talents to develop innovative and valuable solutions. Integrating Bandura's (1982, 1997) antecedents with explanatory style.

P2a: The relationship between entrepreneurial experience and the searching dimension of ESE is positive and moderated by explanatory style.

Morrish (2009) suggests that experience can enhance efficacy in entrepreneurial searching and opportunity recognition. Entrepreneurial opportunities often arise out of innovation and it is important to understand the context with which experience plays a part. She suggests that entrepreneurs view innovation to be intensely context specific. They therefore look for the things in the context that lets them shift innovation to a better space, and always with an expectation of a higher return. Experience in this context allows entrepreneurs to move innovation to market faster and realize returns quickly.

Whereas the above statement suggests less experienced entrepreneurs would apply prescriptive approaches (causation logic), experienced entrepreneurs use other strategies. They may apply a proven system depending on the context or build additional features into existing systems. For example, Starr and Bygrave (1991) argue that experience can be an asset and a liability. The transferability of experience can also straight jacket a potential entrepreneur, keeping them from being able to perceive unrelated opportunities. Experience is then linked in the model to the planning phase of ESE that involves the assessment of the market, the identification of resources to meet the market need (including manufacturing locations and channels), and an understanding of costs. We propose:

P2b: The relationship between entrepreneurial experience and the planning dimension of ESE is positive and moderated by explanatory style.

Marshaling resources involves acquiring and organizing the resources to start a venture, including obtaining start-up funds, hiring staff, and developing a supply base and sales. Unlike causation logic, effectuation holds that entrepreneurial decision making explores contingencies such as resources available to the entrepreneur. These decisions are made in pursuit of some form of return, although may not be fully defined initially. This decision making includes the motivation for starting ventures such as career, opportunity, and lifestyle choices, but it is expected that effectuators will pursue business ideas with the expectation that the result can be any one of many possible outcomes. Therefore:

P2c: The relationship between entrepreneurrial experience and the marshalling dimension of ESE is positive and moderated by explanatory style.

Lacking in all of the previous conceptualizations and operationalizations of ESE is the integration of Sarasvathy's (2001) findings that entrepreneurs tend to be guided not by causal logic but by effectual logic that shapes their business decision making. Augmenting McGee et al. (2009) work with effectuation logic offers a potentially more realistic explanation of how an entrepreneur might frame their self-assessment of their capability to succeed in a new venture.

Effectuation logic is in direct contrast to a causal perspective of business creation, where the entrepreneur was thought to strategically select the product market space that they planned to either create or enter and then by marshalling the required resources proactively leverage innovation to implement a more or less explicit strategy. A causal perspective of business creation suggests a planned outcome. Effectuation logic explicitly accommodates the lack of planning by entrepreneurs during the business formation stage and allows the outcome of the venture to be a function of the entrepreneur's social networks, educational background, business experience, assets, and values. The questions that are fundamental in the effectual logic used in starting a business such as "what do I know," "who do I know," "what resources do I control," and "who I am" moderate a potential entrepreneur's human/social capital's effect on their perceived ability to effectively engage in three dimensions of ESE – searching, planning and resources marshalling. Therefore, we propose that:

P3: The relationship between entrepreneurial experience and an ESE is positive and moderated by effectual reasoning.

2.8.   Conclusion and Discussion

The purpose of this study was to explore the interrelationships between entrepreneurial experience, explanatory style, and effectuation logic in an attempt to better understand the antecedents of ESE for policy and practice. Using work from entrepreneurship and social psychology, we developed a model that may help explain the interrelationship between experience, explanatory style, effectuation, and ESE. In addition, we propose a set of propositions that we hope will help direct future empirical research on the interrelationships between experience, explanatory style, effectuation logic, and ESE.

Experience appears to be the foundation on which both ESE and the capability to engage in effectuation rests. The four components of experience enable an individual to build both the confidence and human/social capabilities to leverage effectuation, intuition, and the joy of entrepreneurial creation. Experience is malleable, with policy makers having the opportunity to create more opportunities for potential entrepreneurs to gain experience through a wide variety of education and management development programs. If experience does hold up in empirical testing across different contexts, it could provide policy makers a tool to better encourage entrepreneurial initiatives.

We suggest that based on this conceptualization, explanatory style may moderate the impact of experience on ESE. Explanatory style can also be influenced. Youth leadership development programs that use positive reinforcement may offer one potential tool to influence explanatory style. However, explanatory style is shaped by many factors such as cultural attitudes toward risk and failure, cultural and individual values, and general economic conditions and may not be subject to explicit policy initiatives.

Effectuation logic can also be a learned technique. While causal logic works well for static organizations in stable predictable environments, effectuation logic is more opportunity seeking, more proactive, more adaptive, more risk accepting, and more innovative. Entrepreneurs that rely on causal logic may never feel as confident in the future, and their ability to successfully exploit future opportunities; unlike effectuation logic driven entrepreneurs who see the future as something that they can shape. In this chapter, we have proposed that the entrepreneurs that exhibit the highest level of ESE will be those whose past experiences provide a solid foundation of entrepreneurial capabilities, are leveraged through an optimistic, opportunity seeking effectual decision-making process.

This chapter contributes to the entrepreneurship literature in two major ways. First, the chapter attempts to explore the rather ambiguous front end of the entrepreneurial process. In addition, the chapter integrates an effectuation perspective into these processes to better capture the primary entrepreneurial initiative – venture creation. We hope that this chapter stimulates further conceptual work and subsequent empirical testing of the framework proposed. In addition, we hope the conceptual framework is further refined and tested for policy makers.

References

Arakawa, D., & Greenberg, M. (2007). Optimistic managers and their influence on productivity and employee engagement in a technology organization: Implication for coaching psychologists. *International Coaching Psychology Review, 2*(1), 78–89.

Arenius, P., & Minniti, M. (2005). Perceptual variables and nascent entrepreneurship. *Small Business Economics, 24*, 233–247.

Bandura, A. (1982). Self-efficacy mechanism in human agency. *American Psychologist, 37*(2), 122–147.

Bandura, A. (1986). *Social foundations of thought and action: A social-cognitive view.* Englewood Cliffs, NJ: Prentice Hall.

Bandura, A. (1988). Organizational applications of social cognitive theory. *Australian Journal of Management, 13*(2), 275–302.

Bandura, A. (1994). Self-efficacy. In V. S. Ramachaudran (Ed.), *Encyclopedia of human behavior* (Vol. 4, pp. 71–81). New York, NY: Academic Press.

Bandura, A. (1997). *Self-efficacy: The exercise of control.* New York, NY: W.H. Freeman and Company.

Bandura, A., & Locke, E. A. (2003). Negative self-efficacy and goal effects revisited. *Journal of Applied Psychology, 88*(1), 87–99.

Baron, R. A. (2008). The role of affect in the entrepreneurial process. *Academy of Management Review, 33*(2), 328–340.

Baron, R. A., & Ward, T. B. (2004). Expanding entrepreneurial cognition's toolbox: Potential contributions from the field of cognitive sciences. *Entrepreneurship Theory and Practice, 28*(6), 553–573.

Baron, R. M., & Kenny, D. A. (1986). The moderator-mediator distinction in social psychological research: Conceptual, strategic, and statistical considerations. *Journal of Personality and Social Psychology, 51*(6), 1173–1182.

Baum, J. R., & Locke, E. A. (2004). The relationship of entrepreneurial traits, skill, and motivation to subsequent venture growth. *Journal of Applied Psychology, 89*(4), 587–598.

Baum, J. R., Locke, E. A., & Smith, K. G. (2001). A multidimensional model of venture growth. *Academy of Management Journal, 44*(2), 292–304.

Betz, N. E. (2001). Career self-efficacy: Exemplary recent research and emerging directions. *Journal of Career Assessment, 15*(4), 403–422.

Bird, B. (1988). Implementing entrepreneurial ideas: The case for intention. *Academy of Management Review, 13*(3), 442–453.

Blanchflower, D. G., & Oswald, A. J. (1998). What makes an entrepreneur? *Journal of Labor Economics, 16*(1), 26–60.

Boyd, N. G., & Vozikis, G. S. (1994). The influence of self-efficacy on the development of entrepreneurial intentions and actions. *Entrepreneurship Theory and Practice, 18*(4), 63–78.

Brockner, J., & James, E. H. (2008). Toward an understanding of when executives see crisis as opportunity. *Journal of Applied Behavioral Science, 44*(1), 94–115.

Carland, J. W., Hoy, F., & Carland, J. C. (1988). Who is an entrepreneur? is a question worth asking. *American Journal of Small Business, 12*(4), 33–39.

Casson, M. (1982). *The entrepreneur*. Towanda, NJ: Barnes and Noble Books.

Chen, C., Greene, P. G., & Crick, A. (1998). Does self-efficacy distinguish entrepreneurs from managers? *Journal of Business Venturing, 13*(4), 295–316.

Chen, G., Gulley, S. M., & Eden, D. (2004). General self-efficacy and self-esteem: Toward theoretical and empirical distinction between correlated self-evaluations. *Journal of Organizational Behavior, 25*(3), 375–395.

Corbett, A. C. (2007). Learning asymmetries and the discovery of entrepreneurial opportunities. *Journal of Business Venturing, 22*(1), 97–118.

Covin, J. G., & Slevin, D. P. (1989). Strategic management of small firms in hostile and benign environments. *Strategic Management Journal, 10*(January), 75–87.

Davidsson, P., & Honig, B. (2003). The role of social and human capital among nascent entrepreneurs. *Journal of Business Venturing, 18*(3), 301–331.

Dayan, M., & Di Benedetto, A. (2011). Team intuition as a continuum construct and new product creativity: The role of environmental turbulence, team experience, and stress. *Research Policy, 40*, 276–286.

DeCarolis, D. M., & Saparito, P. (2006). Social capital, cognition, and entrepreneurial opportunities: A theoretical framework. *Entrepreneurship Theory and Practice, 30*(1), 41–56.

DeCarolis, D. M., Litzky, B. E., & Eddleston, K. A. (2009). Why networks enhance the progress of new venture creation: The influence of social capital and cognition. *Entrepreneurship Theory and Practice, 33*, 527–545. doi: 10.1111/j.1540-6520.2009.00302.x.

Diochon, M., Menzies, T. V., & Gasse, Y. (2008). Exploring the nature and impact of gestation-specific human capital among nascent entrepreneurs. *Journal of Developmental Entrepreneurship, 13*(2), 151–165.

Distributive Education Club of America (2010). Retrieved from http://www.deca.org.

Ensley, M. D., Carland, J. W., & Carland, J. C. (2000). Investigating the existence of the lead entrepreneur. *Journal of Small Business Management, 38*(4), 59–77.

Erez, A., & Isen, A. M. (2002). The influence of positive affect on components of expectancy motivation. *Journal of Applied Psychology, 87*(6), 1055–1067.

Farmer, S. M., Yao, X., & Kung-McIntyre, K. (2011). The behavioral impact of entrepreneur identity aspiration and prior entrepreneurial experience. *Entrepreneurship Theory and Practice, 35*(2), 245–273.

Floin, J., Karri, R., & Rossiter, N. (2007). Fostering entrepreneurial drive in business education: An attitudinal approach. *Journal of Management Education, 31*(1), 17–42.

Forbes, D. P. (2005). The effects of strategic decision making on entrepreneurial self-efficacy. *Entrepreneurship Theory and Practice, 29*(5), 599–626.

Fu, F. Q., Richards, K. A., Hughes, D. E., & Jones, E. (2010). Motivating salespeople to sell new products: The relative influence of attitudes, subjective norms, and self-efficacy. *Journal of Marketing, 74*(November), 61–76.

Gartner, W. B. (1988). Who is an entrepreneur? Is the wrong question. *American Journal of Small Business, 12*(4), 11–33.

Gartner, W. B. (1989). Some suggestions for research on entrepreneurial traits and characteristics. *Entrepreneurship Theory and Practice, 14*(1), 27–37.

Gatewood, E. J., Shaver, K. G., & Gartner, W. B. (1995). A longitudinal study of cognitive factors influencing start-up behaviors and success at venture creation. *Journal of Business Venturing, 10*(5), 371–391.

Gillham, J. E., & Seligman, M. (1999). Footsteps on the road to a positive psychology. *Behavior Research and Therapy, 37*, S163–S173.

Gimmon, E., & Levie, J. (2010). Founder's human capital, external investment, and the survival of new high-technology ventures. *Research Policy, 39*, 1214–1226.

Gist, M. E. (1987). Self-efficacy: Implications for organizational behavior and human resource management. *Academy of Management Review, 12*(3), 472–485.

Gregoire, D. A., Corbett, A. C., & McMullen, J. S. (2011). The cognitive perspective in entrepreneurship: An agenda for future research. *Journal of Management Studies, 48*, 1–35.

Hansen, D. J., Shrader, R., & Monllor, J. (2011). Defragmenting definitions of entrepreneurial opportunity. *Journal of Small Business Management, 49*(2), 283–304.

Hmieleski, K. M., & Baron, R. A. (2009). Entrepreneurs' optimism and new venture performance: A social cognitive perspective. *Academy of Management Journal, 52*(3), 473–488.

Jackson, S. E., & Dutton, J. E. (1988). Discerning threats and opportunities. *Administrative Science Quarterly, 33*(3), 370–387.

Jensen, S. M., & Luthans, F. (2006). Relationship between entrepreneurs' psychological capital and their authentic leadership. *Journal of Management Issues, 18*(2), 254–273.

Judge, T. A., Erez, A., & Bono, J. E. (1998). The power of being positive: The relationship between self-concept and job performance. *Human Performance, 11*(2/3), 167–187.

Kickul, J., Gundry, L. K., Barbosa, S. D., & Whitcanack, L. (2009). Intuition versus analysis? Testing differential models of cognitive style on entrepreneurial self-efficacy and the new venture creation process. *Entrepreneurship Theory and Practice, 33*(2), 439–453.

Kolb, D. A. (1984). *Experiential Learning: Experience as the Source of Learning and Development*. Englewood Cliffs, NJ: Prentice Hall.

Krueger, N. (1998). Encouraging the identification of environmental opportunities. *Journal of Organizational Change Management, 11*(2), 174–183.

Krueger, N. F. (2000). The cognitive infrastructure of opportunity emergence. *Entrepreneurship Theory and Practice, 24*(3), 5–24.

Krueger, N. F. (2005). The cognitive psychology of entrepreneurship. In Z. Acs & D. Audretsch (Eds.), *Handbook of Entrepreneurship Research*. New York, NY: Springer.

Krueger, N. F. (2007). What lies beneath? The experiential essence of entrepreneurial thinking. *Entrepreneurship Theory and Practice, 31*(1), 123–138.

Krueger, N. F., & Dickson, P. R. (1994). How believing in ourselves increases risk taking: Perceived self-efficacy and opportunity recognition. *Decision Sciences, 25*(3), 385–400.

Lumpkin, G. T., & Dess, G. G. (1996). Classifying the environmental orientation construct and linking it to performance. *Academy of Management Review, 21*, 135–172.

Markman, G. D., Balkin, D. B., & Baron, R. A. (2002). Inventors and new venture formation: The effects of general self-efficacy and regretful thinking. *Entrepreneurship Theory and Practice, 27*(2), 149–165.

Markman, G. D., Baron, R. A., & Balkin, D. (2005). Are perseverance and self-efficacy costless? Assessing entrepreneurs' regretful thinking. *Journal of Organizational Behavior*, *26*(1), 1–19.

McGee, J. E., Peterson, M., Mueller, S. L., & Sequeira, J. M. (2009). Entrepreneurial self-efficacy: Refining the measure. *Entrepreneurship Theory and Practice*, *33*(4), 965–988.

Miller, D. (1983). The correlates of entrepreneurship in three types of firms. *Management Science*, *29*(7), 770–792.

Morrish, S. (2009). Portfolio entrepreneurs: An effectuation approach to multiple venture development. *Journal of Research in Marketing and Entrepreneurship*, *11*(1), 32–48.

Peterson, C., & Seligman, M. (1987). Explanatory style and illness. *Journal of Personality*, *55*(2), 237–265.

Peterson, C., Semmel, A., von Baeyer, C., Metalsky, G. I., & Seligman, M. (1982). The attributional style questionnaire. *Cognitive Therapy and Research*, *6*(3), 287–300.

Peterson, C., & Villanova, P. (1988). An expanded attributional style questionnaire. *Journal of Abnormal Psychology*, *97*(1), 87–89.

Read, S., Dew, N., Sarasvathy, S., Song, M., & Wiltbank, R. (2009). Marketing under uncertainty: The logic of an effectual approach. *Journal of Marketing*, *73*(May), 1–18.

Sarasvathy, S. (2001). Causation and effectuation: Toward a theoretical shift from economic inevitability to entrepreneurial contingency. *The Academy of Management Review*, *26*(2), 243–264.

Schulman, P., Castellon, C., & Seligman, M. (1989). Assessing explanatory style: The content analysis of verbatim explanations and the attributional style questionnaire. *Behavior Research and Therapy*, *27*(5), 505–512.

Seligman, M. (1991). *Learned Optimism*. New York, NY: A.A. Knopf.

Seligman, M., Nolen-Hocksema, S., Thornton, N., & Thornton, K. (1990). Explanatory style as a mechanism of disappointing athletic performance. *Psychological Science*, *1*(2), 143–146.

Seligman, M., & Schulman, P. (1986). Explanatory style as a predictor of productivity and quitting among life insurance sales agents. *Journal of Personality and Social Psychology*, *50*(4), 832–838.

Shane, S., Locke, E., & Collins, C. J. (2003). Entrepreneurial motivation. *Human Resource Management Review*, *13*(2), 257–279.

Shane, S., & Venkatraman, S. (2000). The promise of entrepreneurship as a field of research. *Academy of Management Review*, *25*(1), 217–226.

Shaver, K. G., & Scott, L. R. (1991). Person, process, choice: The psychology of new venture creation. *Entrepreneurship Theory and Practice*, *16*(2), 23–26.

Simon, M., Houghton, S. M., & Acquino, K. (1999). Cognitive biases, risk perception, and venture formation: How individuals decide to start companies. *Journal of Business Venturing*, *15*(2), 113–134.

Stajkovic, A. D., & Luthans, F. (1998). Self-efficacy and work-related performance: A meta-analysis. *Psychological Bulletin*, *124*(2), 240–261.

Starr, J., & Bygrave, W. D. (1991). The assets and liabilities of prior start-up experience: An exploratory study of multiple venture entrepreneurs. in *Frontiers of Entrepreneurship Research*, Babson College, Wellesley, MA.

Terjesen, S. (2005). Senior women managers' transition to entrepreneurship: Leveraging embedded career capital. *Career Development International*, *10*(3), 246–259.

Ucbasaran, D., Westhead, P., & Wright, M. (2009). The extent and nature of opportunity identification by experienced entrepreneurs. *Journal of Business Venturing*, *24*, 99–115.

Ucbasaran, D., Westhead, P., Wright, M., & Flores, M. (2010). The nature of entrepreneurial experience, business failure, and comparative optimism. *Journal of Business Venturing*, *25*(6), 541–555.

Unger, J. M., Rauch, A., Frese, M., & Rosenbusch, N. (2011). Human capital and entrepreneurial success. *Journal of Business Venturing*, *26*(3), 341–358.

Ward, T. B. (2004). Cognition, creativity, and entrepreneurship. *Journal of Business Venturing*, *19*(2), 173–188.

Yamakawa, Y., Peng, M., & Deeds, D. L. (2010). How does previous entrepreneurship failure impact future entrepreneurship? *2010 Academy of Management Meeting*, Montreal, Canada, August 8.

Zhao, H., Seibert, S., & Hills, G. E. (2005). The mediating role of self-efficacy in the development of entrepreneurial intentions. *Journal of Applied Psychology*, *90*(6), 1265–1272.

Chapter 3

Contextual Marketing (CM)

Abstract

This chapter is born out of debate and discussions that have been taking place within the sister domains of marketing and entrepreneurship and the call for researchers within those related fields for a "framework, model or paradigm to guide future research at the interface" (Hansen & Eggers, 2010). We propose a conceptualization of the components of "Contextual Marketing" (CM) in light of the outcome of the Charleston Summit (Hansen & Eggers, 2010) through the development of the meaning and operation of language used in context – that is, the language and the associated meaning of words used in a highly socialized setting like a small firm and articulated through conversation. This chapter explores the small firm marketing knowledge gap by looking at the influence of the spoken word on the meaning and practice of marketing in a small firm context. This stream of enquiry has been pursued based on the observation that small firms are a social construct and exist in contextual suspension (after Weick, 1969) and that at such levels of contextualization lexis is developed that conveys meaning within the construct (Chell, 2000; Downing, 2005). This chapter thus contends that an understanding of the lexis of marketing in context can assist in unlocking insight for the development of contemporary understanding and future research within the field of entrepreneurial marketing.

3.1. Introduction

This chapter proposes a conceptualization of the components of "Contextual Marketing" (CM) in light of the outcome of the Charleston Summit (Hansen & Eggers, 2010) through the development of the meaning and operation of language used in context – that is, the language and the associated meaning of words used in a highly socialized setting like a small firm and articulated through conversation.

Entrepreneurial Marketing: Global Perspectives
ISBN: 978-1-78190-786-3

The world of business across the industrialized world has, in the last 25 years or so, undergone continuous and turbulent change. The obvious changes that come to mind are the influence of technology both on firms and the markets they serve, followed closely by the impact of globalization. But perhaps the most dramatic change to affect the way in which business is conducted has been driven by individual small firms, located in local neighborhoods and typically owner/managed. Entrepreneurial small firms have redefined the way business is done (Bjerke & Hultman, 2002; Burns, 2005; Carter & Jones-Evans, 2000). It is a business model that challenges many classically taught economic assumptions: out goes the need to "own" the resources *of* production in favor of a need to "own" knowledge *about* production (Bjerke & Hultman, 2002), ambiguity and change are necessary components for innovation, and complexity and chaos are welcome – long-range planning has become an outdated and paradoxically damaging business task (Stacy, Griffin, & Shaw, 2000), and conceptions of customer centricity are being challenged (Morrish, Miles, & Deacon, 2010).

Some have referred to this change as a revolution (Burns, 2005), while others see such change as cyclical if not evolutionary (Halliday, Deacon, & Palmer, 2005) and others still suggest that business and society are now experiencing a "new economic era," based on the economics of knowledge (Bjerke & Hultman, 2002). Whatever the semantics of the situation, the economic reality is, nevertheless clear: since the mid-1980s entrepreneurial small firms in the UK have created more wealth than all previous industrial periods put together (Burns, 2005), according to the small business service (BIS) there are now twenty million SMEs in Europe. Of those, around four million are UK based (ONS, 2010). Accordingly, there is a consensus among politicians, policy makers, researchers, and business development agencies that the UK is becoming evermore economically dependent on the entrepreneurial small firm sector and that the development of this typology of firm is central to sustained economic recovery as it offers a diversified and innovative basis upon which to build the much sought, "mixed economy."

However, while there is widespread acknowledgement of the importance of the small firm and the individual actors within them for economic well being, there remains a knowledge gap about many of the management actions that small firms take (Carson & Gilmore, 1999; Carson et al., 2002; Carter & Tzokas, 1999; McLarty, 1998). This chapter is born out of debate and discussions that have been taking place within the sister domains of marketing and entrepreneurship and the call for researchers within those related fields for a "framework, model or paradigm to guide future research at the interface" (Hansen & Eggers, 2010).

Such debate has been taking place for over 20 years at annual research meetings where by scholars from both disciplines attempt to discover the uniqueness of research at the interface of the two and disseminate their findings as implications for theory and practice (e.g., University of Illinois at Chicago Research Symposium and the Academy of Marketing Special Interest Group – Small Business and Entrepreneurial Marketing). Pioneering scholars at the interface (Carson, 1985) observed that there were paradigmatic and seminal developments in the distinct fields of marketing and entrepreneurship but little conceptual acknowledgement of the relationship between them. Researchers within the field of entrepreneurial and small business marketing accept that there is a plurality of perspective with regard to how such gaps can be bridged (Carson, 2005). On the one hand, there is an acceptance that some form of adaptation of mainstream marketing management theories can assist our understanding, while on the other, a suggestion that independent theories for entrepreneurial marketing will have to be developed in order to gain clarity of the phenomena (Carson, 2005; McAuley, 2010; Miles & Darroch, 2006; Schindehutte, Morris, & Pitt, 2008). What is observable, however, is that there is a shortfall by the existing, textbook, linear and essentially administrative approach to marketing theory: AM (Administrative Marketing) to assist with a detailed understanding as to what entrepreneurial small firms actually "do" when they "do" marketing (Hills, 2002).

Given the plurality of research view and the historical basis, this chapter explores the small firm marketing knowledge gap by looking at the influence of the spoken word on the meaning and practice of marketing in a small firm context. This stream of enquiry has been pursued based on the observation that small firms are a social construct and exist in contextual suspension (after Weick, 1969) and that at such levels of contextualization lexis is developed that conveys meaning within the construct (Chell, 2000; Downing, 2005). This chapter thus contends that an understanding of the lexis of marketing in context can assist in unlocking insight for the development of contemporary understanding and future research within the field of entrepreneurial marketing.

3.2. Conceptual Antecedence

This research has identified and confirmed the work of others (see, e.g., the proceedings of both the AM SIG 1995–2012 and the UIC symposium 1986–2012) that "traditional" AM marketing methods are not necessarily the most effective way forward for entrepreneurial small firms to "go to market," suggesting that small business entrepreneurs approach market development in a way that has yet to be fully understood by "mainstream" marketing researchers. Further, there is clear identification that aspects of "contextual marketing" stand outside the "accepted," "administrative," or "traditional" view of marketing. These especially include (but not exclusively) the operation and meaning of a language for marketing, through conversation, in the small firm context.

At an early stage of this lexical conceptualization the aim was to develop much of the work of Carson et al. (2002, 2003) in the field of "contextual marketing." The CM concept posits that independant theories of the marketing function exist alongside those which are already known (AM) – however, such an independent, parallel, and emergent paradigm has yet to be fully understood and indeed appear within the marketing texts used within both the academic or small business development fields (Deacon, 2002). It has long been accepted that small firms approach marketing in a different way to that of the larger firm (Bjerke & Hultman, 2002; Blois, 1970; Carson, 1985; Carson, Cromie, McGowan, & Hill, 1995; Gibb & Davies, 1990; Hill, McGowan, & Drummond, 1999; Morrish et al., 2010; Schollhammer & Kuriloff,

1979; Stokes, 2000; Storey, 1994) nevertheless this acceptance has yet to be fully articulated within mainstream marketing or entrepreneurship literature.

Indeed many commentators have attempted to define marketing within the small firm context only to fall foul of the inadequacies of lexicography and conceptualization. As Hills (1995) points out "just as a child is not a small adult a small firm is not a small Fortune 500 company." Therefore, we question the worth of the historical reductionist paradigm (Earls, 2002) when used in the complex, irrational, emotional, egotistical, creative, and conversational world that is the small firm environment – where owners, managers, and entrepreneurs work at the edge of time and chaos, making sense of the world around them through; relationships with others, independent cultural perspectives and language (Earls, 2002; Nilsson, 1995).

Debate within academic symposia as to the nature of marketing within the small firm and marketing's relationship with entrepreneurship appears to be increasing (see for example IJESB and JRME). Areas of debate concern issues relating to: When does a firm start or for that matter cease to be entrepreneurial? What conditions are present to dictate that marketing is taking place? And are there different theoretical constructs relating to marketing, or just differing ways to apply or practice marketing within context?

Perhaps the answers lie not so much with the words we use to describe the theory, application or practice of marketing but the meanings we (and the small firm) associate with these words, and how these meanings are vocalized (or not) in context (Mead, 1934). Mead worked on the concept of "symbolic interactionism" – suggesting that it was the understanding of the minutiae of social interaction that held gravitas rather than a study of societies in their totality. In essence: the small interpretations count. This chapter acknowledges that our "marketing" hearing has been impaired through the ageing process of the marketing concept, but what we are yet to collectively acknowledge is how much of the ongoing contemporary conversation we are missing.

Thus, a confirmation, that there is a growing acceptance of a small firm vernacular for marketing among practitioners is proposed. It is a language system that is based on social interaction and developed within the cooperative activity system that a small firm inhabits (Hakansson & Prenkert, 2004). We therefore set out to suggest further exploration of contextual lexicography and entrepreneurship sociolinguistics, to understand the importance of a linguistic framework that assists in the understanding and meaning and operation of marketing within the informal, self-contextualized and cooperative network-based entrepreneurial small firm. In doing this, researchers may also enable small firms to unlock the potential for entrepreneurial market development and for educators to shake off the deliberating tinnitus of "marketing" rhetoric.

3.3. Contextual Lexicography

Empirical research has illustrated that marketing practitioners within the entrepreneurial small firm environment have their own language or vocabulary for marketing

(Carson et al., 2003) and that the vernacular may well depend on the "tribe" (Cova, 1996; Enright, 2001) to which the practitioner belongs. The "tribe" descriptor may relate to either a sector (for example retail or tourism) or geographic (rural or urban) typology. It is not the use of language here that is of interest, but the use of a language in context. To date much of the theory contained within the marketing literature remains just that – theory. The history of marketing theory would appear, with exploration, to be predicated on a limited number of hard held constructs that have changed little over time, and thus reflect perhaps only the view of academe in relation to practice of marketing (Brown, 2001).

The small firm sector in particular is highly heterogeneous, complicated by social contexts and a high degree of individualism: the rationale of the owner *is* the rationale of the firm (Deacon & Corp, 2004) – in such circumstances the likely success of a standardized approach to marketing practice will be limited. The key actors within small firms, it would appear, like to be treated as individuals and communicated with in *their* own language construct. There appears to be some evidence to support this view, in that the marketing education on offer has been described as rather "theoretical" and of little "practical" use to small firms (Forsyth & Greenhough, 2003) and that the lexicography used reflects that used primarily within the sphere of the fast-moving consumer goods corporate world.

However, the reasoning for such a reductionist view, within "mainstream" marketing theory, perhaps lies in the difficulty in finding a "fit" between theory and practice in the complex small firm environment. There are suggestions that successful learning in this context is linked with the ability of the small firm actor to critically reflect on actions, and thus learn beyond "paradigmatic perspectives" (Mezirow, 1981). In essence the language of the marketing graduate and the language of the owner manager originate from different contextual places. The resulting linguistic operation is the "symbolic interactionism" that Mead (1934) commented on – the "understanding of the minutiae of social interaction" that will inevitably be context specific; shaping as it does the individual's personal "meaning" of marketing (Mezirow, 1981; Walsh, 1995).

There is evidence of a "gap" or "void" of explanation for the differing use and meaning of language when associated with its use within the social setting of the small firm. What is needed then is an understanding of the lived experience of language from those who are using it as a means of both making meaning of thought and communicating with others. The setting therefore requires a social constructivist and interpretivist approach, allowing a mix of ethnographic interpretation, theory elaboration and concept clarification (Rubin & Rubin, 2005) and facilitating an insight to the linguistic construction of reality as experienced by the firms observed: the lived experience. If we accept this approach then a meaning and not the meaning can be interpreted from the narratives heard and interlocution participated in. This approach, it has been argued, (Carson & Gilmore, 1999) is the most appropriate one for investigations concerning the development of understanding within a social setting where multiple realities exist (Guba & Lincoln, 1994). This is especially important where interpretations of social and psychological aspects of language are attempted.

3.4.   Extant Literature at the Interface

A review of the extant literature and contemporary research activities within the field would suggest that there remains a lack of specific knowledge about the contextual nature of the meaning and operation of marketing within the small firm.

As such this is the recognition that small firms base their market development activities – arguably all business decisions – on a knowledge that is derived at a socially constructed level. The socialized nature of this approach and the lack of formality in nearly all areas of business management leads to the acknowledgement that much, if not all, of these actions are at variance with "textbook," "admin-istrative," or "accepted" marketing management practices and therefore gives rise to the concept of "Contextual Marketing" (CM).

3.5.   Marketing in Context

The central feature of much of CM is the concept of a "situation specific" approach and application of marketing, which is contextualized to the individual focal firm and therefore has both a uniqueness and inherent complexity. While this activity is complex, Carson and Gilmore (2000) contend that there are "essential key factors" that can be identified that allow an insight into how marketing is performed within each context. However, these factors are interdependent, interrelated, and synergistically influential in that for successful interface to take place between the firm and the market, firms "simply *have* to perform" (Carson & Gilmore, 2000, p. 5) these activities – they cannot be overlooked by entrepreneurs if they are to launch and develop a venture successfully (Hisrich, 1992).

The next stage of the process is to consider the inherent characteristics of the small firm. These characteristics range from the explicit: the individual personality of the owner/entrepreneur (Chell, Haworth, & Brearley, 1991; Deacon & Corp, 2004; Gibb & Scott, 1985; Macko & Tyszka, 2009) and the influence this trait has on the marketing decision-making process of the enterprise, to the implicit: the limited resources that are available (Birley, 1982; Bjerke & Hultman, 2002; Sarasvathy, 2001). These factors argue Carson and Gilmore (2000, p. 6) "will have an overriding impact on the nature and scope of marketing."

The result is a stratification of influence on how a small firm "does marketing" within the unique context of their specific situation. A pivotal issue is that this uniqueness is not uniqueness to the "generic" small firm but a uniqueness to the "individual" small firm, and hence the importance of acknowledging the social constructive state: the proposed concept represents "how to do marketing rather than what marketing is and as such is highly compatible with SME owner/manager/ entrepreneurs way of thinking, and doing business" (Carson & Gilmore, 2000, p. 6). This chapter, nevertheless, contends that although the "process" of marketing in context has been identified the influence of a language of marketing in context has not been fully considered, Figure 3.1 adapts the original Carson and Gilmore model to suggest areas of linguistic influence.

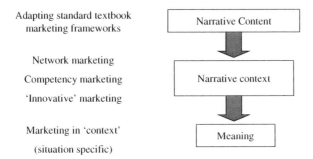

Figure 3.1: Linguistic Stratification of Marketing. Adapted from Carson and Gilmore (1999).

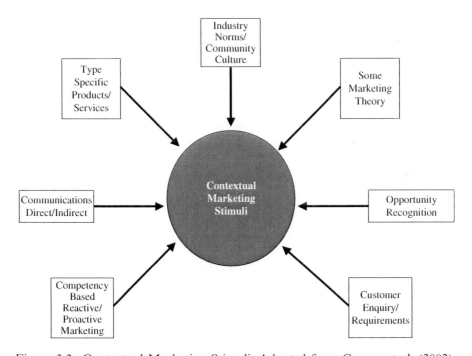

Figure 3.2: Contextual Marketing Stimuli. Adapted from Carson et al. (2002).

A framework of interpretation has been proposed by Carson (2005) to assist with scoping the definition of "Contextual Marketing" (Figure 3.2).

Carson clarifies this framework by stating that the "stimuli" that characterizes and helps to shape "Contextual Marketing" will be the basis of the uniqueness of the context and creates the "situation specific" of the small firm. The framework calls, in part, on earlier conceptual work by Carson and Gilmore (2000) (Figure 3.1) in that it recognizes the subtlety of how small firms "do marketing" by establishing a range of possible factors that underpin, influence, and construct the "doing" of what academe calls "marketing" and small firms call "business." These factors consist of:

i) *Personalities*: that the core of the SME is the personality of the small business owner (Carson et al., 2002); to some extent this will amount to the ultimate differentiator and that the views, personality and even behaviors of the one will manifest themselves in the other. We contend that the personalized use of language will also have an effect on business development and performance.

ii) *Commonalities*: that is factors, which can be recognized as being performed by practicing marketing people, which do not get mentioned in the mainstream marketing literature. Of importance to this study is the clear omission of a contextualized meaning and operation of a language for marketing.

iii) *Triggers*: those factors, which signal or stimulate some form of marketing but which again are not mentioned in the mainstream marketing literature; these often appear as being irrational and "stochastic" as opposed to rational and sequential, Gilmore (2002) suggests that they will also vary from individual to individual owner/manager, and thus present difficulties with interpretation – thus language would fall into such a category.

iv) *Variances*: those factors, which indicate aspects of the marketing difference so that forms of marketing vary because of their influence, the individualistic application of these differentiators again causing difficulties with identification in practice according to Gilmore (2002).

v) *Situation Specifics*: considered to be those factors which dictate that all marketing is in the situation specific and, therefore, is uniquely different to any other marketing because of the situation specific.

vi) *Vocabulary*: the recognition that marketing practitioners have their own vocabulary depending on which "tribe" (Enright, 2001) they belong and as such central to the research issues explored within this study.

(Developed from Carson, 2005)

3.6. Language and Linguistic Content

Language in a social constructivist sense (conversations, narratives, and stories) provides a means for communities to understand the "world" and construct a "reality" (Burr, 1995). Differing relationships within a social setting for example: family, community or a business will require a variation of conversational skill and lexis used. Taking part in such "talking" will adjust the form of the "reality of the world" that we experience and as a consequence of this conversational experience individuals and communities will develop new forms of meaning in context (Shotter, 1993).

Researchers in sociolinguistics (sociolinguistics being the study of language in its social context and the study of life through language), advocate that there are "conversational styles" at play in all our linguistic relationships and within such relationships a framework is developed that enables understanding to take place (Tannen, 1994). The development of understanding will inevitably be based on the wider social relationship that exists between those who are talking – the interlocutors. This relates to whether the relationship is, as Tannen (1994) posits, "private" (one-on-one conversations between intimates and friends) or "public" (the talk that takes place at work). However, there are many influences simultaneously present within conversations:

> Each individual has a unique style, influenced by a personal history of many influences such as geographical region, ethnicity, class, sexual orientation, occupation, religion, and age – as well as a unique personality and spirit. In other words, our ways of talking are influenced by every aspect of our communities ... Yet understanding the patterns of influence on our lives (Tannen, 1994, p.13).

While conversations convey messages, it is contended that within this conveyance a meta-message is also communicated (Bateson, 1972). Bateson suggests that meta-messages contain information about the relationships of the people involved – their attitude toward both the content of the conversation and the other people. Thus, a meta-message acts as a frame or "alignment" for contextualizing meaning within conversation (Goffman, 1974) – critically assisting the interpretation of conversational meaning between locators (Hymes, 1974).

3.7. The Language of Marketing in Context

Much of this chapter thus far has focused on building a picture of the contemporary state of marketing in the context of the small firm – implicit and explicit reference has been made (Carson et al., 2003; Copley, 2002, 2010; Forsyth & Greenhough, 2003; Hulbert, Day, & Shaw, 1998; Stokes & Lomax, 2002) for the need to acquire a "new language" for marketing in context. Indeed Copley arrived at this juncture when reviewing the educational and training expectations of SME practitioners, concluding that while the business environment had changed the modus operandi of educators had remained rooted within the "modernist" (AM) paradigm and thus contextual gaps had arisen that could be overcome perhaps with the development of a "new language" for and of marketing. Copley also propagated the concept that a vocabulary of marketing exists within and without the small firm: in that while there is a need for a "technical" form of language for small firm marketing, within the firm there exists "customer facing" lexicography, the former he suggests is overlooked by the "marketing mix" protagonists and the latter by those supportive of the "Relationship Marketing" paradigm (Carson et al., 2003).

Enright (2001) has suggested that marketing practitioners will use a language dependent to which "tribe" they belong and that the closer one gets to the organization, the more "specific or tribal in nature" the corresponding lexis. Copley refers to this as the "intimate vocabulary" of the focal firm. Enright's work seeks to discover the meanings to those marketing constructs found in mainstream marketing "textbooks" and contrasts these to the meanings ascribed by small firm owner/ managers to contextual "activities of marketing" (Table 3.1). It is work that highlights differences in the interpretation of what marketing is – suggesting that such interpretation will be affected by "localised vocabularies," he concludes: "much remains to be uncovered about such linguistic adaptations."

In their articulation of the language of marketing in SMEs Carson et al. (2003) refer to the phenomena highlighted by Hills and Muzyka (1993) where small firms owner/entrepreneur will respond to questions asked using "textbook" marketing terminology in "textbook" marketing terminology (or more likely an interpretation of it); however, when avoiding such technical language a simpler yet paradoxically more meaningful answer is obtained. The study observes that such simplicity of description often hides very sophisticated marketing activity and suggests that: "in a more general sense, marketing practitioners use marketing terminology in a much more focused and perhaps restricted fashion than the full scope of language contained in the formal marketing literature"... and concludes that: "what tends to happen, is that academe 'interprets' what it sees and recognizes as marketing activity into formal marketing language," further indicating the inadequacies of the current lexicographic framework.

Bjerke and Hultman (2002) make a number of observations concerning the role of language in the entrepreneurial small firm context. They suggest that entrepreneurship is an outcome of three variables: use of language, culture, and entrepreneurial capabilities, the language variable being identified as the way in which meaning at the social level is created.

The view that the development of language or vocabulary for the description of marketing activity is inherently linked to the nature and personality of the owner is further supported by Gilmore (Carson et al., 2003) commenting that owner/ managers "often use an assertive language" and have their "own vocabulary" for marketing activities. However, the normative language used within specific business or technology sectors is also likely to have an effect on the development of community understanding – including the meaning co-created within the market. The development (over time) of a distinct shibboleth within a society can act as a barrier to dissuade entrants (McNamara, 2005) – however, from a marketing point of view it could also be seen to create a barrier for the customer.

As suggested earlier, the importance of a "language" for marketing within the small firm has been referred to both implicitly and explicitly throughout the entrepreneurship, marketing, and SM-related literature. However, literature stops short of further and more detailed investigation – this is perhaps understandable as the study of sociolinguistics has a body of literature of its own. The development of a contextual lexis for the meaning and operation of marketing may be dependent on a number of conditions, which have been supported through the literature so far explored. These conditions can be observed to exist within the dimensions of the individual owner/entrepreneur, the prevailing industry norms, and the strength of formality or informality present in the use of language for marketing within the focal firm.

Table 3.1: The Leviathan approach to assessing difference – Enright, 2003.

Term	Conventional Description	SME Description
Marketing	The identification and satisfaction of customer needs.	Making money by selling. An activity big corporations undertake.
Market orientation	Initiation response frameworks. Intelligence gathering and dissemination.	A boundary free range of opportunities necessarily related to the current, core business.
Business growth	Attainment of predetermined goals that are mutually agreed to across the departments of an organization.	Personal freedom of maneuver expressed as wealth, conspicuous consumption of lifestyle.
Planning	A highly sequenced and complicated combination of activities to attain growth. Marketing is a central tenet of this belief.	A financial matter. Without money there is no future. Marketing may be a means to an end but not necessarily. Survival is a goal.
Customer	An individual, normally under most scrutiny either in the development of the markets or at the end of the supply chain often beyond the effective control of the organization. Most commonly aggregated into target markets and then subjected to highly systemized market targeting.	Can be good, service or idea. Smaller operators tend not to identify difference between customer and product. For them the two concepts merge.
Product	A combination of the marketing mix. Can be a good or a service or an idea. The manifestation of the organization's world view of the market.	Generally smaller organizations are able to differentiate between the concepts of "customer" and "product." Rather they perceive a difference between stock order capacity and the ability to match it to demand.

Table 3.1: (*Continued*)

Term	Conventional Description	SME Description
Price	A component of the marketing mix. Set by markets.	Set by SMEs settled on by market. Price can be difficult to change as product mixes are often shallower and narrower than large organizations, making line pricing modifications difficult.
	The revenue-producing element of the marketing mix.	Price often relates to acquisition costs rather than market price.
Place/distribution	A component of the marketing mix. A marketing function whereby product availability is subjected to varying degrees of selectivity according to desired positioning.	A logical issue rather than a marketing one. Product is usually directly passed on to customers from the premises or distribution points and are selected only so far as such distributors accept the product and the person behind it.
Promotion/ marketing communications	A component of the marketing mix.	A sometimes necessary cost of production in order to achieve sufficient revenue levels.
	A range of activities specifically designed to present the product to the most probable targeted audience in the most convincing way.	Tends to be subsumed under the operation networking activities, associations, and perhaps local memberships.

From Carson et al. (2003).

3.8. Conclusion

This chapter has set out to explore the contemporary research issues posed by the debate and discussions culminating in the outcome report of the Charleston Summit

Table 3.2: Four marketing/entrepreneurship interface research perspectives.

Perspective	Explanation
1. Marketing and entrepreneurship	Commonalities between both disciplines – the normative and historical perspective – where the interface appears at the intersection of the two domains
2. Entrepreneurship in marketing	Entrepreneurship issues framed in the field of Marketing or viewed through a Marketing theoretical lens – in essence "Entrepreneurship" as viewed by researchers in the Marketing field
3. Marketing in entrepreneurship	Marketing issues framed in the field of Entrepreneurship or viewed through a Entrepreneurship theoretical lens – in essence "Marketing" as viewed by researchers in the Entrepreneurship field
4. Unique interface concepts	Concepts that are distinct and unique to the interface and evolve out of the combination of Marketing and entrepreneurship

From Hansen and Eggers (2010).

(Hansen & Eggers, 2010). As part of the debate, four perspectives of the interface were derived as seen here in Table 3.2.

What this chapter concentrates on therefore is a development of a component of "Perspective 4," given that this perspective has been described by Hanson and Eggers as:

> … the fourth perspective could be considered the opposite to the first. Rather than commonalities among marketing and entrepreneurship, this perspective represents that which is unique to the interface – thus: the combination of marketing and entrepreneurship creates something distinctive, like an offspring. During the summit, it was suggested that as a field, we have not made progress because we talk about differing perspectives, but we do not say so explicitly.

Therefore, we suggest that "perspective 4" is "Contextual Marketing" and that as such CM is made up of or contains a number of components – one of which is the meaning and operation of a language for marketing in context. The field of sociolinguistics and the importance of vocal communication may hold the key to unlocking a paradigmatic foundation, which has hitherto been overlooked. Reasons for any academic myopia may be due in part to the reluctance of researchers to engage in this complex field and in part to the reluctance to fully accept an emergent and alternative paradigm (as seen in perspective 4).

Our conceptualization sits thus: at the interface between the concepts of marketing and entrepreneurship and language, where an understanding of a lexis

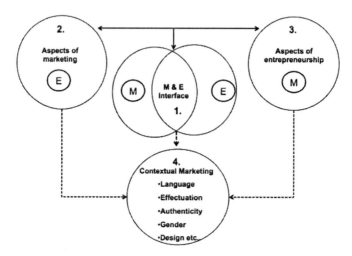

Figure 3.3: A Conceptualization of the Components of "Perspective 4" – An Emergent and Alternative Paradigm of Research at the Interface.

for marketing within the socially constructed and contextual setting allows a detail of insight into the meaning and operation of marketing that develops further the conceptualization of CM. The inclusion of a third notion (in this case language) at the interface explores a level of detail beyond that which has been discovered thus far at the interface of marketing and entrepreneurship alone. The development of lexis for the operation and meaning of marketing in this context is considered, however, one of a number of components of CM that can be found within "perspective 4," a full conceptualization of this perspective can be seen in Figure 3.3.

Further we propose that this perspective has as antecedence, the foundation of philosophical constructs of psychology, sociology, and anthropology and that scholars are encouraged to develop further the linguistic aspect of research and to consider further antecedent inclusions to research at the interface – Figure 3.3 makes some suggestions. We acknowledge that there are limitations with the conceptualization thus far: principally that research in sociolinguistics is a highly sophisticated practice; however, we hope it will encourage others to be conceptually experimental at the interface.

References

Bateson, G. (1972). *A theory of play and fantasy. Steps to an ecology of mind* (pp. 177–193). New York, NY: Ballantine.

Birley, S. (1982). Corporate strategy and the small firm. *Journal of General Management, 8*(2), 82–86.

Bjerke, B., & Hultman, C. (2002). *Entrepreneurial marketing the growth of small firms in the new economic Era*. Cheltenham, UK: Edward Elgar.

Blois, K. J. (1970). The effect of subjective factors on customer/supplier relations in industrial marketing. *European Journal of Marketing, 4*(1), 18–21.

Brown, S. (2001). *Marketing – The retro revolution*. London: Sage.

Burns, P. (2005). *Corporate entrepreneurship – Building an entrepreneurial organisation*. Basingstoke: Palgrave Macmillan.

Burr, V. (1995). *An introduction to social constructionism*. London: Routledge.

Carson, D. (1985). The evolution of marketing in small firms. *European Journal of Marketing, 19*(5), 7–16.

Carson, D. (2005). Research at the interface. *Proceedings of the plenary session of the AM/UIC SIG Entrepreneurial and Small Firms Marketing*, University of Southampton, Southampton, January 1.

Carson, D., Cromie, S., McGowan, P., & Hill, J. (1995). *Marketing and entrepreneurship in SMEs – An innovative approach*. London: Prentice Hall London.

Carson, D., Enright, M., Copley, P., Deacon, J., McAuley, A., & Gilmore, A. (2003). Contextual marketing: The language/vocabulary of marketing in SMEs. *Eighth annual research symposium on the marketing – Entrepreneurship interface*, The University of Gloucestershire Business School, University of Gloucestershire, Cheltenham.

Carson, D., Enright, M., Tregear, A., Copley, P., Gilmore, A., Stokes, D., Hardesty, C., & Deacon, J. (2002). Contextual marketing. *7th annual research symposium on the marketing – Entrepreneurship interface*, Oxford Brookes University, Oxford.

Carson, D., & Gilmore, A. (1999). Characteristics of SME marketing and a conceptual framework. In *Proceedings of the 1999 Academy of Marketing Conference* (pp. 340–358) University of Stirling, Scotland.

Carson, D., & Gilmore, A. (2000). Marketing at the interface: Not "What" but "How". *Journal of Marketing Theory and Practice, 8*(2), 1–7.

Carter, S., & Jones-Evans, D. (2000). *Enterprise and small business – Principles, Practice and Policy*. London: Prentice Hall.

Carter, S., & Tzokas, N. (1999). Marketing activities and the performance of small firms: cross-national study of European SME's *Proceedings of the 22nd ISBA (Institute of Small Business Association) national small firms policy & research conference Leeds: European strategies, growth & development* (pp. 227–243), London, UK.

Chell, E. (2000). Towards researching the 'oportunistic entrepreneur': A social constructivist approach and research agenda. *European Journal of Work and Organisational Psychology, 9*(1), 63–80.

Chell, E., Haworth, J., & Brearley, S. (1991). *The entrepreneurial personality: Concepts, cases, and categories*. London: Routledge.

Copley, P. (2010). Through a discourse analysis lens less darkly: Illuminating how SME principles and support agency practitioners see marketing in SME's. *Marketing Review, 10*(4), 353–368.

Cova, B. (1996). The postmodern explained to managers: Implications for marketing. *Business Horizons, 39(6)*, 15–23.

Deacon, J., (2002). Contextual marketing Commonalties and personalities – Fuzzy experiential excellence. *Proceedings of UIC research symposium: American Academy of Marketing*, San Diego State University, San Diego.

Deacon, J., & Corp, J. (2004). Re Enterprising your warped drive. *Proceedings of the 9th academy of marketing symposium on entrepreneurial and small business marketing – Ensuring a creative future for entrepreneurial marketing*, University of Stirling, Stirling.

Downing, S. (2005). The social construction of entrepreneurship: Narrative and dramatic processes in the co-production of organisations and identities. *Entrepreneurship: Theory and Practice*, 29(2), 185–204.

Earls, M. (2002). *Welcome to the creative age: Bananas, business and the death of marketing.* Chichester: Wiley.

Enright, M. (2001). Approaches to market orientation and new product development in smaller enterprises: A proposal for a context-rich interpretive framework. *Proceedings of the academy of marketing annual conference*, Cardiff.

Forsyth, S., & Greenhough, J. (2003). Marketing and the small business leader: A new perspective. *CIM Study*, Chartered Institute of Marketing Library, Moor Hall, Cookham, England.

Gibb, A., & Davies, L. (1990). In pursuit of frameworks for the development of growth models of the small business. *International Small Business Journal*, 9(1), 15–31.

Gibb, A., & Scott, M. (1985). Strategic awareness, personal commitment and the process of planning in the small business. *Journal of Management Studies*, 22(6), 597–631.

Gilmore, A. (2002). Contextual Marketing. In Carson, D., Enright, M., Tregear, A., Copley, P., Gilmore, A., Stokes, D., Hardesty, C., and Deacon, J., (2002). Contextual Marketing, *7th annual research symposium on the marketing – Entrepreneurship interface*, Oxford Brookes University, Oxford, UK.

Goffman, E. (1974). *Frame analysis.* New York, NY: Harper and Row.

Guba, E., & Lincoln, Y. S. (1994). Competing paradigms in qualitative research. In N. K. Denzin & Y. S. Lincoln (Eds.), *Handbook of qualitative research* (pp. 105–117). Thousand Oaks, CA: Sage.

Hakansson, H., & Prenkert, F. (2004). Exploring the exchange concept in marketing. In Harrison, D. and Waluszewski, A. (Eds), *Rethinking Marketing*, Wiley, Chichester, pp. 75–99.

Halliday, S., Deacon, J., & Palmer, A. (2005). Renaissance marketing. Academy of Marketing Annual Conference, *Marketing: Building Business, Shaping Society*, Dublin Institute of Technology, Dublin: Ireland

Hansen, D., & Eggers, F. (2010). The marketing/entrepreneurship interface: A report on the charleston summit. *Journal of Research in Marketing and Entrepreneurship*, 12(1), pp. 42–53.

Hills, G. (1995). Forward to: Carson, D., Cromie, S., McGowan, P., and Hill, J. *Marketing and entrepreneurship in SMEs – An innovative approach* (pp. xiii–xiv). London: Prentice Hall.

Hills, G. (2002). Forward to: Bjerke, B. and Hultman, C. *Entrepreneurial marketing: The growth of small firms in the new economic era* (pp xi–xiii). Cheltenham: Edward Elgar.

Hill, G., McGowan, P., & Drummond, P. (1999). The development and application of a qualitative approach to researching the marketing networks of small firm entrepreneurs. *Qualitative Market Research: An International Journal*, 2(2), 71–81.

Hills, G., & Muzyka, D. (1993). Introduction, research at the marketing/entrepreneurial interface. *Proceedings of the UIC/AMA symposium on marketing/entrepreneurship interface*, The University of Illinois at Chicago.

Hisrich, R. D. (1992). The need for marketing in entrepreneurship. *The Journal of Consumer Marketing*, 7(3), 53–57.

Hulbert, B., Day, J., & Shaw, E. (1998). Commentary. *Proceedings of the academy of marketing and UIC/MEIG-AMA symposia on the marketing and entrepreneurship Interface*, Nene University College, Northampton.

Hymes, D. (1974). *Foundations in sociolinguistics an ethnographic approach.* London: Tavistock.

Macko, A., & Tyszka, T. (2009). Entrepreneurship and risk taking. *Applied Psychology: An International Review*, 58(3), 469–487.

McAuley, A. (2010). Looking back, going forward: Reflecting on research into the SME internationalisation process. *Journal of Research in Marketing and Entrepreneurship, 12*(1), 21–41.

McLarty, R. (1998). Case study: Evidence of a strategic marketing paradigm in a growing SME. *Journal of Marketing Practice: Applied Marketing Science, 4*(4), 105–117.

McNamara, T. (2005). 21st century shibboleth: Language tests, identity and intergroup conflict. *Language Policy, 4*(4), 351–370.

Mead, G. (1934). *Mind, self and society.* Chicago, IL: University of Chicago Press.

Mezirow, J. (1981). A critical theory of adult learning and education. *Adult Education Quarterly, 32*(1), 3–24.

Miles, M. P., & Darroch, J. (2006). Large firms, entrepreneurial marketing processes and the cycle of competitive advantage. *European Journal of Marketing, 40*(5/6), 485–501.

Morrish, S. C., Miles, M. P., & Deacon, J. H. (2010). Entrepreneurial marketing: acknowledging the entrepreneur and customer-centric interrelationship. *Journal of Strategic Marketing, 18*(4), 303–316.

Nilsson, T. (1995). *Chaos marketing – How to win in a turbulent world.* Maidenhead: McCraw-Hill.

ONS. (2010). *UK Business: Activity, size and location 2010.* Office for National Statistics, UK.

Rubin, H., & Rubin, I. (2005). *Qualitative interviewing – The art of hearing data.* Thousand Oaks, CA: Sage.

Sarasvathy, S. (2001). Causation and effectuation: Toward a theoretical shift from economic inevitability to entrepreneurial contingency. *Academy of Management Review, 26*(2), 243–263.

Schindehutte, M., Morris, M. H., & Pitt, L. (2008). *Rethinking marketing: The entrepreneurial imperative.* Englewoods Cliffs, NJ: Prentice Hall.

Schollhammer, H., & Kuriloff, A. (1979). *Entrepreneurship and small business management.* Chichester: Wiley.

Shotter, J. (1993). *Conversational realities: Constructing life through language.* London: Sage.

Stacy, R., Griffin, D., & Shaw, P. (2000). *Complexity and management – Fad or radical challenge to systems thinking?* Oxford: Routledge.

Stokes, D. (2000). Entrepreneurial marketing: A conceptualisation from qualitative research. *Qualitative Marketing Research, an International Journal, 3*(1), 47–54.

Stokes, D., & Lomax, W. (2002). Taking control of word of mouth marketing: The case of an entrepreneurial hotelier. *Journal of Small Business and Enterprise Development, 9*(4), 349–357.

Storey, D. (1994). *Understanding the small business sector.* London: Routledge.

Tannen, D. (1994). *Talking from 9 to 5 – Women and Men at Work: Language, sex and power.* London: Virago.

Walsh, J. (1995). The process of small firm internationalisation in Ireland: An exploration of human resource issues. *Academy of Entrepreneurship Journal, 1*(1), 65–81.

Weick, K. (1969). *The social psychology of organizing.* New York, NY: McGraw Hill.

Chapter 4

The Role of Marketing Rational and Natural Business Start-Ups

Abstract

This chapter is about the role marketing plays in various business start-ups. It makes a distinction between rational and natural business start-ups. To understand this distinction, the chapter starts by outlining a recent development of the subject of entrepreneurship as we see it, that it is possible to talk about a narrow and a broad view of the field of entrepreneurship today. The chapter ends by discussing which role marketing can play in different business start-ups in general and in rational and natural business start-ups in particular.

4.1. The Narrow and the Broad View of Entrepreneurship

Interest in and research on entrepreneurship has simply increased exponentially during the past 10 years or so. It is also possible now to see different theoretical orientations and their differences. Two important orientations, containing definitely different "views" on the subject of entrepreneurship in the society at large, are (Bridge, O'Neill, & Cromie, 2003):

a. *The narrow view*: Entrepreneurship is basically an economic phenomenon and is a matter of tracing and exploiting opportunities and of creating something *new*, thereby satisfying *demand in different markets*, new or not. Some representatives of this view are, for instance, Dees, Emerson, and Economy (2001), Amin, Cameron, and Hudson (2002), and Dart (2004).
b. *The broad view*: Entrepreneurship belongs to the whole society, not only to its economy and is a question of creating something *new* and thereby satisfying *demands and/or needs*, new or not. This view is represented by, for instance, Hardt (2002), Hjorth and Steyaert (2003), Johannisson (2005), and Bjerke (2007).

Entrepreneurial Marketing: Global Perspectives
Copyright © 2013 by Emerald Group Publishing Limited
All rights of reproduction in any form reserved
ISBN: 978-1-78190-786-3

Some authors refer to this as the American (US) and the Scandinavian view (e.g., Bill, Jansson, & Olaison, 2010). There are often differences in the definition of the phenomenon in United States and Scandinavian textbooks. First some US examples:

> Entrepreneurship is the process whereby an individual or a group of individuals use organized efforts and means to pursue opportunities to create value and grow by fulfilling wants and needs through innovation and uniqueness, no matter what resources are currently controlled. (Coulter, 2001, p. 6)

> An entrepreneur is one who creates a new business in the face of risk and uncertainty for the purpose of achieving profit and growth by identifying opportunities and assembling the necessary resources to capitalize on them. Although many people come up with great business ideas, most of them never act on their ideas. Entrepreneurs do. (Zimmerer & Scarborough, 2005, p. 4)

> Entrepreneurship is a dynamic process of vision, change, and creation. It requires an application of energy and passion towards the creation and implementation of new ideas and creative solutions. Essential ingredients include the willingness to take calculated risks – in terms of time, equity, or career; the ability to formulate an effective venture team; the creative skill to marshal needed resources; the fundamental skill of building a solid business plan; and finally, the vision to recognize opportunity where others see chaos, contradiction, and confusion. (Kuratko & Hodgetts, 2004, p. 30)

Compare this with some Scandinavian definitions:

> Entrepreneurial processes are about identifying, challenging and breaking institutional patterns, to temporarily depart from norms and values in the society. (Lindgren & Packendorff, 2007, p. 29; our translation)

> Entrepreneurship is tangible action as creative organizing in order to realize something different. (Johannisson, 2005, p. 371; our translation)

> Entrepreneurship = to satisfy user values and/or needs – new or old – in new ways. (Bjerke, 2007, p. 17)

It is obvious that the broad view defines entrepreneurship less specifically than what the narrow view does (compare the definitions from United States and from Sweden above). In other words:

The broad view, unlike the narrow one, does not think it is possible to specify in any detail which personality and which behavior that is *generally speaking* associated with (successful) entrepreneurs.

Furthermore:

1. "New" as related to entrepreneurial results does not accord to the broad view, unlike the narrow view, have to be interpreted as something radically new. "New" in the former view, is most of the time a marginal improvement of what is there already, for instance, that a solution is more accessible or more user-friendly. Most entrepreneurial efforts do not change our lives to any major degree.
2. The narrow view asserts that entrepreneurs are some kind of extraordinary people; the broad view does not.

Lindgren and Packendorff (2007, p. 18) point out that there are some weaknesses in existing entrepreneurship research (i.e., what we refer to as the narrow view of entrepreneurship):

- It suggests that entrepreneurship can be measured, predicted and stimulated in an objective and neutral way, which leads to a number of problems because the phenomenon of entrepreneurship is characteristically complex.
- It almost always lets individuals embody entrepreneurship, in spite of the fact that most entrepreneurial acts are performed by people in cooperation.
- Entrepreneurship is operationalized – lacking better data – as freshly registered new firms, which excludes a number of entrepreneurial acts that take place within existing firms and/or do not lead to the start of traditional companies.
- The focus is too narrow most of the time that excludes, for instance, female entrepreneurs and ethnic minorities and what is referred to the cultural sector (see Chapter 9 for further commentary on this area, by Zubin Sethna).

Most entrepreneurship theories are of the narrow type and *market based*. Historically, the entrepreneurship discourse is built on the economic discourse (Steyaert & Katz, 2004). Most of these theories rarely position themselves in terms of *where, in what culture and during which time they are valid* (Bjerke, 2010). Some examples are as follows:

- Entrepreneurs are achievement motivated, have a risk-taking propensity, have an internal locus of control, have a need for autonomy, are determined, creative and self-confident, and take initiative (Bridge et al., 2003).
- Many entrepreneurs seem to think counter-factual, live more in the present and in the future than in the past, become more involved when making decisions and evaluating things, underestimating costs as well as time required succeeding (Baron, 1998).
- Positive consequences for entrepreneurs of starting a business include creating one's own future, having a high degree of independence, being responsible only to oneself and following in the family's footsteps (Coulter, 2001).

Three things become natural with these types of theories:

1. To look at "growth" as something primary (Allen, 2010; Coulter, 2001; Wickham, 2006).

2. To see "opportunity recognition" as a distinct and fundamental entrepreneurial behavior (Gaglio, 1997; Kirzner, 1979; Stevenson & Jarillo, 1990; Venkataraman, 1997).
3. To view entrepreneurship as a (special) type of management (Drucker, 1985; Stevenson & Jarillo, 1990; Wickham, 2006).

The narrow view of entrepreneurship sometimes claims that the founder of a small new firm should have a growth ambition in order for him or her to be looked at as entrepreneur. The broad view looks at this requirement as too strict and even useless. It is a fact that most start-up business firms do not grow over and above a certain level (Davidsson, 1989; Wiklund, 1998), nor do all entrepreneurs share the same ability to grow. *It is possible* to ask some questions, like Sexton and Bowman-Upton (1991) do: What makes the business starter to put his or her firm in a growth cycle that happens among less than 10% of the firms in a country? Why is the typical business starter oriented toward change and growth and is this something that separates the entrepreneur from the manager? Are those factors already there when the firm starts? If that is the case, can it then be seen in decisions and acts that take place to start the operation or do all firms start the same way, where later only the lucky ones survive and grow? Sexton and Bowman-Upton (1991) assert that growth is not automatic. It must, in their opinion, be carefully planned for it to take place and actions must be taken for it to be reached. They look at growth as a controllable factor. It is a decision made by some to act forcefully in order to achieve it, for some to start more slowly and for some to avoid.

It *is* possible to separate the entrepreneur from the normal small firm on the basis of growth orientation (Sexton & Bowman-Upton, 1991, p. 8). Growth orientation can, in their opinion, be measured in terms of the owner(s) intention when the firm is starting, his or her (or their) propensity to support growth, or design strategic plans to encourage growth. They also note that growth-oriented managers in large firms share this orientation. So, growth orientation *can* be seen as a way to separate an entrepreneurial firm from any other small firm and note that this does not separate the entrepreneur from growth-oriented persons in the same company or in a larger firm. Based on this, Sexton and Bowman-Upton (1991, p. 14) suggest the matrix below (Figure 4.1).

However, the above discussion is of interest only in the narrow view of entrepreneurship, not in the broad view, where growth is not seen as a necessary entrepreneurial inclination.

According to Gaglio and Katz (2001, p. 95), "understanding the opportunity identification process represents one of the core intellectual questions for the domain of entrepreneurship." Mariotti and Glackin (2010, p. 13) assert that there is a simple definition of "entrepreneur" that captures the essentials: "An entrepreneur recognizes opportunities where other people see only problems." According to Baron and Shane (2008, p. 5), entrepreneurship involves the key actions of identifying an opportunity that is potentially valuable in the sense that it can be exploited in practical business terms and yield sustainable profits. "The entrepreneur always searches for change, responds to it, and exploits it as an opportunity"

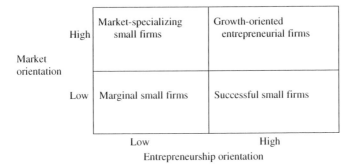

Figure 4.1: Small Firms in Terms of Growth.

(Drucker, 1985, p. 25). Kirzner (1979) asserts that the mentality of entrepreneurs differs because they are driven by *entrepreneurial alertness*, which he suggests is a distinctive set of perceptual and cognitive processing skills that directs the opportunity recognition process.

An opportunity is seen by Barringer and Ireland (2006, p. 28) as "a favorable set of circumstances that creates a need for a new product, service, or business." Coulter (2001, p. 53) sees opportunities as "positive external environment trends or changes that provide unique and distinct possibilities for innovating and creating value."

The opportunities themselves often emerge from changes in economic, techno-logical, governmental, and social factors. When entrepreneurs notice links or connections between these changes, ideas for new ventures may quickly follow (Baron & Shane, 2008, p. 13).

Timmons (1999) defines a business opportunity as an idea, plus four characteristics:

1. It is attractive to customers.
2. It will work in your business environment.
3. It can be executed in the window of opportunity (which is the amount of time you have to get your business idea to the market) that exists.
4. You have the resources and skills to create the business or you know someone who does and who might want to form a business with you.

Opportunities are often seen as noticeable circumstances. Such circumstances may be (Mariotti & Glackin, 2010, p. 16):

1. *Problems* that your business can solve.
2. *Changes* in laws, situations or trends.
3. *Inventions* of totally new products or services.
4. *Competition.* If you can find a way to beat the competition on price, location, quality, reputation, reliability or speed, you may create a very successful business with an existing product or service.
5. *Technological advances.* Scientists may invent new technology, but entrepreneurs figure out how to use and sell new products based on it.

Opportunities are claimed to generally arise from two major sources – the information people have that helps them to notice new business opportunities, and changes in the external world that generate opportunities (Baron & Shane, 2008, p. 39). According to one economist, Ács (2002, p. 12), opportunities for discovering or creating goods and services in the future exist precisely because of the dispersion of information. This dispersion creates the opportunity in the first place. Second, the very same dispersion presents hurdles for exploiting the opportunity profitably, because of the absence or failure of current markets for future goods and services. It is, therefore, according to Ács (*ibid.*) necessary to understand (1) how opportunities for the creation of new goods and services arise in a market economy, and (2) how and in what ways individual differences determine whether hurdles in the dis-covering, creating and exploiting opportunities are overcome.

There has been a debate in the field of entrepreneurship whether opportunities exist in the external world or are created by human minds (see, for instance, Forbes, 2005). Baron and Shane (2008, p. 84) believe that there is no basis for controversy over this issue. Opportunities, according to them, as *potentials*, come into existence in the external world as a result of changes in conditions in the society. However, they remain merely potentials until they are recognized by somebody's perceptual and cognitive skills. In a sense, therefore, according to these two authors, opportunities both exist "out there" and are a creation of human thought. Maybe a solution to whether opportunities are there to be discovered or created could be to talk about *opportunity formation*. Hjorth and Johannisson (2003) refer to this process as "articulation."

The broad view of entrepreneurship does not look at opportunity recognition as a necessary entrepreneurial quality. This view even points at two aspects *within the narrow view of entrepreneurship* that support this criticism:

1. The highly recognized Global Entrepreneurship Monitor studies on the variation of entrepreneurship inclination across countries have come to the conclusion (e.g., Bosma & Harding, 2007), that early-stage entrepreneurship is more likely to be *necessity-based* in middle or low-income countries, where entrepreneurship in many cases may be the only option for making a living, than *opportunity-driven* that is the case in high-income countries.
2. A more serious criticism against the usefulness of looking at opportunity recognition, and exploitation as a *necessary* entrepreneurial characteristic is probably that the success of that type of research on which the narrow view of entrepreneurship is based and thereby supporting the opinion that opportunity recognition skill as a primary and necessary entrepreneurial quality is judged by its ability *to make a forecast*. The broad view of entrepreneurship thinks it is *possible* to look at opportunity recognition and exploitation as a variable in a model of entrepreneurial behavior, but that is most of the time *after the fact* and this is often *not a very adequate explanation for what has actually been going on.* To claim that opportunity recognition and exploitation is a *necessary* requirement to succeed as an entrepreneur (logically related to having a good business plan, aiming for growth and having the skills of a good manager) *before* you go for a

business start-up, the broad view of entrepreneurship simply finds very doubtful, in practice as well as in theory. One study in the tradition of the narrow view of entrepreneurship (Gartner & Carter, 2003) even claims that the desire to start a business more often than not comes *before* looking for a business opportunity.

One consequence of the narrow view of entrepreneurship is like Wickham (2006, p. 16) who claimed that it is possible to say with confidence that an entrepreneur is a *manager*, that is, somebody who manages in an entrepreneurial way. Entrepreneurial management, as he sees it, is characterized by three features: a focus on change, a focus on opportunity, and organization-wide management. Drucker (1985, p. 131) suggests that no matter where entrepreneurship is happening in a society, the rules governing it are pretty much the same, the things that work and those that do not are pretty much the same, and so are the kinds of innovation and where to look for them. He claims that in every case there is a discipline that can be called *entrepreneurial management*.

Along the same line is the view that successful entrepreneurship starts by coming up with a *good business plan*.

Unless a new venture develops into a business and makes sure of being "managed," it will not survive no matter how brilliant the entrepreneurial idea, how much money it attracts, how good its products, nor even how great the demand for them (Drucker, 1985, p. 172).

The broad view claims, as mentioned before, that it sees a clear difference between entrepreneurship and management. Steyaert (2004) is a proponent of the broad view of entrepreneurship. Imitations for the future and necessary mundane aspects of entrepreneurship, he refers to as the prosaic with entrepreneurship. Having such a focus as a researcher, you leave a dominating focus of building models by using general concepts, which is usually encouraged in the area (Steyaert, 2000) and enter a road of studying the conversation process that does not neglect the everydayness of entrepreneurial processes.

As pointed out, the most fundamental or at least natural consequence of the broad view of entrepreneurship is to make a clear difference between traditional ways of doing business and entrepreneurship – between "managerialism" and "entrepre-neurialism" in Hjorth and Johannisson's terminology (1998). Management and organizational theory preserves according to Hjorth and Steyaert (2003, pp. 298–299) a special place for entrepreneurship, but this depends on its usefulness as a solution in management theory. The entrepreneurship boom became part of the management view in the 1980s (Kanter, 1983; Peters & Waterman, 1982). The enterprising discourse moved forward on a broad front and comprehended what was called the Thatcherism and the Reaganism in the 1980s as well as making the employee an enterprising individual in the 1990s (du Gay, 1997; Peters, 1994a, 1994b). To be enterprising (Burchell, Gordon, & Miller, 1991) represents what is entrepreneurial according to managerialism (du Gay, 1997) and is therefore spread quickly in the society in all places where managerialism has become the governing basis for rationality. It was important to the enterprising discourse in the 1990s that it was almost impossible to define the limit for managerialism: "attempts to construct a culture of enterprise have proceeded through the progressive enlargement of the territory of the market – the realm of private enterprise and economic rationality – by a series of redefinitions of its objects" (du Gay, 1997, p. 56).

The result became a new target for management knowledge – the employees themselves. They were seen in entrepreneurial terms or at least as parts of an entrepreneurial company. All that can be influenced – in order to become effective – should then function as parts of an entrepreneurial management. To be successful and to contribute to the success of the company or, the care center or, the primary school, or the public institution all employees should develop a self-knowledge (Townley, 1995) that centers around the management version of the entrepreneur: the one who takes initiatives, the one who looks for opportunities, the one who takes responsibility, the one who is reliable, that individual who is enterprising. When Drucker (1985) wrote that he wanted to do the same for entrepreneurship as he did for management in the 1950s – to turn it into a successful discipline – he was forecasting both how entrepreneurship in its enterprising form became the ruling power of the new technology of self (Deetz, 1998; Martin, Gutman, & Hutton, 1988; Townley, 1995) and how entrepreneurship was developing as an academic discipline during the 1990s (Katz, 1998). How to behave and how to make something of your life was now answered more and more in enterprising terms: manage your life as an entrepreneurial company and become an enterprising individual.

The broad view of entrepreneurship sees no point in creating conceptual systems to explain entrepreneurship. If entrepreneurship is to be treated as an economic concept only, the fear among those who want to apply a broad view of it is that the subject would have nothing of its own to give. The broad view instead asserts that what is needed is a new way to speak of the entrepreneurial, so that it includes more of the society, not just the economic part of it.

One aspect of the broad view of entrepreneurship, as mentioned already, is not to have a focus on discovery of opportunities but on the creative process in itself, which could be emphasized by using its verb as the present participle, as something ongoing, that is "entrepreneuring" (Steyaert, 2007). Lindgren and Packendorff (2007) also assert that entrepreneurship research to an increasing extent is focusing on entrepreneurial action processes. Entrepreneurial studies must then build on a process philosophy (Steyaert, 1997). By this, entrepreneurship could be called *the science of the art of imagination* (Gartner, 2007). Two proponents of the broad view of entrepreneurship, that is, Hjorth and Steyaert, have had such a point of departure in their so-called movement books (Hjorth & Steyaert, 2004, 2009; Steyaert & Hjorth, 2003, 2006).

One important difference between the two views of entrepreneurship is that the broad view inevitably looks at entrepreneurship as an activity embedded in a special social (historical, cultural, economic) context, that is, embedded in a place. The innovative power of entrepreneurship can then not be taken as "creative destruction" in the Schumpeter sense but rather as a presentation that is filled by an attitude in which "the high value of the present is indissociable from a desperate eagerness to imagine it, to image it otherwise than it is, and to transform it not by destroying it but by grasping it in what it is" (Foucault, 1997, p. 311).

Criticism of the broad view of entrepreneurship has come from the narrow view of entrepreneurship, claiming that entrepreneurship research needs to limit itself and come up with what the narrow view considers to be the distinctive aspects of entrepreneurship, to find the domain or so-called *core* of entrepreneurship, that is, asserting that the subject needs to be consolidated (Baron & Shane, 2008; Davidsson, 2003; Low, 2001; Venkataraman, 1997).

Some scholars suggest a broader view of entrepreneurship, without completely excluding the narrow view. What should be considered in a broad view of entrepreneurship is to them at least the following:

- Entrepreneurship is as much a continuous improving imitation as a genuine creation of something new (Johansson, 2010).
- It is too simplistic to say that entrepreneurship needs freedom to prosper. It really needs resistance to be stimulated to great things (Berglund & Gaddefors, 2010).
- There is a risk to claim that entrepreneurship requires spectacular behavior and then excluding the more mundane reality-based activities (Bill et al., 2010).

To summarize, there are some concepts related to the narrow view of entrepreneurship:

- Need for achievement
- An economic phenomenon
- Growth
- Exploiting opportunities
- A special type of management
- Business planning
- *Extraordinary behavior among extraordinary people*

Some concepts related to the broad view of entrepreneurship are:

- A phenomenon dependent on culture and place
- Not only an economic phenomenon
- To act as if and make a difference
- The power of imagination
- Entrepreneurs are not a kind of managers
- Too much planning can stifle creativity
- *Extraordinary actions among ordinary people*

4.2. Rational and Natural Entrepreneurial Start-Ups

The narrow view of entrepreneurship tends to build rational models. This has expressed itself when starting entrepreneurial activities in a *goals-rational way* ("causation") or in a *means-rational way* ("effectuation") (Sarasvathy, 2001). Goals-rationality looks at establishment of an activity such that goals and ambitions with its start are rather explicit and that the entrepreneur is looking for alternative

Goals and market   Means   The start of the operation

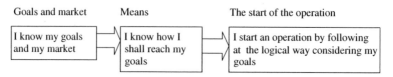

Figure 4.2: Goals-Rationality ("causation").

Means   Goals   The start of the operation

Figure 4.3: Means-Rationality ("effectuation").

possibilities to fulfill its goals and ambitions. He or she is then choosing those means that seems to provide the largest chances for him or for her to reach what he or she wants. This requires that the entrepreneur has great analytical skills, that he or she is putting much time and efforts into what he or she wants and that he or she has a reasonable ability to forecast the future.

A goal-rational person decides by trusting his or her ability to forecast the future and to reach his or her goals by using that set of means that are available and/or can be acquired. Much of the narrow view of entrepreneurship is based on this thought. Those who think goal-rational assert that "if I can forecast the future I can control it." Goal-rational starts of entrepreneurship are illustrated in Figure 4.2.

Means-rationality ("effectuation") is rational as well, but the procedures are determined by available means, not by the desired goals. Those who think means-rational assert that "if I can control the future, I do not need to forecast it." Means-rationality is a rational logic, which both new and experienced entrepreneurs can use in the largely unpredictable start-up phase of an entrepreneurial operation. Means-rationality is illustrated in Figure 4.3.

According to *Wikipedia* (2012-07-03), means-rationality consists of four principles:

- *Bird in Hand Principle* – Start with what you have. Don't wait for the perfect opportunity. Start taking action based on what you have readily available: who you are, what you know and who you know.
- *Affordable Loss Principle* – Set affordable loss. Evaluate opportunities based on whether the downside is acceptable, rather than on the attractiveness of the predicted upside.
- *Lemonade Principle* – Exploit your situation as much as you can. Welcome surprises that may arise in uncertain situations and remain flexible rather than sticking to existing goals.
- *Crazy-Quilt Principle* – Form partnerships with people and organizations willing to make a real commitment to build a future together with you – product, firm, market. Don't worry so much about competitive analyses or strategic planning.

There is reason to believe that entrepreneurial new operations often start naturally rather than rationally (which does not mean, of course, that rational businesses are completely unnatural or that natural businesses are completely irrational). This can be discussed in terms of *bricolage*, which means to start something new by involving actors in a process, where genuinely new combinations come up and existing resources are transformed for old or for new purposes (Baker & Nelson, 2005; Garud, Kumaraswamy, & Nayyar, 1998). Lévi-Strauss, who brought up the concept, did not provide any specific definition of this, but bricolage is often described as "making it with what is at hand" (Lévi-Strauss, 1966, pp. 16–17; Miner, Bassoff, & Moorman, 2001; Weick, 1993).

Bricoleurial activities mean a set of actions that are "driven by the pursuit of existing and often scarce resources that can be recombined to create novel and interesting solutions of value that affect their respective markets" (Kickul, Griffiths, & Gundry, 2010, p. 232). The concept of bricolage can help us understand how some new entrepreneurial operations take on challenges under circumstances, where resources are very limited.

Rational models of nascent entrepreneurial operations look at the economic payoff that entrepreneurs come to expect. Bricolage is instead focusing on more natural behavior, supporting neighborhoods, which usually are poor on resources and mainly offer new challenges without providing new resources. Bricolage is often about exploiting physical, institutional, social and other inputs that other firms reject or ignore. To realize new results by being innovative can be a matter of the extent to which entrepreneurs can apply and combine resources that are at their disposal when they face new problems and want to come up with new possibilities with what they have (Baker & Nelson, 2005).

Lévi-Strauss (1966) makes a distinction between "the engineer" and "the bricoleur," which in our case can be seen as the difference between developing new entrepreneurial operations rationally or naturally. These are two different ways of thinking, where the engineer always attempts to find ways and means to get out of those limitations that exist at the moment when the bricoleur has an inclination or looks at it as necessary to always remain within these limitations. One important difference between the two or between rational and natural thinking is that the bricoleur always gives something of himself or herself to what he or she is doing (Lévi-Strauss, 1966, p. 21).

The importance of the relationships between a business company and its environment has been discussed for a long time. Penrose (1959) argued that business companies having very similar material and human resources can offer distinctly different service to markets because of differences in imaging different use of these resources. Models for open systems started to appear about the same time (Boulding, 1956), and it was then a discussion about the need for business companies to behave differently in different environments. These models of open systems were later developed by, for instance, Katz and Kahn (1978) and Scott (1998). These models gave however no answer to *how* specific business processes take place nor, above all, how business companies can create something from what seems to be nothing. This is what theories of bricolage do.

"Orderly sequential processes may be the exception in entrepreneurship" (Baker & Nelson, 2005, p. 358). Bricolage, creativity and improvising often seem to be closely related. This differs from traditional linear and rational social planning and focuses instead on design processes in the society and on the extent of relationships between resources in the environment and resources within the business firm. Bricolage is an important way to counteract organizational tendencies to accept limitations without testing them. This means that a constructionistic approach to resource environments sometimes is more fruitful than objectivistic and rational approaches. An objective, rational view of resource environments is ruling within much of entrepreneurship research today (Baker, Gedjlovic, & Lubatkin, 2005). The social construction of the resource environment, which can lead to another picture or simply denying the ruling definitions of resources, is basic for the bricoleurial process. This opens up new areas for entrepreneurship research and, which is of interest to us, a new way to discuss how entrepreneurs apply marketing when they start-up. In the literature business actions when facing limited resources have been discussed in financial terms (e.g., as so-called bootstrapping) and, to some extent, in terms of nonlinear process designs (Bhave, 1994). When we define those resources that are at hand, we should include resources that are available at very low costs or even for free, even if others consider them as useless or below acceptable standards. This is rarely done in rational entrepreneurship research.

It may look like "effectuation" and "bricolage" are the same, but there are several differences:

- "Effectuation" attempts to provide a more correct explanation of how business firms start, "bricolage" attempts to understand how business firms start by looking at entrepreneurs as agents in social construction.
- Somebody who is means-rational is as, in Sarasvathy's picture (2001), is like cooking a dinner using what is at hand in terms of ingredients and skills at the moment the cooking takes place. A bricoleur starts far earlier by collecting things, which he or she has come across – it may be an interesting ingredient or way of cooking, which he or she buys or remembers because he or she has a feeling that it may be useful sometime in the future.
- A bricoleur can be very good at improvising. To continue with Sarasvathy's picture about cooking a dinner, a bricoleur, who does not look at his situation as factual but as a social construction and thereby questions what an opportunity means, may in a clever way use an ingredient in a way that very few or even no one had thought of before.
- An effectual start means that what you know in terms of resources and skills could, in principle, be applied anywhere or anywhere special. A bricoleur is tied to a specific place and time and he or she may use this at his or her advantage. Johnstone and Lionais (2004) provide several examples of this in their discussion of how entrepreneurs in what they call "depleted communities" may succeed in their efforts to revitalize their place:

> They may accept very low returns on what they do, because they may not only have financial goals;

They probably have a much larger variation in how they organize themselves;
They could have access to local volunteers as a resource; this is very unlikely for business entrepreneurs, who only have their own private financial gain in focus,
They may be able to convince people in their neighborhood to invest in their efforts due to the fact that what they do may be seen as something promoting their local place; such resources may not be available to traditional business entrepreneurs;
They may be able to convince locals to be their customers due to the fact that these customers might prefer to buy locally rather than supporting some (nonlocal) businesses.

- Examples of how a bricoleur may be able to benefit from his place in the picture of cooking a dinner (at the same time as they are examples of generations of "new" resources out of "nothing") could be that he or she may use flowers from his or her own garden as decorations of his or her food (creation of material). He or she may also, for instance, ask his or her guests to arrive earlier and participate in the joy of cooking a meal (creation of labor).

Something from nothing is in many ways an extreme version of more from less. According to Baker and Nelson (2005) can this be done in three ways:

- Resources at hand
- Recombination of resources for new purposes
- Making do

4.2.1 Resources at Hand

Lévi-Strauss (1966) observed that bricoleurs are collecting physical artifacts, skills and ideas according to the principle that they may possibly become useful rather than as with an engineer, who looks at in a contrasting way, and is collecting resources as an answer to what is needed in an actual project. Previously acquired skills and ways to make it are for a bricoleur used in a pragmatic repertoire in order to handle challenging new situations. Earlier or existing institutions or elements from institutions that have failed will be the building material for new institutions – institutions that are not built *on* the ruins but *by using* the ruins from earlier situations. Above all are contacts in existing social networks resources to develop new businesses (Baker et al., 2005).

4.2.2. Recombination of Resources for New Purposes

Bricolage can mean to combine and reuse resources in other applications than those, in which they were originally intended to be used. Systems designers may possibly "paste together a few components into 'something,' see how it looks like, play with it, check if it works, evaluate, modify or reject. This bricolage activity is not directed to any specific solution or configuration in particular, because [nobody] knows in advance what the final configuration is going to be" (Lanzara, 1999, p. 337). Evolution is "always a matter of using the same elements, of adjusting them, of altering here and there, of arranging various combinations to produce new objects of increasing complexity" (Jacob, 1977, pp. 1164–1165). Bricolage means an "ingenious reconciliation of existing organizational mechanisms and forms, picked by management according to subjective plans and interpretations" (Ciborra, 1996, p. 104).

4.2.3. Making Do

To make do, implies a bias toward action and active engagement in problems rather than lingering over questions of whether a workable outcome can be created from what is at hand. It means necessarily to test those limitations that seem to exist. Many cases of bricolage mean skillful acts of improvisation (Miner et al., 2001; Weick, 1993).

A model for the bricoleurial way to start an entrepreneurial operation is provided in Figure 4.4 (this is an adaptation from Baker & Nelson, 2005, p. 353). There are many differences between this figure and Figures 4.1 and 4.2, but the most important one is perhaps that the environment is not here seen as objective and factual (which is the case for causation as well as effectuation) but as a set of social constructions.

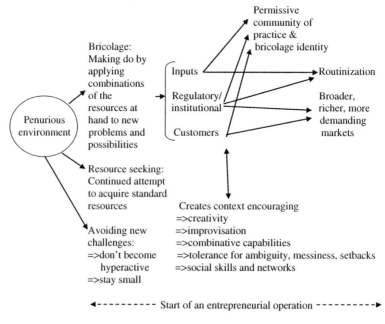

Figure 4.4: Bricolage.

Operations develop in a kind of natural way here. One important reason for this is that bricoleurs apply networking as genuine co-creation. Fyall and Garrod (2005, p. 154) talk about applying networking at four different levels:

4: Co-creation
3: Cooperation
2: Planning something together
1: Talking to each other

Much of networking stops at the first level. Bricoleurs deliberate exploit the fourth level to the fullest. Baker and Nelson (2005, p. 349) provide several examples of this:

Domain	Description
Inputs: physical	By imbuing forgotten, discarded, worn or presumed "single-application" materials with new user value, bricolage turns valueless or even negatively valued resources into valuable materials.
Inputs: labor	By involving customers, suppliers, and hangers-on in providing work on projects, bricolage sometimes creates labor inputs.
Inputs: skills	By permitting and encouraging the use of amateur and self-taught skills (electronics repair, soldering, road work, etc.) that would otherwise go unapplied, bricolage creates useful services.
Customers/markets	By providing products or services that would otherwise be unavailable (housing, cars, billing systems, etc.) to customers (because of poverty, thriftiness, or lack of availability), bricolage creates products and markets where none existed.
Institutional and regulatory environment	By refusing to enact limitations with regard to many "standards" and regulations, and by actively trying things in a variety of areas in which entrepreneurs either do not know the rules or do not see them as constraining, bricolage creates space to "get away with" solutions that would otherwise seem impermissible.

Bricolage notions of making do and using whatever is at hand links with a fundamental shift of developing smart, sustainable, projects that are integral to social change. This represents a shift from a consumption-based to a conservation-based way of doing things better through an improved understanding of existing resources, their form, function, and fungibility (Kickul et al., 2010, p. 237).

4.3.   The Narrow and the Broad View of Marketing

So far we have focused the discussion on entrepreneurship. We will now discuss marketing and overlaps between entrepreneurship and marketing. Entrepreneurship and marketing are often regarded as related disciplines that mirror different aspects of similar phenomena. Many studies have investigated and reported alignments between entrepreneurial orientation and marketing orientation (e.g., Atuahene-Gima & Ko, 2001; Morris & Sexton, 1996; Zahra & Garvis, 2000). And there is not a bold statement to say that there are many similarities. But also very distinct differences, all depending on how the two disciplines are defined. The overlap between entrepreneurship and marketing, called entrepreneurial marketing, will be further discussed in the context of new ventures and different forms of entrepreneurship later in this chapter.

Despite similarities to parts of entrepreneurship marketing as a domain, it is also very pluralistic (Achrol & Kotler, 2012). Consequently, marketing is a complex phenomenon and there are many ways the discipline can be characterized. Within the discipline of marketing, as in the discipline of entrepreneurship, there are many views of what marketing is and how it can be implemented in organizations (and elsewhere).

When looking at views of how marketing is to be implemented in organizations, a narrow as well as a broad view can be identified – similar to our previous discussion on entrepreneurship.

In the narrow view, marketing is regarded as a business function among other business functions, like production, personnel, and finance. In the American Marketing Association's definition of marketing from 2004 this is clearly stated:

> Marketing is an organizational function and a set of processes for creating, communicating and delivering value to customers and for managing customer relationships in ways that benefit the organization and its stakeholders.

This definition was replaced in 2007[1]; however, the idea of marketing as a business function has been very strong for very long, especially among US scholars, and it is the dominating perspective in many marketing management textbooks. This type of marketing theory is often called administrative marketing or managerial marketing.

---

1. The present AMA-definition of marketing is from 2007: Marketing is the activity, set of institutions, and processes for creating, communicating, delivering, and exchanging offerings that have value for customers, clients, partners, and society at large.

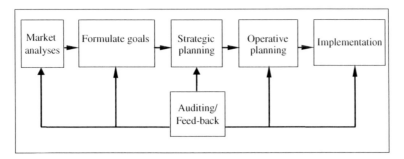

Figure 4.5: Administrative Marketing with a Rational Marketing Planning Process.

Such marketing literature is based on a fairly rational perspective and a planning paradigm. The perspective is that marketing decisions are made based on analytically accurate information and that "well known alternatives" can be ranked in advance. Marketing activities should be planned years in advance and the business plan and the marketing plan are important tools, not only to convince banks and other capital providers but also as a guide for the daily work. Decisions can be dealt with as if there are maximize- or minimize- solutions in sequential processes, Figure 4.5.

In principle, this view of marketing follows the goal-rationality logic (causation) for how marketing is to be implemented, see the discussion related to Figure 4.2. The marketer analyzes and forecasts the market in advance, formulates goals to be reached, and develops strategic plans to be implemented some years later. This thinking is originally based on large firm behavior but is expected to be valid for new firms as well. Similar thinking is to be found in many how-to-do-it seminars with a theme like "How to start your own company." One of the initial actions can be start with create your own business and/or marketing plan.

A very different and broader perspective has existed in parallel, especially among scholars in UK and in the Nordic countries. Marketing is expected to penetrate all business activities. All staff are involved in the different processes of customer value creation. The firms future existence depend on the ability of the whole organization to be able to compete and deliver offers to the market that is equal – or superior– to other sellers' offers at the marketplace. This view is, for example, represented by Grönroos (2000, p. 302) when he writes:

The marketing process includes all resources and activities that have direct or indirect impact on the establishment, maintenance and strengthening of customer relationships, irrespective of where they are in the organization.

Consequently marketing is not a specialist function. It is something much broader, like a philosophy that must penetrate the whole organization and includes everybody. In new ventures, with few individuals involved, most personnel may be directly involved with marketing activities such as customer contacts and after sale-service. Gummesson (1991) has named this phenomenon the *part-time marketer* because most of the staff in a new venture [or in his writing the service firm] may be in direct contact with the market.

Hills and Hultman (2005) had a similar view when they summarized several empirical studies of *entrepreneurial marketing behavior* by identifying a number of characteristics of such behavior:

- Marketing permeates all levels and functional areas of the firm
- Marketing decisions are linked to personal goals and long-time performance
- Flexible, customization approach to market
- Speedy reaction to shifts in customer preference
- Exploit smaller market niches
- Customer knowledge based on market immersion/interaction
- Marketing tactics are often two-way with customers
- Planning, or lack of, occurs in short, incremental steps
- Vision and strategy are driven by tactical successes
- Founder and other personalities are central to marketing
- Marketing decisions based on daily contact and networks
- Formal market research is rare
- Focused on proactively creating and exploiting markets
- Inherent focus on recognition of opportunities
- Calculated risk taking in new ventures
- Reliance on intuition and experience
- Product/venture development is interactive, incremental, informal and with little research/analysis
- A role for passion, zeal, and commitment
- Strives to lead customers
- Value creation through relationships and alliances
- Marketing based on personal reputation, trust, and credibility
- Innovation in products/services and strategies
- Heavy focus on selling and promotion

This thinking reveals a different view of marketing and how it is implemented. The process is based on means-rationality (effectuation) or the bricolage way and is flexible and intermittent. This type of marketing follows the discussion related to Figure 4.3 or Figure 4.4 above. The marketer looks at what is to be found in the close environment and is driven by a vision and short time success; exploiting smaller niches, planning (if any) is short and incremental, and influenced by the actor's personality and is accomplished with the resources and means that are presently available; one step at a time and led by a vision that is emergent and develops based on tactical success.

4.4.   The Role of Marketing in Different Business Start-ups

The business leader Jan Carlzon (1987) named a famous book in service marketing "the moment of truth." This is the time when the customer is exposed to the service and all the promises in the seller's service-offer. It is very much the situation when a start-up is going from ideas to real actions in a market – the situation when the value-proposition to the market, the offer, is evaluated. The seller gets a very obvious feed-back – a yes or a no. Although, many times there is a long process even when the outcome is positive and the final response from the customer is a "yes." To get the first order is important but often there are many barriers and delays to the first successful sale, especially for start-ups in industries with high technological complexity.

The role of marketing is, if possible, more crucial in this phase of a business development than in later phases. And marketing is linked to entrepreneurship by definition. However, all start-ups, like all mature businesses, are not alike. There are huge variations between start-ups due to industry, type of competitive environment, type of entrepreneur as well as key-actor's experience in the start-up situation together with many other factors.

It is obvious that there are several different patterns of how marketing is to implemented and what marketing actions are to be taken in a new venture. Clearly there is not just one best way of implementing marketing in a start-up. And what kind of marketing there will be is dependent on the entrepreneur, his/her personality and personal goals, etc. A bricoleur versus manager/engineer type of starter of a new venture will act differently in their approach to marketing issues. However, one type of behavior is not necessarily better than the other. There is definitely an equifinality in the sense that many different patterns and behavior can lead to similar outcomes and there is nothing definitive to suggest the best way of taking marketing actions in a new venture. But there are differences that can be identified and used as mental models that make us understand important differences in approaches to marketing in start-ups.

The two perspectives of marketing, broad and narrow, can be used as archetypes of how marketing is implemented in an organization. Since these archetypes are linked to the two forms of entrepreneurship we have identified in previous sections we have discussed different views of entrepreneurship and also different types of entrepreneurs. The bricoleur versus the managerial/engineering type of entrepreneur will not let marketing play the same role in a start-up phase.

The first is the administrative view of marketing. Existing literature about marketing in start-ups is dominated by the archetype of administrative marketing. Most of the "checklist" — and "how-to-do it" — books also have their theoretical foundations in the administrative view. A very common myth is that marketing in start-ups is generally regarded to suffer from lack of resources. Many books offer advice on how to deal with this, for early examples see *Guerrilla marketing* (Levinson, 1984); *Marketing on a Shoestring* (Davidson, 1994); *Off-the-Wall Marketing Ideas* (Michaels & Karpowicz, 2000). Such views are based on traditional thinking of administrative marketing. New firms have a lack of resources compared with what is generally regarded as necessary to do in a standard business or marketing plan. Naturally, a new firm often has less financial resources available compared with many mature firms. But a start-up may have more personal enthusiasm and commitment; more creativity among its staff that can compensate the lower level of financial resources. Further, it is the idea of a complete marketing plan that must be

Table 4.1: Characteristics of administrative and entrepreneurial marketing.

	Narrow View: Administrative Marketing	**Broad View: Entrepreneurial Marketing**
General role	Marketing is a specialist function among other specialist functions	Marketing and Entrepreneurship mirror similar phenomenon and partly overlap. Sometime it is impossible to categorize entrepreneurial action in marketing or entrepreneurship
	Marketing can be outsourced to functional specialist firms	
	The role of marketing collects correct information on customer demand and other relevant information to the firm's decision makers as well as create as selling (outgoing) information so it is possible to position products and services and convince customers	Marketing cannot be outsourced since it is penetrates all parts of the firm (however, different specialist parts of marketing, for example advertising can be outsourced)
	Opportunities are identified through market analyses	Marketing's role is to coordinate all efforts in the process of formulating and delivering value–creating product – and services to customers
	Strategic goals and annual targets lead daily activities	
	Strategic and tactical actions are planned in advance	
	Contact with customers is mainly through salesmen and customer contact departments	Opportunity recognition that is both intended and emergent is a central and unique component of both entrepreneurial and marketing processes
	All marketers are specialists	
	Innovation is sometimes necessary to maintain competitive advantage	Actions are led by vision and is driven by short time success and available resources
	Plans are based on forecasting. Dynamism is co-opted by re-planning and revised rolling plans	Actions are taken one-step at a time and the intensity of marketing activities depend on available resources
		Continuous contact and cooperation with customers and others outside the firm is an important part in all marketing processes
		Everyone in the firm is a marketer
		Innovation is a way to continuously improve the firms' value-creating ability, this leads to competitive advantage
		Continuous contacts with the market and willingness to change and cooperate with dynamic markets

Table 4.1: (*Continued*)

	Narrow View: Administrative Marketing	**Broad View: Entrepreneurial Marketing**
Value creation	Superior products and services ensure that customers get best value for money	Close relations and a mental willingness to solve customers' problem secure that customer value is co-created with customers
Measure of success	Financial metrics are important indicators of success	Customer satisfaction and ability to maintain relationships is key indicator for successful marketing. Profit and positive cash flow are necessities for this. Competitive advantage is gained by close relations and understanding of customers' needs

implemented and that resources must be available, and has its roots in administrative marketing. Activities like market analyses, market positioning, and entry strategies are also originated from traditional marketing management. This is the type of thinking and behavior we can expect in a rational start-up with the engineer-type entrepreneur.

However, in traditional university textbooks, administrative marketing is not the only existing model but also the best way of dealing with marketing in start-ups. In a natural start-up, and the bricoleur as a starter, the marketing thinking and actions taken can rather be expected to follow the broad, entrepreneurial marketing model. Actions are taken and lessons are learned during the process. The important step is to take action to start the process and to learn by doing. The natural start-up starts the process with resources available and starts learning who can be the customer by exploring own and other personal network. It is a causation process with mean-rationality and follows entrepreneurial marketing characteristics. Entrepreneurial marketing is defined as:

> Entrepreneurial marketing is a spirit, an orientation as well as a process of passionately pursuing opportunities and launching and growing ventures that create perceived customer value through relationships by employing innovativeness, creativity, selling, market immersion, networking and flexibility. (Hills & Hultman, 2006)

Entrepreneurial marketing in a natural start-up is a vision driven, incremental, and informal learning process that permeates all levels in the firm; value creation is a two-way interactive, flexible co-creation process with a speedy reaction to shift in customer preference and use innovations to improve customer value. Market decisions are based on intensive contacts and networks; intuition and experience are also ingredients and there is a role for passion, zeal, trust, and personal commitment. There is an inherent focus on recognition of opportunities as well as proactively creating and exploiting markets, preferably smaller markets.

In Table 4.1, the two perspectives on marketing are exemplified.

4.5. Conclusion

Both entrepreneurship and marketing have many definitions. In this chapter, two main perspectives were taken on both disciplines: a narrow and a broad view. The narrow view of entrepreneurship is basically an economic phenomenon and is a matter of exploiting opportunities. The broad view defines entrepreneurship less specifically and stresses outcome more than anything else.

Related to these views of entrepreneurship, two types of start-ups were discussed: the rational versus the natural entrepreneurial start-up. Based on Sarasvathy (2001), the first-type entrepreneurial activities are formed in a goals-rational way (causation) or in the means-rationality way (effectuation). Decisions are made based on forecasts of the future and activities are regarded as possible to plan in advance. We link this view of entrepreneurship to the thinking behind a rational start-up. It is much in line with the main logic and content of mainstream administrative marketing. These theories illustrate the marketing behavior among rational start-ups.

The natural start-up is linked to a broader view of entrepreneurship. The entrepreneur takes actions with means and information available, incrementally, and step-by-step learning. This is much in line with the logic behind entrepreneurial marketing but is different from administrative marketing behavior.

In both cases, the outcome of all marketing (and entrepreneurship) processes is to interpret environmental information and transform these interpretations into perceived opportunities. Then to exploit innovations, create superior value propositions, develop competitive market offers, and develop and maintain business relations, be able to seal all this in a business deal and finally to secure that customers are able to create their customer value in a co-creation environment. For sure not a simple role but this is what it takes for doing business!

Fortunately, there are many routes to success for a start-up. Empirical evidence of both these marketing archetypes can be found. Marketing in start-ups are very much determined by the key actors' way of thinking. Therefore, it is important to realize that there are parallel images of marketing behavior that coexist. And the marketing behavior may follow a causation-rationality as well as a means-rationality logic.

References

Achrol, R. S., & Kotler, P. (2012). Frontiers of the marketing paradigm in the third millennium. *Journal of the Academy of Marketing Science, 40*(1), 35–52.

Ács, Z. J. (2002). *Innovation and the Growth of Cities*. Northampton, MA: Edward Elgar.

Allen, K. R. (2010). *New venture creation* (5th International ed.). Mason, OH: South-Western.

Amin, A., Cameron, A., & Hudson, R. (2002). *Placing the social economy*. London: Routledge.

Atuahene-Gima, K., & Ko, A. (2001). An empirical investigation of the effect of market orientation and entrepreneurship orientation alignment on product innovation. *Organization Science, 12*(1), 54–74.

Baker, T., Gedjlovic, E., & Lubatkin, M. (2005). A framework for comparing entrepreneurship processes across nations. *Journal of International Business Studies, 36*, 492–504.

Baker, T., & Nelson, R. E. (2005). Creating something from nothing: Resource construction through entrepreneurial bricolage. *Administrative Science Quarterly, 50*, 329–366.

Baron, R. A. (1998). Cognitive mechanisms in entrepreneurship: Why and when entrepreneurs think differently than other people. *Journal of Business Venturing, 12*, 275–294.

Baron, R. A., & Shane, S. A. (2008). *Entrepreneurship. A process perspective* (2nd ed.). Mason, OH: Thomson.

Barringer, B. R., & Ireland, R. D. (2006). *Entrepreneurship. Successfully launching new ventures*. Upper Saddle River, NJ: Pearson Education, Inc.

Berglund, K., & Gaddefors, J. (2010). Entrepreneurship requires resistance to be mobilized. In F. Bill, B. Bjerke & A. W. Johansson (Eds.), *(De)mobilizing the entrepreneurship discourse. Exploring entrepreneurial thinking and action*. Northampton, MA: Edward Elgar.

Bhave, M. P. (1994). A process model of entrepreneurial venture creation. *Journal of Business Venturing, 9*(3), 223–242.

Bill, F., Jansson, A., & Olaison, L. (2010). The spectacle of entrepreneurship: A duality of flamboyance and activity. In F. Bill, B. Bjerke & A. W. Johansson (Eds.), *(De)mobilizing the entrepreneurship discourse. Exploring entrepreneurial thinking and action*. Northampton, MA: Edward Elgar.

Bjerke, B. (2007). *Understanding entrepreneurship*. Northampton, MA: Edward Elgar.

Bjerke, B. (2010). Entrepreneurship, space and place. In F. Bill, B. Bjerke & A. W. Johansson (Eds.), *(De)mobilizing the entrepreneurship discourse. Exploring entrepreneurial thinking and action*. Northampton, MA: Edward Elgar.

Bosma, N., & Harding, R. (2007). *Global entrepreneurship*. GEM 2006 Summary Results, Babson College, Babson Park, MA, USA and London Business School: London, UK.

Boulding, K. E. (1956). General systems theory: The skeleton of science. *Management Science, 2*, 197–208.

Bridge, S., O'Neill, K., & Cromie, S. (2003). *Understanding enterprise, entrepreneurship and small business* (2nd ed.). New York, NY: Palgrave Macmillan.

Burchell, G., Gordon, C., & Miller, P. (Eds.). (1991). *The foucault effect: Studies in governmentality*. Chicago, IL: University of Chicago Press.

Carlzon, J. (1987). *Moment of truth*. New York, NY: Harper & Row.

Ciborra, C. U. (1996). The platform organization: Recombining strategies, structures, and surprises. *Organization Science, 7*, 103–118.

Coulter, M. (2001). *Entrepreneurship in action*. Upper Saddle River, NJ: Prentice Hall.

Dart, R. (2004). The legitimacy of social enterprise. *Non-Profit Management & Leadership, 14*(4), 411–424.

Davidson, J. (1994). *Marketing on a shoestring*. New York, NY: Wiley.

Davidsson, P. (1989). *Continued entrepreneurship and small firm growth*. Doctoral dissertation, Stockholm School of Economics, Stockholm, Sweden.

Davidsson, P. (2003). The domain of entrepreneurship research: Some suggestions. In D. Shepherd & J. Katz (Eds.), *Cognitive approaches to entrepreneurship research*. Amsterdam: Elsevier.

Dees, J. G., Emerson, J., & Economy, P. (2001). *Enterprising nonprofits. A toolkit for social entrepreneurs*. New York, NY: Wiley.

Deetz, S. (1998). Discursive formations, strategized subordination and self-surveillance. In A. McKinley & K. Starkey (Eds.), *Foucault, management and organization theory*. London: Sage.

Drucker, P. (1985). *Innovation and entrepreneurship. Practice and principles*. London: Heineman.

du Gay, P. (Ed.). (1997). *The production of culture – Cultures of production*. London: Sage.

Forbes, D. P. (2005). Are some entrepreneurs more overconfident than others? *Journal of Business Venturing, 20*, 623–640.

Foucault, M. (1997). What is enlightenment? In P. Rabinow (Ed.), *Michel foucault. ethics, subjectivity and truth*. New York, NY: The New Press.

Fyall, A., & Garrod, B. (2005). *Tourism marketing – A collaborative approach. Aspects of Tourism 18*. Clevedon, UK: Channel View Publications.

Gaglio, C. M. (1997). Opportunity recognition: Review, critique and suggested research directions. In J. Katz & R. H. Brockhaus (Eds.), *Advances in entrepreneurship, firm emergence and growth*. Greenwich, CT: JAI Press.

Gaglio, C. M., & Katz, J. A. (2001). The psychological basis of opportunity identification: Entrepreneurial alertness. *Small Business Economics, 16*, 95–111.

Gartner, W. B. (2007). Entrepreneurial narrative and a science of the imagination. *Journal of Business Venturing, 22*(5), 613–627.

Gartner, W. B., & Carter, N. M. (2003). Entrepreneurial behavior and firm organizing processes. In Z. J. Ács & D. B. Audretsch (Eds.), *Handbook of entrepreneurship*. Dordrecht, NL: Kluwer.

Garud, R., Kumaraswamy, A., & Nayyar, P. (1998). Real options of fool's gold. Perspective makes the difference. *Academy of Management Review, 3*(2), 212–214.

Gummesson, E. (1991). Marketing revisited: The crucial role of the part-time marketers. *European journal of Marketing, 25*(2), 60–67.

Grönroos, C. (2000). *Service management and marketing – A customer relationship management approach*. Chichester: Wiley.

Hardt, M. (2002). *Gilles Deleuze. An Apprenticeship of Philosophy*. Minneapolis, MN: University of Minnesota Press.

Hills, G., & Hultman, C. (2005). Marketing, Entrepreneurship and SMEs: Knowledge and education revisited. Paper presented at the Academy of Marketing Special Interest Group on Entrepreneurial and SME Marketing, Southampton, UK.

Hills, G., & Hultman, C. (2006). Entrepreneurial marketing. In S. Lagrosen & G. Svensson (Eds.), *Marketing – Broadening the horizons* (pp. 220–234). Lund: Studentlitteratur.

Hjorth, D., & Johannisson, B. (1998). Entreprenörskap som skapelseprocess och ideologi [Entrepreneurship as a creative process and ideology]. In B. Czarniawska (Ed.), *Organisationsteori på svenska [Organization theory in Swedish]*. Malmö: Liber Ekonomi.

Hjorth, D., & Johannisson, B. (2003). Conceptualising the opening phase of regional development as the enactment of "collective identity". *Concepts and Transformations, 8*, 69–92.

Hjorth, D., & Steyaert, C. (2003). Entrepreneurship beyond (a new) economy: creative swarms and pathological zones. In C. Steyaert & D. Hjorth (Eds.), *New movements in entrepreneurship*. Northampton, MA: Edward Elgar.

Hjorth, D., & Steyaert, C. (Eds.). (2004). *Narrative and discursive approaches in entrepreneurship. A second movements in entrepreneurship books.* Northampton, MA: Edward Elgar.

Hjorth, D., & Steyaert, C. (Eds.). (2009). *The politics and aesthetics of entrepreneurship. A fourth movements in entrepreneurship book.* Northampton, MA: Edward Elgar.

Jacob, F. (1977). Evolution and tinkering. *Science, 196*(4295), 1161–1166.

Johannisson, B. (2005). *Entreprenörskapets väsen [The essence of entrepreneurship].* Lund: Studentlitteratur.

Johansson, A. W. (2010). Innovation, creativity and imitation. In F. Bill, B. Bjerke & A. W. Johansson (Eds.), *(De)mobilizing the entrepreneurship discourse. Exploring entrepreneurial thinking and action.* Northampton, MA: Edward Elgar.

Johnstone, H., & Lionais, D. (2004). Depleted communities and community business entrepreneurship: revaluing space through place. *Entrepreneurship and Regional Development, 16*(May), 217–233.

Kanter, R. M. (1983). *The change masters – Innovation and entrepreneurship in the American corporation.* New York, NY: Simon and Schuster.

Katz, D., & Kahn, R. L. (1978). *The social psychology of organizations* (2nd ed.). New York, NY: Wiley.

Katz, J. A. (1998). A brief history of tertiary entrepreneurship education in the United States. Paper presented at the Entrepreneurship Education Workshop, Stockholm.

Kickul, J., Griffiths, M. D., & Gundry, L. (2010). Innovating for social impact: Is bricolage the catalyst for change? In A. Fayolle & H. Matlay (Eds.), *Handbook of research on social entrepreneurship.* Northampton, MA: Edward Elgar.

Kirzner, I. M. (1979). *Perception, opportunity, and profit.* Chicago, IL: University of Chicago Press.

Kuratko, D. F., & Hodgetts, R. M. (2004). *Entrepreneurship. Theory, process, practice* (6th ed.). Stanford, CT: Thomson South-Western.

Lanzara, G. F. (1999). Between transient constructs and persistent structures: Designing systems in action. *Journal of Strategic Information Systems, 8,* 331–349.

Levinson, J. C. (1984). *Guerrilla marketing: Secrets for making big profits from your small business.* Boston, MA: Houghton Mifflin.

Lévi-Strauss, C. (1966). *The savage mind.* Chicago, IL: The University of Chicago Press.

Lindgren, M., & Packendorff, J. (2007). *Konstruktion av entreprenörskap. Teori, praktik och interaktion [Construction of entrepreneurship. Theory, practice and interaction].* Stockholm: Forum för Småföretagsforskning.

Low, M. B. (2001). The adolescence of entrepreneurship research: Specification of Purpose. *Entrepreneurship Theory and Practice, 25*(4), 17–25.

Mariotti, S., & Glackin, C. (2010). *Entrepreneurship* (2nd ed.). Upper Saddle River, NJ: Prentice Hall.

Martin, L. H., Gutman, H., & Hutton, P. H. (1988). *Technologies of the self – A seminar with michel foucault.* Amherst, MA: University of Massachusetts Press.

Michaels, N., & Karpowicz, D. (2000). *Off-the-wall marketing ideas: Jump-start your sales without busting your budget.* Avon, MA: Adams Media.

Miner, A. S., Bassoff, P., & Moorman, C. (2001). Organizational improvisation and learning. A field study. *Administrative Science Quarterly, 46,* 304–337.

Morris, M. H., & Sexton, D. L. (1996). The concept of entrepreneurial intensity: Implications for firm performance. *Journal of Business Research, 36*(1), 5–13.

Penrose, E. G. (1959). *The theory of the growth of the firm.* New York, NY: Wiley.

Peters, T. (1994a). *The Pursuit of WOW! Every person's guide to topsy-turvy times.* London: Pan Books.

Peters, T. (1994b). *The Tom Peters seminar. Crazy times call for crazy organizations.* London: Pan Books.

Peters, T., & Waterman, R. (1982). *In search of excellence.* London: Harper and Row.

Sarasvathy, S. (2001). Causation and effectuation: Toward a theoretical shift from economic inevitability to entrepreneurial contingency. *Academy of Management Review, 26*(2), 243–263.

Scott, W. R. (1998). *Organizations: Rational, natural, and open systems* (4th ed.). Upper Saddle River, NJ: Prentice Hall.

Sexton, D. L., & Bowman-Upton, N. B. (1991). *Entrepreneurship. Creativity and growth.* New York, NY: Macmillan Publishing Company.

Stevenson, H. H., & Jarillo, J. C. (1990). A paradigm for entrepreneurship: Entrepreneurial management. *Strategic Management Journal, 11,* 17–27.

Steyaert, C. (1997). A qualitative methodology for process studies of entrepreneurship. Creating local knowledge through stories. *International Studies of Management and Organization, 27*(3), 13–33.

Steyaert, C. (2000). Entre-concepts: conceiving entrepreneurship. Paper presented at the RENT-conference XIV, Prague.

Steyaert, C. (2004). The prosaic of entrepreneurship. In D. Hjorth & C. Steyaert (Eds.), *Narrative and discursive approaches to entrepreneurship. A second movements in entrepreneurship books.* Northampton, US: Edward Elgar.

Steyaert, C. (2007). "Entrepreneuring" as a conceptual attractor? A view of process theories in 20 years of entrepreneurship studies. *Entrepreneurship and Regional Development, 19*(6), 453–477.

Steyaert, C., & Hjorth, D. (Eds.). (2003). *New movements in entrepreneurship.* Northampton, MA: Edward Elgar.

Steyaert, C., & Hjorth, D. (Eds.). (2006). *Entrepreneurship as social change. A third movements in entrepreneurship book.* Northampton, MA: Edward Elgar.

Steyaert, C., & Katz, J. (2004). Reclaiming the space of entrepreneurship in society: Geographical, discursive and social dimensions. *Entrepreneurship and Regional Development, 16*(May), 179–196.

Timmons, J. A. (1999). *New venture creation. Entrepreneurship for the 21st Century* (5th ed.). New York, NY: Irwin McGraw-Hill.

Townley, B. (1995). "Know thyself": Self-awareness, self-formation and managing. *Organization, 2*(2), 271–289.

Venkataraman, S. (1997). The distinctive domain of entrepreneurship research. In J. A. Katz & R. Brockhaus (Eds.), *Advances in entrepreneurship, firm emergence and growth* (Vol. 3). Greenwich, CT: JAI Press.

Weick, K. E. (1993). The collapse of sensemaking in organizations: The Mann Gulch Disaster. *Administrative Science Quarterly, 38,* 628–652.

Wickham, P. A. (2006). *Strategic entrepreneurship* (4th ed.). Essex: Pearson Education Limited.

Wiklund, J. (1998). *Small firm growth and performance.* JIBS Dissertation Series No. 003. Jönköping International Business School, Jönköping, Sweden.

Zahra, S., & Garvis, D. (2000). International corporate entrepreneurship and firm performance: The moderating effect of international environmental hostility. *Journal of Business Venturing, 15*(5), 469–492.

Zimmerer, T. W., & Scarborough, N. M. (2005). *Essentials of entrepreneurship and small business management* (4th ed.). Upper Saddle River, NJ: Prentice Hall.

Chapter 5

Entrepreneurial Marketing Orientation in SMEs

Abstract

This chapter describes entrepreneurial marketing in small and medium-sized enterprises (SMEs). The way in which smaller firms and entrepreneurial new ventures take products and services to market is often very different from large organizations. SMEs face a number of internal and external business challenges that they overcome by implicitly using an entrepreneurial marketing orientation (EMO). EMO is particularly visible in knowledge intensive high-technology sectors where the marketplace is globalized and rapidly changing, with frequent new product development (NPD) launches and with high competition from other large players and smaller competitors launching innovative new technologies. The chapter begins by explaining and conceptualizing EMO and then describing a qualitative framework with which to explore entrepreneurial marketing. The purpose of qualitative research investigation and the findings from the application of the framework are articulated and explained. Finally, comparative data is discussed from Silicon Valley, United States and from Wales, United Kingdom which shows that firm focus on marketing is different in each region and that firm orientation is often different, which impacts on firm development and growth. Lastly, conclusions are drawn and implications for future research are proposed.

5.1. Introduction

As PhD researchers during the period of 2005–2009, both authors of this chapter were exploring the phenomena of marketing in technology firms and investigating how this was carried out. Unaware of each other's work at first, consecutively Suoranta was researching in the United States (US) and Jones was studying in

Wales, United Kingdom (UK). Both researchers worked very closely and intensively with software technology firms in their respective university regions, and this gave opportunity for generation of some unique insights into how these firms operate.

As a theoretical platform, existing small and medium-sized enterprise (SME) research provided vital data and findings related to SME marketing. This is particularly so with the growth of new firms in the new economic era (Bjerke & Hultman, 2002) where new ventures are created in globalized markets with ever-increasing uncertainty, and with ever more demanding consumers. Hill (2001) was one of the first to observe from a large-scale study of manufacturing firms that small firms are not simply smaller versions of large firms, but they also carry out marketing activities very differently. There is now an acknowledgement that although the SME's approach to marketing may not fit established theories (Freel, 2000), successful SMEs are able to capitalize on their unique benefits of "smallness." Carson, Cromie, McGowan, and Hill (1995) proposed that SME marketing was in fact entrepreneurial marketing, a distinctive style characterized by a range of factors that included an inherently informal, simple, and haphazard approach. This approach is a result of various factors including small size, business and marketing limitations, the influence of the entrepreneur, and the lack of formal organizational structures or formal systems of communication with sometimes no systems at all when it comes to marketing. This form of marketing tends to be responsive and reactive to competition and opportunistic in nature (Carson et al., 1995). It also tends to be highly dependent on networking (Gilmore & Carson, 1999; Gilmore, Carson, & Grant, 2001; Miller, Besser, & Malshe, 2007) and the opportunities it provides for the generation of social capital (Bowey & Easton, 2007; Cope, Jack, & Rose, 2007; Miller et al., 2007; Shaw, 2006). Networks facilitate the formation and generation of customer contacts where word-of-mouth recommendation is facilitated through use of interorganizational network relationships and personal contact networks (Gilmore et al., 2001; Hill & Wright, 2001). As Chapter 1 (Gilmore, McAuley, Gallagher, and Carson) point out, the activities of entrepreneurship and marketing researchers in the UK, the US, and now globally have firmly established a growing base of knowledge around how SMEs do business and how entrepreneurs carry out entrepreneurial marketing activities (Hills, Hultman, & Miles, 2008; Kraus, Filser, Eggers, Hills, & Hultman, 2012).

In an effort to understand how marketing was carried out in entrepreneurial, innovative high-tech ventures, the work of Jones in the UK draws on the experiences of working with one software technology firm and marketing for it as part of the PhD, and by also scanning well known quantitative scales and measures in the entrepreneurial orientation (EO), market orientation (MO), innovation orientation (IO), and customer orientation (CO) literatures. From this literature, Jones proposed a conceptual model for entrepreneurial marketing that identifies the components of such a model, together with specific indications of the overlap between scales in the different areas. The Jones and Rowley model (2011) implicitly suggests that marketing in SMEs is intertwined with other activities and behaviors in the small business enterprise, and argues that in order to understand marketing in SMEs it is essential to understand its context, specifically in relation to customer engagement, innovation, and entrepreneurial approaches to marketing.

Marketing and, more specifically, MO has been identified as an important contributor to business performance (Deshpande, Farley, & Webster, 1993; Jaworski & Kohli, 1993; Narver & Slater, 1990). Conversely, several researchers have identified the absence of MO and skills in SMEs that often leads to lower performance levels and higher risks of business failure (Alpkan, Yilmaz, & Kaya, 2007; Blankson & Stokes, 2002; Brooksbank, Kirby, & Taylor, 2004; Hill & Blois, 1987; Huang & Brown, 1999; McCartan-Quinn & Carson, 2003). Davis, Hills, & LaForge, (1985, p. 31) suggested that: "marketing academicians have almost entirely neglected investigations at the small enterprise/marketing interface."

Fortunately, given the importance of small business to the economy, there has been a much greater level of activity in relation to marketing in SMEs over the last 20 years (Blankson & Omar, 2002; Blankson & Stokes, 2002; Brooksbank, 1991; Brooksbank, Kirby, Taylor, & Jones-Evans, 1999, 2004; Carson, 1990; Carson et al., 1995; Gilmore et al., 2001; Hill, 2001; Stokes, 1998), and this has led to a developing body of knowledge around SMEs and their marketing strategies, planning and activities, as discussed later in this chapter. However, much of this research has taken as its foundation the disciplinary perspectives of marketing and/or strategy, and has been published in journals and books in these fields. It is therefore timely to seek to energize the debate about marketing and MO within the mainstream small business literature.

More recently, Morris, Schindehutte, & La Forge (2002, p. 5) have defined EM as "the proactive identification and exploitation of opportunities for acquiring and retaining profitable customers through innovative approaches to risk management, resource leveraging and value creation." Researchers also view EM behavior as being derived from entrepreneurial thinking, entrepreneurs being innovative, calculated risk takers, proactive, and opportunity oriented (Kirzner, 1979), while Hills and Hultman (2006, p. 222) identified EM behavioral characteristics that included "marketing tactics often two way with customers' and 'marketing decisions based on daily contacts and networks."

It has also been proposed that marketing has much to offer the study of entrepreneurship (Hills, 1987; Murray, 1981) and, conversely, entrepreneurship can look to marketing as the key function of the firm, which can encompass innovation and creativity (Collinson & Shaw, 2001). Indeed, empirical evidence suggests that there exists a significant correlation between an enterprise's marketing and entrepreneurial orientations, both widely being responsible for corporate success (Miles & Arnold, 1991). The relatively recent development of EM theory has generated a substantial body of literature surrounding the interface between marketing and entrepreneurship. Yet, Carson (2005) cited in Hills and Hultman (2006, p. 232) put the case for a more holistic approach to the domain: "I think we need a holistic interpretation of the domain, rather than focusing on an either/or scenario."

This chapter then proposes that the EM paradigm should be advanced to include an approach to marketing that is grounded in the knowledge bases of not only marketing but also innovation, entrepreneurship, and customer engagement and relationships. This philosophical standpoint is operationalized through a focus on "orientations." Thus, the conceptual model (Jones & Rowley, 2011) seeks to integrate key facets of the MO scales, with facets from CO, EO, and innovation orientation (IO). In particular, the case is argued for the inclusion of the notion of CO as a distinct component of EM, rather than being subsumed under MO. This chapter describes the key themes in the EM literature from the SME perspective, together with a review of the EO, MO, IO, and CO literatures that on this basis a new entrepreneurial marketing orientation (EMO) model is proposed.

5.2.   Strategic Orientations and SMEs

As discussed in the previous section, there is increasing interest in EM theory, and an established recognition of its grounding in both marketing and entrepreneurship theory and practice. This section will argue that on the basis of an analysis of the EM literature any consideration of EM must embrace innovation and customer engagement and relationships. Accordingly, in this section, previous work MO, EO, CO, and IO scales is summarized and conceptualized, where possible, with respect to SMEs. In addition, the scales that were used to inform the components in the proposed EMO model are identified and discussed.

5.2.1.   Market Orientation

MO is widely recognized as having a positive effect on business performance (Deshpande, 1999; Jaworski & Kohli, 1993; Kotler, 1984; Kotler & Anderson, 1987; Narver & Slater, 1990, 1999; Webster, 1988). Although literature has provided a variety of definitions of MO, most authors appear to adopt one of two perspectives (Tajeddini, Trueman, & Larsen, 2006; Verhees & Meulenberg, 2004), that of Kohli and Jaworski (1990) or Narver and Slater's (1990) definition. Kohli and Jaworski adopt a behavioral perspective, using marketing intelligence rather than a customer focus as the central element. In contrast, the Narver and Slater scale is based on a cultural perspective, identifying three behavioral components: CO, competitor orientation, and interfunctional coordination. Both models are rigorously tested for reliability in large firms research but opinion remains divided as to which is the more suitable (Pitt, Carauna, & Berthon, 1996; Tajeddini et al., 2006). Deshpande et al. (1993) developed a MO scale, which embodied a CO focus and later, Deshpande and Farley (1998) developed the "MORTN" scale, based on elements of Narver and Slater's (1990) scale, Kohli, Jaworski, and Kumar (1993) "MARKOR" scale and Deshpande et al.'s (1993) scale.

Owing to their robustness, reliability, and validity, Narver and Slater's (1990) MO scale and Kohli et al.'s (1993) "MARKOR" scale are used in the MO element of the proposed EM orientation model. The MO dimensions that inform the EMO model are market intelligence generation (Kohli et al., 1993), responsiveness toward competitors (Kohli et al., 1993), and integration of business processes (Narver & Slater, 1990).

5.2.2. Customer Orientation

CO has its roots in early services marketing literature in which the importance of customer-focused employees was a tangible sign of quality for the firm and its services (Gronroos, 1982). Since then, the concept of CO within firms has been investigated by a number of authors and researchers; indeed, some authors view CO as the "pillar of marketing" (Deshpande et al., 1993; Jaworski & Kohli, 1993; Slater & Narver, 1995). Narver and Slater (1990) observed that CO requires a sufficient understanding to create products or services of superior value, defining CO as a culture that accentuates the creation of customer value as the overriding organizational goal, while Cardwell (1994) argues that a company's very survival will depend on moving closer to the customer, fully understanding the customer's needs and wants, building a relationship and, therefore, developing an attitude of consistent customer dedication.

Zontanos and Anderson (2004) assert that a small firm's marketing advantage is precisely linked to the close relationships between the entrepreneur and the customers, in contrast to larger firms where it is much more difficult to embed entrepreneurship and a CO into its organizational culture. Small firms' generally narrow and localized customer base creates a much shorter line of communication between the firm and its customers (Weinrauch, Man, Robinson, & Pharr, 1991), with entrepreneurs often knowing their customers personally. As a result of such a close interactive relationship, benefits arise such as higher customer loyalty and higher levels of customer satisfaction (Carson, 1985; Lindman, 2004). Long-term relationships between the customer and entrepreneurs are often cemented by the small firm's ability to react to customer needs quickly as they are more likely to be flexible in their ability to respond to customer inquiries (Carson et al., 1995).

CO has been identified and investigated by a number of researchers in a range of disciplines. Some authors regard CO as central to the marketing concept and view CO and MO as interchangeable concepts (Deshpande et al., 1993; Shapiro, 1988; Webster, 1988). Narver and Slater (1990) regard CO as a culture that accentuates the creation of customer value as the overriding organizational goal, while others such as Jones, Busch, and Dacin (2003) maintain MO and CO orientation as separate concepts and, according to Day and Wensley (1988), a balance must be found between the two orientations. From a slightly different perspective Drucker (1954) defined CO as a philosophy and a set of behaviors directed toward determining and understanding the needs of the target customer and adapting the selling organization's response in order to satisfy those needs better than the competition.

CO also features in the services management and marketing literature in which companies that adopt a customer satisfaction perspective are considered more able to attain organizational goals with greater effectiveness than their competitors (Reichheld & Sasser, 1990). Conversely, Saura, Contri, Taulet, and Velazquez (2005) identify CO as resting in both the sales literature and the MO literature. The sales literature promotes customer centrality for service excellence and uses such measures as Saxe and Weitz's (1982) service orientation and customer orientation SOCO scale, which examines the relationship between service and COs. This scale is still frequently used and adapted in the sales literature. Deshpande et al.'s

(1993) MO scale is known as a customer-oriented scale based on corporate culture and organizational innovativeness while Saura et al. (2005) developed scales that are more representative of Drucker's definition. The scales of Despande et al., Saura et al., and Saxe and Weitz, are used in the proposed new model as they represent central elements of the CO concept from a range of perspectives and this work is proven for its reliability and validity. CO dimensions from the scales that inform the CO aspect of the model are: responsiveness toward customers (Kohli et al., 1993); communication with customers (Narver & Slater, 1990); understanding and delivering customer value (Deshpande et al., 1993; Saura et al., 2005; Saxe & Weitz, 1982).

5.2.3. Entrepreneurial Orientation

Entrepreneurial personality traits that are identified in the body of entrepreneurship literature largely inform the EO measurement scales and constructs. Therefore, the dimensions of risk taking, proactiveness, and innovation are often incorporated (Covin & Slevin, 1991; Ginsberg, 1985; Khandwalla, 1977; Lumpkin & Dess, 1996; Miles & Arnold, 1991; Morris & Paul, 1987; Naman & Slevin, 1993). Investigation of EO related to research in SMEs includes Salavou and Lioukas' (2003) investigation of market focus, technological posture, and EO. Furthermore, Kreiser, Marino, and Weaver (2002) propose that EO research should include culture, innovation, risk taking, and proactiveness. Khandwalla (1977) developed the "ENTRESCALE" that has subconstructs of innovation and proactiveness, entrepreneurial proclivity, and a propensity for risk taking. This scale has been subsequently refined (Covin & Slevin, 1989; Miller & Friesen, 1978) and much cited in the EO literature, being noted for its reliability and validity in numerous studies (Covin & Slevin, 1989; Khandwalla, 1977; Miles & Snow, 1978). More recently, Knight (1997) adapted the "ENTRESCALE" scale, while Matsuno, Mentzer, and Özsomer (2002) also developed an EO scale adapted from earlier EO research studies (Covin & Slevin, 1989; Miller, 1983; Morris & Paul, 1987). Matsuno et al.'s scale considers receptiveness to innovation, risk-taking attitude, and proactiveness toward opportunities. Knight's and Matsuno et al.'s scales reflect the consensus view of the EO literature preferring orientation scales that are known for their reliability and validity. They inform the EMO model with the following dimensions: research and development (Knight, 1997), speed to market (Knight, 1997), risk taking (Matsuno et al., 2002), and proactiveness (Matsuno et al., 2002).

5.2.4. Innovation Orientation

While the interface between marketing and entrepreneurship has generated debate, the MO literature has also identified a relationship between innovation, MO, and company performance (Connor, 1999; Hurley & Hult, 1998; Jaworski, Kohli, & Sahay, 2000; Slater & Narver, 1998; Verhees & Meulenberg, 2004). Narver & Slater (1990) propose that the practice of continuous innovation remains an ever-present element of all three identified components of a MO (Tajeddini et al., 2006), while many entrepreneurial activities, such as the identification of new opportunities, the application of innovative techniques, the conveyance of goods to the marketplace, and the successful meeting of customer needs in the chosen market, are also elementary aspects of marketing theory (Collinson & Shaw, 2001). They propose a more in-depth approach to EM that takes into account the characteristics of the entrepreneur, whereby marketing and entrepreneurship are seen to have three areas of interface: change focused, opportunistic in nature, and innovative in their approach to management. Kuratko (1995) describes an entrepreneur as "an innovator or developer who recognizes and seizes opportunities, converts those opportunities into workable/marketable ideas, adds value through time, effort, money or skills, assumes the risks of the competitive marketplace to implement these ideas and realizes the rewards from these efforts." Miles and Darroch (2004) consider EM activities to be closely coupled with creating superior advantage by using innovation to create products, processes and strategies that better satisfy customer needs (Covin and Miles, 1999), while Hills and Hultman (2006, p. 222) describe EM characteristics that reflect such activities as "a flexible, customization approach to market" and "innovation in products, services and strategies." Hills and Hultman (2006) view innovation as a fundamental element of EM, proposing a theoretical model of the research field of EM that incorporates entrepreneurship, marketing and innovation as the core elements.

There are limited IO measures to draw upon because of the strong focus on innovation as an output (patents and so on) rather than as a firm behavior. Hurley and Hult (1998) and Aldas-Manzano, Küster, and Vila (2005) examined innovation in relation to MO, but they failed to consider innovation as a culture or behavioral orientation of the organization. Siguaw et al.'s IO (2006) scale was judged to be the most appropriate for the EMO model as they conceptualize IO using a set of interfirm innovative behaviors that are drawn together from pertinent strands of the innovation literature. Dimensions drawn from this scale that are incorporated into the EMO model are: overarching knowledge infrastructure (Siguaw, Simpson, & Enz, 2006); and encouraging, stimulating and sustaining innovation (Siguaw et al., 2006).

5.3. The EMO Conceptual Model

In the previous section a number of MO, CO, IO, and EO scales were identified as being central to the understanding of these orientations. On the basis of these scales, coupled with the characteristics of EM identified in the literature, the EMO model in Figure 5.1 is proposed. The model shows four key orientations, and argues that any concept of EM that is an accurate reflection of the way in which successful small businesses market must embrace aspects of behaviors that have traditionally been researched in the entrepreneurship, innovation, and customer engagement and relationship fields. In other words, in small businesses it is impossible and not fruitful to seek to differentiate between marketing, innovation, entrepreneurship and

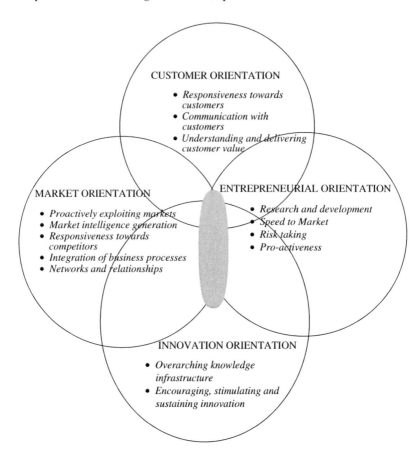

Figure 5.1: The SME Entrepreneurial Marketing Orientation (EMO) Conceptualized Model. *Source:* Model extracted from Jones and Rowley (2011).

customer engagement. The evidence for this assertion is most powerfully evident in the overlaps between orientation scales in these different fields. In Figure 5.1, such overlaps have been resolved as illustrated in the model, in order to offer a clear set of dimensions for EMO. Construction of the model and proposed dimensions of the model under each "orientation" are fully explained in Jones and Rowley (2011).

5.4. The EMICO Framework

Subsequent development of the conceptual EMO model for SMEs resulted in development of the EMICO framework (Jones & Rowley, 2009), EMICO being an anachronism for entrepreneurship, marketing, innovation, and CO. For those readers questioning why the conceptual model was published in 2011, later than the EMICO framework, this was due to differences in timings of publications for different journals.

The EM theory used in the EMICO framework (Box 5.1) includes the elements that informed the EMO conceptual model; Morris et al.'s (2002) EM dimensions, and some of the 23 characteristics of EM identified by Hills and Hultman (2006). These elements were chosen for the framework as they were considered most applicable to the research context of entrepreneurial small hi-tech firms in Wales, UK. In addition, the framework draws on the aforementioned popular scales known for their rigor, reliability, and validity in numerous studies. For MO these include Kohli et al. (1993) and Narver and Slater's (1990) scale. EO scales that inform the framework include Knight (1997) and Matsuno et al. (2002), whilst the IO scale used is that of Siguaw et al. (2006). CO and SO scales that inform the framework include Deshpande et al. (1993), Saura et al. (2005), and Saxe and Weitz (1982). The framework is also informed by the following researchers of networks in the SME, firm learning orientation, and EM contexts: Carson et al. (1995), Cegarra-Navarro and Rodrigo-Moya (2007), and Morris et al. (2002).

The refined and tested EMICO framework was constructed and synthesized into fifteen dimensions in the manner of other scale constructions (Hart & Diamanto-poulos, 1993; Strutton & Lumpkin, 1994). Dimensions were chosen from established scales and literature using aspects from the EM, EO, MO, IO, SO, and CO literature. The proposed framework draws on pertinent aspects of EM theory and specifically identifies both network theory and the CO/SO literature as essential for the research of technology firms who create bespoke software for their customers. These research findings that have been surfaced are interesting because the EM literature recognizes entrepreneurial activity and influence, use of networks and network relationships together with marketing and innovation. However, despite the fact that researchers recognize that entrepreneurs develop close customer relationships as part of their marketing activity, and EM views customer relationships as part of a co-creative activity and a value creation process (Hills & Hultman, 2006; Stokes, 2000) the importance of a CO is not core to the EM concept. Accordingly, this research has sought to extend the knowledge of EM by investigating a sample of small software technology firms in relation to CO and SO. In this way, investigation of software firm's EM activities and behaviors has drawn into the debate the importance of customer relationships for the marketing of software in small entrepreneurial firms, a key factor identified and challenged in the early stages of the research.

The EM literature has informed the EMICO framework by incorporating key elements of EM identified by researchers. Two of the framework dimensions of "exploiting markets" and "sales and promotion" were taken directly from the list of characteristics identified by Hills and Hultman (2006) as they were considered highly applicable to research in this context. Other important elements formed under-pinning descriptors for eleven of the EMICO dimensions (Hills & Hultman, 2006; Morris et al., 2002). In all, thirteen of the dimensions have been informed by the EM literature (with the exception of "research and development" and "speed to market," which are derived from the EO literature). Box 5.1 shows the "EMICO" framework and the 15 dimensions and underpinning descriptors that are drawn from the EM and the wider literature and have been tested for their suitability and validity for the research of EM in the SME context. The process of consolidation and validation of

---

Box 5.1. The EMICO Framework

Entrepreneurial Orientation = EO dimensions
Research and Development-*Descriptors*-Level of emphasis on investment in R&D; technological leadership and innovation.
Speed to Market-*Descriptors*-Stance of the firm; competitive; collaborative; follower; leader; defensive.
Risk Taking-*Descriptors*-Calculated risk taking; preparedness to seize opportunities; preference for both incremental and transformational acts; reliance on intuition and experience.
Proactiveness-*Descriptors*-Commitment to exploiting opportunities; inherent focus of recognition of opportunities; passion, zeal and commitment.

Market Orientation = MO dimensions
Exploiting Markets-*Descriptors*-Vision and strategy are driven by tactical successes; planning, or lack of, in short incremental steps; proactively exploiting smaller market niches; flexible, customization approach to market; marketing decisions linked to personal goals and long-term performance.
Market Intelligence Generation-*Descriptors*-External intelligence gathering; informal market research generation; gathering marketing intelligence through personal contact networks (PCNs) and web-based networks.
Responsiveness toward Competitors-*Descriptors*-Reactive to competitor's new products (NPDs); niche marketing strategies; differentiation strategies using product quality; software innovation; quality and responsiveness of software service support; competitive advantage based on understanding of customer needs.
Integration of Business Processes-*Descriptors*-Closely integrated functions, R&D, marketing etc.; sharing of resources; product/venture development is interactive; formal processes, project planning, project management; marketing that permeates all levels and functional areas of the firm.
Networks and Relationships-*Descriptors*-Resource leveraging; capacity for building network and business competence; use of personal contact networks (PCNs); creation of value through relationships/alliances; intra-firm networks; market decision making based on daily contact and networks.

Innovation Orientation = IO dimensions
Knowledge Infrastructure-*Descriptors*-Formalized IT-based knowledge infrastructures; formal and informal policies, procedures, practices and incentives; gathering and disseminating information.
Propensity to Innovate-*Descriptors*-Processes for sustaining and shaping the organization's culture to stimulate and sustain creativity and innovation; covering all innovation types- new product, services, process and administration.

Customer Orientation = CO dimensions
Responsiveness toward Customers-*Descriptors*-Responsiveness to customer feedback and behavior; speedy reaction to shifts in customer preference.

Communication with Customers-*Descriptors-*Strives to lead customers; formal and informal feedback gathering mechanisms; ongoing dialogue with customers to build long-term relationships; successful delivery to customers that builds customer confidence, with marketing based on personal reputation, trust and credibility.
Understanding and delivering customer value-*Descriptors-*Organization driven by customer satisfaction; understanding of how customers value products/services; closely linked to innovation practices; often two-way marketing with customers; customer knowledge often based on market immersion/interaction.
Promotion and Sales-Descriptors-*Organizational focus on sales and promotional activities.
Source: Figure extracted from Jones & Rowley (2009).

dimensions and underpinning descriptors during the testing and refinement of the framework is explainedand described in Jones and Rowley (2009), as are the firms and the respondents used in the sample.

What is of note here, is that while the EMICO framework was constructed using dimensions that were based on the prior research from EM and SME researchers and research of relevant strategic orientations, the descriptors for each dimension were not only developed from prior research but also from the "en vivo" descriptions of both entrepreneurs and employees from a purposive sample of firms (Shaw, 1999). A purposive sample was expected to be more useful for this research as this group of six firms would be more likely to offer commonalities for the framework's development and generate insights into the key issues for marketing in small bespoke software technology firms. It was important that firms were either micro or small firms, had a software product offering and also service offering so that reasonable comparisons could be drawn across the group of firms. It was also important that firms were over five years old so that long-term growth and sustainability could be observed and that the factor of growth volatility, which is normally associated with start-up phases in the first four years of trading, could be eliminated (Storey, 1989).

5.5. EMO Comparisons Between Silicon Valley, US, and Wales, UK

More recently, Jones, Suoranta, and Rowley (2013a) applied the EMICO framework to explore EMO activities, attitudes and behaviors exhibited by two groups of small software technology firms based in North Wales, UK and Silicon Valley, US, focusing specifically on the following;

a) overall firm orientation in relation to EMO and firm growth (in respect to: EO, IO, MO, and CO).
b) Similarities between the UK and US samples in relation to the fifteen dimensions of EMO.
c) Differences between the UK and US samples in relation to the fifteen dimensions of EMO.

Table 5.1: Firm growth classifications.

	High	**Medium**	**Incremental**
UK firms	1	1	4
US firms	3	3	0

Table 5.2: Specialist sales/marketing resource per firm groupings.

	High	**Medium**	**Incremental**
UK firms	2	1	0
US firms	28	23	

5.5.1. Firm Orientation and Growth

UK firms were very customer oriented and focused on incremental innovations while US firms were entrepreneurially oriented and focused on new product developments (NPDs) and market leading innovations. UK firms appeared generally much less proactive in the marketplace. The firms chosen were categorized following data collection. Firms were classified either being high growth, medium growth and incremental (slower) growth. Classification was by growth of employees, annual sales, and percentage increase in profit of the last 5 years. UK and US firm growth is illustrated in Table 5.1.

The US firms had a higher ratio of high growth firms. Four UK firms were incremental (slow growth firms) while the US had no firms in the incremental category.

5.5.2. Marketing and Sales Employees

Table 5.2 shows the amount of sales and marketing employees per firm classification. Firms with incremental growth in the UK sample had no designated specialist marketing or sales resource. The two UK firms with medium and high growth categories had specialist sales and marketing resources at a senior level. In the US sample there was a marked difference in that firms had significantly larger teams of sales and marketing employees.

5.5.3. Similarities

Research & Development (R&D) – Both UK and US firms invested and continually reinvested a significant amount of their funds into R&D. Both groups of firms considered this dimension to be very important to the extent that it was seen as central to all the firm's activities. It was also described by both groups as indistinguishable from all other activities taking place in the firm, including marketing activities. Put simply *everything's R&D here*. Investment in R&D was seen as a way to operate blue ocean strategies in the US, in creating new markets by pivoting in the marketplace, beating off their competitors to become market leaders and innovators. In the UK R&D focus was just as important but, R&D impact on UK firm growth was seemingly diffused for the reasons outlined below.

Market Intelligence Generation – Formal market intelligence was not carried out as it is expensive and time consuming. Software technology markets are high speed, competitive and, require frequent NPDs to market in order to secure growth in new markets. Firms in the US and UK samples viewed market intelligence gathering as much less important overall as firms were less concerned about competitor offerings and more focused on their own product/service strategies. UK firms had a limited focus on NPDs. They differentiated their software product from their competitors by providing high levels of service quality and developing bespoke software products with customers. US firms focused much more on creating radical innovations and making current software products on the market obsolete. Any marketing intelligence that was carried out was an implicit activity, using networks and relationship contacts, and hence, it was not a formalized process.

Responsiveness to Competitor Actions – As technology markets are fast-moving, global and fragmented, awareness of competitor actions is very difficult unless information is gathered by personal and business relationship contacts and networks. The US sample of firms were much more competitor and product aware than UK firms and knew which competitors they wished to beat. But these US firms chose to be proactive rather than reactive toward competitors by creating new products quickly onto the market ahead of their competitors. Both groups focused on creating value for their customers via innovation rather than take note of what competitors are doing. Research findings indicate that both US and UK firms view being responsive toward competitors as a reactive activity not a proactive activity and so it is not their focus or priority.

Integration of Business Processes – Both samples acknowledged that as the firms grew larger and took on more customers then, there was a need for more effective management of projects and, more formalized business processes to be embedded within the firm. This was an activity that UK firms began to focus on as they grew so that they could manage and control their projects more effectively. Despite the US firms stating that they also required effective, integrated business processes they preferred to prioritize R&D and launching products to market quickly.

Networks & Relationships – Networking is vital for both groups of firms, both at and before inception of the firm and for the firm's future growth. Silicon Valley offers more obvious opportunities to network given the geographic size of the area and proximity to other technology firms. Networks provide firms with the ability to leverage vital additional resources for smaller firms. Identified networks include: personal contact networks (PCNs), customer relationships and industry networks, partnering with large firms to generate new business opportunities in terms of additional project funding, marketing opportunities and innovation opportunities. Within these firms are effective intrafirm networks rather than departments, as these small flexible firms are nonhierarchical in nature. Employees are also a valuable source of informal market intelligence, sourcing information via PCNs and IT networks.

Knowledge Infrastructure – In software technology firms having an organized infrastructure to retain and keep tacit knowledge in the firm is important and reduces the risk of knowledge loss when an employee leaves, which has a significant impact on a small firm. Data repositories are used to hold information on project designs; this means that a certain amount of replication of products can be done and this saves the firm time and money on project design. Responses to this activity was similar to that for *integration of business processes* in that this is seen as very useful but becomes more so when the firm grows and has more employees. This aspect of the research also confirms that some dimensions of EM are used more or less depending on the stage/growth of the firm.

Propensity to Innovate – Both UK and US firms have a culture of innovating and were predisposed to being creative in terms of new products (US), incremental software developments and limited NPDs (UK), and innovative processes, services and administration often supported by their own in house software developments. This dimension was considered extremely important and research participants linked this concept to other dimensions of EMO such as "Pro-activeness," "R&D," "Communications with Customers" and "Understanding and Delivering Customer Value." However, there was a stronger focus on radical innovation in the US sample.

Communications with Customers – This dimension was considered very important in both US and UK firms and participants considered that this was closely linked to the notion of "Understanding & Delivering Customer Value." Without effective communications with customers, who are business customers, software technology firms would be unable to understand what value meant for the customer. Continued dialogue with customers meant that technology firms grew to understand what customers wanted in the industry that they were in. Participants in both samples acknowledged that they often had difficulties in communicating effectively with customers in order to manage customer expectations.

Understanding & Delivering Customer Value – Of critical importance to both sample groups. Firms in the US sample see this dimension as core to facilitating innovation and providing new (radical) innovations that will have a degree of market acceptance because they have anticipated customer demand. Although this was also the most important of all dimensions in UK firms and was also linked to innovation, it was described more in terms of delivering incremental product and service offerings and improving the overall service experience. It was used to differentiate companies from other firms in the UK while new innovations in firms in the US were created with the objective of making the firm a market leading innovator.

5.5.4. Differences

Speed to Market – In the US group "Speed to Market" was considered extremely important for competitiveness and market growth. This was not so in UK, participants considered it a low priority and much less important. In terms of competitive stance, the US firms took a leadership stance in the market, striving to create and deliver NPDs as quickly as possible ahead of competitors, pivoting in the market to change strategic direction. UK firms took a collaborative stance to the market, often partnering with other companies on projects and working to deliver projects with larger organizations.

Risk Taking – This was very much embedded in the culture of the US firms where both individuals in the firm and, entrepreneurs, were predisposed to taking risks. Risk was identified as a general attitude in behavior and life style of entrepreneurs and employees. Investing time, resources and money on a project that could fail was the risk for all these firms. In the UK entrepreneurs in the sample and hence the firm, were calculated risk takers and rated risk as low in importance. Although on reflection two of the owner-managers observed that in being risk averse they had impeded their firm's growth by failing to take opportunities. The implications so far are that this may be due in part to a lack of venture capital availability in UK and also generally a different attitude to entrepreneurial risk. Entrepreneurs based in Wales often funded start-up businesses with their own funding and with limited venture capital. Also technology parks in Wales, UK are geographically remote while technology parks are small and dispersed across rural and urban regions in Wales rather than part of large competitive geographic region and network as with the Silicon Valley region.

Proactiveness – UK firms are much less proactive, in general, and typically less proactive in terms of marketing and in seeking market opportunities. While there was an organizational willingness or propensity toward proactiveness there was a lot of procrastination about needing to refocus and need to make sure that in the future they should carry out more of the activities identified on the EMO framework. UK Firms were often encumbered with too many resource limitations; limited finances, limited time and limited marketing knowledge and expertise. Conversely, US firms rated this dimension very highly and displayed proactive attitudes toward innovating and selling NPDs. Proactive behaviors were embedded, as with a positive attitude to taking risks not only in the firms but also visible in individual employees and entrepreneurs in the US firms.

Exploiting Markets – UK-based firms viewed "Exploiting Markets" as much "less important"; they tended to develop software that was bespoke but incremental in terms of innovation using niche marketing, bottom up approaches to marketing and word-of-mouth (WOM). Interestingly, in the US WOM was used but not relied upon as a marketing or sales tool. Here, there was a very close link of innovation-to-market with firms demonstrating Schumpeterian behavior by their own descriptions during interviews in attitudes toward provoking markets, creating new markets by creating market demand, by innovating and taking risks.

Responsiveness Toward Customers – Here the US firm attitude was markedly different from firms in the UK. The UK sample acknowledged that performance had suffered due to over-responsiveness toward demanding customers and being highly customer oriented. This is turn limits their ability to innovate, because too much software developer time is dedicated to dealing with demanding customers. US-based firms were deliberately less responsive and must prepare products for new markets, "leading customers" to innovations. One entrepreneur observed that their customers did not always know what was that they needed or know what is possible in terms of developing software innovations.

Sales & Promotion – UK firms generally viewed sales and promotion as "less important" than other dimensions. Consequently they had few if any dedicated sales or marketing employees. UK firms relied on developing a niche market and cross-selling across similar industries that were not dominated by the larger firms while generating new business by using WOM. US firms used their sales teams and their networks to find the decision maker in the prospective client company and to get new leads. Also Silicon Valley firms used sales teams situated in the major US cities, for example, Chicago and New York. Therefore, these US firms had a much less localized approach and greater global reach. There was also a clear software engineering-to-sales relationship in the US firms that was not visible in the UK firms.

5.6. Discussion and Conclusion

This chapter has presented ongoing research exploration of EMO appropriate to the SME context. Details of the qualitative research methodologies outlined within this chapter are contained in the referenced journal papers. Use of the qualitative EMICO framework as opposed to measuring strategic orientations using scales and constructs has allowed for uncovering of implicit entrepreneurial marketing activities, attitudes, and behaviors in firms. It is what is known as going underneath the surface (Blankson, Jaideep, & Levenburg, 2006) and attempting to undertand the "hows" and the "whys" of the research phenomena rather than testing by hypothesis using assertions based on traditional marketing activities carried out by large firms in mass marketing environments.

We hope that further analysis will uncover the reasons behind the differences in the strategic orientations of these firms and firm activities, attitudes, and behaviors in the US and UK samples. Certainly the research so far points toward the significance of networks and relationships for doing business (Carson et al., 1995; Jones, Suoranta, & Rowley, 2013b; Shaw, 1999) and for ensuring an appropriate focus of strategic orientations and, more specifically, an EMO. For example, a high focus on CO seems to act as an inhibitor to innovation and IO. The findings also imply that different EM activities are more important at different stages of firm growth, such as "knowledge infrastructure," while the focus on some dimensions is required to remain constant, for example, on "R&D" and "sales and promotion." In particular it is interesting to note that US firms and their entrepreneurs embody much that is described in the EM literature; exhibiting Schumpeterian behavior, provoking change, creating new markets, innovating by leading customers and with an inherent sales focus. Firm performance in these samples implies that US firms in this sample have much swifter growth, greater profitability, and introduce more frequent products to market. Hence, we consider that this research will inevitably provide useful managerial implications by reporting successful growth strategies for small software technology firms based on the EMICO framework and its dimensions, while taking into account the different opportunities offered to entrepreneurs in two country contexts.

It is proposed that theEMICO framework may be used with little adaptation as a generic framework with which to explore EM in other firms and in other business sectors, therefore further extending opportunities for research in the SME marketing and EM field.

The EMICO framework should be applied to a heterogeneous sample of technology SMEs to compare the differences in EM activities and behaviors in small firms in high speed markets. Small software firms in this research project offered a bespoke software product and a support service. Firms were all customer oriented rather than market oriented. It would be interesting to apply the framework in the qualitative research of small software firms who offer solely NPDs in the form of off-the-shelf products to enable comparisons to be drawn.

It is proposed that the refined EMICO framework should be pilot tested and if necessary adjusted in an unrelated SME business sector. It would be very interesting to compare the findings between the software sector and another more stable market. In particular it would be interesting to see whether the demand for innovation was similar and to investigate the importance of networks in these firms. It would also be interesting to see the difference between service- and product-based firms in different sectors. This may further inform the SME research as to whether some small firms are more customer oriented than others and why.

It is proposed that this framework be developed into a quantitative analysis tool for EM measurement. Using this method, analysis of EM across a range of sectors and in different countries could be undertaken. It would be useful to apply the EMICO framework to large firms that appear entrepreneurial in nature, in order to gauge effectiveness of the EMICO in the large firm context and how far the framework would need adaptation. It would also be interesting to see whether any of the dimensions are affected by firm size. If the EMICO scale is found to be suitable then this would be likely to help inform researchers as to the behavior associated with corporate entrepreneurship.

References

Aldas-Manzano, J., Küster, I., & Vila, N. (2005). Market orientation and innovation: An inter-relationship analysis. *European Journal of Innovation Management, 8*(4), 437–452.

Alpkan, L., Yilmaz, C., & Kaya, N. (2007). Marketing orientation and planning flexibility in SMEs. *International Small Business Journal, 25*(2), 152–172.

Bjerke, B., & Hultman, C. M. (2002). *Entrepreneurial marketing – The growth of small firms in the new economic era.* Cheltenham, England: Edward Elgar.

Blankson, C., Jaideep, G. M., & Levenburg, N. M. (2006). Understanding the patterns of market orientation among small businesses. *Marketing Intelligence and Planning, 24*(6), 572–590.

Blankson, C., & Omar, O. E. (2002). Marketing practices of African and Caribbean small business in London. *Qualitative Market Research: An International Journal, 5*(2), 132–134.

Blankson, C., & Stokes, D. (2002). Marketing practices in the UK small business sector. *Marketing Intelligence and Planning, 20*(1), 49–61.

Bowey, J. L., & Easton, G. (2007). Entrepreneurial social capital unplugged. *International Small Business Journal, 25*(3), 272–306.

Brooksbank, R. (1991). Defining the small business: A new classification of company size. *Entrepreneurship and Regional Development, 3*(1), 17–31.

Brooksbank, R., Kirby, D., & Taylor, D. (2004). Marketing in survivor medium-sized British manufacturing firms: 1987–1997. *European Business Review, 16*(3), 292–306.

Brooksbank, R., Kirby, D. A., Taylor, D., & Jones-Evans, D. (1999). Marketing in medium sized manufacturing firms: The state of the art in Britain, 1987–1992. *European Journal of Marketing, 33*(1/2), 103–120.

Cardwell, M. (1994). *Customer care strategy for the '90s*. Cheltenham, England: Nelson Thorne.

Carson, D. (1985). The evolution of marketing in small firms. *European Journal of Marketing, 19*(5), 7–16.

Carson, D. (1990). Some exploratory models for assessing small firms' marketing performance (a qualitative approach). *European Journal of Marketing, 24*(11), 8–51.

Carson, D. (2005). Towards a research agenda – 2005. Conference discussion paper, the *UK Academy of Marketing/Entrepreneurship Interface SIG*, Southampton, 5–7 January.

Carson, D., Cromie, S., McGowan, P., & Hill, J. (1995). *Marketing and entrepreneurship in SMEs – An innovative approach*. Essex: Prentice Hall.

Cegarra-Navarro, J. G., & Rodrigo-Moya, B. (2007). Learning culture as a mediator of the influence of an individual's knowledge on market orientation. *The Services Industries Journal, 27*(5), 653–669.

Collinson, E., & Shaw, E. (2001). Entrepreneurial marketing – A historical perspective on development and practice. *Management Decision, 39*(9), 761–766.

Connor, T. (1999). Customer-led and market orientated: A matter of balance. *Strategic Management Journal, 20*(12), 1157–1163.

Cope, J., Jack, S., & Rose, M. B. (2007). Social capital and entrepreneurship: An introduction. *International Small Business Journal, 25*(3), 213–219.

Covin, J. G., & Miles, M. P. (1999). Corporate entrepreneurship and the pursuit of competitive advantage. *Entrepreneurship Theory and Practice, 23*(3), 47–63.

Covin, J. G., & Slevin, D. P. (1989). Strategic management of small firms in hostile and benign environments. *Strategic Management Journal, 10*(1), 75–87.

Covin, J. G., & Slevin, D. P. (1991). A conceptual model of entrepreneurship as firm behavior. *Entrepreneurship: Theory and Practice, 16*(1), 7–24.

Davis, C. D., Hills, G. E., & LaForge, R. W. (1985). The marketing small enterprise paradox: A research agenda. *International Small Business Journal, 3*(3), 31–42.

Day, G. S., & Wensley, R. (1988). Assessing advantage: A framework for diagnosing competitive superiority. *Journal of Marketing, 52*(2), 1–20.

Deshpande, R. (1999). *Developing a market orientation*. Thousand Oaks, CA: Sage Publications.

Deshpande, R., & Farley, J. U. (1998). Measuring market orientation: Generalization and synthesis. *Journal of Market Focused Management, 2*, 213–232.

Deshpande, R., Farley, J. U., & Webster, F. (1993). Corporate culture, customer orientation, and innovativeness in Japanese firms: A quadrat analysis. *Journal of Marketing, 57*(1), 23–37.

Drucker, P. F. (1954). *The Practice of management*. New York, NY: Harper and Row.

Freel, M. S. (2000). Barriers to product innovation in small manufacturing firms. *International Small Business Journal, 18*(2), 60–80.

Gilmore, A., & Carson, D. (1999). Entrepreneurial marketing by networking. *New England Journal of Entrepreneurship*, *12*(2), 31–38.

Gilmore, A., Carson, D., & Grant, K. (2001). SME marketing in practice. *Marketing Intelligence and Planning*, *19*(1), 6–11.

Ginsberg, A. (1985). Measuring changes in entrepreneurial orientation following industry deregulation: The development of a diagnostic instrument. *Proceedings of the first biennial conference of the U.S. Affiliate of the International Council for Small Business*.

Gronroos, C. (1982). *Strategic management and marketing in the service sector*. Cambridge, MA: Marketing Science Institute.

Hart, S., & Diamantopoulos, A. (1993). Marketing research activity and company performance: Evidence from the manufacturing industry. *European Journal of Marketing*, *27*(5), 54–72.

Hill, J. (2001). A multidimensional study of the key determinants of effective SME marketing activity: Part 1 and 2. *International Journal of Entrepreneurial Behaviour& Research*, *7*(5-6), 171–204.

Hill, J., & Wright, L. T. (2001). A qualitative research agenda for small to medium sized enterprises. *Marketing Intelligence and Planning*, *19*(6), 432–443.

Hill, S. M., & Blois, K. (1987). New small technically-based firms and industrial distributors. *International Small Business Journal*, *5*(3), 61–65.

Hills, G. E. (1987). Marketing and entrepreneurship research issues: Scholarly justification. In GE Hills (Ed.), *Research at the marketing/entrepreneurship interface* (pp. 3–15). Chicago IL: University of Illinois.

Hills, G. E., & Hultman, C. M. (2006). Entrepreneurial marketing. In S. Lagrosen & G. Svensson (Eds.), *Marketing, broadening the horizons*. Denmark: Studentlitteratur.

Hills, G. E., Hultman, C. M., & Miles, M. P. (2008). The evolution and development of entrepreneurial marketing. *Journal of Small Business and Marketing*, *46*(1), 99–112.

Huang, X., & Brown, A. (1999). An analysis and classification of problems in small business. *International Small Business Journal*, *18*(1), 73–85.

Hurley, R. F., & Hult, T. M (1998). Innovation, market orientation, and organisational learning: An integration and empirical examination. *Journal of Marketing*, *62*(3), 42–54.

Jaworski, B. J., & Kohli, A. K. (1993). Market orientation: Antecedents and consequences. *Journal of Marketing*, *57*(3), 53–70.

Jaworski, B. J., Kohli, A. K., & Sahay, A. (2000). Market-driven versus driving markets. *Journal of the Academy of Marketing Science*, *28*(1), 45–54.

Jones, E., Busch, P., & Dacin, P. (2003). Firm market orientation and salesperson customer orientation: Interpersonal and intrapersonal influences on customer service and retention in business-to-business buyer-seller relationships. *Journal of Business Research*, *56*(4), 323–340.

Jones, R., & Rowley, J. (2009). Presentation of a generic 'EMICO' framework for research exploration of entrepreneurial marketing in SMEs. *Journal of Research in Marketing and Entrepreneurship*, *11*(1), 5–21.

Jones, R., & Rowley, J. (2011). Entrepreneurial marketing in small businesses: A conceptual exploration. *International Small Business Journal*, *29*(1), 25–36.

Jones, R., Suoranta, M., & Rowley, J. (2013a). Entrepreneurial marketing: A comparative study. *The Services Industries Journal*, *33*(7–8), pp. 705–719.

Jones, R., Suoranta, M., and Rowley, J. (2013b). Strategic network marketing in technology SMEs. Academy of Marketing Special Issue. *Journal of Marketing Management*, *29*(5–6).

Khandwalla, P. N. (1977). *The design of organizations*. New York, NY: Harcourt Brace Jovanovich.

Kirzner, I. M. (1979). *Perception, opportunity, and profit: Studies in entrepreneurship.* Chicago, IL: University of Chicago Press.

Knight, G. A. (1997). Cross-cultural reliability and validity of a scale to measure firm entrepreneurial orientation. *Journal of Business Venturing, 12*(3), 213–225.

Kohli, A. K., & Jaworski, B. J. (1990). Market orientation: The construct, research propositions, and managerial implications. *Journal of Marketing, 54*(4), 1–18.

Kohli, A. K., Jaworski, B. J., & Kumar, A. (1993). MARKOR: A measure of market orientation. *Journal of Marketing Research, 30*(4), 467–477.

Kotler, P. (1984). *Marketing essentials.* Englewood Cliffs, NJ: Prentice Hall.

Kotler, P., & Anderson, A. (1987). *Strategic marketing for non-profit organizations.* Englewood Cliffs, NJ: Prentice Hall.

Kreiser, P., Marino, L. D., & Weaver, K. M. (2002). Assessing the psychometric properties of the entrepreneurial scale: A multi-country analysis. *Entrepreneurship, Theory and Practice, 26*(4), 71–94.

Kraus, S., Filser, M., Eggers, F., Hills, G. E., & Hultman, C. M. (2012). The entrepreneurial marketing domain: A citation and co-citation analysis. *Journal of Research in Marketing and Entrepreneurship, 14*(1), 6–26.

Kuratko, D. (1995). Entrepreneurship. In: *International Encyclopedia of Business and Management.* London: International Thomson Press.

Lindman, M. T. (2004). Formation of customer bases in SMEs. *The Marketing Review, 4*(2), 134–156.

Lumpkin, G. T., & Dess, G. G. (1996). Clarifying the entrepreneurial orientation construct and linking it to performance. *Academy of Management Review, 21*(1), 135–172.

Matsuno, K., Mentzer, J. T., & Özsomer, A. (2002). The effects of entrepreneurial proclivity on business performance. *Journal of Marketing, 66*(3), 18–32.

McCartan-Quinn, D., & Carson, D. (2003). Issues which impact upon business markets in the small firm. *Small Business Economics, 21*, 201–213.

Miles, M. P., & Arnold, D. R. (1991). The relationship between market orientation and entrepreneurial orientation. *Entrepreneurship Theory and Practice, 15*(4), 49–65.

Miles, M. P., & Darroch, J. (2004). Large firms, entrepreneurial marketing processes, and the cycle of competitive advantage. *European Journal of Marketing, 40*(5–6), 485–501.

Miles, R. E., & Snow, C. C. (1978). *Organizational strategy, structure and process.* New York, NY: McGraw-Hill.

Miller, D. (1983). The correlates of entrepreneurship in three types of firms. *Management Science, 29*(7), 770–791.

Miller, D., & Friesen, P. H. (1978). Archetypes of strategy formulation. *Management Science, 24*(9), 921–933.

Miller, N. J., Besser, T., & Malshe, A. (2007). Strategic networking among small businesses in small US communities. *International Small Business Journal, 25*(6), 631–665.

Morris, M. H., & Paul, G. W. (1987). The relationship between entrepreneurship and marketing in established firms. *Journal of Business Venturing, 2*(3), 247–259.

Morris, M., Schindehutte, M., & La Forge, R. W. (2002). Entrepreneurial marketing: A construct for integrating emerging entrepreneurship and marketing perspectives. *Journal of Marketing Theory and Practice, 10*(4), 1–19.

Murray, J. (1981). Marketing is home for the entrepreneurial process. *Industrial Marketing Management, 10*, 93–99.

Naman, J. L., & Slevin, D. P. (1993). Entrepreneurship and the concept of fit: A model and empirical tests. *Strategic Management Journal, 14*(2), 137–153.

Narver, J. C., & Slater, S. F. (1999). The effect of a market orientation on business profitability. In R. Deshpande (Ed.), *Developing a market orientation* (pp. 45–77). Thousand Oaks, CA: Sage.

Narver, J. C., & Slater, S. F. (1990). The effect of a market orientation on business profitability. *Journal of Marketing, 54*, 20–35.

Pitt, L., Carauna, A., & Berthon, P. R. (1996). Market orientation and business performance: Some European evidence. *International Marketing Review, 13*(1), 5–18.

Reichheld, F. F., & Sasser Jr., W. E. (1990). Zero defections: Quality comes to services. *Harvard Business Review, 68*(5), 105–111.

Salavou, H., & Lioukas, S. (2003). Radical product innovations in SMEs: The dominance of entrepreneurial innovation. *Creativity and Innovation Management, 12*(2), 94–108.

Saura, I. G., Contri, G. B., Taulet, A. C., & Velazquez, B. M. (2005). Relationships amongst customer orientation, service orientation and job satisfaction in financial services. *International Journal of Service Industry Management, 16*(5), 497–525.

Saxe, R., & Weitz, B. A. (1982). The SOCO scale: A measure of the customer orientation of salespeople. *Journal of Marketing Research, 19*(3), 343–351.

Shapiro, B. (1988). What the hell is market orientated? Harvard Business Review. *November/December*, 119–125.

Shaw, E. (2006). Small firm networking: An insight into contents and motivating factors. *International Small Business Journal, 24*(1), 5–29.

Shaw, E. (1999). A guide to the qualitative research process: evidence from a small firm study. *Qualitative Market Research: An International Journal, 2*(2), 59–70.

Siguaw, J. A., Simpson, P. M., & Enz, C. A. (2006). Conceptualizing innovation orientation: A scale for study and integration of innovation research. *Journal of Product Innovation Management, 23*(6), 556–574.

Slater, S. F., & Narver, J. C. (1995). Market orientation and the learning organization. *Journal of Marketing, 59*(3), 63–74.

Slater, S. F., & Narver, J. C. (1998). Customer-led and market orientated: Let's not confuse the two. *Strategic Management Journal, 19*(10), 1001–1006.

Stokes, D. (1998). *Small business management* (3rd ed.). London: Letts.

Stokes, D. (2000). Putting Entrepreneurship into marketing: The process of entrepreneurial marketing. *Journal of Research in Marketing and Entrepreneurship, 2*(1), 1–6.

Storey, D. J. (1989). Firm performance and size: explanations from the small firm sector. *Small Business Economics, 1*(3), 175–180.

Strutton, D., & Lumpkin, J. R. (1994). Problem and emotion-focused coping dimensions and sales presentation effectiveness. *Journal of the Academy of Marketing Science, 22*(1), 28–37.

Tajeddini, K., Trueman, M., & Larsen, G. (2006). Examining the effects of market orientation on innovativeness. *Journal of Marketing Management, 22*(5/6), 529–551.

Verhees, F. J. H. M., & Meulenberg, T. G. (2004). Market orientation, innovativeness, product innovation, and performance in small firms. *Journal of Small Business Management, 42*(2), 134–154.

Webster Jr., F. E. (1988). Rediscovering the marketing concept. *Business Horizons, 31*(May–June), 29–39.

Weinrauch, J. D., Man, K., Robinson, P. A., & Pharr, J. (1991). Dealing with limited financial resources: A marketing challenge for small businesses. *Journal of Small Business Management, 29*(4), 44–54.

Zontanos, G., & Anderson, A. R. (2004). Relationships, marketing and small business: An exploration of links in theory and practice. *Qualitative Market Research: An International Journal, 7*(3), 228–236.

Chapter 6

Globalization of Markets: Implications for the Entrepreneurial Firm in the 21st Century

Abstract

This chapter attempts to cover the crux of the material on globalization, and then provides fresh perspectives on how entrepreneurial firms can thrive in an inevitably global world. After briefly reviewing the pros and cons, the drivers of the globalization process are discussed, emphasizing the role of technology and population growth over the traditional factors of cost, market, government, and competition. In particular, the enabling role of technology to co-create value should be embraced to overcome the challenges of population growth (or lack thereof). This is followed by a discussion on evaluating market potential and appropriate market selection. The chapter then integrates prevailing views on global marketing strategy and brand development. It concludes with implications for the entrepreneurial firm based on extant research insights on advertising media and the Rule of Three theory.

6.1. Introduction

"May you live in interesting times" is indeed a proverbial Chinese curse. And the curse is certainly being fulfilled. People are more connected than ever before socially, culturally, and economically (if not physically). Information and capital flow more quickly and seamlessly than ever. Goods and services produced in a far side of the world are available in the rest of the world's markets. Cherished brands are loyally sought by consumers from different continents. The nature of our interesting times is best captured in the phrase *globalization*, a primarily economic wave that sweeps over the entire world. Globalization cannot be stopped, and there will be winners and losers in the transformation to a global marketplace (Sheth, 1986; Sheth, Uslay, & Sisodia, 2008; Mooij de, 2010). Globalization has been defined as a process of

Entrepreneurial Marketing: Global Perspectives
ISBN: 978-1-78190-786-3

the result of human innovation and technological progress that increases the integration of economies around the world through trade and financial flows (IMF, 2000) (http://www.amazon.com/The-Rule-Three-Surviving-Competitive/dp/074320560X). Globalization has provided means for the fittest of firms to thrive in a new world where suppliers, competitors, and customers are no longer bounded by their national or regional locations.

Global economic integration is not a new phenomenon. For seven centuries, since the travels of Marco Polo, global activities through trade movements, communication, and technology transfer have been on the rise. In a broader sense, globalization is the process by which people and their ideas and activities in different parts of the world become interconnected or integrated.

The process of globalization has been observed to be a tedious path of incremental steps toward global rationalization (Yeniyurt, 2009). According to traditional models of internationalization of firms, marketers first engage in exporting activities, then establish foreign subsidiaries, and engage in strategic partnerships over time (Malhotra, Agarwal, & Ulgado, 2003; Yeniyurt, Townsend, Cavusgil, & Ghauri, 2009). After firms develop regional presence, they may then gradually evolve into a multiregional and finally into a global company (Yeniyurt, 2009). However, the traditional approach is too rigid to cope with the pace of emerging markets. Entrepreneurial rather than conventional marketing efforts are critical to succeed in such dynamic environments. For example, some entrepreneurs turn the conventional model on its head and launch "born-global" firms. Still other domestic firms suddenly emphasize rapid international expansion and are "born-again global" (Bell, McNaughton, & Young, 2001; Knight & Cavusgil, 1996; Knight & Cavusgil, 2004). Thus, the way the world's markets are connected is also reflected in their overall dynamic state. No consumers are spared from the transformational force of globalization. Events transpiring in one part of the world can also have dramatic effects on the rest of the world. For example, the Asian financial crisis in 1997 has severely affected businesses around the world (McLean, 2001) and the outbreak of SARS in 2003 has shown how globalization permits the rapid spread of disease, which affects travel, the hospitality industry, and other businesses around the globe (Meredith, 2003). More recently, the 2011 tsunami disaster in Japan has disrupted supply chains in dozens of sectors.

Proponents of globalization argue that it makes the world a better place. It promotes global economic growth, generates jobs, makes companies more competitive, lowers prices, and improves quality of life for consumers. Globalization can also help developing countries through the infusion of foreign direct investment and know-how, and by spreading prosperity to create the conditions in which democratic ideals and respect for human rights may flourish (Sheth et al., 2008). For example, global e-commerce is growing steadily since the 1990s, and according to the Interactive Media in Retail Group, it will surpass 1.25 trillion euros by 2013 (Montaqim, 2012). Nevertheless, skeptics of globalization argue that it has not proven to be a vehicle for prosperity. As pointed out in the book *The Dark Side of Globalization*, the growth in transnational flows has not been matched by an equivalent growth in global governance mechanisms to regulate them (Heine & Thakur, 2011). These authors argue that aggressive liberalization, deregulation, and relaxation of border controls have not led to self-sustaining growth and greater wealth. We note that benefits of globalization have lagged in markets with limited heritage of entrepreneurship. Therefore, entrepreneurship can serve as the catalyst to advance globalization and democratize its benefits.

In terms of consumer behavior, firms increasingly witness a convergence in consumer attitudes and actions that enable them to standardize and market beyond traditional geographic and cultural boundaries. *The New York Times* columnist Thomas Friedman (2005) observes in his book *The World is Flat* that information technology has generated a unlimited possibilities for individuals and firms to compete and to collaborate globally. Our deeply networked world makes even six degrees of separation appear redundant. Moreover, as people move about and easily access different regions and cultures, their tastes and preferences also get more adventurous. That is not to say that no customization is required. *Globalization* is the new imperative. Globalization drives overall strategy and implementation but at times firms find locally-tailored products boost performance best. Lasting success relies on entrepreneurial marketers' ability to identify and serve attractive markets, connect with their customers, and provide superior value all the while seeking that elusive balance of mass-customization.

Implications of globalization, cross-cultural dynamics (differences across borders, emerging and mature market dynamics as well as subsistence economies and multi-cultural environments) remain among the research priorities for the marketing-entrepreneurship interface (Uslay & Teach, 2008). A large body of research has focused on the impact of globalization on firms' structure, marketing functions, and strategic performance (e.g., Cavusgil, Yeniyurt, & Townsend, 2004; Kirca, Hult, Deligonul, Perry, & Cavusgil, 2012; Townsend, Yeniyurt, Deligonul, & Cavusgil, 2004; Wan, 2005; Wan & Hoskisson, 2003; Wiersema & Bowen, 2008). Many of these have emerged as a collection of independent streams of research with little cross examination of broader stakeholder outcomes in across cultures. For example, more conceptual and empirical research on mindful marketing and consumption is required for counter-balance (Malhotra, Lee, & Uslay, 2012). The developments facilitated by globalization also need to be gauged for their long-term sustainability. While it is not possible to review the literature on globalization or international entrepreneurship in a single chapter, we made an attempt to cover the crux of the material yet still provide fresh perspectives within our space limitations. In this chapter, first we discuss the main drivers of globalization and the globalization process. Second, we cover the challenges of evaluating market attractiveness and market selection in a global world. Third, we discuss global brands and global marketing strategies. We conclude with implications for the entrepreneurial firm.

6.2.   The Driving Forces of Globalization

Multinational companies are faced with opportunities and threats deriving from economic, social, cultural, political, legal, and technological forces, to an ever-increasing variety of products and geographical areas, growing in both number and complexity. Geographical distance, cultural differences, and proliferating competitors make the development and administration of global marketing strategies inherently complex.

The main forces driving globalization are governments, cost, markets, and competition (Townsend et al., 2004; Yip & Hult, 2011). We discuss these first and then emphasize two more critical factors: technology utilization and population growth (or their lack of).

6.2.1. Government as a Driver of Globalization

Governments play a key role as they regulate the markets, set the technical standards and trade policies. Government owned organizations are customers and at times direct competitors to global firms. While most governments are globalization friendly, internal politics can cause them to take hostile action against certain country's multinationals. However, the most important dimension of governmental activity pertaining globalization is through trade agreements and economic unions. Public policy in developed and developing countries significantly influence the nature and pace of global economic integration (Sheth & Sisodia, 2006). Recent financial crises have demonstrated that local economies rely more and more on the world market, with less room for government control. A trade agreement is a contract or agreement between two or more countries that contains working terms and conditions to eliminate trade barriers so that they can mutually benefit from trade and investment. Trade barriers in consideration include tariffs, which have been primarily put in place to protect domestic manufacturers or to raise revenue. Agreements may involve collaboration and co-operation, lower import duties, guarantees of capital or labor investments made by trading partners, preferential tax treatment, and more. They can mean escalating levels of co-operation from free trade areas, common monetary area, customs union, common market, monetary union, to full economic union. Although trading blocs act as a means of reducing trade restrictions between participating countries, they are often perceived as a trade barrier by non-members. It has been suggested by Drucker (2001) and observed by others that regional blocks (e.g., EU, NAFTA, Mercosur) will gain more importance and boost free trade internally but become protectionist externally (Drucker, 2001; Sheth & Sisodia, 2006; Uslay, Morgan, & Sheth, 2009). Understanding of international regulations, agreements and blocks is vital for those engaging in international entrepreneurship.

6.2.2. Cost as a Driver of Globalization

The case for globalization through the cost argument is relatively straightforward. Global markets enable tremendous economies of scale and scope as well as quick accumulation of experience (curve). These cost benefits naturally include sourcing and logistics but also extend to lower foreign country costs including labor and raw materials. Furthermore, global markets can help firms extend their product life cycles, decrease their product developments costs and/or speed to market. Beyond cutting labor costs that can vary based on production levels, in many sectors firms find that the fixed cost (capital) investments needed to develop and launch new products approach billions of dollars (e.g., semiconductors). Engaging in global marketing helps to recoup high fixed product development costs. Overall, there is increasing pressure for firms to reduce costs, and going global represents an enduring solution (Townsend et al., 2004).

6.2.3. *Market as a Driver of Globalization*

As firms transcend national borders, global consumers have become the product of cultural convergence. Even for attitudes regarding entrepreneurship, Uslay, Teach, and Schwartz (2002) reported more similarities than differences among students from US, Turkey, and Spain. In his seminal article "The Globalization of Markets," Theodore Levitt (1983) argued for *economics of simplicity*, — standardized marketing efforts based on homogeneous customer needs and wants, and their willingness to sacrifice customization for lower prices at high quality. He also observed that serving global markets can generate substantial economies of scale in production. He underlined that global marketing would enable firms achieve unequaled success.

However, globalization does not mean that consumers around the world uniformly share the same taste or values. Cultural differences across country markets have a significant impact on consumer behavior and can influence the process of globalization (Yeniyurt & Townsend, 2003). National cultural characteristics have a significant effect on the adoption of new products, and services, and therefore are important factors that shape the global diffusion process of new ideas, technologies, and the development of global brands. However, while brands may be perceived differently across cultures, quality signal, global myth, and social responsibility were found to explain 60% of variance in global brand preferences (Holt, Quelch, & Taylor, 2004). In addition, a market's socioeconomic status, such as the development level of the educational infrastructure and the degree of urbanization, moderates the effect of culture. In essence, to become truly globalized, firms must take an integrated approach across all markets to leverage global reach. Planning and resource allocation need to be considered on a global basis in order to take advantage of worldwide manufacturing capabilities and marketing opportunities to implement a globally integrated strategy (Yeniyurt & Townsend, 2003). In their exploratory examination of global company performance, Townsend et al. (2004) found that the global consumer is an effective factor in driving the success of marketing programs, and in turn overall financial performance. Thus, international marketers/entrepreneurs need to first acquire in-depth customer insights for success in global markets.

6.2.4.   *Competition as a Driver of Globalization*

The level and nature of competitive dynamics influences the transformation to a global marketplace. The *rule of three* theory (Sheth & Sisodia, 2002) offers unique insights regarding globalization of markets particularly on how three major players emerge to dominate the market in mature and competitive industries, with the balance filled by specialist niche players (Sheth et al., 2008). Evidence suggests that three full-line, volume-driven competitors eventually capture the vast majority of market share in a given market (Uslay, Altintig, & Winsor, 2010). Using a diverse sample of over 160 US industries, two base-time periods, and numerous performance measures, Uslay et al. (2010) reported strong support for Sheth and Sisodia's (2002) theory. Firms evolve into two complementary strategic groups: generalists that cater to large, mainstream groups of customers, and specialists well-focused on catering to niche markets. Any company stuck-in-the-middle between these strategic groups is likely to experience major financial difficulties and be swallowed up through M&A or disappear altogether. Therefore, *rule of three* has strategic choice implications for firms competing globally. A firm that is market leader in its home market may still find itself ill-sized to compete globally or even in a particular foreign market. Interestingly, the theory can also apply at the global level (Uslay et al., 2010). There are plenty of examples of three main players in international markets (e.g., Matsushita, Sony, Toshiba (Japanese electronics manufacturers); Deutsche Bank, Dresdner Bank, Commerzbank (German banks)) (Sheth & Sisodia, 2002). Finally, as markets get deregulated and mature, we will be observing the *global rule of three* emerge in numerous sectors (e.g., Michelin, Bridgestone, and Goodyear among tire manufacturers) (Sheth et al., 2008).

6.2.5.   *Technology as Global Competitive Advantage*

Technological progress from transportation to IT has allowed for faster and less costly control of distance and factors of production. This geographic expansion is further accelerated by savings from low-cost sourcing of materials. Efficient manufacturing and R&D can now be stretched throughout the value chain across regions and borders and results in growth, particularly due to emerging markets. For example, communication and transportation technologies enable Toyota and Dell to set up operations in different parts of the world in order to access new markets and resources in order to decrease production and distribution costs.

Technology serves as a driver in every facet of globalization at a velocity never before experienced. It impacts every global company on a daily basis. Whether it is simple communication, online tracking of suppliers' deliveries, managing e-commerce websites, or providing self-service capabilities, the use of technology is revolutionizing the increasingly service dominant economies as new technologies and millennial lifestyles converge. Technology is truly borderless as there are typically no cultural boundaries limiting its application. Entrepreneurs provide and international marketers integrate technology into their operations to improve efficiency, extend customer connectivity, manage capacity, enable customization, technological innovation, and ultimately to co-create value (Lee, Uslay, & Meuter, 2013; Sheth & Uslay, 2007). As technology gains legitimacy in marketing processes, marketers energetically employ these technologies to facilitate marketing goals, generate economies of scale, and manage customer relationships. When a firm leverages technologies to co-create value with consumers, it can apply appropriate marketing techniques, improve its processes, generate market intelligence, create customized solution bundles or use real-time data to put itself ahead of its competitors (Uslay, Malhotra, & Citrin, 2004; Sheth & Uslay, 2007).

Perhaps the most important development with respect to globalization was the advent of the internet and the advances in telecommunications. Information now travels around the world in milliseconds, facilitating the diffusion of ideas, trends, brands, products and services. The result is an ever increasing global customer segment that demands globally standardized products and services. The internet has also expanded the market access for new start-ups. While in the past the only way to reach global customers was by developing global distribution networks, start-ups can now utilize the internet and the global shipping services to market and distribute their products and services to the world. This drastically lowered capital requirements for born-globals. Similarly, global social network platforms like Facebook and Twitter and online stores such as Ebay, Amazon, and the Apple App-store present unique opportunities for global entrepreneurs, regardless of their geographic location and nationality. A teenager located in Middle East, Asia, or Africa can now design and develop a game or application, and offer it to the world on several of these global platforms. In short, use of technology can let entrepreneurs/marketers create and sustain competitive advantages globally.

6.2.6. *Population as Global Competitive Advantage*

Interestingly, population (skilled workforce) turns out to be a factor in the race for global geopolitical realignment (Sheth & Sisodia, 2006). While 19th century was dominated by the European and the 20th century was dominated by the US economies, it is increasingly certain that the 21st century (or at least the first half of it) will be remembered for the growth and dominance of Asian economies, primarily those of China and India (Sheth, 2011). While both China and India will continue to grow their economies at a high pace during the next decade, China's growth is predicted to slow down after 2020 (Sheth, 2011). China has one thing in common with Japan and other developed nations: due to its one child per family policy, it has an ageing population. The birth rates in most developed nations are not enough to replace their existing populations, and as a consequence their absolute population numbers will shrink during the 21st century (Sheth & Sisodia, 2006). Couple this phenomenon with increasing life expectancies, and you have relatively fewer young/highly productive workers trying to support more elderly/retirees. This will underline the need for proportionately young employees and this is what India (in contrast with China) has no shortage of. Thus, once it resolves its infrastructure and policy issues, India is expected to assume the lead in growth during the second quarter of the 21st century (Sheth, 2011). Finally, Sheth (2011) argues that China, India and developed nations will focus their attention to the continent with the most workforce potential: Africa. Its population boom and workforce will turn into an advantage after African nations resolve their infrastructure and policy issues and educate their workforce with investment and training help from China and India (and other developed nations that will need access to emerging markets to sustain themselves). Thus, nations of Africa may take the spotlight away from India in the second half of the 21st century. These interesting turn-of-events have significant implications for firms planning to be/remain global in the not-so-distant future.

6.3.   Globalization Process

Firms that aim to become global have to employ radical changes in their processes and organizational structures in order to establish themselves in global markets (Yeniyurt, 2003). Exporting and creating a regional presence have been considered among the first two steps of the global expansion process. However, many firms are finding that the path toward globalization is more accessible with international marketing alliances (Yeniyurt et al., 2009) in the process of new product development (Townsend et al., 2004), product launch (Yeniyurt, Townsend, & Talay, 2007), and for a global brand architecture (Townsend, Yeniyurt, & Talay, 2009). Such alliances enable firms to leverage their unique resources and develop specialized skills to build competitive advantages, establish stronger market positions, and manage competitive threats brought about by globalization (Hamel, 1991; Ireland, Hitt, & Vaidyanath, 2002). In that sense, a firm must reach a mature stage in the globalization process, be geocentric, adopt a standardized market strategy, have a globally inter-connected structure, and must retain appropriate skills, organization culture and managerial processes to be truly global (Cavusgil et al., 2004).

6.3.1.   Market Attractiveness and Selection

International expansion is a risky endeavor due to the firm's limited knowledge about the context of the host country (Johansson, 1997). In order to mitigate the effects of uncertainty, international marketers can assess the potential of a market using relative attractiveness measures. Location advantages are fundamental when evaluating international expansion opportunities and include examining variables such as economic stability and market potential to determine the relative attractiveness of a country (Dunning, 1988). In order to measure the relative level of global engagement of countries, the *Globalization Index* released by Ernst & Young (2012) in cooperation with the Economist Intelligence Unit (EIU) uses five evaluative criteria: openness to trade, capital movements, exchange of technology and ideas, labor movements, and cultural integration. The index covers the period from 1995 to 2015 with each criterion's weighting validated by the business leaders surveyed (Ernst & Young, 2012). Hong Kong, Ireland, and Singapore made the top three, with the US in 23rd and China 39th place in 2011.

Another way to measure market attractiveness is by the market related factors that provide motivation for launching a brand in a specific country. Relative market attractiveness is a significant factor considered in managerial decision-making for product introductions in new markets (Guiltinan, 1999). It has been suggested that prosperity, size, infrastructure and accessibility are appropriate indicators of market attractiveness (Mitra & Golder, 2002). Under conditions of uncertainty, market size is a significant predictor of a brand's propensity to enter a new market (Yeniyurt et al., 2007). Risk tolerance of the entrepreneurs is also a consideration since emerging markets such as Indonesia offer high growth with matching risk.

Traditional market selection analysis relies on purely macroeconomic and political factors to assess dynamic global markets and their future potential. Primary research on emerging market potential is costly and comparative research efforts are immediately confronted with diverse markets for which there is a dearth of existing studies. As a result, market selection using ranking or clustering techniques is widely adopted to identify countries with the assumption that all customers in the same set can be reached effectively with a similar marketing mix. Firms that aim to standardize offerings and marketing strategy across different markets benefit from cluster analysis since it provides insights into structural similarities among markets (Cavusgil & Nevin, 1981). On the other hand, a firm that wants to identify the best possible market to enter should lean toward the ranking approach as a way to determine the few that deserve the greatest attention (Sakarya, Eckman, & Hyllegard, 2007). For example, GlobalEdge provides market potential and ranking of countries including volatile developing markets using various metrics (www. globaledge.org).

Hybrid approaches that synthesize the strengths of both clustering and ranking techniques are also possible. For example, Cavusgil, Kiyak, and Yeniyurt (2004) developed a country market potential evaluation procedure by combining clustering and indexing techniques. They reported that country markets can be ranked and grouped according to the strength of their infrastructure, economic well-being, standard of living, market size, and market dynamism. Using only secondary data sources, their study constitutes a good tool for the early stages of global exploration since it requires a minimal amount of investment.

6.3.2. Global Marketing Strategies

The preeminent view of global marketing strategy is based on standardization (Ohmae, 1989; Samiee & Roth, 1992). As such, standardization has been given much attention as reflected by the large volume of publications in this area (e.g., Cavusgil & Zou, 1994; Laroche, Kirpalani, Pons, & Zhou, 2001). Proponents argue that a firm is pursuing a global marketing strategy if its marketing programs across different countries are standardized with regard to its product offering, promotional mix, price, and supply chain structure (Johansson, 1997). Standardization can extend to the selection of product line range or employment of specific marketing mix elements. Mesdag (2000) pointed out that some products are more suitable to market globally due to their duration of usage.

Another perspective of global marketing strategy focuses on firms' efforts in coordination and configuration of their value-chain activities. Advocates of such view embrace the means to exploit the synergies that exist across different markets and the comparative advantages associated with various host countries. It has been suggested that optimal configuration enables a firm to exploit location-specific advantages through specialization (Craig & Douglas, 1997; Porter, 1986; Roth, Schweiger, & Morrison, 1991). A key aspect of configuration is the degree of concentration (Porter, 1986; Roth et al., 1991; Zou & Cavusgil, 1996). Since different countries have unique comparative advantages, concentration of value-chain activities in places where marketing activities can be performed most efficiently allows firms to maximize efficiency, eliminate cost inefficiencies and reduce duplicate operational efforts in national and regional divisions. Global integration implies playing a role in many different world markets that are relevant to the business. Integrating firm operations typically requires some markets to utilize the resources of others to achieve success and vice versa. It also involves balancing resources and risks to consider competitive initiatives in all areas. For example, product development and engineering activities can be concentrated in a limited number of countries where world-class engineering skills exist, whereas labor-intensive manufacturing can be concentrated in countries with low-cost labor. As such, global integration and coordination, across geographic markets and across the value chain is becoming increasingly important (Yeniyurt, Cavusgil, & Hult, 2005). Only companies that can develop the necessary global market knowledge competencies would be able to survive the global battle for market domination that is taking place in many industries. Understanding global customer trends, as well as local differences is a crucial requirement for achieving global responsiveness. Similarly, firms now have to keep constant watch on their global competitors, as well as local competitors, and react to competitive moves on a global scale.

It has been shown that cultural and cognitive factors such as global orientation (Workman, Homburg, & Gruner, 1998; Zou & Cavusgil, 2002) and global mindset (Kedia & Mukherji, 1999; Murtha, Lenway, & Bagozzi, 1998) of the managerial team affect the global strategy, structure, and processes of organizations. In addition, standardizing a marketing program does not necessarily mean that all marketing efforts and implementation strategy will be the same. Being market-oriented (adaptive) can be beneficial to organizational learning, entrepreneurial orientation, and overall performance across cultures (Uslay & Sheth, 2008). When firms operate in different countries, they commit to developing and changing plans on a country-by-country or region-by-region basis. Nevertheless, there will be still common factors in strategy and practice that allow for some form of standardization (Kotabe & Helsen, 2010).

6.3.3. *Global Brand Development*

Global branding deserves special attention as it constitutes a key competitive advantage for global companies. A global brand is defined as one that is marketed across the world, preserving the same core essence even though the marketing activities can be adapted to locally (de Chernatony, Halliburton, & Bernath, 1995). A global brand name can serve as universal signal for product quality. This is achieved by shaping branding through advertising, multimedia, word-of-mouth, and interactive communication of products and services. Great efforts are exerted into branding including naming products, designing logos, and ensuring that the service offering is uniform throughout the business. Through continued exposure, global brands resonate with potential and existing customers (Aaker & Joachimsthaler, 1999; Dawar & Parker, 1994; Townsend et al., 2009). For example, Apple can charge more for its computers than its competitors because of its in innovative design, consistent quality, and global ecosystem. Coca-Cola continues has been considered the most valuable global brand for decades and its brand equity alone is worth some $77.8B! (www.interbrand.com). Interestingly, global marketing can even enable brands to achieve a higher status in international markets than in its home market (e.g., Jeep in China; McDonald's in Russia).

6.4. Marketing and Strategy Implications for Entrepreneurship and Small Business

It is no surprise that small firms do not have the marketing resources to compete with incumbent firms. The notion of guerilla marketing (Levinson, 1998) was conceived because of the need of small firms with limited budgets to compete with large firms (Uslay, 2002). In a global marketplace, small firms can benefit from engaging in entrepreneurial (rather than traditional) marketing in a couple of ways. First, due to their lower fixed costs small firms are inherently more flexible. They can take advantage of standardized product and service strategies of global players and provide customization at levels that global players are unable or unwilling to provide. This should lead to niche-customer loyalty and allow for the emergence of global specialists. Second, small firms have less to lose from experimentation and must strive to take risks with social media, viral/buzz marketing, and other evolving marketing media. For example, even though most firms engage in it, only a minority of product placements are paid for in cash and gratis and barter arrangements are still common (Karniouchina, Uslay, & Erenburg, 2011). Appropriate product placement in a hit movie (or even a Youtube video) can enable a small firm instantly reach a global audience. Furthermore, it has been observed that marketing media also have a life-cycle (Karniouchina, Uslay, & Erenburg, 2011). Early adoption of emerging/viral methods can generate tremendous returns for start-ups at low or no cost. Wait-and-see approach will not create any advantages for small firms because the hyper-returns begin to level off with early adopters and eventually diminish by the time late adopters are engaged in new media.

The "rule of three" theory (Sheth & Sisodia, 2002) also has important implications for start-ups. Uslay et al. (2010) found that firms with less than 1% share significantly underperformed other firms with 1–5% market share. Therefore, firms with a specialist (niche) strategy must plan their growth accordingly and exceed the 1% share threshold as quickly as possible (Uslay, Karniouchina, Altintig, & Hultman, 2011). Furthermore, Uslay et al. (2010) reported that firms stuck in the middle with 5–10% market share significantly underperformed both specialists with less share and generalists with larger share. This finding has two key implications: first, specialists need to ensure that they grow "healthily." Uncontrolled growth has detrimental bottomline consequences if the firm ends up getting stuck-in-the-middle. For example, People Express fell victim to its fast growth when its booking capabilities failed to meet the challenges brought forward by the computerized systems and revenue management schemes of American Airlines and other major carriers (Sheth, Allvine, Uslay, & Dixit, 2007). Furthermore, generalists must plan on achieving the 10% share general threshold accordingly. However, this may be easier said then done during market entry to mature foreign markets, necessitating M&A as well as alliances (Yeniyurt et al., 2009). Based on their firm strategy, it is important for firms to plan for optimal scale in each market based on the level of their product and marketing standardization. We precaution that simply relying on marketing-driven organic growth may not prove healthy when operating in mature foreign markets.

The *rule of three* also has implications for developing markets. Early entrants to emerging markets are typically small in size and they can be numerous. It is important for entrepreneurs to strategize if they plan to be one of the three generalists standing as the market matures. If that is not the case, divestment with attractive terms or restructuring/downsizing to a specialist strategy are more attractive options than getting stuck-in-the-middle in the long run.

Finally, even if a firm qualifies as one of the top three in strategic market(s), it is important to think about whom the top three global players will be, and what potential alliances and customer/supplier relationships can be developed. It is increasingly likely that many more Chinese (e.g., Haier) and Indian brands (e.g., Tata) will become global. It has been observed that firms can create global brands sooner if they enter three major continents as part of their early international expansion (Townsend et al., 2009). This requires a more B2B oriented research in its many facets and our understanding of B2B entrepreneurship is lagging (Malhotra & Uslay, 2009). We think that it is important for entrepreneurs and marketers to conceive expanded roles for buyers and sellers as partners for success in mature and developing markets in an inevitably global marketplace (Malhotra, Uslay, & Ndubisi, 2008).

References

Aaker, D., & Joachimsthaler, E. (1999). The lure of global branding. *Harvard Business Review, November–December*, 137–144.

Bell, J., McNaughton, R., & Young, S. (2001). Born-again global firms: An extension to the 'Born-Global' phenomenon. *Journal of International Management, 7*(3), 173–189.

Cavusgil, S. T., & Nevin, J. R. (1981). State-of-the-art in international marketing: An assessment. In B. M. Enis & K. J. Roering (Eds.), *Review of Marketing* (pp. 195–216). Chicago, IL: American Marketing Association.

Cavusgil, S. T., Kiyak, T., & Yeniyurt, S. (2004). Complementary approaches to preliminary foreign market opportunity assessment: Country clustering and country rankings. *Industrial Marketing Management*, *33*(7), 607–617.

Cavusgil, S. T., Yeniyurt, S., & Townsend, J. D. (2004). The framework of a global company: A conceptualization and preliminary validation. *Industrial Marketing Management*, *33*(8), 711–716.

Cavusgil, S. T., & Zou, S. (1994). Marketing strategy-performance relationship: An investigation of the empirical link in export market ventures. *Journal of Marketing*, *58*(1), 1–21.

Craig, C. S., & Douglas, S. P. (1997). Managing the transnational value chain – Strategies for firms from emerging markets. *Journal of International Marketing*, *5*(3), 71–84.

Dawar, N., & Parker, P. (1994). Marketing universals: Consumers' use of brand name, price, physical appearance, and retailer reputation as signals of product quality. *Journal of Marketing*, *58*(April), 81–95.

de Chernatony, L., Halliburton, C., & Bernath, R. (1995). International branding: Demand or supply driven opportunity. *International Marketing Review*, *12/2*, 9–22.

Dunning, J. H. (1988). *Internationalization and market entry mode*. London: Allen and Unwin.

Drucker, P. F. (2001). The next society. *The Economist* (November 3), 3–20.

Ernst & Young. (2012). Singapore takes third spot on globalization index 2011. Retrieved from http://www.ey.com/SG/en/Newsroom/News-releases/News-release_20120208_Singapore-takes-third-spot-on-Globalization-Index-2011. Accessed on October 25, 2012.

Friedman, T. L. (2005). *The world is flat*. New York, NY: Farrar, Straus and Giroux.

Guiltinan, J. P. (1999). Launch strategy, launch tactics, and demand outcomes. *Journal of Product Innovation Management*, *16*, 509–529.

Hamel, G. (1991). Competition for competence and inter-partner learning within international strategic alliances. *Strategic Management Journal*, *12*, 83–103.

Heine, J., & Thakur, R. C. (2011). *The dark side of globalization*. Tokyo: United Nations University Press.

Holt, D. B., Quelch, J. A., & Taylor, E. L. (2004). How global brands compete. *Harvard Business Review*, *82*(9), 68–75.

IMF. (2000). Globalization: Threat or opportunity? Retrieved from http://www.imf.org/external/np/exr/ib/2000/041200to.htm. Accessed on October 8, 2012.

Ireland, R. D., Hitt, M. A., & Vaidyanath, D. (2002). Alliance management as a source of competitive advantage. *Journal of Management*, *28*(3), 413–446.

Johansson, J. K. (1997). *Global marketing: Foreign entry, local marketing, and global management*. Chicago, IL: Richard D. Irwin.

Karniouchina, E. V., Uslay, C., & Erenburg, G. (2011). Do marketing media have life cycles? The case of product placement in movies. *Journal of Marketing*, *75*(3), 27–48.

Kedia, B. L., & Mukherji, A. (1999). Global managers: Developing a mindset for global competitiveness. *Journal of World Business*, *34*(3), 230–251.

Kirca, A., Hult, T. M., Deligonul, S., Perry, M. Z., & Cavusgil, S. T. (2012). A multilevel examination of the drivers of firm multinationality: A meta–analysis. *Journal of Management*, *38*(2), 502–530.

Knight, G. A., & Cavusgil, S. T. (1996). The born global firm: A challenge to traditional internationalization theory. In S. T. Cavusgil & T. Madsen (Eds.), *Advances in international marketing* (Vol. 8, pp. 11–26). Greenwich, CT: JAI Press.

Knight, G. A., & Cavusgil, S. T. (2004). Innovation, organizational capabilities, and the born-global firm. *Journal of International Business Studies, 35,* 121–141.

Kotabe, M., & Helsen, K. (2010). *Global marketing management: The international business* (5th ed.). Wiley.

Laroche, M., Kirpalani, Y. H., Pons, F., & Zhou, L. (2001). A model of advertising standardization in multinational corporations. *Journal of International Business Studies, 32*(2), 249–266.

Lee, O. F., Uslay, C., & Meuter, M. L. (2013). Antecedents and consequences of technology orientation (TECHOR) for small firms. In N. O. Ndubisi & S. Nwankwo (Eds.), *Enterprise development in SMEs and entrepreneurial firms: Dynamic processes.* IGI Global (pp. 214–238). doi:10.4018/978-1-4666-2952-3

Levinson, J. C. (1998). *Guerilla marketing: Secrets for making big profits from your small business* (3rd ed.). Boston, MA: Houghton Mifflin.

Levitt, T. (1983). The globalization of markets. *Harvard Business Review, 61*(May-June), 92–102.

Malhotra, N. K., Ulgado, F. M., & Agarwal, J. (2003). Internationalization and entry modes: A multitheoretical framework and research propositions. *Journal of International Marketing, 11*(4), 1–31.

Malhotra, N. K., Uslay, C., & Ndubisi, N. O. (2008). Commentary on "The essence of business marketing theory, research and tactics: Contributions by the journal of business-to-business marketing," by Lichtenthal, Mummalaneni, and Wilson: A paradigm shift and prospection through expanded roles of buyers and sellers. *Journal of Business-to-Business Marketing, 15*(2), 204–217.

Malhotra, N. K., & Uslay, C. (2009). Relative presence of business-to-business research in the marketing literature: The demand-oriented path forward. *Journal of Business-to-Business Marketing, 16*(1/2), 23–30.

Malhotra, N. K., Lee, O. F., & Uslay, C. (2012). Mind the gap: The mediating role of mindful marketing between market and quality orientations, their interaction, and consequences. *International Journal of Quality & Reliability Management, 29*(6), 607–625.

McLean, R. (2001). Globalization and the Asian financial crisis. *Atlantic Economic Journal, 29*(3), 471.

Meredith, R. (2003). Even with SARS, globalization marches on. Forbes. Retrieved from http://www.forbes.com/2003/04/10/cz_rm_0410globalization.html. Accessed on October 10, 2012.

Mesdag, M. (2000). Culture-sensitive global adaptation and standardization: The duration of usage hypothesis. *International Marketing Review, 17*(1), 74–84.

Mitra, D., & Golder, P. N. (2002). Whose culture matters? Near-market knowledge and its impact on foreign market entry timing. *Journal of Marketing Research, 39*(3), 350–365.

Montaqim, A. (2012). Global E-commerce sales will top 125 trillion in 2013. Retrieved from http://www.internetretailer.com/2012/06/14/global-e-commerce-sales-will-top-125-trillion-2013. Accessed on October 12, 2012

Mooij de, M. (2010). *Consumer behavior and culture: Consequences for global marketing and advertising.* Thousand Oaks, CA: Sage.

Murtha, T. P., Lenway, S. A., & Bagozzi, R. P. (1998). Global mindsets and cognitive shift in a complex multinational corporation. *Strategic Management Journal, 19*(2), 97–114.

Ohmae, K. (1989). Managing in a borderless world. *Harvard Business Review, 67*(May/June), 152–161.

Porter, M. E. (1986). Changing patterns of international competition. *California Management Review, 28*(Winter), 9–40.

Roth, K., Schweiger, D., & Morrison, A. (1991). Global strategy implementation at the business unit level: Operational capabilities and administrative mechanisms. *Journal of International Business Studies, 22*(3), 369–402.

Samiee, S., & Roth, K. (1992). The influence of global marketing standardization on performance. *Journal of Marketing, 56*(2), 1–17.

Sakarya, S., Eckman, M., & Hyllegard, K. H. (2007). Market selection for international expansion: Assessing opportunities in emerging markets. *International Marketing Review, 24*(2), 208–238.

Sheth, J. (1986). Global markets or global competition? *Journal of Consumer Marketing, 3*(2), 9–12.

Sheth, J. N., & Sisodia, R. S. (2002). *The rule of three: Surviving and thriving in competitive markets.* New York, NY: The Free Press.

Sheth, J. N., & Sisodia, R. S. (2006). *Tectonic shift: The geoeconomic realignment of globalizing markets.* Thousand Oaks, CA: Response.

Sheth, J. N., Allvine, F. C., Uslay, C., & Dixit, A. (2007). *Deregulation and competition: Lessons from the airline industry.* Thousand Oaks, CA: Sage.

Sheth, J. N., & Uslay, C. (2007). Implications of the revised definition of marketing: From exchange to value creation. *Journal of Public Policy & Marketing, 22*(2), 302–307.

Sheth, J. N., Uslay, C., & Sisodia, R. S. (2008). The globalization of markets and the rule of three. In P. J. Kitchen (Ed.), *Marketing Metaphors and Metamorphosis* (pp. 26–41). London: Palgrave-Macmillan.

Sheth, J. N. (2011). *Chindia rising: How China and India will benefit your business* (2nd ed.). New Delhi: Tata-McGraw Hill India.

Townsend, J. D., Yeniyurt, S., Deligonul, Z. S., & Cavusgil, S. T. (2004). Exploring the marketing program antecedents of performance in a global company. *Journal of International Marketing, 12*(4), 1–24.

Townsend, J. D., Yeniyurt, S., & Talay, M. B. (2009). Getting to global: An evolutionary perspective of brand expansion in international markets. *Journal of International Business Studies, 40*(4), 539–558.

Uslay, C. (2002). Buzz marketing: Secrets they don't teach you at the business school. *Glokal, Spring,* 38–41.

Uslay, C., Teach, R. D., & Schwartz, R. G. (2002). Promoting entrepreneurship for economic development: A cross-cultural analysis of student attitudes. *Journal of Research in Marketing & Entrepreneurship, 4*(2), 101–118.

Uslay, C., Malhotra, N. K., & Citrin, A. V. (2004). Unique marketing challenges at the frontiers of technology: An integrated perspective. *International Journal of Technology Management, 28*(1), 8–30.

Uslay, C., & J. N. Sheth (2008). Exploring the relationship between market orientation, entrepreneurial orientation, and learning orientation. Annual research symposium on marketing and entrepreneurship, Stockholm, Sweden.

Uslay, C., & Teach, R. D. (2008). Marketing/entrepreneurship interface (MEI) research priorities (2010–2012). *Journal of Research in Marketing & Entrepreneurship, 10*(1), 70–75.

Uslay, C., Morgan, R. E., & Sheth, J. N. (2009). Peter Drucker on marketing: An exploration of five tenets. *Journal of the Academy of Marketing Science, 37*(1), 47–60.

Uslay, C., Altintig, Z. A., & Winsor, R. D. (2010). An empirical examination of the "Rule of Three": Strategy implications for top management, marketers, and investors. *Journal of Marketing, 74*(March), 20–39.

Uslay, C., Karniouchina, E. V., Altintig, Z. A., & Hultman, C. M. (2011). Entrepreneurial chasm: An empirical examination of the 1% share threshold. Global research symposium on marketing, entrepreneurship, and entrepreneurship education, Rio de Janeiro, Brazil.

Wan, W. P. (2005). Country resource environments, firm capabilities, and corporate diversification strategies. *Journal of Management Studies, 42,* 161–171.

Wan, W. P., & Hoskisson, R. E. (2003). Home country environments, corporate diversification strategies, and firm performance. *Academy of Management Journal, 46,* 27–45.

Wiersema, M., & Bowen, H. P. (2008). Corporate diversification: The impact of foreign competition, industry globalization, and product diversification. *Strategic Management Journal, 29,* 115–132.

Workman, J. P. J., Homburg, C., & Gruner, K. (1998). Marketing organization: An integrative framework of dimensions and determinants. *Journal of Marketing, 62*(3), 21–41.

Yeniyurt, S. (2003). A literature review and integrative performance measurement framework for multinational companies. *Marketing Intelligence and Planning, 21*(3), 134–142.

Yeniyurt, S., & Townsend, J. D. (2003). Does culture explain acceptance of new products in a country? An empirical investigation. *International Marketing Review, 20*(4), 377–396.

Yeniyurt, S., Cavusgil, S. T., & Hult, G. T. M. (2005). A global market advantage framework: The role of global market knowledge competencies. *International Business Review, 14*(1), 1–19.

Yeniyurt, S., Townsend, J. D., Cavusgil, T. S., & Ghauri, P. N. (2009). Mimetic and experiential effects in international marketing alliance formations of US pharmaceuticals firms: An event history analysis. *Journal of International Business Studies, 40*(2), 301–320.

Yeniyurt, S., Townsend, J. D., & Talay, M. B. (2007). Factors influencing brand launch in a global marketplace. *Journal of Product Innovation Management, 24,* 471–485. doi: 10.1111/j.1540-5885.2007.00264.x

Yeniyurt, S. (2009). Reflections on the research path towards the global company. In S. T. Cavusgil (Ed.), *Advances in international marketing: MSU contributions to international business* (Vol. 19, pp. 201–211). Bingley, UK: Emerald Group Publishing Limited.

Yip, G. S., & Hult, T. M. (2011). *Total global strategy* (3rd ed). Upper Saddle River, NJ: Prentice-Hall.

Zou, S., & Cavusgil, S. T. (1996). Global strategy: A review and an integrated conceptual framework. *European Journal of Marketing, 30*(1), 52–69.

Zou, S., & Cavusgil, S. T. (2002). The GMS: A broad conceptualization of global marketing strategy and its effects on firm performance. *Journal of Marketing, 66*(4), 40–56.

Chapter 7

Opportunity and the Entrepreneurial Marketer

Abstract

Opportunity is raison d'être of entrepreneurial marketing. This includes seeking, recognizing, fostering, expanding, and creating opportunity, together with the activities involved in value creation and capture when exploiting opportunity. In this chapter, the complex nature of opportunities is examined, and a temporal, nonlinear, and emergent perspective is encouraged. The view that opportunities exist, and one must simply undertake research to discover them, is overly restricting. Opportunities can be created and they move, change, fragment, and morph into new shapes and forms. Entrepreneurial marketing exists at the juncture of opportunity discovery/creation and exploitation. Marketers must take heightened responsibility for a firm's opportunity horizon, place a primacy on entrepreneurial alertness, and adopt an enlightened perspective on value creation and capture. The marketer is dealing with two highly variable and subjective phenomena when ensuring the fit between value and opportunity. Both are subject to creation, enhancement, and manipulation, and each affects the other.

7.1. Introduction

Discussions of commonalities between marketing and entrepreneurship emphasize the fact that both involve a process and are concerned with value creation (e.g., Kerin, Hartley, & Rudelius, 2012; Stevenson, Roberts, & Grousbeck, 1989). While certainly true, it is our position that the more fundamental nexus between the two involves recognition and exploitation of opportunity. Neither marketing nor entrepreneurship can exist without an opportunity. The marketing mix is designed based on the marketer's delineation and understanding of an opportunity. Similarly, a venture is launched and developed based on the entrepreneur's belief that an opportunity exits that lends itself to exploitation. Our contention is that entrepreneurial

Entrepreneurial Marketing: Global Perspectives
Copyright © 2013 by Emerald Group Publishing Limited
All rights of reproduction in any form reserved
ISBN: 978-1-78190-786-3

marketing, which represents the interface between these two disciplines, should stress opportunity as its cornerstone. For example, Morris, Schindehutte, and LaForge (2002) have defined entrepreneurial marketing as "the proactive identification and exploitation of opportunities for acquiring and retaining profitable customers through innovative approaches to risk management, resource leveraging and value creation."

In the published work appearing in both disciplines, the understanding of opportunity is relatively limited. Marketing scholars have tended to define opportunities in terms of customers and their needs, differences among market segments, and competitor vulnerabilities (Urban & Hauser, 2004; Webb, Ireland, Hitt, Kistruck, & Tihanyi, 2011). Considerable attention is devoted to generating intelligence about customer opportunities and the use of that intelligence in decision making (Kohli & Jaworski, 1990). Within entrepreneurship, while opportunity-related issues have received heightened focus over the past decade, the primary focus has been on opportunity recognition as a personal orientation or skill (e.g., how alert to opportunity is the individual, in how much opportunity seeking behavior is the individual engaged).

Missing in the extant work is a richer sense of the underlying nature of opportunities, their associated properties, their sources and how they come about, and the roles marketers and entrepreneurs play in defining an opportunity as it emerges. In this chapter, we explore these issues in more depth. The implications of an opportunity-centric perspective on entrepreneurial marketing are examined.

7.2.   What Is an Opportunity?

New ventures, products, and processes start as a concept – a concept that someone thinks will create more value than currently exists in the market. Whether the concept is a success or a failure does not depend, however, just on the quality of the idea or the passion and enthusiasm of the marketer. What ultimately determines success is the extent to which the business idea is based on a genuine opportunity in the marketplace.

In broad terms, an opportunity is an appropriate or favorable time or occasion, a situation or condition favorable for the attainment of a goal, or a good position, chance, or prospect, for advancement or success. From an entrepreneurial perspective, we follow Morris (1998) in defining an opportunity as a favorable set of circumstances in the external environment that creates a need or opening for a new concept or venture. An opportunity is the chance of fulfilling unmet consumer demand, or satisfying currently unsatisfied needs or wants, whether those demands, needs, or wants are currently realized or not (Hulbert, Brown, & Adams, 1997). An opportunity, in short, is a gap in the current marketplace that provides the potential for value creation. It exists in the environment and is embedded in market conditions (Shane, 2012).

One way of thinking about opportunities is by acknowledging what they are not. Opportunities are not ideas for new businesses or products. In fact, most new products and services fail because of a lack of alignment with market opportunities, which leads to limited customer demand based on a flawed value proposition. Opportunities are also not constant. They are inextricably linked to the environmental conditions and timeframes in which they exist. This is where the expression "window of opportunity" comes from; opportunities exist as transient openings in the market for value to be created, based on features of the market that are constantly in flux.

In Figure 7.1, we attempt to capture the defining elements that contribute to a market opportunity. We begin with the forces that create an opportunity. This is a set of environmental forces that combine in some way to create a market opening. Examples include changes or developments in technology, regulation, social trends, the economy, the labor force, customers, competitors, the supply chain, distributors, and other components of the environment. The customer need is next, and is concerned with the problem being solved, the pain being removed, or the benefit being provided for a user. Opportunities are further delineated in terms of particular types of customers, where the parameters of the market and individual user segments are defined. These parameters will determine market potential and size, where potential is the upper limit on demand in dollars or units in terms of customers with the willingness and ability to buy, and size is the amount of that potential that has been realized. Primary demand (or opportunity) is the difference between potential and current size. Changing customer perceptions is another constituent part of opportunity, as these perceptions influence the both nature of the customer's need and the acceptability of various solutions. The extent of customer loyalties, satisfaction levels, and switching costs with regard to currently available solutions further

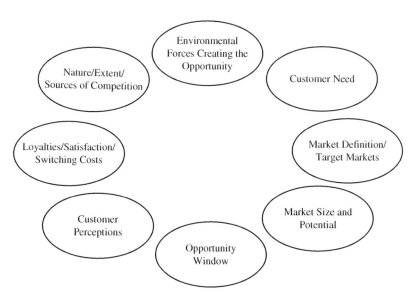

Figure 7.1: Eight Emergent Elements That Define Market Opportunities.

defines new opportunities. Competition is also a factor, both direct and indirect, and includes number of competitors and their relative aggressiveness. Finally, opportunities tend to have a life, in that they are uncovered at some point, and can be depleted over time as they are exploited. The concept of a window of opportunity suggests opportunities open and close. Again, and as we will explore below, these elements are subject to change.

The overarching function of business is to exploit opportunity. This means capitalizing on the opportune market conditions (unmet demand, unsatisfied wants, underserved needs, etc.) as presented to the business or entrepreneur with the purpose of generating profits. But before one is able to exploit the opportunity, it is useful to further understand the sources of opportunities and how they are uncovered.

7.3. Sources and Types of Opportunities

The process of opportunity creation and identification starts with a deep assessment and understanding of the market environment. There are a plethora of analytical tools and frameworks available for such purposes, ranging from the "five forces" industry analysis commonly used in strategy (Porter, 2008) and the "5C" situation analysis commonly used in marketing, to pattern identification methodologies (Fiet, 2002), lead user research (Von Hippel, 1986), and the techniques of futurology (e.g., Popcorn, 1991; Toffler & Toffler, 2006). Such tools allow the marketer to clearly outline and articulate the nature of openings in the external environment from which one might profit.

In the entrepreneurial marketing field, numerous potential sources of opportunities can present themselves through market analysis (Drucker, 1985; see also Morris, 1998; Hulbert et al., 1997). Key examples include

1. Unexpected external events in the marketplace, whether positive or negative, that may result from the limitations of assumptions or understandings about the market or consumers.
2. Incongruities between generally accepted assumptions or notions about the marketplace or consumers, and actual reality.
3. Requirements within the processes of a business or industry where a current task is not being adequately or efficiently performed.
4. Significant changes in industry or market structures (e.g., due to competition, regulation or technology).
5. Significant shifts in the demographics of a market population (e.g., age, composition, educational status, income or tastes).
6. Significant changes in perception, mood or meaning where, regardless of reality (see #2), changes in perceptions influence needs, wants, and expectations.
7. Development and dissemination of new knowledge and information, based on science, technology or other factors.

Consideration of these sources leads to an important conclusion. While opportunity can be created by forces in the external environment beyond the control of individuals or companies, the actions of the marketer can also have an impact on the development of an opportunity. This brings us to the question of how opportunities are discovered.

7.4. Are Opportunities Identified or Created?

There are at least three ways of thinking about why and how opportunities come to exist, or come to present themselves to the entrepreneur. On one hand, we can approach opportunities as existing "out there" in the world, somewhere, awaiting *discovery*. Here opportunities appear as real phenomena in the market that the entrepreneur must first identify, then exploit (Alvarez & Barney, 2008). Opportunities here are objective, and distinct from the entrepreneur (Hansen, Shrader, & Monllor, 2011; Shane, 2003). A venture or new product is created in response to this opportunity.

On the other hand, we can approach opportunities as *creations* of the entrepreneur based on that individual's understanding of the marketplace and world around them. In this context, the opportunities do not exist "out there" in the world until someone acts to create them (Alvarez & Barney, 2008). The entrepreneur takes actions that change the external environment, in effect creating new openings. Opportunities here are subjective, and inextricably linked to the entrepreneur (Hansen et al., 2011; Sarason, Dean, & Dillard, 2006). Moreover, new products or ventures can play a role in creating the opportunity.

Yet a third perspective finds elements of the external environment *interacting* with elements of the entrepreneur's behavior over time to produce an opportunity. Hence, an iterative process is involved where the entrepreneur attempts to connect a business concept to existing environmental conditions, and lack of fit leads to modifications both to the concept and to the market and need being addressed. Whether opportunities are ultimately identified or created before they can be exploited is less a binary for debate and more an opening or chance for the entrepreneur to think about value creation in several, often overlapping, ways. As we will discuss, thinking about opportunities as both things we can find *and* things we can create simply increases the potential for the entrepreneur to create value.

The degree to which opportunities are existent and simply must be discovered, or result from actions and insights of the marketer brings us to qualities is tied, at least in part, to the nature of the opportunity in question, and its underlying properties, a subject to which we now turn.

7.5. Core Properties of Opportunities: Temporality, Dynamism, and Emergence

Opportunities have a temporal quality. The existence of a given opportunity can be short-lived (e.g., the need for alternative sources of clean water or energy after a natural disaster strikes an urban community), of an intermediate term (e.g., the need for public pay telephones in the same urban community), or seemingly unending (e.g., the ongoing need for energy sources to heat homes and businesses in that urban community). It is difficult to know in advance how long an opportunity will last.

This temporal dimension also involves the extent to which the focal opportunity is subject to meaningful change or emergence. In this regard, at least five scenarios are possible:

- Some opportunities are discrete and relatively well-defined, with a short (sometimes fleeting) or intermediate life. Once discovered and capitalized upon, they may offer no apparent path to subsequent opportunities.
- Other opportunities might be labeled perennial in the sense that they are relatively continuous or ongoing, and do not change in fundamental ways. The need for personal grooming in a given community produces an ongoing opportunity for hair salons. In a similar vein, in many instances, there are ongoing opportunities for those who can improve quality, reduce costs, or enhance service levels within an existing market.
- A different scenario finds the initial opportunity unfolding as the marketer gains more experience with it and learns more about it. Thus, the opportunity itself takes on whole new dimensions or components. Such a situation could entail all or part of the opportunity actually being created by the marketer.
- A fourth scenario involves a kind of "opportunity corridor" (Ronstadt, 1988), where the experiences with a given opportunity make it possible to uncover other possibilities that are directly or indirectly tied (and may be unrelated) to the initial opportunity.

Opportunities can also have a dynamic quality. People have a host of needs that surround eating. Opportunities emerge as other factors interact with the need for sustenance. Being overweight, being on the go, having little time, needing to entertain, wanting to save the planet, being rich, the rising costs of ingredients, being unable or unwilling to leave one's home, changing consumer tastes, and having particular nutritional requirements are but a few examples. In these examples, the dynamic quality is driven by interactions between the basic opportunity and environmental developments.

Yet, if we consider the latter two of the scenarios described above, the dynamic quality is fueled by interactions between the marketer and the opportunity. Discovery is not just about what one observes or perceives, but also involves the actions and behaviors of the marketer and the subsequent learning and sensemaking that take place. Hence, opportunities can have an emergent property that is situated in the unfolding experiences as opportunity and agent interact. We believe that emergence represents the single most distinguishing characteristic of most opportunities.

7.6.   The Nature of Opportunity Emergence

Emergence has been defined as "the arising of novel and coherent structures, patterns and properties during the process of self-organization in complex systems"

(Goldstein, 1999, p. 54). It involves the identification of a new context where elements of the previous state continue to exist together with new elements. It is not simply pursuing a new path or direction, but instead is a new type of order. The entity is in the process of becoming something it was not before. Hence, it is more than change or modifications to what exists (Lichtenstein, Dooley, & Lumpkin, 2006).

Emergence is not simply the result of the process of interactions (i.e., a new state or entity). Rather, it takes place *during* the process of interacting (McKelvey, 2001). A fluid structure emerges from a "soup" of interacting components that are themselves in flux. As the emergence of order in structures, processes and routines is a messy process, the emergence of any given phenomenon can be difficult to explain. This difficulty is traceable to the underlying properties of emergence, which themselves are context dependent. Examples of these properties include time irreversibility, dynamic instability and tensions, nonlinear change with small inputs producing large outcomes, component parts co-evolving, components combining in unpredictable ways, reciprocal interactions between micro-level events and behaviors and emergent macro-structures, and surprise, where nonobvious or unexpected behaviors come from the object in question. These properties are novel when they are unpredictable, unexplainable and irreducible to component parts (Humphreys, 1997).

As emergent phenomena, opportunities that ultimately sustain a business can substantively differ from the opportunity that initially instigated the marketer to act (Dimov, 2011; Dutta & Crossan, 2005). Emergence suggests that the entrepreneurial process may not always begin with a well-defined or attractive opportunity but is instead nonlinear: opportunities and the actions used to define and exploit opportunities emerge together and as a consequence of each other.

Apple's iPod Touch provides an excellent example of emergence. When Apple launched the iPod Touch the company was not sure what it was for – so they let it loose and observed what happened. On Christmas Day 2009, sales of apps (applications that run on Apple's iPhone and the Touch) on the Apple Store soared 1000% – mostly due to people downloading games for their new Touch they'd received as a gift (Wired, 2009). Indeed in December 2009, 280 million apps were downloaded for the Touch – generating $250 million in revenues for Apple (GigaOM, 2010). Apple CEO Steve Jobs reflected: "Originally, we weren't exactly sure how to market the Touch. Was it an iPhone without the phone? Was it a pocket computer? What happened was, what customers told us was, they started to see it as a games machine. We started to market it that way, and it just took off. And now what we really see is it's the lowest-cost way to the App Store" (*New York Times*, 2009).

The Touch is far from being an isolated instance of this phenomenon. Consider Facebook, Second Life, or Twitter. Each is a platform in which users create content and determine purpose – which is often highly heterogeneous. Facebook was not expressly developed to be the massive, international social networking site it is today. Mark Zuckerberg and his fellow computer science students started Facebook so that their college roommates and students at Harvard University could interact with each other, catch up on news, and share photographs. The website's membership was initially limited by the founders to Harvard students, but then expanded to other universities in the Massachusetts area, and then other schools and colleges. Today the site has almost a billion members, and has become a forum for doing all the things the founders intended, but also a vehicle to share links and videos, chat, and run cause groups ranging from electing Obama to raising funds for Haiti or the Victims of Hurricane Sandy.

Opportunity emergence is driven both by objective and subjective elements (Eckhardt & Shane, in press). It is a product of the reciprocal interactions between the environment (i.e., objective) and entrepreneur (i.e., subjective). Let us first consider objective emergence. Endogenous changes to the market comprise the first mechanism through which opportunities emerge. Marketers and entrepreneurs begin exploiting opportunities based on "facts on the ground" related to the market, such as the market size, customer demographics and needs, industry characteristics and competitors, and existing products and services. However, these facts are not constant, and events such as the entrance of new competitors, suppliers, or competitor's introduction of innovative technologies or business models may change in a way that substantively reshapes the objective foundation of opportunity. As markets evolve, so do opportunities. For example, Borders bookstores initially exploited an opportunity related to customers' desire for a store that sold books related to their personal tastes and their ability to customize each store's inventory based on customer purchases (Raff, 2000). However, the entrance of an innovative competitor altered the opportunity perceived by Borders. Amazon.com, by simultaneously offering customers a customized book selection alongside a massive inventory and lower prices, changed the bookselling market. While the opportunity being exploited by Borders did not evaporate – customers still preferred a customized selection – it emerged to incorporate customer needs Borders was unable to fulfill, forcing them into bankruptcy.

Demographic shifts can also drive opportunity emergence (Shane, 2003). Organizations often discover that their customers' needs and reasons for buying evolve with time, creating tensions between the market and the marketer and altering the opportunities they exploit. For example, universities have found the opportunity for educational services has emerged to incorporate needs of younger generations used to consuming information electronically, resulting in the explosion of online education, even at institutions previously wedded to the in-class teaching format and resistant to change, such as Harvard and Berkeley (Mayadas, Bourne, & Bacsich, 2009).

In other instances, businesses may find themselves engaging in new activities to serve customers they did not initially target. In these instances, opportunities are emerging to include customers for whom the business may create value using products or services already deployed in another market segment. For instance, Greenwood and colleagues (2005) describe how accounting firms' emerging market conditions led them to expand their consulting services toward customers for whom they were already providing auditing services. Elsewhere, Baker and Sinkula (2005) describe an environmental services entrepreneur who, as a "lark" to increase his revenue, decided to tentatively pursue smokestack emission analysis. Through this act of improvisation based on a sketch of an idea, the entrepreneur was surprised to find an abundance of available government contracts and came to believe that this line of work would prove to be highly lucrative, and he ultimately dropped all other revenue drivers to focus on this new, unexpected opportunity. In both examples, changing market conditions – the accounting firms encountered new needs, and the environmental services entrepreneur encountered new customers – influenced the emergence of the opportunity.

Turning to subjective emergence, perceptions are a key driver of decisions and behaviors. Marketers and entrepreneurs are themselves developing over time, leading to changes in the manner in which they perceive objective reality. They may develop competencies or learn through experience, which can alter how they come to perceive opportunities. They constantly acquire new information and create new knowledge, from which they may draw enhanced opportunity inferences (Tang, Kacmar, & Busenitz, 2012). Moreover, they enhance their cognitive abilities through use, which may make them better able to ascertain and conceptualize opportunities (Gaglio & Katz, 2001; Haynie, Shepherd, Mosakowski, & Earley, 2010). As individuals develop the cognitive schemas and behaviors necessary to fully conceptualize an opportunity, they can become better at evaluating market conditions and drawing conclusions, reshaping how they perceive an opportunity. Similarly, as they become better able to associate disparate pieces of information, they may more quickly perceive the importance of some new market condition, hastening the pace of opportunity emergence.

A similar process driving opportunity emergence is the simple acquisition of information and knowledge. For example, a marketer with a robust social network may act to exploit an opportunity through interacting with customers, suppliers, and bankers. In so doing, the individual may find that their selected target market for a product innovation is incorrect or that the selected means of distribution is wrong. In these instances, opportunity emergence constitutes the "fleshing out" of an idea and the reduction of uncertainty through venture creation (Dimov, 2011). It is unlikely that marketers or entrepreneurs instantly and fully perceive the market conditions constituting an opportunity. Instead, through interactions with others, they acquire knowledge that reshapes how they understand what customer needs their products or services fulfill, who their customers are, or where and how to reach them (Levie & Lichtenstein, 2010).

7.7.   Facilitating Emergence

An important question concerns how one maximizes the opportunities occasioned by emergence. Berthon, Pitt, and Watson (2008) suggest that entrepreneurial marketers need to understand three elements: openness, programmability, and interconnectivity.

7.7.1.   *Openness*

Traditionally marketers seek "closed" opportunities: that is, where others are discouraged or prevented from changing, modifying or repurposing offerings. This has the effect of destroying variance (the characteristics or traits of offerings cannot be changed) and heritability (improvements that could have been made to offerings cannot be passed on). So those who view emergence as an opportunity will value openness, to a greater or lesser extent. Openness encourages variation and, if the variation is *in turn* open, heritability. Indeed the greater the openness, the faster and more extensive will be the level of emergence.

7.7.2. Programmability

Variation, and thus innovation, is a function of how easily the elements of an offering can be recombined into novel arrangements. This is known as programmability or composability (*cf.* Pratt, Ragusa, & von der Lippe, 1999). For example, the ability to create apps on the iPod Touch enables it to be anything from a mobile phone (by using the Skype app), through a gaming device (see the Grand Theft Auto app) to a sphygmomanometer (see the iHealth blood pressure measurement app). Thus, the ease with which an offering can be programmed or reprogrammed determines its emergent potential.

7.7.3. Interconnectivity

Interconnectivity through networks allow customers to self-organize in terms of production of new ideas (variation), the dissemination and modification of new designs (heritability), and the consumption of new offerings (selection). Simply, the spread of reinvention of an emergent offering depends on an infrastructure that allows talented individuals, who might be globally distributed, to collaborate. The Internet and associated cooperative technologies (e.g., cloud computing, web sites, cell phones) enable those with a common interest to participate in the reinvention of an offering and the dispersion of innovations. Social interconnectivity is thus central in determining the emergent potential of an offering.

The primary challenge facing entrepreneurial marketers who pursue emergent opportunities is of course, monetization. Emergent offerings often create value that is difficult to monetize, but it is value nonetheless. For example, Facebook, Wikipedia, Twitter, YouTube, and Craig's List all provide huge value to consumers, but (currently) little return to the organizations themselves. However, this is not to say that emergent offerings cannot be monetized. The trick is to finding *what* to monetize. For example, Google search (its primary offering) was, and still is, free – the monetary potential came from linking other things to the fundamental activity of search. No one would have paid, or would pay for search, but as it turned out someone was prepared to pay for something associated with it (links, ad words, etc.). Facebook's fundamental activity is social networking, but so far the company has not been able to monetize that (and it is unlikely people will pay for it). So the firm's challenge is to get firms or consumers to pay for something about social networking.

7.8. The Creation of Opportunities

In some instances, the actions of the marketer result in creation of new opportunities. Creation suggests no market currently exists or is about to emerge, and no market-based need has been specified. The need is at best nascent or lies within some generic problem. Elements that could contribute to the opportunity may or may not be in place but they have yet to combine in ways that produce a potential market.

The marketer launches an innovation that represents a significant disruption of equilibrium and opportunities appear in response. Whereas the marketer responding to an existing market is creating dissonance between known solutions and some improvement or revision, with creation dissonance is being created between an individual's or organization's current situation and the unknown. The marketer is opening up entirely new possibilities, representing a disruption to the potential customer's sense of the world and ways in which value can be created. Marketing action triggers people or organizations to identify needs they did not know they have or identify needs they did not heretofore have. As the market starts to form, the customer is determining a new set of relevant attributes and a means to assess them.

A key factor explaining the creation of new opportunities is the development of new knowledge and leading edge technologies. Scientists and inventors may be driven by curiosity, a sense of possibility, or the drive to solve a particular technical challenge. The airplane was invented based on relentless pursuit of the theoretical notion that a machine heavier than air could be kept aloft, or more simply by the fantasy that man could fly like a bird. Many opportunities appeared in response to the first successful air flight (military defense, consumer travel, agriculture, logistics, and shipping). Similarly, a pioneer who is first to master the advancement of laser technology and its application to enhancing eyesight is effectively creating a market that did not exist before. The value proposition makes possible things that heretofore were not possible, and those possibilities create new demand for eye surgery, while also opening new possibilities for a range of new product and infrastructure development.

With opportunity creation, the marketer usually has a vision of a market that could exist. Yet, the idea that marketers can create opportunities does not mean that they actually control them. Risks are high, and the ability to accurately measure the market is often problematic. At the same time, the returns may not be commensurate with these risks, as one is dealing with the unknown.

7.9. Opportunity and Entrepreneurial Marketing

Entrepreneurial marketing is fundamentally opportunity-driven behavior. It entails a dual set of responsibilities. First, it involves creating new opportunities as well as identifying existing and facilitating emerging opportunities. Hence, the marketer is creating markets and leading customers as well as deciphering existing markets. Second, marketing actions are instrumental in exploiting opportunities, regardless of how the opportunity came about.

Up to this point, we have examined issues surrounding the discovery or creation of opportunities. To complete the picture, we must consider opportunity exploitation, which involves two core facets of successful business practice: value creation and value capture.

Value creation concerns the ability of an individual or organization to engage in activities that produce benefit or utility as perceived by a target user or buyer. The user or buyer is subjectively assessing the qualities of an item (e.g., a product, service, or process) in relation to their needs and wants. Importantly, value is created not simply through the item itself, but through a host of other marketing variables in the so-called marketing mix.

Value capture or appropriation occurs when an exchange takes place and some return or gain is realized by the value creator. The amount of value captured can be less than that created (i.e., a consumer surplus), for at least three reasons: (a) supply and demand conditions dictate a market price that is lower than the value a customer is actually receiving (and hence the value created is being shared with competitors); (b) the value creator must share the value created with other stakeholders (e.g., employees and society); and (c) the value creator intentionally charges a lower price (in currency or some other form of return) than the value conveyed for altruistic reasons or based on some personal objective. The user or buyer subjectively estimates the value they perceive in a given item, while the competitive marketplace determines how much is actually paid for the item. Also, it should be noted that sometimes the value creator is able to engage in exchange where the price that is wrought exceeds the amount the value creator was willing to accept (i.e., a producer surplus).

The amount of value the marketer captures is determined not just by the existence and actions of any competitors, but also the isolating mechanisms they are able to develop (Lepak, Smith, & Taylor, 2007). Isolating mechanisms are defined as phenomena that limit the ex post equilibration of rents among individual firms (Rumelt, 1984). They enable the value creator to limit the amount of value captured that is shifted to other competitors or stakeholders. Examples of such phenomena include controlling unique resources others cannot mimic, developing proprietary knowledge and holding patents or other forms of intellectual property protection, the creation of customer switching costs, establishing a strong brand image or reputation, and locking up sources of supply or channels of distribution.

To better understand how value creation and capture interact with opportunity, consider Figure 7.2. Here, we have extended our earlier conceptualization to distinguish opportunity at three levels: generic, industry level, and company level. Generic opportunities represent broad-based conceptualizations of a need or market opening. They are defined in more general and inclusive terms, and are more conjectural or speculative in nature, making them impossible to quantify with any precision. Consider the opportunities represented by a growing social pattern such as families engaged in home schooling of their children, or a demographic trend such as the growing numbers of citizens who are over 75 years of age, healthy in body and mind, reasonably well-off financially, with time on their hands (what is labeled a "multiple-cause" opportunity). At the industry-level, the opportunity is defined in terms of more tangible needs that relate to the technologies, resources, and

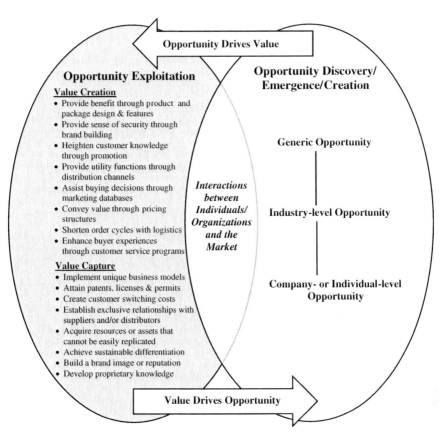

Figure 7.2: Entrepreneurial Behavior at the Interface Between Opportunity Recognition and Exploitation.

capabilities of a particular industry. The opportunity now lends itself to general measurement and assessment of its relative attractiveness. With home schooling, we might consider the educational software industry, and its ability to address the need for assessment methods for parents who are teaching their own children. For the senior citizen opportunity, if approached by the social networking industry, the focus might be on the need for social experiences on the part of those in the stage of the family life cycle who are retired solo survivors. Turning to the company- or individual-level, the opportunity is now defined in terms of the (relatively) precise potential for particular value creating solutions to a problem or need together with the individual's or firm's capacity for value capture. Hence, the resources, capabilities and entrepreneurial actions at the level of the individual or firm are instrumental in determining just how large the opportunity is. With the home schooling example, the potential for a software product that is based on a patented algorithm for assessing student learning in math and sciences and has been sanctioned by a leading educational accrediting body would be a case in point. For the senior citizens, the opportunity might be defined by a company that develops a concept of "extreme sports for seniors" and gets an exclusive permit from a municipal airport to offer tandem parachuting experiences. It should also be kept in mind that, when the individual or firm is a first mover, they may well be the industry (a monopolist), at least for a time. In such circumstances, the concept of opportunity will be a bit more general.

The core argument behind Figure 7.2 concerns the dynamic interplay between opportunity discovery/creation and value creation/capture. The initiation of the interaction can happen in any number of ways. Consider three of the many possibilities:

1. Awareness or understanding of the opportunity may be relatively loose or general, existing primarily at the generic level, and based on this understanding, the marketer develops a value proposition
2. The marketer has an innovative idea for a venture, product or process, and goes in search or possible opportunities at the industry-level that might be a good fit for the innovation.
3. The marketer carefully examines the extant opportunity at the individual- or company level, identifying where there are holes or gaps in terms of what is currently being done by key players in the market (including their approaches to both value creation and value capture), and then develops some new value proposition to capitalize on these holes or gaps.

As a generalization, opportunity recognition and exploitation are rarely two discrete activities. Rather, it is a messy process where opportunities are most typically uncovered as one pursues some innovative idea for a business or product. The opportunity is emerging just as the value proposition is emerging. Each is feeding off of the other.

The marketer becomes a central actor in the dynamics that underlie Figure 7.2. They must navigate the corridor that connects opportunity recognition and value creation/capture, and it is not typically a linear path. Instead, the corridor is filled with side paths, dead ends, surprises, and openings that are disguised or hard to see. It is a journey lacking a clear map or plan, with few if any dependable signposts along the way. Most challenging is the fact that the marketer rarely knows if and when they have arrived at their intended destination. While they may well uncover a profitable market and successfully exploit it with a viable value proposition, there is uncertainty regarding whether there were key aspects of the opportunity they missed or failed to properly understand, and whether they in fact captured all of the available value. This uncertainty would seem especially in situations where value creation and capture are not simply vehicles for exploitation of a fairly well-defined opportunity, but instead lead to opportunity discovery or creation.

Entrepreneurial marketing is concerned with the interactions between the opportunity at any of these levels and both value creation and capture by a given individual or organization. Those involved with it are responsible for creating and capturing value in response to an opportunity, interacting with the market to enable an opportunity to emerge, and sometime actually creating new opportunities. The skill set of the entrepreneurial marketer centers around vision, innovation, risk mitigation, resource leveraging, creative problem-solving, adaptation (Morris et al., 2002). These capabilities must be continuously applied to opportunity recognition, value creation and value capture, and frequently in tandem.

The key to the opportunity recognition component is entrepreneurial alertness, defined as "a process and perspective that helps some individuals to be more aware of changes, shifts, opportunities, and overlooked possibilities" (Tang et al., 2010). The marketer is able to build on a range of inputs, including their developing knowledge base, past experiences, mental maps, information processing and pattern recognition skills, and social interactions to recognize or develop opportunities (Baron, 2006). Tang et al. (2012) argue that alertness has three complementary dimensions: scanning and searching for new information, connecting previously disparate information, and evaluating whether the new information represents an opportunity. To the extent that opportunities are not preexisting and well defined, the searching, connecting and evaluating cannot consider the opportunity in isolation, but must incorporate information and insights on current and potential possibilities with regard to a value proposition and means of value capture.

With regard to value creation, Figure 7.2 provides examples of a number of key ways in which the marketer can contribute to the value proposition. It is critical to note here is that opportunities aren't only capitalized upon with products or services, but also with new processes and business models. This is important in a marketing context, as it suggests opportunities can be exploited via new packaging, distribution, logistics, selling, promotion, pricing, payment methods, and customer service approaches. They are doing these things in a manner that is either responsive to a deep understanding of an existing opportunity, or that is continually seeking to adapt value elements to potential opportunities. Typically, they are also doing it in ways that reflect resource leveraging, bricolage, guerrilla actions, improvisation, and nonconventional tactics. As such competencies are developed, opportunities that might otherwise have been perceived as too difficult or costly to exploit begin to receive attention.

Finally, we must consider the marketer's or entrepreneur's role in value capture. Examples of tools or approaches for limiting value slippage are provided in Figure 7.2. Again, creativity is the key as one attempts to create switching costs (e.g., longer term customer contracts), build deeper ties with distributors (e.g., with shared databases), or acquire assets that are difficult to replicate (e.g., personnel with a unique ability to close sales or deliver service), or any of the other value capture approaches. Arguably, as one is able to capture relatively more value, the potential exists for greater market interaction and more lessons learned, which can translate into richer insights regarding how opportunities are evolving and new elements that may be emerging.

7.10. Opportunity Assessment

The pure, simple indicator of whether something can be truly considered an opportunity is if it offers potential – potential customers, potential users, potential revenue, potential cost savings, and so on (Morris, 1998). Potential underscores that the opportunity is something one *can* do rather than something one *could* do. Opportunities consider the marketplace at two time horizons, now and in the future, and offer the entrepreneur a sustainable and profitable means of converting the former to the latter. The distinction between possibility and probability cannot be overemphasized. It is a distinction that requires a deep awareness of the marketplace in its current manifestation, and a motivation to construct a different, better, future manifestation of that marketplace (Webb et al., 2011).

Regardless of how much value is created, the potential to capture value is delimited by the parameters that define an opportunity. The clarity of these parameters is tied to how fixed or emergent the opportunity is. This brings us to an unsettling reality: a true opportunity – reliant on potential, rather than just possibility – cannot truly be validated as such until after we attempt to exploit it. The market is the true test, and only in hindsight can we confirm whether what we perceived and acted on was indeed an opportunity (i.e., market success) or a simply an idea that was not an opportunity (i.e., market failure) (Eckhardt & Shane, 2003). Especially where they are emergent, opportunity assessment can involve retrospective sensemaking (Weick, Sutcliffe, & Obstfeld, 2005), where a relatively attractive market opening is understood only after it has been capitalized upon.

In spite of these challenges, a number of means exist for assessing the validity of an opportunity. There are several reliable indicators and criteria for evaluation than can help us ascertain whether or not there is an opportunity for a given idea or concept (see Timmons, 1990). Below are some approximate benchmarks that can serve as a "test" for potential:

- Market Indicators: Reachable and receptive customers with an identified need; High potential for value creation in part due to low perceived risk of adoption and rapid customer payback period (less than one year).
- Industry Indicators: Disorganized competition and/or emerging industry (emerging industries generally exist where market growth rates exceed 30%).
- Target Criteria: 40%+ sustainable gross margins; 10%+ durable net margins; 25%+ ROI; 20%+ market share.
- Economic Criteria: Breakeven and cash flow positive within two years; Low to moderate capital requirements; Low risk, fundable business model with existing or easily accessible harvest/exit mechanisms.
- Competitive Advantage Criteria: Low fixed and variable costs (production, marketing, distribution) with moderate to strong degrees of control (prices, costs, supply chains, distribution channels); Ability to erect barriers to entry through IP protection, contractual exclusivity and/or first-mover advantages (as per "Target Criteria") in technology, market innovation, resources, capacity or product.
- Differentiation Criteria: Sources are numerous, substantive and sustainable; Ideally, multiple sources of differentiation are interrelated and interdependent, which further blocks imitability.
- Management Criteria: Strong, proven performance records for an existing team, with well-developed, high quality and accessible networks.

These benchmarks represent ideal conditions that may not be fully satisfied to the extent noted herein. Yet, assessing the potential of the business opportunity against these indicators and criteria can provide both an initial litmus test for the validity of the opportunity and a roadmap for strategic development should certain conditions be met.

7.11. Conclusions and Implications

Opportunity is raison d'être of entrepreneurial marketing. This includes seeking, recognizing, fostering, expanding, and creating opportunity, as well as the range of activities involved in value creation and value capture when exploiting opportunity. In this chapter, we have attempted to examine the complex nature of opportunities, and encourage a more temporal, nonlinear, and emergent perspective. The conventional view that opportunities exist or are out there, and one simply needs to undertake the necessary research and discover them, is overly narrow and restricting. Marketers who adopt such a view will likely fail to perceive large components of existing opportunities while also not recognizing many opportunities that could have been. The contemporary global environment is one in which opportunities are not static. They move, change, fragment, and morph into entirely new shapes and forms. Any one conceptualization of an opportunity is increasingly short-lived.

In a similar vein, we reject the conceptualization of marketing as activities that create value and exchange simply in response to opportunity. Rather, entrepreneurial marketing exists at the juncture of opportunity discovery/creation and exploitation. Marketers must take heightened responsibility for a firm's opportunity horizon. This not only means placing a primacy on entrepreneurial alertness but also requires a much more enlightened perspective on value creation and capture. In trying to ensure the fit between value and opportunity, the marketer is in effect dealing with two highly variable and subjective phenomena. Both are subject to creation, enhancement and manipulation. Both can affect the other.

For their part, scholars must help guide this new conceptualization of marketing's role. More work is required to understand the nature of opportunity emergence and creation. Case studies are needed to map the evolution and emergence of opportunities in different kinds of industries and markets. Building on our initial characterization of different temporal paths for opportunities, it may be possible to develop typologies of opportunities and to establish defining characteristics and behaviors of each type. Further, insights must be developed on the underlying factors that enable a given opportunity to develop new dimensions or to emerge into something fundamentally different than it was before. Of course, part of our argument is that the marketer is one of these factors. Yet, we know relatively little about how marketing actions (value creation and capture) influence the development or demise of nonexistent or emerging opportunities. Insights are also needed regarding how independent stakeholders operating in parallel effectively co-create new opportunities. These are but a few of provocative questions awaiting scholarly attention.

Finally, an opportunity-centric perspective raises questions regarding how marketers are educated and trained. An examination of the marketing curriculum in universities and the training programs in companies would uncover scant evidence of courses, modules or learning materials focused on opportunity-related skills and capabilities. More attention should be devoted to how marketers can better recognize new opportunities and emerging changes and transformations in existing opportunities. Trend analysis, pattern recognition, gap analysis, visioning, nonlinear, and lateral thinking, and the ability to challenge and relax assumptions would seem especially pertinent capabilities. In addition, the marketer must learn how to engage in more trial and error with a constant stream of new value experiments, and to couple these efforts with rapid learning and quick adaptation as new opportunities are be uncovered and emerging opportunities are chased.

References

Alvarez, S. A, & Barney, J. B. (2008). Opportunities, organizations and entrepreneurship. *Strategic Entrepreneurship Journal, 2*, 171–173.

Baker, W. E., & Sinkula, J. M. (2005). Environmental marketing strategy and firm performance: Effects on new product performance and market share. *Journal of the Academy of Marketing Science, 33*, 461–475.

Baron, R. (2006). Opportunity recognition as pattern recognition: How entrepreneurs connect the dots to identify business opportunities. *Academy of Management Perspectives, 20*(1), 104–119.

Berthon, P., Pitt, L., & Watson, R. T. (2008). From genesis to revelations: The technological diaspora. *Communications of the ACM, 51*(12), 1–14.

Dimov, D. (2011). Grappling with the unbearable elusiveness of entrepreneurial opportunities. *Entrepreneurship Theory and Practice, 35*(1), 57–81.

Drucker, P. (1985). *Innovation & entrepreneurship.* New York, NY: Harper & Row.

Dutta, D. K., & Crossan, M. M. (2005). The nature of entrepreneurial opportunities: Understanding the process using the 4I organizational learning framework. *Entrepreneurship Theory and Practice, 29*(4), 425–449.

Eckhardt, J. T., & Shane, S. A. (2003). Opportunities and entrepreneurship. *Journal of Management, 29*(3), 333–349.

Fiet, J. (2002). *The systematic search for entrepreneurial discoveries.* Westport, CT: Quorum.

Gaglio, C. M., & Katz, J. A. (2001). The psychological basis of opportunity identification: Entrepreneurial alertness. *Small Business Economics, 16*, 95–111.

GigaOM. (2010). Retrieved from http://gigaom.com/2010/01/12/the-apple-app-store-economy/

Goldstein, J. (1999). Emergence as a construct: History and issues. *Emergence, 1*(1), 49–72.

Greenwood, R., Li, S. X., Prakash, R., & Deephouse, D. L. (2005). Reputation, diversification, and organizational explanations of performance in professional service firms. *Organization Science, 16*(6), 661–673.

Hansen, D. J., Shrader, R., & Monllor, J. (2011). Defragmenting definitions of entrepreneurial opportunity. *Journal of Small Business Management, 49*(2), 283–304.

Haynie, J. M., Shepherd, D., Mosakowski, E., & Earley, P. C. (2010). A situated metacognitive model of the entrepreneurial mindset. *Journal of Business Venturing, 25*(2), 217–229.

Hulbert, B., Brown, R. B., & Adams, S. (1997). Towards an understanding of "Opportunity." *Marketing Education Review, 7*(3), 67–73.

Humphreys, P. (1997). How properties emerge. *Philosophy of Science, 64*(1), 1–17.

Kerin, R., Hartley, S., & Rudelius, W. (2012). *Marketing.* New York, NY: McGraw-Hill-Irwin.

Kohli, A. K., & Jaworski, B. J. (1990). Market orientation: The construct, research propositions, and managerial implications. *Journal of Marketing, 54*(2), 1–18.

Lepak, D. P., Smith, K. G., & Taylor, M. S. (2007). Value creation and value capture: A multilevel perspective. *Academy of Management Review, 32*(1), 180–194.

Levie, J., & Lichtenstein, B. B. (2010). A terminal assessment of stages theory: Introducing a dynamic states approach to entrepreneurship. *Entrepreneurship Theory and Practice, 34*(2), 317–350.

Lichtenstein, B. B., Dooley, K. J., & Lumpkin, J. T. (2006). Measuring emergence in the dynamics of new venture creation. *Journal of Business Venturing, 21*(2), 153–175.

Mayadas, A. F., Bourne, J., & Bacsich, P. (2009). Online education today. *Science, 323*(5910), 85–89.

McKelvey, B. (2001). Energizing order-creating networks of distributed intelligence: Improving the corporate brain. *International Journal of Innovation Management, 5*(2), 181–212.

Morris, M. H. (1998). *Entrepreneurial intensity: Sustainable advantages for individuals, organizations, and societies.* Westport, CT: Quorum Books.

Morris, M. H., Schindehutte, M., & LaForge, R. (2002). Entrepreneurial marketing: A construct for integrating emerging entrepreneurship and marketing perspectives. *Journal of Marketing Theory & Practice, 10*(4), 1–19.

New York Times. (2009). Retrieved from http://bits.blogs.nytimes.com/2009/09/09/in-qa-steve-jobs-snipes-at-amazon-and-praises-ice-cream/

Popcorn, F. (1991). *The popcorn Report: Faith popcorn on the future of your company, your world, your life.* New York, NY: Doubleday.

Porter, M. (2008). The five competitive forces that shape strategy. *Harvard Business Review, 86*(1), 78–93.

Pratt, D. R., Ragusa, L. C., & von der Lippe, S. (1999). Composability as an architecture driver. *Proceedings of the 1999 interservice/industry training, simulation and education conference*, Orlando, FL.

Raff, D. M. G. (2000). Superstores and the evolution of firm capabilities in American bookselling. *Strategic Management Journal, 21*(10–11), 1043–1059.

Ronstadt, R. (1988). The corridor principle. *Journal of Business Venturing, 3*, 31–40.

Rumelt, R. P. (1984). Towards a strategic theory of the firm. In R. B. Lamb (Ed.), *Competitive strategic management* (pp. 556–570). Englewood Cliffs, NJ: Prentice-Hall.

Sarason, Y., Dean, T., & Dillard, J. F. (2006). Entrepreneurship at the nexus of individual and opportunity: A structuration view. *Journal of Business Venturing, 21*(3), 286–305.

Shane, S. (2003). *A general theory of entrepreneurship: The individual-opportunity nexus.* Cheltenham: Edward Elgar.

Shane, S. (2012). Reflections on the 2010 AMR Decade Award: Delivering on the promise of entrepreneurship as a field of research. *Academy of Management Review, 37*(1), 10–20.

Stevenson, H., Roberts, M. J., & Grousbeck, I. (1989). *New business ventures and the entrepreneur* (3rd ed.). Homewood, IL: Irwin Publishing.

Tang, J., Kacmar, K. M., & Busenitz, L. (2012). Entrepreneurial alertness in the pursuit of new opportunities. *Journal of Business Venturing, 27*(1), 77–94.

Timmons, J. A. (1990). *New venture creation: Entrepreneurship in the 1990s.* Homewood, IL: Irwin Publishing.

Toffler, A., & Toffler, H. (2006). *Revolutionary wealth*. New York, NY: Alfred A. Knopf.

Urban, G. L., & Hauser, J. R. (2004). Listening in to find and explore new combinations of customer needs. *Journal of Marketing, 68,* 72–87.

Von Hippel, E. (1986). Lead users: A source of novel product concepts. *Management Science, 32*(7), 791–806.

Webb, J. W., Ireland, R. D., Hitt, M. A., Kistruck, G. M., & Tihanyi, L. (2011). Where is the opportunity without the customer? An integration of marketing activities, the entrepreneurship process, and institutional theory. *Journal of the Academy of Marketing Science, 39,* 537–555.

Weick, K. E., Sutcliffe, K. M., & Obstfeld, D. (2005). Organizing and the process of sensemaking. *Organization Science, 16*(4), 409–421.

Wired. (2009). Retrieved from http://www.wired.com/gadgetlab/2009/12/ipod-touch-app-sales-jumped-1000-on-christmas-day/

Chapter 8

Entrepreneurial Capital and Networks

Abstract

While it is accepted that the creation, development, growth, and sustainability of entrepreneurial ventures is predicated on more than the availability of financial researches, it is only more recently that researchers have sought to explore both the process of entrepreneurship including actors other than the founding entrepreneur involved in establishing and growing new ventures and also the mix of resources critical to this process. The chapter opens by briefly considering the entrepreneurial process before exploring, in some detail, the different types of resources needed to support the entrepreneurship process. Following this, the chapter considers in more detail the role and contribution of entrepreneurial networks in providing access to these resources and so supporting the process of entrepreneurship.

8.1. The Entrepreneurial Process

When researching entrepreneurship, significant attention has been afforded to founding entrepreneurs, their motivations, aspirations, and characteristics. As such, while we know much about entrepreneurs drive, vision, need for autonomy, and preference to take control (Chell, 1985; McClelland, 1961), we know much less about the process of entrepreneurship, especially over time. As a process, entrepreneurship is commonly associated with creating something new: an enterprise, an innovation, and a new way of looking at things. As such, the process of entrepreneurship can be channeled toward the creation of a new venture as well as occur within the context of a larger, more established firm keen to remain competitive by embracing and encouraging innovation, creative thinking, and new ideas. Regardless of the focus of or the context within which entrepreneurship takes place, entrepreneurship is recognized as an interactive process that, to be effective, must involve a wider range of individuals, groups, and organizations than founding, or within an established

Entrepreneurial Marketing: Global Perspectives
Copyright © 2013 by Emerald Group Publishing Limited
All rights of reproduction in any form reserved
ISBN: 978-1-78190-786-3

organization, leading entrepreneurs. Conceived of in this way, we can identify and discuss entrepreneurship at a number of different levels of analysis:

8.1.1.   The Entrepreneur

This and narrowest level of analysis considers the individuals driving new ventures, new thinking, innovations, new business models, and new technologies. Well-known examples include Richard Branson (Virgin), Sergey Brin (Google), James Dyson (Dyson), Martha Lane Fox (Lastminute.com), Doris Fisher (GAP), Sahar Hashemi (Coffee Republic), Larry Page (Google), Pierre Morad Omidya (Ebay), and Mark Zuckerberg (Facebook). Interestingly, the organizations established by each of these individuals have grown to become large and, in today's context, established organizations. What is common across each of these individuals is their ability to spot opportunities, often when others cannot see an opportunity (think of Facebook); to approach these opportunities with creative, sometimes innovative thinking; to weigh up these opportunities against the challenges they present and to take calculated risks and, to engage with others to make their visions and ambitions a reality. As such, while much of the research on entrepreneurs has concentrated on their characteristics suggesting they have a high need for achievement, internal locus of control and autonomy (McClelland, 1961), these examples and many others suggest that the practice of successful entrepreneurship is reliant upon the entrepreneurs interactions, collaborations, partnerships, and alliances with others.

8.1.2.   The Entrepreneurial Team

This second and slightly wider level of analysis broadens out to consider other working closely with the entrepreneur. Common to each of the successful entrepreneurs identified above is their involvement with others and the partnerships and teams that they create to help support and deliver their entrepreneurial vision. Despite a research history that has focused on investigating and characterizing individual entrepreneurs, the practice of entrepreneurship necessitates that entrepreneurs engage, interact, and work with others. Indeed many of today's successful organizations were established by an entrepreneurial partnership or team rather than an individual entrepreneur. Examples of successful entrepreneurial teams and partnerships include Ben and Jerry's (Ben Cohen and Jerry Greenfield), Google (Sergey Brin and Larry Page) and Apple (Steve Jobs, Ronald Wayne and Steve Wozniak). Research indicates that an important benefit of entrepreneurial partnerships and teams is that a wider variety and amount of financial and nonfinancial resources are available to support the process of entrepreneurship than if an individual entrepreneur were involved (Wilson, Shaw, & Grant, 2010). A second way of thinking about entrepreneurial teams is within the context of more established organizations. Sometime referred to an "intrapreneurship," entrepreneurial teams often exist within larger, established organizations keen to maintain their competitive edge by embracing an entrepreneurial orientation. A well-known example of such an organization might be 3M. Within these organizations, entrepreneurial teams often work across departments and functions on multidisciplinary projects. Often critical to the success of these types of entrepreneurial teams is the bringing together of different skills, experiences, and contacts of the team.

8.1.3. The Entrepreneurial Venture

At a third level of analysis the entrepreneurial venture can be identified as the focus of the analysis. For smaller and especially newer organizations this might include new ventures and all those individuals involved in establishing the new venture. Within the context of a larger more established firm, the entrepreneurial venture might be regarded as a spin out or a spin off. This might happen when the project an entrepreneurial team has been working on can be successfully commercialized and the parent organization and the team agree that to be competitive, the project should be taken out of the parent firm and created as a standalone venture. This often takes place within Universities when technologies scientists have been working on are discovered to have commercial capabilities – rather than continuing to house the project within the structures of the university, the project becomes a standalone spin out company. Well known examples of such university spin out ventures include Hewlett Packard, Polaroid, and more recently Google, Netscape.

8.1.4. Entrepreneurship as a Socially Embedded Process

The fourth and broadest level of analysis considers entrepreneurship as a socially embedded process. This perspective regards entrepreneurs and the process of entrepreneurship as being embedded in a rich socioeconomic and cultural context (De Clercq & Voronov, 2009; Gartner & Starr, 1993; Jack, 2010; Sarason, Dean, & Dillard, 2006; Zahra, 2007) and views entrepreneurs as social animals. Recognizing this, Granovetter (1985, 1992) has argued that when researching economic exchanges and the mechanisms supporting such exchanges such as the process of entrepreneurship, it is important to consider the social context in which such exchanges and are located or embedded. De Clercq and Voronov (2009) agree that entrepreneurship is a "profoundly socially embedded process" (p. 395) and it is recognized that interactions between entrepreneurs, entrepreneurial teams and entrepreneurial ventures, and the environments within which they are embedded are critical to entrepreneurial successes and experiences yet remain an under-researched area.

8.2. Entrepreneurship in Context

Accepting that the process of entrepreneurship is embedded within a social context, this suggests that this context presents both opportunities and challenges for entrepreneurship such as launching new products, gaining acceptance of new thinking about, for example, about a business process and introducing new business models. Importantly, this context contains all the resources needed to support entrepreneurship. In contrast, entrepreneurs and their teams do not possess all of the resources needed to engage in entrepreneurship. Instead they rely upon making use of the resources that are contained within the context in which they are embedded. Specifically, research suggests that the networks in which entrepreneurs, entrepreneurial teams, and entrepreneurial ventures are embedded are critical in presenting entrepreneurial opportunities and providing access to entrepreneurial resources (Aldrich & Zimmer, 1986; Birley, 1985; De Carolis, Litzky, & Eddleston, 2009). Particularly for new and entrepreneurial organizations, research indicates that the context in which such firms are embedded can have a disproportionate impact on their survival, sustainability, and growth (Gulati & Gargulio, 1999, Hite, 2005; Scase & Goffee, 1980; Stanworth & Curran, 1976). For this reason, the context within which entrepreneurial ventures are embedded must be closely observed by researchers and entrepreneurs if entrepreneurial opportunities are to be spotted and the resources needed to exploit these opportunities are to be acquired.

8.3. Entrepreneurial Resources

It is recognized that the process of entrepreneurship is predicated on the availability of and access to financial and nonfinancial resources (Erikson, 2002; Firkin, 2003; Morris, 1998; Shaw, 2006; Shaw, Lam, & Carter, 2008; Shaw, Gordon, Harvey, & Maclean, 2011). Whether the process of entrepreneurship is channeled toward creating a new venture or is focused on new product development within the context of an established organization, it does require access to and use of a variety of resources, both tangible and intangible. Responding to this, entrepreneurship scholars have embraced the concept of entrepreneurial capital (Erikson, 2002; Firkin, 2003; Harvey, Maclean, Gordon, & Shaw, 2011). This concept regards the resources needed to support entrepreneurship as different forms of capital and, research indicates that the variety and the amount of capital possessed by and available to entrepreneurs, entrepreneurial teams and entrepreneurial organizations, can significantly impact on both experiences of entrepreneurship and the performance of firms (Davidsson & Honig, 2003; Stringfellow & Shaw, 2009). Building on the resource-based (RB) perspective of entrepreneurship (Penrose, 1968), the notion of entrepreneurial capital suggests that in addition to financial capital, the entrepreneurial process is affected by the other forms of capital possessed by entrepreneurs and available to them through networks and relationships (Firkin, 2003; Shaw et al., 2011). Entrepreneurship scholars have variously identified nonfinancial capital as including the physical, organizational, technological, human, cultural, social, and symbolic capital of business owners and their firms (Boden & Nucci, 2000; Carter, Brush, Greene, Gatewood, & Hart, 2003; Casson & Giusta, 2007; Cope, Jack, & Rose, 2007; Davidsson & Honig, 2003; Firkin, 2003; Haber & Reichel, 2007).

While a more recent theoretical development within entrepreneurship research, the concept of capital is however not new to the social sciences (*cf.* Giddens, 1991). Capital theory (Bourdieu, 1986) identifies individuals as possessing four types of capital: economic (financial), social (networks), cultural (including human), and symbolic; both Gorton (2000) and Firkin (2003) have provided detailed accounts of the value of capital theory for developing our understanding of the relevance of different forms of capital for sustainable, successful entrepreneurship.

8.3.1. Economic Capital

This form of capital is often regarded as financial capital and is clearly important to entrepreneurship as all ventures whether new and independent or located within established organizations require financial investment if they are to be successful. Indeed, research indicates that initial under capitalization can have a detrimental impact on a venture's sustainability and growth (Carter & Rosa, 1998; Carter, Shaw, Wilson, & Lam, 2007). Indeed, research on women's entrepreneurship indicates not only that women-owned firms are routinely under-capitalized by up to two thirds less than those of their male counterparts but also, that as a consequence, their firms experience different, slower, and lower growth that in turn weakens their competitiveness. Bourdieu (1986) describes economic as including all tangible and intangible forms of capital that can immediately and directly be converted into money. This suggests that in addition to financial assets, economic capital can include tangible resources such as factories, plant, and equipment, as well as intangible assets such as patents, both of which can accrue an economic value.

8.3.2. Human Capital

Writing on Capital theory, Bourdieu (1986) conceived of three forms of cultural capital: *embodied* that refers to personal dispositions; *objectified* that takes the form of "cultural goods" including books, pictures, and instruments, and *institutionalized* that he refers to as educational qualifications. Within entrepreneurship research, scholars have adopted a more focused definition of cultural capital and have narrowed their studies to consider the impact that different forms of human capital can have on the process of entrepreneurship. Typically, entrepreneurship researchers have employed Becker's (1964) definition of human capital to investigate what impact differences in age, education and work, and family experiences can have on entrepreneurship.

8.3.3. Social Capital

While social capital has been variously defined (Bourdieu, 1986; Lin, 2001; Portes, 1988), entrepreneurship scholars tend to use a perspective shared by most definitions that identify an individual's possession of and access to social capital as being dependent upon the size, contents, and relational dimensions of their personal contact networks (Anderson, Park, & Jack, 2007; Cope et al., 2007; Davidsson & Honig, 2003; Firkin, 2003; Lechner, Dowling, & Welpe, 2006; Shaw, 2006). More recently, there has also been recognition within the entrepreneurship literature that social capital is essential if entrepreneurs are to become embedded within the field of business ownership and recognized as legitimate, credible entrepreneurs (De Clercq & Voronov, 2009; Jack, 2010; Jack & Anderson, 2002). A broader perspective on social capital is that it is comprised of social obligations, connections, relationships, and networks and as such is critical in providing access to information and resources and to bridging structural holes (Burt, 1992).

8.3.4. Symbolic Capital

Symbolic capital includes those signals and signs that generate trust and approval in others, for example, business partners, customers, employees, and investors. While difficult to grasp and of a particularly subjective nature, this form of capital can have powerful effects: perceptions of the symbolic capital possessed by individuals, team, and entrepreneurial ventures can enhance their legitimacy and encourage customers and others within the market to "buy into" and believe in the products, services, and ideas that they offer (Harvey & Maclean, 2008; Maclean, Harvey, & Press, 2006). Regarded in this way and applied to entrepreneurship, symbolic capital gives some indication of entrepreneurial reputation, credibility, and legitimacy (De Clercq & Voronov, 2009) and as such can be a powerful resource to help new and young ventures overcome the liabilities of newness and smallness (Stinchcombe, 1965). While symbolic capital is conceptually powerful, it can be challenging to operationalize and, to date, there have only been limited discussions of this form of capital within the entrepreneurship literature (*cf.* Shaw et al., 2008; Shaw et al., 2011). Typically, such studies have been guided by Maclean et al. (2006) approach to operationalizing symbolic capital which suggests that when using publicly available data, titles, honors, and awards can serve as useful indicators of symbolic capital. This suggests that customers, suppliers, and other stakeholders relevant to the sustainability of entrepreneurs, entrepreneurial teams, and entrepreneurial ventures may use industry awards, patents, and other similar awards when assessing and gauging their reputational capital and considering whether to do business with them and, within larger organizations, to support and champion their new products, services, and ideas. However, even accepting this there is a need for further development of how symbolic capital can be operationalized to assist in studies of the impact that such capital can have on the sustainability of entrepreneurs, entrepreneurial teams, and their ventures.

8.4. Interactions Between Forms of Capital

Each form of capital is interdependent and convertible. This interdependence means that while entrepreneurs may possess various forms of capital, it may be difficult to isolate and separate each individual form of capital that they possess. Complicating this further is by what Firkin (2003, p. 5) refers to as the convertibility of capital; that is, "how each form of capital can be converted from and into other forms of capital." For example, if an individual possesses high levels of cultural capital in terms of their education and experience, it might be expected that this will convert into high levels of social capital in terms of networks and contacts. Of all these forms of capital, Bourdieu (1986) argues that economic capital is especially relevant, as its possession can facilitate and leverage access to all other forms of capital that, individually and collectively, can enhance the agentic power of individual wealth holders (Maclean et al., 2006). That is an individual's ability to exert control over their immediate environment and to use their individual actions and behaviors to achieve their targets such as successful new venture creation is enhanced by the forms and amounts of capital they possess and, through their networks, can access. Closer consideration of symbolic capital can help further explain the convertibility of forms of capital. Bourdieu (1986) regards symbolic capital as the form that different types of capital take once they are perceived and recognized by others as legitimate. This suggests then that even when entrepreneurs possess identical amounts and types of economic, human and social capital, others in their environment may place differing "values" on the "package" of entrepreneurial capital that they possess. Extending this, Firkin (2003, p. 65) explains that the "concept of entrepreneurial capital is based on the total capital that an individual possesses" and the value placed on this composite form of capital. While Bourdieu (1986) argued that ultimately, each form of nonfinancial capital converts to economic capital, he drew particular attention to the convertibility of social into symbolic capital. This interplay between social and symbolic capital has particular relevance for understanding entrepreneurial reputation and legitimacy. It indicates that the networks through which entrepreneurs build their reputation and that of their venture may convert to differing amounts and value of symbolic capital. Conceived of in this way, it may be that dependent upon the value created when social capital is converted into symbolic capital, the reputation of the entrepreneur and their venture be enhanced or diminished.

8.5. Forms of Capital and Entrepreneurship Research

While at an early stage of empirical investigation, entrepreneurship research has been quick to adopt theories of capital and a growing number of studies have sought to explore the impact of various forms of capital on the process of entrepreneurship (Adler & Kwon, 2002; Boden & Nucci, 2000; Brush, Carter, Greene, Hart, & Gatewood, 2002; Carter et al., 2003; Cope et al., 2007; Davidsson & Honig, 2003; Hospers & van Lochem, 2002). Common to most of these studies is an examination of the interplay between one or at most two forms of capital and the entrepreneurial process. Such studies have revealed that the amount and forms of capital possessed by and available to entrepreneurs can have significant effects on entrepreneurial sustainability and success and also on experience of entrepreneurship. In particular, researchers have concentrated on exploring the dynamic between entrepreneurship and economic, human, and social capital. For example, Boden and Nucci (2000) have drawn attention to differences in the amount and quality of human capital possessed by nascent and new entrepreneurs. Their findings indicate that women's fewer years of work experience, reduced exposure to managerial occupations and different education profiles — all indicators of human capital (Becker, 1964) have restricted women entrepreneurs' possession of and access to finance and provide some explanation of a bimodal funding pattern between male and female-owned businesses. Similarly, Carter et al. (2003) examined the influence of social and human capital on entrepreneurs' likely access to various forms of finance. Using Becker's (1964) definition of human capital and Coleman's (1988) definition of social capital to establish the influence of the entrepreneur's social network on their access to venture capital, their study found that only human capital, particularly graduate education, had any significant influence. In contrast, Brush et al. (2002) found social rather than human capital to be significant in formulating venture capital "deals" and concluded that even when the entrepreneur and their team had the necessary financial and human capital coupled with goals that meet the requirements of equity investors, the deal is unlikely to progress without the necessary social capital, indicated by relevant network connections.

Importantly, such research reveals that while the environment within which entrepreneurship is embedded can provide access to each forms of capital, possession of and access to these capital forms are dependent on interactions between entrepreneurs and their environments that result in entrepreneurs acquiring varying amounts and forms of capital. The dynamic between entrepreneurial agency and social structures helps explain this. Capital theory suggests that individual, and therefore entrepreneurial positions within emerging social structures are determined both by the amounts and forms of capital possessed by individuals, and also by the value placed on such capital by others (Bourdieu, 1977). Simply put, depending on the context (what Bourdieu refers to as "field"), certain types of capital may be more sought after and valued than others. For example, it is likely that within the field of business and enterprise, knowledge of social media for brand building purposes is a valued form of human capital whereas in the field of competitive sports, fitness, speed, and power together with hand–eye or hand–foot coordination are likely to be perceived as high value dimensions of human capital. This suggests that entrepreneurs may be able to enhance their experiences of entrepreneurship if, within their chosen field, they understand that forms of capital are most valued and engage in interactions within that field which can help build and acquire those forms and amounts of capital perceived to be most relevant and therefore valuable. This assumes however that by identifying differences between what entrepreneurial capital they possess and what forms and amounts are required to succeed within their chosen field, entrepreneurs are able to use their networks to close any such gaps. The reality of course is that for many entrepreneurs, accessing the forms and amounts of capital needed to close such gaps in entrepreneurial capital is often complex and challenging. The reason for this is that social structures are both *objective* and *subjective* (Bourdieu, 1977; Bourdieu & Wacquant, 1992). Objective structures contain and can provide access to entrepreneurial resources and capitals. In contrast, subjective structures are created by the subconscious systems of classification that all individuals use as symbolic roadmaps for engaging in and interpreting practical activities. Such structures are created by human interactions and reflect tacitly taken-for-granted assumptions. Take, for example, society's "natural" attitude toward gender differences. Bourdieu (1977) argues that such assumptions create attitudes that connote women with negative qualities (such as weakness) and men with positive (such as strength) and, as a consequence, emerging social structures can benefit men, for example, by creating opportunities for them to acquire greater economic capital, while disadvantaging women.

Applied to entrepreneurship, Bourdieu's (1977) perspectives suggest that social phenomena (entrepreneurship) emerge from a complex interplay between human interactions (entrepreneurial agency) and both objective and subjective structures. Simply put, as subjective social structures are created by individual values and perceptions of individuals and their interactions, they can both support and constrain access to resources and capital contained within objectives social structures. Shaw et al. (2008) illustrate this dynamic by applying Bourdieu's thinking to the nexus between entrepreneurial capital and the financing of entrepreneurial ventures. They reason that as a consequence of the interplay between entrepreneurial agency and objective and subjective structures, not only is it likely that male and female entrepreneurs will possess different forms and amounts of capital but also, that even when male and female entrepreneurs possess similar levels and forms of capital, the value this commands among their stakeholders may differ and such differing values will impact upon male and female experiences of business ownership creating perhaps more opportunities for those entrepreneurs in possession of a mix of capitals that command greater value.

To date however very few studies have explored the effects of the synergistic characteristic of entrepreneurial capital on the process of entrepreneurship. While theoretically convincing, the effects of entrepreneurial symbolic capital and the impact of the overlapping, convertible nature of different forms of capital on the process and experiences of entrepreneurship have received scant research attention. Exceptions to this include Shaw et al. (2008) investigation of the role of entrepreneurial capital on building entrepreneurial reputation and emerging studies considering the role of entrepreneurial philanthropists in contemporary society (Harvey et al., 2011; Shaw et al., 2011). These initial studies have established that the interplay between economic, human, and social capital can generate the symbolic capital relevant for service reputation and so contribute to enhanced firm performance (Shaw et al., 2008) and have empirically revealed a dynamic between social and symbolic capital supportive of Bourdieu's (1986) proposition of the convertibility of social into symbolic capital (Shaw, Wilson, Grant). Significantly, these studies have revealed the relevance of the entrepreneurial capital framework for understanding the relevance of financial and nonfinancial forms of entrepreneurial capital and both the interdependence and convertibility of these and the significant impact that this mix of forms of capital can have on the process of entrepreneurship.

8.6. Entrepreneurial Networks

The discussion presented has emphasized two important points. The first is that entrepreneurship is predicated on possession of and access to financial and non-financial forms of capital. The second is that entrepreneurs' use their networks to access those forms of capital that they do not possess but are aware of being contained within networks; both with which they are directly connected and those they can reach indirectly via network contacts. As such, networks are recognized as a critical resource that have been found to accrue multiple benefits for entrepreneurial ventures. Particularly as a consequence of their often restricted resource base, "networks have been shown to improve entrepreneurial effectiveness by providing access to resources and competitive advantage without capital investment" (Slotte-Kock & Coviello, 2009, p. 33) and have been described as *the* most important entrepreneurial resource (Johannisson, 1986; Ostgaard & Birley, 1996). Indeed, entrepreneurs and their firms have been urged to engage in networking if their firms are to survive (Huggins, 2000). Clearly, for small and entrepreneurial ventures networks and networking are critically important and for this reason the chapter now turns to a discussion of networks and networking.

8.7. Social Networks Theory

In framing studies of entrepreneurial networks, scholars have drawn from Social Network Theory (SNT). Developed within the domains of sociology and anthropology (Mitchell, 1969) this well established theory has been used by business and management researchers including entrepreneurship scholars (Jack, 2010; Slotte-Kock & Coviello, 2009) to understand both how firms interact with the environment in which they are embedded and to explore the possibilities of networks as an entrepreneurial marketing resource. SNT conceives of society as possessing a network structure of overlapping relationships that connect individuals, groups and organizations and as such can be used to analyze the networks of differing analytical units including individual entrepreneurs, entrepreneurial teams and entrepreneurial ventures. As such SNT offers a useful way of conceiving the relational environment within which owners and their firms are embedded (Mitchell, 1969). Specifically, this theory asserts that as social networks are created by processes of on-going interactions, their structures fluctuate and their boundaries are "fuzzy" (Johannisson, 1986). Building on this, it has been reasoned that if relationships between social networks and small firms are to be understood, both their structural and interactional dimensions have to be considered (Hoang & Antoncic, 2003). Structural dimensions refer to features that determine the size and shape of network and include the "anchor" or focus of a network that can be the entrepreneur, the entrepreneurial team or the entrepreneurial venture; "reachability" that is a measure of how far and easily an anchor is able to contact others in their network; "density" is a measure of the extent to which actors within a network are connected to one another and is used to indicate whether networks are "loose" or "tight-knit" and, "range" provides an indication of the extent to which the anchor is embedded within a diverse or homogenous.

SNT argues that to understand social behaviors it is important to also consider the interactional dimensions of networks must also be explored of which five are identified: content, intensity, frequency, durability, and direction. Of these, content is often regarded as most important as this refers to the meanings that people attach to relationships and the understandings they have about how they should behave with regard to different relationships. This suggests, for example, that if an entrepreneur defines a relationship as a "friendship," they will engage in activities and behaviors they understand to be fitting to those of a "friend." As contents are not directly observable, SNT proposes that the meanings attached to relationships can be interpreted in terms of their information, communication, economic or emotional contents. SNT also suggest that stronger relationships will be "multiplex" containing a variety of contents. Discussion of the content of entrepreneurial networks has sparked debate over whether "economic" networks can be distinguished separately from those comprised of "information" and "emotional" contents (cf. Curran, Jarvis, Blackburn, & Black, 1993; Szarka, 1990). SNT suggests that while relationships can be described as multiplex, each content is not representative of a separate network and that given such mutiplexity, entrepreneurial behavior vis-a-vis networks and relationships is analyzed by considering the various contents exchanged within a relationships. Intensity provides an indication of the importance of a relationship and gives some insight into the complexity of entrepreneurial relationships. For example, where a relationship contains both economic and friendship contents, the interactions involved in its economic content will be influenced by the friendship that is also shared. Like contents, the intensity of a network relationship cannot be directly observed and because of this, estimates of frequency and durability are often used as proxy indicators of intensity. Frequency is the amount of time entrepreneurs' spend interacting in relationships and sometimes referred to as "networking." A high frequency of interaction can sometimes represent an intense relationship. However, relationships containing friendship contents can often be intense despite infrequent interactions while frequent interactions between entrepreneurial ventures and their key clients can often be required to increase their switching costs and increase repeat business. "Durability" is an indication of the length of time over which a relationship continues and can also provide an indication of the intensity of relationships. Durability is influenced relationship contents and the extent to which those involved perceive the relationship to be mutually satisfying. The final interactional dimension, "direction" refers to the entrepreneur or venture from which a relationship is orientated. Direction can provide an indication of the power orientation of a relationship and is of particular relevance to firms involved in co-operative relationships involving strategic alliances and co-production. For example, where organizations share a partnering relationship, the orientation of the relationship may be such that the smaller of the firms holds a more vulnerable position.

8.8. Entrepreneurial Networks as an Important Entrepreneurial Marketing Resource

By identifying network structure, network interactions and the interplay between these as critical to the analysis of entrepreneurial networks (Mitchell, 1969), SNT can be useful in understanding the dynamic between entrepreneurial agency and structures. This interplay between network structures and interactions has emerged as a popular if debated topic within the entrepreneurship literature. Building on "strength of weak ties" proposition, researchers suggest that entrepreneurial ventures may benefit by being centrally located within loosely connected networks (structural dimension) comprised of mainly weak relationships (interactional network). Studies have suggested that the benefit of this particular structure-agency dynamic is that entrepreneurs embedded within loose networks may have access to greater amounts and diversity of information and resources than those located within close-knit networks comprised of many strong relationships (Aldrich & Zimmer, 1986; Birley, 1985; Granovetter, 1985). The reality of entrepreneurship dictates however that most ventures are embedded within networks containing a variety of weak and strong ties and areas of both network density and structural holes (Burt, 1992) and the findings of recent empirical studies have challenged the strength of weak ties thesis (Hoang & Antoncic, 2003; Jack, 2010; Shaw et al., 2008).

Particular to marketing, entrepreneurial networks are recognized as a critical EM tool (Hills, Hultman, & Miles, 2008) that can assist ventures in a number of important ways. Networks have been found to provide access to market opportunities and information (Aldrich & Zimmer, 1986; Birley, 1985; Casson & Giusta, 2007; Hite & Hesterley, 2001; Nahapiet & Ghosal, 1998; Ozcan & Eisenhardt, 2009), contribute to enhanced innovation (Batterink, Emiel, Lerkx, & Omta, 2010; Saxenian, 1990), assist organizational learning (Lee & Jones, 2008; Rae, 2005) and, ultimately help ventures protect a sustainable, competitive advantage (Joyce, Woods, & Black, 1995; Ostgaard & Birley, 1996; Uzzi, 1996). As mentioned above, at the broadest level of analysis, entrepreneurship is a socially embedded process involving a variety of social actors. As such, entrepreneurship can only happen if entrepreneurs, entrepreneurial teams and entrepreneurial ventures interact and network with others in their environment. For many entrepreneurial ventures, this environment is unique as, given their often smaller scale and limited resource base, it can elicit a disproportional effect over their sustainability. Recognizing this, a key mechanism used by entrepreneurial ventures as protection from the effects of their environment are the networks of relationships in which they are embedded. Entrepreneurial ventures often possess little market share and can be vulnerable to competitive market pressures. Particularly in tough economic climates when competitors with more plentiful resources are able to implement price cuts and employ aggressive promotional tactics, entrepreneurial ventures must rely upon different approaches. For such firms, established relationships within the local, industrial and regional networks in which they are embedded are often critical to their survival and sustainability (Jack & Anderson, 2002; Shaw, 2006). If entrepreneurial ventures nurture relationships within these networks by engaging in reciprocal behaviors, such networks can help small, entrepreneurial firms remain competitive even when facing significant competitive pressures. In particular, established relationships with networks of customers and suppliers can provide entrepreneurial ventures with an important defense against challenging competitive dynamics. Such relationships have been found to guarantee regular business as well as provide referrals and the supply of informed, relevant market and competitive information (Carson, Cromie, McGowan, & Hill, 1995; Shaw, 2006). Considered collectively, research evidence regarding entrepreneurial networks suggests that entrepreneurial ventures do not need to engage in traditional approaches to environmental scanning and market research. Instead, market and competitive information is provided by networks at a cost below which they would have to pay were they to acquire such information and research through market mechanisms. Writing on this, Hills, Hiltman, & Miles (2008, p. 222) argue that for entrepreneurial ventures, marketing tactics are often based upon two-way communications with customers and that marketing decisions are typically informed by daily contact with customers and other relevant stakeholders in venture's environment.

8.9.   Research Gaps and Future Directions

8.9.1.   Future Research Topics

Discussion so far confirms entrepreneurial networks as an established area of research that has confirmed that the networks of relationships within which entrepreneurs, entrepreneurial teams and entrepreneurial ventures are embedded are critical resources entrepreneurial marketing resources that can significantly contribute to the sustainability and competitiveness of small and entrepreneurial firms. This body of research indicates that by networks can provide entrepreneurs and entrepreneurial ventures with access to diverse resources and forms of capital and by so doing, can provide a cost effective mechanisms for extending the restricted resource base of small, entrepreneurial firms. Despite this, it is acknowledged that a number of enduring research gaps are yet to be addressed (Anderson, Drakopoulou Dodd, & Jack, 2010; Dodd Drakopoulou, Jack, & Anderson, 2002; Jack, 2010; Jack, Anderson, & Drakopolou Dodd, 2008; Jack & Anderson, 2002; Slotte-Kock & Coviello, 2009; Shaw, 2006). Where researchers have employed SNT, the research evidence indicates they have concentrated on measuring the structural dimensions, particularly of individual entrepreneurs' networks (Aldrich & Zimmer, 1986; Birley, 1985; Carson et al., 1995). As a consequence, much less is known about interactional network dimensions or the interplay between these and structural network dimensions (Jack, 2010; Slotte-Kock & Coviello, 2009). We also know very little about the broader networks involved in entrepreneurship such as the collective networks created when entrepreneurial partnership, teams, and ventures come together and pull their respective networks or, given the fluctuating nature of networks, the processes by which networks evolve and the implications of network evolution over time (Anderson et al., 2010; Hoang & Antoncic, 2003; Jack et al., 2008; Shaw, 2006). Research gaps also surround the context within which entrepreneurship occurs (Zahra, 2007), and the implications that industry and region may have on the use of networks as an entrepreneurial marketing resource. Similarly, as networking is by its very essence an interactive process, the implications that advance in technology including on-line environments such as Twitter and LinkedIn are likely to have for the entrepreneurial use of networks for marketing purposes require investigation (Fischer & Reuber, 2011). Regarding entrepreneurial capital, there are opportunities to explore the interplay between and convertibility of different forms of capital and for researchers to more fully understand the nature and impact of symbolic capital.

8.9.2. Research Approaches and Methodologies

To progress research in these areas researchers will need to embrace a variety of research approaches and methods including the use of mixed methods to develop insights in both structural and interactional network dimensions and the interplay between each of these (Jack, 2010; Slotte-Kock & Coviello, 2009). To date, research on entrepreneurial networks has been dominated by the use of quantitative methods often involving large scale surveys with a broad cross section of entrepreneurs. While such methods have generated a large body of empirical evidence that has been used to inform discussions surrounding the size and shape of entrepreneurial networks and consideration of whether strong or weak ties are preferable, they are less suited for examining interactional network dimensions. Network contents, relationship intensity and reasons for durability are better suited to qualitative methods such as case studies and depth interviews particularly over time. Of course such research is more time consuming, can be difficult to analyze and is often if difficult to publish in peer reviewed journals that prefer the generalizations possible when network structures are measured and quantitatively analyzed. Cognizant of this, researchers are likely to be able to contribute and advance out knowledge and understanding of entrepreneurial networks and capital if they engage in mixed methods research that employs a range of data collection methods and seeks to collect data from others involved in the process of entrepreneurship over time. By shifting the unit of analysis away from a narrow focus on individual entrepreneurs to consider entrepreneurial partnerships, teams, and small ventures, the research field will benefit by gaining insights into the multiple, overlapping and complex nature of entrepreneurial networks and the impact and implications of this and such networks on entrepreneurship over time. A further dimension to consider when deciding upon the unit of analysis is that of diversity. Historically, studies of entrepreneurship have concentrated on understanding entrepreneurship from the single point of one entrepreneur who has typically been a male. Currently, entrepreneurship is an activity undertaken by a diverse range of individuals and groups and there is a need for entrepreneurship researchers to recognize this diversity within their research samples. Only by collecting data from a wider range of entrepreneurial groups that include, for example, women, young people, ethnic minority entrepreneurs, entrepreneurs with disabilities and special needs can researchers provide research evidence of relevance to the diverse range of entrepreneurs, entrepreneurial teams, and entrepreneurial ventures that engage in entrepreneurial marketing and make use of resources such as entrepreneurial networks for developing and expanding the entrepreneurial capital needed to make their venture sustainable and successful.

References

Adler, P. S., & Kwon, S. (2002). Social capital: Prospects for a new concept. *Academy of Management Review*, 27(1), 17–40.

Aldrich, H. E., & Zimmer, C. (1986). Entrepreneurship through social networks. In H. E. Aldrich (Ed.), *Population perspectives on organizations* (pp. 13–28). Uppsala: Acta Universitatis Upsaliensis.

Anderson, A., Park, J., & Jack, S. (2007). Entrepreneurial social capital: Conceptualising social capital in new high-tech firms. *International Small Business Journal*, 25(3), 245–272.

Anderson, A. R., Drakopoulou Dodd, S., & Jack, S. (2010). Network practices and entrepreneurial growth. *Scandinavian Journal of Management*, 26, 121–133.

Batterink, M. H., Emiel, F. M., Lerkx, L., & Omta, S. W. F. (2010). Orchestrating innovation networks: The case of innovation brokers in the agri-food sector. *Entrepreneurship and Regional Development*, 22(1), 47–76.

Becker, G. (1964). *Human capital*. Chicago, IL: University of Chicago Press.

Birley, S. (1985). The role of networks in the entrepreneurial process. *Journal of Business Venturing*, 11, 107–117.

Boden, R., & Nucci, A. (2000). On the survival prospects of men's and women's new business ventures. *Journal of Business Venturing*, 15(4), 347–362.

Bourdieu, P. (1977). *Outline of a theory of practice*. Cambridge: Cambridge University Press.

Bourdieu, P. (1986). The forms of capital. In J. Richardson (Ed.), *Handbook of theory and research for the sociology of education* (pp. 241–258). New York, NY: Greenwood Press.

Bourdieu, P., & Wacquant, L. (1992). *An invitation to reflexive sociology*. Cambridge: Polity Press.

Brush, C., Carter, N., Greene, P., Hart, M., & Gatewood, E. (2002). The role of social capital and gender in linking financial suppliers and entrepreneurial firms: A framework for future research. *Venture Capital*, 4(4), 305–323.

Burt, R. S. (1992). *Structural holes*. Cambridge, MA: Harvard University Press.

Carson, D., Cromie, S., McGowan, P., & Hill, J. (1995). *Marketing and entrepreneurship in SMEs: An innovative approach*. Prentice Hall International.

Carter, S., & Rosa, P. (1998). The financing of male and female-owned businesses. *Entrepreneurship & Regional Development*, 10(3), 225–241.

Carter, N., Brush, C. B., Greene, P. G., Gatewood, E., & Hart, M. (2003). Women entrepreneurs who break through to equity financing: The influence of human, social and financial capital. *Venture Capital*, 5(1), 1–28.

Carter, S., Shaw, E., Wilson, F., & Lam, W. (2007). Gender, entrepreneurship and bank lending: The criteria and processes used by bank loan officers in assessing applications. *Entrepreneurship, Theory and Practice*, 31(3), 427–444.

Casson, M., & Giusta, M. D. (2007). Entrepreneurship and social capital: analysing the impact of social networks on entrepreneurial activity from a rational action perspective. *International Small Business Journal, 25*(3), 220–244.

Chell, E. (1985). The entrepreneurial personality: A few ghosts laid to rest? *International Small Business Journal, 3*(3), 43–54.

Coleman, J. (1988). Social capital in the creation of human capital. *American Journal of Sociology*, Supplement: Organisations and Institutions Sociological and Economic Approaches to the Analysis of Social Structure, *94*, 95–102.

Cope, J., Jack, S., & Rose, M. B. (2007). Social capital and entrepreneurship: An introduction. *International Small Business Journal, 25*(3), 213–219.

Curran, J., Jarvis, R., Blackburn, R. A., & Black, S. (1993). Networks and small firms: Constructs, methodological strategies and some findings. *International Small Business Journal, 11*(2), 13–25.

Davidsson, P., & Honig, B. (2003). The role of social and human capital among nascent entrepreneurs. *Journal of Business Venturing, 18*(3), 301–331.

De Carolis, D. M., Litzky, B. E., & Eddleston, K. A. (2009). Why networks enhance the progress of new venture creation: The influence of social capital and cognition. *Entrepreneurship, Theory and Practice* (March), 527–545.

De Clercq, D., & Voronov, M. (2009). Towards a practice perspective of entrepreneurship: Entrepreneurial legitimacy as habitus. *International Small Business Journal, 27*(4), 395–419.

Dodd Drakopoulou, S., Jack, S., & Anderson, A. R. (2002). Scottish entrepreneurial networks in the international context. *International Small Business Journal, 20*(2), 213–219.

Erikson, T. (2002). Entrepreneurial capital: The emerging venture's most important asset and competitive advantage. *Journal of Business Venturing, 17*, 275–290.

Firkin, P. (2003). Entrepreneurial capital. In A. De Bruin & A. Dupuis (Eds.), *Entrepreneurship: New perspectives in a global age* (pp. 57–75). Aldershot: Ashgate Publishing Limited.

Fischer, A., & Reuber, R. (2011). Social interaction via new social media: (How) can interactions on Twitter affect effectual thinking and behavior? *Journal of Business Venturing, 26*(1), 1–18.

Gartner, W. B., & Starr, J. A. (1993). The nature of entrepreneurial work. In S. Birley & I. C. MacMillan (Eds.), *Entrepreneurship research: Global perspectives*. Amsterdam: Elsevier Science Publications.

Giddens, A. (1991). *Modernity and self-identity*. Cambridge: Polity Press.

Gorton, M. (2000). Overcoming the structure-agency divide in small business research. *International Journal of Entrepreneurial Behaviour and Research, 6*(5), 276–292.

Granovetter, M. S. (1985). Economic action and social structure: The problem of embeddedness. *American Journal of Sociology* (November), *91*, 55–81.

Granovetter, M. S. (1992). Networks and organisations: Problems of explanation in economic sociology. In N. Nohria & R. G. Eccles (Eds.), *Networks and organisations: Structure, form and action* (pp. 26–56). Boston, Ma: Harvard Business School Press.

Gulati, R., & Gargulio, M. (1999). Where do interorganizational networks come from? *American Journal of Sociology, 103*(5), 177–231.

Haber, S., & Reichel, A. (2007). The cumulative nature of the entrepreneurial process: The contribution of human capital, planning and environment resources to small venture performance. *Journal of Business Venturing, 22*(1), 119–145.

Harvey, C., & Maclean, M. (2008). Capital theory and the dynamics of elite business networks in Britain and France. *The Sociological Review, 56*(S1), 105–120.

Harvey, C., Maclean, M., Gordon, J., & Shaw, E. (2011). Andrew Carnegie and the foundations of contemporary entrepreneurial philanthropy. *Business History, 53*(3), 425–450.

Hills, G. E., Hultman, C., & Miles, M. (2008). The evolution and development of entrepreneurial marketing. *Journal of Small Business Management, 46*(1), 99–112.

Hite, J. M. (2005). Evolutionary processes and paths of relationally embedded network ties in emerging entrepreneurial firms. *Entrepreneurship Theory and Practice, January*, 113–144.

Hite, J. M., & Hesterley, W. S. (2001). The evolution of firm networks: From emergence to early growth of the firm. *Strategic Management Journal, 22*, 275–286.

Hoang, H., & Antoncic, B. (2003). Network-based research in entrepreneurship: A critical review. *Journal of Business Venturing, 18*(2), 165–187.

Hospers, G-L., & van Lochem, M. V. (2002). Social capital and prosperity: Searching for the missing link. *New Economy, 9*(1), 52–56.

Huggins, R. (2000). The success and failure of policy-implanted inter-firm network initiatives: Motivations, processes and structure. *Entrepreneurship and Regional Development, 12*(2), 11–135.

Jack, S. (2010). Approaches to studying networks: Implications and outcomes. *Journal of Business Venturing, 25*(1), 120–137.

Jack, S. L., & Anderson, R. A. (2002). The effects of embeddedness on the entrepreneurial process. *Journal of Business Venturing, 17*(5), 467–487.

Jack, S. L., Anderson, A. R., & Drakopolou Dodd, S. (2008). Time and contingency in the development of entrepreneurial networks. *Entrepreneurship and Regional Development, 20*(2), 125–159.

Johannisson, B. (1986). Network strategies: Management, technology, and change. *International Small Business Journal, 5*(1), 19–30.

Joyce, P., Woods, A., & Black, S. (1995). Networks and partnerships: managing change and competition. *International Journal of Innovation Management, 2*, 11–18.

Lechner, C., Dowling, M., & Welpe, I. (2006). Firm networks and firm development: The role of the relational mix. *Journal of Business Venturing, 21*(4), 514–540.

Lee, R., & Jones, O. (2008). Networks, communication and learning during business start-up: The creation of cognitive social capital. *International Small Business Journal, 26*(5), 559–593.

Lin, N. (2001). *Social capital – A theory of structure and action.* New York, NY: Cambridge University Press.

Maclean, M., Harvey, C., & Press, J. (2006). *Business elites and corporate governance in France and the UK.* London: Palgrave Macmillan.

McClelland, D. C. (1961). *The achieving society.* Princeton, NJ: Van Nostrand.

Mitchell, J. C. (1969). The concept and use of social networks. In J. C. Mitchell (Ed.), *Social networks in urban situations* (pp. 1–50). Manchester: University of Manchester Press.

Morris, M. (1998). *Entrepreneurial intensity: Sustainable advantages for individuals, organisations, and societies* (1st ed.). Westport, CT: Quorum Books.

Nahapiet, J., & Ghosal, S. (1998). Social capital, intellectual capital, and the organizational advantage. *Academy of Management Review, 23*(2), 242–266.

Ostgaard, A., & Birley, S. (1996). New venture growth and personal networks. *Journal of Business Research, 36*(1), 37–50.

Ozcan, P., & Eisenhardt, K. M. (2009). Origin of alliance portfolios: Entrepreneurs, network strategies, and firm performance. *Academy of Management Journal, 52*(2), 246–279.

Penrose, E. T. (1968). *The theory of the growth of the firm* (Fourth impression). Oxford: Basil Blackwell. (First published in 1959.)

Portes, A. (1988). Social capital: Its origins and the application in modern sociology. *Annual Review of Sociology, 24,* 1–24.

Rae, D. (2005). Entrepreneurial learning: A narrative-based conceptual model. *International Journal of Entrepreneurial Behaviour and Research, 12*(3), 323–335.

Sarason, Y., Dean, T., & Dillard, J. (2006). Entrepreneurship as the nexus of individual and opportunity: A structuration view. *Journal of Business Venturing, 21*(3), 286–305.

Saxenian, A. L. (1990). Regional networks and the resurgence of silicon valley. *California Management Review, 33*(1), 89–112.

Scase, R., & Goffee, R. (1980). *The real world of the small business owner.* London: Croom Helm.

Shaw, E. (2006). Small firm networking: An insight into outcomes and motivating factors. *International Small Business Journal, 24*(1), 5–29.

Shaw, E., Gordon, J., Harvey, C., & Maclean, M. (2011). Exploring contemporary entrepreneurial philanthropy. *International Small Business Journal.*

Shaw, E., Lam, W., & Carter, S. (2008). The role of entrepreneurial capital in building service reputation. *The Service Industries Journal, 28*(7), 883–898.

Slotte-Kock, S., & Coviello, N. (2009). Entrepreneurship research on network processes – A review and ways forward. *Entrepreneurship, Theory and Practice* (January), 31–57.

Stanworth, J., & Curran, J. (1976). Growth and the small firm – An alternative view. *Journal of Management Studies, 13,* 95–110.

Stinchcombe, A. L. (1965). Organizations and social structure. In J. G. March (Ed.), *Handbook of organizations* (pp. 153–193). Chicago, IL: Rand McNally.

Stringfellow, L., & Shaw, E. (2009). Conceptualising entrepreneurial capital for a study of performance in small professional service firms. *International Journal of Entrepreneurial Behaviour and Research, 15*(2), 137–161.

Szarka, J. (1990). Networking and small firms. *International Small Business Journal, 8*(2), 10–22.

Uzzi, B. D. (1996). The sources and consequences of embeddedness for the economic performance of organizations: The network effect. *American Sociological Review, 61,* 674–689.

Wilson, J., Shaw, E., & Grant, I. (2010). The role and impact of business networks on marketing in the creative industries: Evidence from case study research, paper presented to the IMP Conference, Budapest, September.

Zahra, S. A. (2007). Contextualizing theory building in entrepreneurship research. *Journal of Business Venturing, 22,* 443–452.

Chapter 9

Are We Going Around in Circles? Diasporic SMEs: A Conceptual Pattern in the Field of Entrepreneurial Networks

Abstract

This chapter reviews the past literature from a cultural, global perspective to present a thought piece and a new perspective on the relationship between "modern-day" networks and SMEs. Starting from the viewpoint of historical globalization, then examining ethnicity as a conceptual culture emulsifier, the chapter then moves on to discuss cultural values, absorption and "multi-local" identities and the issue of diasporic meaning, and its relevance to contemporary SMEs. The chapter introduces the key notion of trust and its role as a binding agent of diaspora and networking activity and proposes that despite the fact that interrelated factors such as market conditions, selective migration, culture, social networks, and group strategy (i.e., the relationship between opportunity and ethnic characteristic) have developed over a long period of time, the resulting conceptual patterns drawn in the field of entrepreneurial networks by the diasporic SME is very similar to the patterns being drawn by SMEs in 2013, a suggestion that we are "going around in circles."

9.1. Introduction

Over the past 300–400 years we have borne witness to a succession of regional and longer-distance "trade diasporas" (Cohen, 1971) or "trading networks." These first came to fruition in Asia and Europe and eventually expanded across the seas, oceans, and many landscapes; the very fields from within which the entire world came to work on what we now know as *globalization*; an area of study with which there seems to be much preoccupation in terms of marketing strategy and global business strategies. The concept of Entrepreneurial Marketing has at its heart, the notion of

Entrepreneurial Marketing: Global Perspectives
Copyright © 2013 by Emerald Group Publishing Limited
All rights of reproduction in any form reserved
ISBN: 978-1-78190-786-3

entrepreneurial networks and the entrepreneur's use of "resource leveraging" via personal contacts networks (PCNs) or social networks (Collinson & Shaw, 2001). However, it remains fact that many global networks were formed and in existence prior to the beginning of the 20th century. Interestingly, apart from the entrepreneurial marketing fraternity which has only recently developed an interest (Carson, Cromie, McGowan, & Hill, 1995) from the marketing perspective, colleagues in the various fields from social and commercial history (Aghassian & Kevonian, 1999; Kardasis, 2001), to sociology and economics (Curtin, 1984; Masters, 1988), but to name a few, hold an avid interest in the study of such networks.

But in order to understand these "ethnic trade diasporas," we first need to understand the full meaning of the word diaspora in this context. Abner Cohen in 1971 specifically referred to *a nation of socially interdependent, but spatially dispersed communities*:

> A diaspora of this kind is distinct as a type of social grouping in its culture and structure. Its members are culturally distinct from both their society of origin and from the society among which they live. Its organisation combines stability of structure but allows a high degree of mobility of personnel.

Jonathan Israel's definition (2005) ...

> scattered people dispersed — often in some degree forcibly — from their original homeland but not entirely cut off from it, and which then remain sharply distinct from their host societies, and united among themselves, by strong ties of religion, language and ethnicity

... goes someway to explaining the significance of the diaspora in developing societies and cultures.

9.2. Historical Lessons and Current Applications

There are many examples which can be drawn upon from various disciplines to show the power of the diasporic community. For instance, in early Enlightenment Europe, journalism, theological debates, and publishing were all something that the Huguenots excelled in. The scholarly activity exuded by the Greeks during renaissance Italy was almost second to none. The Jews believed vehemently in accurate translation, medicine, and philosophical debate in medieval Islam. However, none of this explains the exemplary role that diasporas have played in conquering empires and thus developing long-distance trade routes which have led to our current global network. Gourgouris (2005) comments on this by way of distinguishing the large diasporic populations from the *fringes of Europe* (Jews, Greeks, Armenians) as entrepreneurial networks which prospered socially, culturally, and economically as well because of the Imperial framework within which they operated (e.g., Beerbuhl & Vogele, 2004; Curto & Molho, 2002). The colonialist economies of the then industrial-capitalist nations were avid breeding grounds for the back-lash from a proliferation of family-centric mercantile enterprises, which flourished by taking advantage of the somewhat unrestricted and imprecise administrative organizations run by their Host state (e.g., note the lenient attitude of the Habsburgs or the Osmanic Empire; Chatziioannou, 1999; Hassiotis, 1993)

Thus we can see that in the contemporary scholarly world, *diaspora* has managed to develop a conceptual status which encompasses references of a philosophical, linguistic, literary, and psychological nature. However, it is the very juxtaposition of *diaspora* with other, more recent, conceptual frameworks such as migration, transnationalism, nomadism, exile, displacement, cosmopolitanism, and hybridity, which leads to the belief that we have come full circle.

9.3. Ethnicity as a Conceptual Culture Emulsifier

Invariably and undoubtedly, the discussion surrounding diasporas, will always include some reference to ethnicity and ethnic communities, ethnic groupings, and ethnic networks. Indeed, it is intriguing how researchers from different eras, disciplines, and with differing interests will indicate and conclude comparable examples of ethnic entrepreneurial behavior. According to Chatziioannou (2005) "an ethnic network based on group solidarity, kinship and common culture provides to its members economic advantages plus economic resources" (*commenting on the Greek community*). A view which is further corroborated by Becchetti and Trovato (2002) in their reference to "collaborative relationships" (*commenting on the Italian community*). Whilst this scenario is easily identifiable during the "colonialist economies," it is also still prevalent today. Notably, Crick and Chaudhury (2010) concluded that Asian transnational entrepreneurs increase their competitiveness by maximizing their relationships with contacts in their country of origin and by use of a strong and trusted network. In an article in *Business History* from 1998, Choi Chi-Cheung wrote, *Family, together with kinship, region and dialect ties, construct the inner circles of the fiduciary community which serve as prime criteria for recruiting employees, securing a firm's internal harmony and establishing business relations. Overall, the consensus of opinion is that wherever successful Chinese businesses have been found they have operated within extensive networks based on kinship.*

We should note here that the modern interpretation of the word culture as an "external process of evolution of the 'culture' of a nation" is somewhat too confined in its outlook. It is preferable to use a more holistic approach. For example, an approach outlined by Raymond Williams (1961) encompassed the "internal" process of evolution through religion, art, family, and personal life, which formulate the institutions, practices, values, and ways of thinking of a society. It is the maintenance of such "being" which Bourdieu (1977) defines in his concept of *habitus* as "shared ways of interiorizing exteriority and exteriorizing interiority." Perhaps this provides the notion of a common culture which members of a diaspora share?

Most of the definitions of ethnicity found in the sociological and anthropological literature tend to agree that, at a general level, the concept refers to the character or quality encompassing various indicators that are used to assign people to groupings (Gordon, 1964). The two most consistently suggested elements included in the definition of ethnicity are: (1) common origin; and (2) shared cultural traits (Barth, 1969; Keyes, 1976; Vallee, 1982; Yinger, 1985). When ethnicity is defined by a common origin, it tends to be more permanent and basic than social class, which is largely defined by common interests and lifestyles of different people (Van Den Berghe, 1987). Ethnic origin is a *de facto* characteristic of the individual. On the other hand, cultural traits are a combination of a person's cultural background and his/her acculturation experience resulting from continuous contacts with another ethnic group (Greeley, 1971).

Shared cultural values can be defined as "people's conceptions of the goals that serve as guiding principles in their lives" and transcend specific situations (Schwartz, 1990, p. 142). What is desirable, or utopian, is the criterion of preference (Cotgrove & Duff, 1981). Rokeach (1973, p. 13) observes that values are prescriptive, and "guide conduct in a variety of ways" because they are standards by which people evaluate themselves. This assertion that entrepreneurial formations are the result of social and cultural factors is also argued by Shapero and Sokol (1982). In addition, ethnic culture (and the underlying cultural values) can influence the structure and process of a person's cognition, making it an antecedent of entrepreneurial cognition (Abramson, Lane, Nagai, & Takagi, 1993; Redding, 1980). Hence, the inherent or prevailing cultural values may influence whether or not entrepreneurial thought and activity is encouraged within cultural networks.

9.4. Cultural Values, Absorption, and Multi-Local Identities

Understanding ethno-cultural values is a necessary step to understanding ethnic diasporas. However, as we already saw in Chapter 4 earlier, *existing entrepreneurship research focus is too narrow most of the time which excludes, for instance, female entrepreneurs and ethnic minorities and what is referred to the cultural sector* (Bjerke & Hultman, 2013).

Consequently there is a need to provide a schema for identifying ethnic subcultures when researching ethnicity and networks globally, especially within an SME context. To explore this, the literature on acculturation offers a useful conceptual base (Faber & O'Guinn, 1987; Penloza, 1989). In the study of interpersonal relationships, a strong research tradition has been established in the realms of network analysis (e.g., Brown & Reingen, 1987; Granovetter, 1982). Most useful is Porters and Sensenbrenner's (1993) modification of the idea of social capital for application in a migration context. Their study focuses on diasporic immigrant groups, and offers an interesting recasting of social capital in a more "ethnic" light. Of particular interest is their idea of "bounded solidarity" (*a collective consciousness that compels people to behave in a certain way; bounded because it is restricted to members of a particular group who are similar and contemporarily affected by common events*) as a kind of social capital which minority immigrant groups have to offer.

This view is backed by much research; according to Basu and Goswami (1999), a stereotypical view of Asian business "success" in Great Britain is that those who succeed (in surviving or expanding their businesses) do so by virtue of their cultural characteristics which encourage thrift, hard work, and the reliance on family labor (Werbner, 1990). These are the "internal mechanisms of self-help" referred to by Soar (1991) which give Asian businesses a competitive edge over other minority businesses. A more formal explanation for the emergence and survival of Asian entrepreneurship in Great Britain is offered by immigrant entrepreneurship theory (Mars & Ward, 1984; Waldinger, Aldrich, & Ward, 1990) in the context of ethnic resources and opportunities created by an enclave economy. Empirical research on Asian businesses in Great Britain (Ballard, 1994; Werbner, 1990) generally supports this view. Conversely, other studies (Metcalfe, Modood, & Virdee, 1996; Ram, 1994) find that cultural factors may restrict growth by creating excessive reliance on the local ethnic community market, informal sources of finance, and family control of the businesses. Using Waldinger et al.'s (1990) model it is possible therefore, to conceptualize a "typical" Asian entrepreneur as one who makes productive use of cultural resources; for example, cheap and readily available family labor, finance from within the community, and cultural values that emphasize hard work and thrift.

Early ethnicity studies can be criticized for simplifying their approaches in an attempt to make generalizations. This contrasts with the very introspective (often even psycho-analytical) approach taken to the subject of entrepreneurship. The positive research drivers in entrepreneurial studies are the researchers' attempts to understand entrepreneurial resources, psychological motivational factors, and mind-sets (often) as determinants of success. Researchers, by incorporating an increasing array of factors, have produced more informed and potentially more comprehensive ways to look at the ethnic entrepreneur (e.g., Cleveland, 2007; Cleveland, Papadopoulos, & Laroche, 2011; Cleveland, Laroche, & Hallab, 2013). Different research strategies have evolved over the years and the evolutionary process may be highlighted using three approaches:

(1) The straight-line assimilation perspective suggests that an unchanging set of dominant values exists in a society (Sandberg, 1974; Warner & Srole, 1945). Entrepreneurs will eventually succumb to the forces of assimilation and become one with the host society. In this respect, ethnic markets would be but a fleeting, transient kind of phenomenon; thus, flying in the face of "diasporic usefulness."

(2) An ethnic resilience perspective which suggests that some ethnic entrepreneurs retain much of their original cultural values (Portes, 1984). Now it becomes important for these ethnic businesses to understand and demonstrate what these values might be, so as to develop sound marketing and communication strategies for internal and external stakeholders. In this view, segmentation based on diasporic groups is both useful and practical. Demographic variables help identify these segments. SMEs can now segment the market based on various ethnic or national groups (e.g., Indians, Chinese, Afro-Caribbean, etc.).

(3) The ethnic identification perspective informs the SME that individuals within an ethnic group may differ in the degree they identify with the ethnic [diasporic] group (Donthu & Cherian, 1992). In other words, some people are more ethnic than others (one end of the acculturation theory continuum). By finding out how individuals feel about their ethnicity (Sethna, 2006), the entrepreneur arrives at a better understanding of the market in question.

Based on the more recent research, it can be seen that entrepreneurs differ in their degree of *ethnicness* not only with respect to their level of ethnic identification, but also in regard to whom they have social relationships with, for example, the company they keep.

9.5.   Trust

Many commentators have explicitly referred to "trust" as one of the key binding agent of diaspora/network activity. Baladouni and Makepeace (1998) talked about the *ethos of trust* among Armenian enterprises. This was echoed by Chaudhry & Crick (2005) who noted *networks of trust, shared information and mutual support based on the fact that they were a distinct ethnic and religious minority*. We can further make sense of this from an SME context by incorporating notes from Kotkin (1993) who observed, that, it is for the very reason that because diasporas incorporate global networks of mutual trust, that this provides member of diasporas with a competitive advantage over people lacking such links. A recent example of this is the anecdotal evidence that may be seen with the current emergence of new Eastern European community enterprises becoming established in Britain as changes in European Union (EU) regulations allow new countries to enter the EU common market.

Subrahmanyam (1996) noted that during the era of western European capitalism some ethnic minorities (e.g., Jews, Greeks, Armenians) *found themselves better equipped to provide economic services, thanks to their scattered geographical presence and to the strong bonds of mutual trust that develop in such communities*.

Another way of describing trust in this context is portrayed by Harlaftis (1996) who commented ... *inner cohesiveness of these ethnic diasporas was exceptionally effective in overcoming the disruption in long-distance trades*.

9.6.   The Diasporic SME Typology

A review of the literature provides clear indications that the notion of networks, entrepreneurship, and ethnicity has not been fully explored. While interest in networks in the entrepreneurial marketing context is gathering momentum, it is useful to stand back and to reflect on the work of researchers who may contribute to entrepreneurial marketing and entrepreneurial networks from the globalization and ethnicity perspective.

It would seem that from the evidence thus far, that the "SME diaspora" can be viewed as a cohesive body. The accomplishment achieved by these particular SMEs is not one by mistake. Rather, diasporic SMEs have developed in tandem with an entrepreneurial typology, suggesting a close interrelationship between the two occurrences, and the inference that perhaps the typology itself brought about the "accomplishment."

Commentators on the evolution of 19th century business, such as Boyce (1995) and Jones (1996), have noted that a lot of the activity is conducted through "collaborative or network arrangements" which is in stark contrast to the notion that traditionalists have promulgated; the notion that business expansion was largely due to the "rise of the impersonal market, which in turn was seen as a function of the emergence of the anonymous businessman as an important economic agent" (Condliffe, 1951). Hence the focus on human and sociocultural capital, and the economics of diasporas in providing some comparative advantage, are of equal importance (Brenner & Keifer, 1981; Light & Gold, 2000; Schrover, 2001).

It also appears that another key aspect to be included in this typology should be the fact that diasporic SMEs value the creation of multiple identifications. They now, more so than ever before, incorporate elements from different cultures into these identities before they reoffer "globalized ethnicities" in various geographical areas.

Given that many diasporic SMEs had originally been excluded from gaining access to resources which were guarded by the wider business community in the *host* society, their fallback position was to rely on their diasporic network. This is not to say that the aspirations of wanting to enter the *host* society network did not exist. To ensure that these aspirations were somewhat fulfilled, it can be seen that the diasporic SME has adopted elements from the *host's* culture. Thus with a combination of common characteristics (Figure 9.1) from both host and co-ethnic culture, the diasporic SME is able to not only call upon the skills and resources available from

Figure 9.1: Common characteristics and key themes.

within both networks, but use this knowledge to leverage the external perception of being a sophisticated, international, and a cosmopolitan outfit.

9.7. Conclusion

Researchers are encouraged to "take the gauntlet" now thrown down, and to explore in greater depth entrepreneurial marketing, ethnicity, culture, and values and the effect on entrepreneurial activity and networks, as it has been merely alluded to in the SME marketing context. Investigations into entrepreneurship have touched upon areas which need further exploration (notably the three research strategies identified here in this chapter). Globalization of business and marketing has made this topic of even greater impact than before, witness the mass movement of people in the last century and the subsequent globalization of firms and markets. Yet, we have little understanding of ethnic networks and, how we can understand and, effectively harness this knowledge.

Whilst the interrelated factors of market conditions, selective migration, culture, social networks, and group strategy (meaning, the relationship between opportunity and ethnic characteristic) have developed over a long period of time and, in different geographic areas across the globe, the resulting patterns which may be drawn in the field of entrepreneurial networks by the diasporic SMEs are very similar to the patterns being drawn by SMEs in 2013; a suggestion that perhaps we ARE going all around in circles.

An Entrepreneurial Epilogue (Harlaftis, 2005)

> We can trace certain common characteristics among the development of the business practices of historical diasporas whose practices facilitated the integration of the new economic world system of the modern capitalist era. They all developed in big-multiethnic empires and, apart from the Greeks, they are all Asian. They all speak languages that are not Latin-based, they are all ancient people who have retained their own culture, religion and language, they are all multi-lingual with an "overinvestment" in education. They are all organised in enclave groups based on kinship and intermarriage wherever they established themselves. And we can distinguish in all of them a continuity of old structures and success in transnational business.

Further confirmation that we are indeed going around in circles.

Acknowledgments

This chapter acts mainly as a thought-piece which brings together issues of ethnicity, networks, history, and trust in the context of EM. It is evident that there is a lot to research in this fruitful area. Thanks are due to my dear friends Dr. Roz Jones and Professor Jim Blythe for their contributions to this chapter and valuable time in reviewing previous versions.

References

Abramson, N. R., Lane, H. W., Nagai, T., & Takagi, H. (1993). A comparison of Canadian and Japanese cognitive styles: Implications for management interaction. *Journal of International Business Studies, 24*(3), 575–587.

Aghassian, M., & Kevonian, K. (1999). The Armenian merchant network: Overall autonomy and local integration. In S. Chaudhury & M. Morineau (Eds.), *Merchants, companies and trade: Europe and Asia in the early modern era*. Cambridge: Cambridge University Press.

Baladouni, V., & Makepeace, M. (Eds.). (1998). *Armenian merchants of the seventeenth and early eighteenth centuries: English East India Company sources*. Philadelphia, PA: American Philosophical Society.

Ballard, R. (1994). Emergence of Desh Pardesh. In R. Ballard et al. (Eds.), *Desh Pardesh: The South Asian presence in Britain*. London: Hurst and Co.

Barth, F. (1969). *Ethnic groups and boundaries: The social organization of culture difference*. London: Allen and Unwin.

Basu, A., & Goswami, A. (1999). South Asian entrepreneurship in Great Britain: Factors influencing growth. *International Journal of Entrepreneurial Behaviour and Research, 5*(5), 251–275.

Becchetti, L., & Trovato, G. (2002). The determinants of growth for small and medium sized firms: The role of the availability of external finance. *Small Business Economics, 19*(4), 291–300.

Beerbuhl, M., & Vogele, J. (Eds.). (2004). *Spinning the commercial web. International trade, merchants, and commercial cities, c. 1640–1939*. Frankfurt: Peter Lang.

Bjerke, B., & Hultman, C. M. (2013). The role of marketing rational and natural business start-ups. In Z. Sethna, R. Jones & P. Harrigan (Eds.), *Entrepreneurial marketing: Global perspectives*. Bingley, UK: Emerald Publishing. Chapter 4.

Bourdieu, P. (1977). *Outline of a theory of practice*. London: Cambridge University Press.

Boyce, G. H. (1995). *Information, mediation and institutional development: The rise of large-scale enterprise in British shipping, 1870–1919*. Manchester: Manchester University Press.

Brenner, R., & Keifer, N. M. (1981). The economics of the diaspora: Discrimination and occupational structure. *Economic Development and Cultural Change, 29*(3), 517–534.

Brown, J. J., & Reingen, P. H. (1987). Social ties and word-of-mouth referral behaviour. *Journal of Consumer Research, 14*(December), 350–362.

Carson, D., Cromie, S., McGowan, P., & Hill, J. (1995). *Marketing and entrepreneurship in SMEs — An innovative approach*. Essex: Prentice Hall.

Chatziioannou, M. C. (1999). L'emigrazione commerciale greca dei secoli XVIII–XIX: una sfida imprenditoriale. *Proposte e ricerche, 42*(1), 22–38.

Chatziioannou, M. C. (2005). Greek merchant networks in the age of empires. In I. B. McCabe, G. Harlafis & I. P. Minoglou (Eds.), *Four centuries of history*. London: Berg Publishing.

Chaudhry, S., & Crick, D. (2005). An exploratory investigation into the entrepreneurial activities of Asian-owned franchises in the UK. *Journal of Strategic Change, 14*(6), 349–356.

Cleveland, M. (2007). *Globals, locals, and creoles: Acculturation to global consumer culture, ethnic identity, and consumptionscapes.* Germany: VDM Verlag Dr. Müller.

Cleveland, M., Papadopoulos, N., & Laroche, M. (2011). Identity, demographics, and consumer behaviors: International market segmentation across product categories. *International Marketing Review, 28*(3), 244–266.

Cleveland, M., Laroche, M., & Hallab, R. (2013). Globalization, culture, religion, and values: Comparing consumption patterns of Lebanese Muslims and Christians. *Journal of Business Research, 66*(8), 958–967.

Collinson, E., & Shaw, E. (2001). Entrepreneurial marketing – A historical perspective on development and practice. *Management Decision, 39*(9), 761–766.

Crick, D., & Chaudhury, S. (2010). An investigation into UK-based Asian entrepreneurs' perceived competitiveness in overseas markets. *Entrepreneurship and Regional Development, 22*(1), 5–23.

Chi-Cheung, C. (1998). Kinship and business: Paternal and maternal kin in Chaozhou Chinese family firms. *Business History, 40*(1), 26–49.

Cohen, A. (1971). Cultural strategies in the organization of trading diasporas. In C. Mesailloux (Ed.), *L'evolution du commerce en Afrique de l'Ouest.* London: Oxford University Press.

Condliffe, J. B. (1951). *The commerce of nations.* London: George Allen & Unwin.

Cotgrove, S., & Duff, A. (1981). Environmentalism, values, and social change. *British Journal of Sociology, 32*(1), 92–110.

Curtin, P. (1984). *Cross-cultural trade in World history.* Cambridge: Cambridge University Press.

Curto D. R., & Molho A. (Eds.). (2002). *Commercial networks in the early modern world.* Florence Working Paper No. 467/2002/2, European University Institute.

Donthu, N., & Cherian, J. (1992). Hispanic coupon usage: The impact of strong and weak ethnic identification. *Psychology and Marketing, 9*(6), 501–510.

Faber, R., & O'Guinn, T. (1987). Ethnicity, acculturation, and the impact of product attributes. *Psychology and Marketing, 4*, 121–134.

Gordon, M. (1964). *Assimilation in American life.* New York, NY: Oxford University Press.

Gourgouris, S. (2005). Concept of 'diaspora' in contemporary world. In I. B. McCabe, G. Harlaftis & I. P. Minoglou (Eds.), *Diaspora entrepreneurial networks: Four centuries of history.* London: Berg Publishers.

Granovetter, M. S. (1982). The strength of weak ties; a network theory revisited. In P. V. Marsden & N. Lin (Eds.), *Social structure and network analysis* (pp. 105–130). Beverley Hills, CA: Sage.

Greeley, A. M. (1971). *Why can't they be like us?* New York, NY: E.P. Dutton.

Harlaftis, G. (1996). *A history of Greek-owned shipping: The making of an international tramp fleet, 1830 to the present day.* London: Routledge.

Hassiotis, I. K. (1993). *A survey of the history of Modern Greek Diaspora.* Thessalonika: Vanias.

Israel, J. (2005). Diasporas Jewish and non-Jewish and the world maritime empires. In I. B. McCabe, G. Harlaftis & I. P. Minoglou (Eds.), *Diaspora entrepreneurial networks: Four centuries of history.* London: Berg Publishers.

Jones, G. (1996). *The evolution of international business: An introduction.* London: Routledge.

Kardasis, V. (2001). *Diaspora merchants in the Black Sea: The Greeks in Southern Russia, 1775–1861.* New York, NY: Lexington Books.

Keyes, C. F. (1976). Towards a new formulation of the concept of ethnic group. *Ethnicity, 3*, 202–213.

Kotkin, J. (1993). *Tribes: How race, religion and identity determine the success in the new global economy.* New York, NY: Random House.

Light, I., & Gold, S. (2000). *Ethnic economies*. San Diego, CA: Academic Press.

Mars, G., & Ward, R. (1984). Ethnic business development in Britain: Opportunities and resources. In R. Ward & R. Jenkins (Eds.), *Ethnic communities in business: Strategies for economic survival*. Cambridge: Cambridge University Press, in Basu and Goswami (1999).

Masters, B. (1988). *Merchant diasporas and trading "nation". The origins of Western economic dominance in the Middle East*. New York, NY: New York University Press.

Metcalfe, H., Modood, T., & Virdee, S. (1996). *Asian self-employment: The interaction of culture and economics in England*. London: Policy Studies Institute.

Penloza, L. (1989). Immigrant consumer acculturation. In T. Scrull (Ed.), *Advances in consumer research* (Vol. 16, pp. 110–118). Provo, UT: Association for Consumer Research.

Porters, A., & Sensenbrenner, J. (1993). Embeddedness and immigration: Notes on the social determinants of economic action. *American Journal of Sociology, 98*(6), 1320–1350.

Portes, A. (1984). The rise of ethnicity: Determinants of ethnic perceptions among Cuban exiles in Miami. *American Sociological Review, 49*, 383–397.

Ram, M. (1994). *Managing to survive: Working lives in small firms*. Oxford: Blackwell.

Redding, S. G. (1980). Cognition as an aspect of culture and its relation to management process: An exploratory view of the Chinese case. *Journal of Management Studies, 17*, 127–148.

Rokeach, M. (1973). *The nature of human values*. New York, NY: Free Press.

Sandberg, N. C. (1974). *Ethnic identity and assimilation: The Polish-American Community*. New York, NY: Preager.

Schrover, M., (2001). *Entrepreneurs and ethnic entrepreneurs: What is the difference? German entrepreneurs in the Netherlands in the nineteenth century*. Unpublished paper, N.W. Posthumus Institute, Netherlands Graduate School for Economic and Social History.

Schwartz, S. H. (1990). Individualism-collectivism: Critique and proposed refinements. *Journal of Cross-Cultural Psychology, 21*(2), 139–157.

Sethna, Z. (2006). An investigation into how individual and organisational consumption is affected when dealing with SME organisations from emerging economies. *Asia Pacific Journal of Marketing and Logistics, 18*(4), 266–282.

Shapero, A., & Sokol, L. (1982). The social dimension of entrepreneurship. In C. A. Kent, D. L. Sexton & K. H. Vesper (Eds.), *Encyclopedia of entrepreneurship* (pp. 72–90). Englewood Cliffs, NJ: Prentice-Hall.

Soar, S. (1991). Business development strategies. TECS and Ethnic Minorities Conference Report, Home Office Ethnic Minority Business Initiative, University of Warwick, in Basu and Goswami (1999).

Subrahmanyam, S. (Ed.). (1996). *Merchant networks in the early modern world*. Aldershot: Variorum.

Vallee, F. G. (1982). Inequalities and identity in multi-ethnic societies. In D. Forcese & S. Richer (Eds.), *Social issues*. Toronto, Canada: Prentice-Hall.

Van Den Berghe, P. (1987). Ethnicity and class: Bases of sociality. In L. Driedger (Ed.), *Ethnic Canada* (pp. 242–255). Toronto: Copp Clark Pitman.

Waldinger, R., Aldrich, H., & Ward, R. (Eds.). (1990). *Ethnic entrepreneurs*. London: Sage.

Warner, W. L., & Srole, L. (1945). *The social systems of American ethnic groups*. New Haven, CT: Yale University Press.

Werbner, P. (1990). Renewing and industrial past: British Pakistani entrepreneurship in Manchester. *Migration, 8*, 17–41.

Williams, R. (1961). *The long revolution*. London: Chatto and Windus.

Yinger, M. J. (1985). Ethnicity. *Annual Review of Sociology, 11*, 151–180.

Part B — Approaches to Entrepreneurial Marketing

Chapter 10

Market Creation as an Entrepreneurial Marketing Process

Abstract

Market creation is a fundamental business activity in dynamic and competitive free markets that can provide large corporations a potential growth trajectory. Creating new needs and wants is, as we will demonstrate, central to market creation. However, we believe that marketing has drifted too far away from market creation as an intended strategic decision and, instead, presents market creation simply as a consequence of satisfying latent needs which many would agree is a by-product of effective marketing, and not a strategic decision. This chapter suggests that market creation is an intended strategy and is different from market creation as an emergent phenomenon. Accordingly, we propose an entrepreneurial marketing approach to market creation that more fully embraces current work in both marketing and entrepreneurship where market creation is presented as intended strategy and at the core of the marketing and entrepreneurship interface. Even though marketing did once acknowledge market creation as a source of competitive advantage, we argue that marketing has become more silent in recent decades and has instead developed tools and techniques to identify explicit consumer needs and wants, many of which will not lead to market creation. We observe, however, that the entrepreneurship literature has continued to embrace and encourage market creation as a source of competitive advantage. Accordingly, we encourage a blended approach, one that draws from current practice in marketing and entrepreneurship and we present this in a model we call "A dynamic model of market creation."

10.1. Introduction

Market creation is a fundamental business activity in dynamic and competitive free markets that can provide large corporations a potential growth trajectory. With the

Entrepreneurial Marketing: Global Perspectives
Copyright © 2013 by Emerald Group Publishing Limited
All rights of reproduction in any form reserved
ISBN: 978-1-78190-786-3

marketplace overflowing with competitors offering similar value propositions, a firm seeking to create competitive advantage is often faced with three alternatives: (1) drive costs down to create a lower cost structure than competitors in the present product/market space (difficult in an era of widespread lean production and global outsourcing); (2) differentiate their marketing mix to create a superior value proposition in the present product/market space; or (3) leverage a shift in consumer behavior or/and radical, disruptive, proactive innovation to develop a competitive advantage based upon the creation of a new product market space. Firms that follow the third alternative seek new product market spaces that allow the firm to move from overcrowded hypercompetitive markets to markets with little or no competitive threats into a new commercial and technological ecosystem (see Kim & Mauborgne, 2004). Table 10.1 illustrates this third form of competitive advantage and its potential consequences.

In comparison, entrepreneurship has taken a different path. Instead of a business strategy that focuses upon "play(ing) the game better than competitors," entrepreneurial business strategy attempts to change the rules and "play the game better than competitors *or* play your own game" (Covin & Slevin, 2002, p. 321). Market creation offers a way to shift the competitive landscape and play your own game in a new product/market space.

Venkataraman (1997, p. 120) defines the central issue of entrepreneurship as being "fundamentally concerned with understanding how, in the absence of current markets for future goods and services, these goods and services manage to come into existence." Shane and Venkataraman (2000) further argue that entrepreneurship is a process involving (1) discovery or creation; (2) assessment; and (3) exploitation of economic opportunities by opportunity driven, enterprising entities that often as a consequence create new product-markets. Like entrepreneurship, marketing has also placed market creation within the boundaries of its discipline, but this was done early in the development of the discipline of marketing, with minimal interest in this area of research lately. For example in the first issue of the first volume of the

Table 10.1: Market creation as positional advantage.

Sources of advantage	Positional advantages	Performance outcomes
1. Superior skills + 2. Superior resources	1. Cost-based advantage 2. Differentiation-based advantage 3. Market creation-based advantage – changing the playing field!	1. Superior economic performance 2. Superior marketing performance 3. New markets created

Source: Day and Wensley (1988).

Journal of Marketing, Coutant (1936) identified the importance of market creation by stating that

> ... the flow of business depends mostly upon natural supply and demand. Once that was roughly true, when supply never quite equaled the capacities of markets to absorb them .... A great thinker named Millikan pointed the way out of such a blockade, however, when he observed that progress comes from creating new wants in people and satisfying them. (Coutant, 1936, p. 28, emphasis added)

Creating new needs and wants is, as we will demonstrate, central to market creation. However, we believe that marketing has drifted too far away from market creation as an intended strategic decision and, instead, presents market creation simply as a consequence of satisfying latent needs which many would agree is a by-product of effective marketing, and not a strategic decision. Levitt (1960) suggests that firms will tend to enjoy better performance through "planned marketing innovation." We suggest that market creation is an intended strategy and is different from market creation as an emergent phenomenon. Accordingly, we propose an entrepreneurial marketing approach to market creation that more fully embraces current work in both marketing and entrepreneurship (see, for example, Miles & Darroch, 2006; Morris, Schindehutte, & LaForge, 2002; Schindehutte, Morris & Kocak, 2008) where market creation is presented as intended strategy and at the core of the marketing and entrepreneurship interface (see Hills & LaForge, 1992 for additional discussion on the marketing/entrepreneurship interface). Our approach is consistent with the position taken by Miles and Darroch (2006, p. 498) who, in a paper discussing entrepreneurial marketing processes (EMP) and competitive advantage, contend that

> firms that adopt EMPs are better suited to discover and create, assess, and exploit attractive entrepreneurial opportunities, and that this enhanced level of corporate entrepreneurship enables the EMP firm to more effectively and efficiently create and renew competitive advantage.

Thus by adopting an entrepreneurial marketing approach to market creation, managers are in a better position to develop new means-end relationships, rather than working within existing means-end frameworks (Kirzner, 1997; Shane & Venkataraman, 2000). We begin by exploring the terms "market" and "market creation." We then outline demand side and supply-side approaches to market creation. Next we critique the way in which market creation is currently presented in the marketing discipline before offering a more comprehensive and blended solution that draws from both marketing and entrepreneurship. We argue that a blended approach is important for effective entrepreneurial marketing and suggest that market creation can provide valuable assets to the firm upon which sustainable competitive advantages are based.

10.2.   What Is a Market and How Are Markets Created?

Markets have had a somewhat mythical existence in Western culture and the managerial and social sciences (Coase, 1988). Markets can be conceptualized in a similar way to quality, you know quality when you see it (Persig, 1974) – and we suggest the same can be said of markets — you know one when you see one. Markets can be conceptualized as free and open (Friedman, 1962) or highly controlled, domesticated, and regulated (Arndt, 1979a, 1979b).

Markets can be examined from a "supply-side" perspective, in which the focus is on the products or services firms are willing to supply (Sarasvathy & Dew, 2004). Competitor products are seen as direct competitors; therefore, products that can be categorized as having the same product form or use similar technology. The purpose of market analysis then is to identify which firms belong in the market so as to make inferences about market power and anticompetitive actions, often as part of a broader assessment of anti-trust issues. Markets defined using a supply-side perspective would consist of the competitive set of firms within the marketer's relevant ecosystem (Alsem, 2007) all of which produce products that more or less satisfy the same needs and wants of consumers (Mason, 1990). An example of a supply-side approach to a market creation definition is the automobile industry. As a value proposition automobile manufacturers more or less create the same set of values for the customer — in that they offer a personal transportation method and do so with enough variation of offer to appeal to a wide range of desired functionality and budget. The critique that in most markets there is a growing similarity of automotive design can be somewhat attributed to the use of "global platforms," upon which a variety of models are built (e.g., the VW A5 platform — Golf variants, Audi A3 and TT, and Seat variants).

Alternatively, markets can be defined from a consumer or "demand-side" perspective. Here, a market comprises a set of consumers who have homogeneous revealed preferences for a certain combination of attributes (Lancaster, 1971). These preferences might be for existing products or "yet-to-be-invented" products. An example of a demand-side perspective could be the fitness market — with alternative products serving this emerging need from home rowing equipment to Nordic walking equipment to health clubs, to liposuction to weight watchers.

Therefore, we suggest that a market is either (1) a group of consumers with the same needs and wants; or (2) a group of products that satisfy the same needs and wants. Common to both definitions of a market is the homogeneity of consumers' needs and wants. However, the difference lies in whether any analysis of the market begins with the consumer (i.e., the demand side) or the product (i.e., the supply side). Since our unit of analysis is market creation, we propose that markets are created when a consumer group with a new set of homogenous needs and wants is identified and served. Furthermore, the process of market creation begins with either the consumer or product — we have labeled these approaches as either (1) a demand-side approach to market creation; or (2) a supply-side approach to market creation. These two approaches to market creation are captured in Figure 10.1.

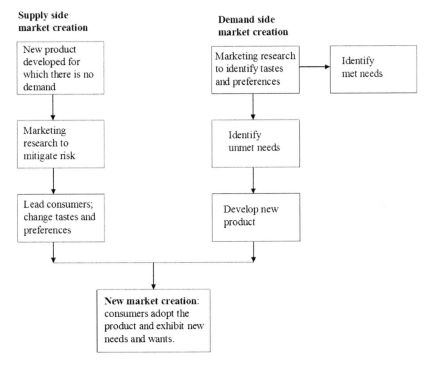

Figure 10.1: Demand-side and supply-side approaches to market creation.

According to the demand-side approach to market creation, managers begin by identifying emerging tastes and preferences that typically arise due to social, technological, or regulatory environmental changes. These tastes and preferences manifest themselves as unmet needs and wants, for which managers develop new products. Within this framework, it is assumed that consumers can state tastes and preferences but may not be able to articulate their needs and wants. In fact, it is quite likely that consumers harbor latent but detectable unmet needs and so can describe a problem they have with an existing product but not offer a solution (e.g., the digital picture frame as a solution to displaying digital photographs). Importantly though, a homogeneous set of tastes and preferences exists and this provides the incentive for managers to develop new products. Thus, one task of marketing management is to detect consumer preferences in order to identify unmet latent needs (Kotler, 1973). Kotler (1973, p. 44) notes that

> latent demand exists when a substantial number of people share a strong need for something which does not exist in the form of an actual product. The latent demand represents an opportunity for the marketing innovator to develop the product that people have been wanting.

The more latent the need, the more sophisticated managers' market sensing capabilities need to be and the more entrepreneurial the manager must act in order to make the linkages between unmet needs and possible product solutions. One potential downside risk of this approach however is that products may be developed that are at odds with the core business. In addition, managers might acquire and invest in new resources and diversify the core business based on the promise of potential profits, eventual market creation, and a possible sustainable competitive advantage.

Alternatively, a market can be created by first developing a new product and then leading consumers to that product. Here the focus is on leveraging innovations around existing products, processes, strategies, domains, or business opportunities (see Morris, Kuratko, & Covin, 2008). For many managers, this internally driven option is often more certain, manageable, and economically attractive (see, for example, Burgelman & Doz, 2001; Campbell & Park, 2004) because these entrepreneurial initiatives are linked to the core business. However, new product development may not be coupled with strong market sensing capabilities and so the risk is that consumers may not adopt the product because managers have misread the market. If the firm does succeed in creating demand for the new product, a new group of consumers with homogeneous needs and wants emerges and a market is eventually created. We call this the supply-side approach to market creation. An example of this approach to market creation is provided by Akio Morita, the founder of Sony, who pursued his idea for a portable cassette player (the Sony Walkman) on the basis that "Sony does not serve markets, it creates them" (Kotler & Keller, 2006, p. 353). With the Walkman, Sony gained an early position of market leadership in a newly created market and, in so doing, influenced emerging industry standards and enjoyed strategically significant cost advantages.

No matter which approach is followed, we believe a market is created *ex post*, that is, sometime *after* the new product is developed because in order to adopt the new product, consumers need to alter their preference structures and exhibit a new set of needs and wants. Thus, market creation occurs after a new product is launched (i.e., once new tastes and preference are formed) and so cannot be considered part of the new product development process. Therefore, central to our position is the view that market creation is not immediate and may not occur until sometime after a new product is launched, if at all (Gort & Keppler, 1982). The temporal nature of market creation is reflected in the work of (Danneels, 2004) who suggested a disruptive technology is often only labeled as such once it has disrupted the businesses of incumbent firms. However, we contend that this temporal element has been largely overlooked in the extant literature on market creation.

10.3.   What Do We Teach in Marketing?

We suggest that supply-side market creation has only made sporadic appearances in marketing. For example, supply-side market creation appeared in the very first edition of the *Journal of Marketing* (Coutant, 1936). Later on, Smith (1956, p. 5) positioned marketing as a mechanism to enable the convergence of heterogeneous demand functions into a set of "several demand schedules where only one was recognized before." Similarly, Dickson and Gintner (1987) demonstrated the importance of segmentation to create unique segments (i.e., markets) in order to provide the firm with a unique competitive advantage. In 1971, Kaldor noted that consumers often do not really know or acknowledge their needs and therefore effective marketers must create new markets through leveraging the firm's competencies. This perspective was reinforced by Houston (1986) who suggested that in the future (e.g., a decade henceforth) marketers need to use their capabilities to create future markets since customers are not necessarily good sources of information about their needs and that firms adopt innovative marketing practices to persuade and educate consumers about new product/market opportunities. Houston (1986, p. 86) further argued that "anticipating future needs and wants are consistent with the marketing concept."

By contrast, much of what is written about marketing practice is biased toward demand-side market creation and we have a plethora of tools and techniques aimed at keeping current customers at the center of the business, managing customer relationships, and surveying customers in order to measure attitudes and opinions, usually with the intention of satisfying customers and uncovering unmet needs. In addition, there is an increasing emphasis on superior market sensing capabilities (Day, 1994) in order to uncover latent needs and this is often translated into the use of alternative, non-survey-based methodologies such as demographic trend analysis (Drucker, 1985) or anthropological studies (see, for example, Arnould & Wallendorf, 1994). This demand-side approach to market creation is embedded in the value creation approach to marketing, described in Kotler and Keller's *Marketing Management* textbook and offered as the most effective approach to marketing (Kotler & Keller, 2006, p. 36). By following the value creation approach, managers first do their homework by conducting marketing research in order to identify market segments that exist, thereby identifying consumers with homogenous tastes and preferences. Next, managers choose a segment or segments upon which to focus and create a value proposition for each segment. Managers then develop a product that will provide value to consumers. Once launched, marketers embark upon a campaign to communicate the product's value to consumers. We contend that this demand-side perspective of market creation is reflected in the current American Marketing Association (2007) definition of marketing, which emphasizes value creation:

> Marketing is the activity, set of institutions, and processes for creating, communicating, delivering, and exchanging offerings that have value for customers, clients, partners, and society at large.

In the remainder of this section, we critique this demand-side approach to market creation and, in so doing, demonstrate why an over-emphasis on a demand-side approach to market creation is not always in the organization's best strategic interests.

As we have already suggested, we teach marketing students that "marketing involves satisfying customers' needs and wants" (Kotler & Keller, 2006). Further, we explain to students that historically, demand exceeded supply and that if a firm was to develop products (supply) it would create its own demand (this is also known as Say's Law from 1803). Thus, managers developed new products knowing that, in order to make a profit, the firm simply needs to sell sufficient quantities of the product at the right price. Here, marketing occurred as part of the sales process (i.e., once the product was conceived and made), and the task of marketing was to find and stimulate buyers to enter into an exchange (Kotler & Levy, 1969). This administrative approach has since been labeled the "traditional approach" to marketing (Kotler & Keller, 2006). As already noted, Kotler and Keller (2006) continue by recommending an alternative approach to marketing, one more appropriate in today's conditions, and call it the "value creation" approach. Here managers identify the preference structures of existing market segments, develop products to suit those needs, and then embark upon a campaign to communicate the product's value to consumers.

This value creation approach to marketing (which we have named the demand-side approach to market creation) is based upon a number of assumptions: (1) a market exists and is fixed and exogenous to the firm; (2) managers can conceive of a marketing research study that will measure consumers' tastes and preferences to ultimately allow managers to predict demand; (3) consumers are sufficiently rational and articulate and can state their tastes and preference; (4) the research study is an accurate reflection of consumer tastes and preferences; (5) tastes and preferences are stable and needs and wants are generally manifest — once identified they become boundaries within which managers work; and (6) managers are rational decision makers, can assess the results of a marketing research study, and make decisions that will provide some kind of competitive advantage to the firm. The following paragraphs expand upon a number of these points.

A market exists and is exogenous to the firm (Lewin & Voberda, 1999; Wiltbank, Dew, Read, & Sarasvathy, 2006). A physical market generally refers to a place where buyers and sellers engage in an exchange. However, putting boundaries around parts of a physical market in order to talk about markets in relation to tastes and preferences is, at the very least, arbitrary (Day, Shocker, & Srivastava, 1979) and perhaps nothing more than a management strategy, rather than a market condition (Dickson & Gintner, 1987). In fact Mises (1949, pp. 258–259) suggests that markets are a process:

> The market is not a place, a thing or a collective entity. The market is a process, actuated by the interplay of the actions of the various individuals cooperating under the division of labor. The forces determining the – continually changing – state of the market are the value judgments of these individuals and their actions as directed by these value judgments. There is nothing inhuman or mystical with regard to the market. The market process is entirely a resultant of human actions. Every market phenomenon can be traced back to definite choices of the members of the market society.

Even if a market exists, central to this first assumption is the view that a market sits "out there," or exogenous to the firm. In addition, preferences are also exogenous and so changes in preferences remain exogenous to the market creation process and will simply present as new opportunities for the firm (Sarasvathy & Dew, 2004). What becomes important is the ability of managers to identify and exploit these opportunities (Kirzner, 1973; Venkatraman, 1997).

However, preferences can also be considered endogenous, coevolving with the market creation process rather than being exogenous and fixed — if you like, they are somewhat of a moving target (Carpenter & Nakamoto, 1989, 1994; Kahneman & Snell, 1988). For example, a firm introduces a new product and teaches consumers new behaviors to facilitate the adoption process (e.g., touch screen technology). Thus, the innovating firm shapes tastes and preferences and this becomes central to the market creation process (Sarasvathy & Dew, 2004). These new preference structures form new consumer ideal points against which all other products are compared (Carpenter & Nakamoto, 1989). Done well, "owning" the new ideal point in the new market becomes a valuable asset that underpins a competitive advantage for the firm (Carpenter & Nakamoto, 1994).

Consumers are sufficiently rational and articulate and can state their tastes and preferences. Embedded in this assumption is the notion that consumers want to know how to and indeed do maximize their utility (Daniel, 1970). Furthermore, consumers have complete and certain knowledge of their requirements and understand exactly how to go about satisfying them (Daniel, 1970).

However, we also know that consumers tastes and preferences are ill defined and ambiguous, especially when dealing with new potentially new products (Kaldor, 1971; Sarasvathy & Dew, 2005a, 2005b). Thus, if tastes and preferences are ill defined, consumers are unlikely to be able to articulate their needs and wants or express likely demand for the new product (Sarasvathy & Dew, 2005b) because they simply do not understand the product concept being tested (Kirzner, 1979; Robertson & Yu, 2001). Furthermore, consumers find their needs change as they learn by using a new product (Robertson & Yu, 2001). Thus, preliminary research studies, in which the emphasis is on new product development, are not necessarily accurate reflections of current and future consumer tastes and preferences. Again, a supply-side approach to market creation accepts the possibility that there is no demand for a new product and managers then must take substantial risks in order to launch a product for which there is an uncertain future.

Tastes and preferences are stable; once identified they become boundaries within which managers work. Under this assumption, changes in preferences are generally only minor or haphazard (Hirschman, 1984) and changes in demand only occur due to changes in income or prices, not because tastes and preferences have changed (Daniel, 1988). However, just as Coutant (1936) argued that progress comes from creating new wants in people and satisfying them, Penrose (1959, p. 80) once said that "the really enterprising entrepreneur has not often, so far as we can see, taken demand as a 'given' but rather as something that he ought to be able to do something about." Furthermore, we know that tastes and preferences can change once innovations are introduced (Daniel, 1988) and so stated tastes and preferences should not become boundary conditions within which to innovate.

Managers are rational decision makers, can assess the results of a piece of marketing research, and make decisions that will provide some kind of competitive advantage to the firm. Under this assumption, managers can control the future of the firm and decide where the firm should be in five or ten years' time (Robertson & Yu, 2001). Armed with tools such as Ansoff's growth matrix (Ansoff, 1957), Schoemaker's scenario planning analysis (Schoemaker, 1991, 1995), segmentation (Smith, 1956), and Porter's five forces (Porter, 1979), managers work hard to predict the future and position of the firm and its products more accurately (Wiltbank et al., 2006). Managers assume that by predicting the future they can control it (Dew & Sarasvathy, 2003). Superior outcomes of the planning process are anticipated when managers learn and adapt and make use of superior market sensing capabilities (Day, 1994) in order to rapidly adjust to changes in their external environment (see, for example, Teece, Pisano, and Shuen's (1997) dynamic capabilities approach; Eisenhardt's (1989, 1990) fast decision-making; or Mintzberg and Waters's (1985) work on emergent strategy). Therefore, by making good use of planning tools, and responding quickly to changes in the environment, managers hope to make superior predictions about the future (in relation to their competitors) that will provide a competitive advantage to the firm (Wiltbank et al., 2006).

We offer two main counterpoints to the argument above. First, do managers really have any control over the future of the firm? Population ecologists would argue that they do not; any attempts by managers to restructure and transform the organization are futile and reduce chances of firm survival (Lewin & Voberda, 1999). Therefore, the best that managers can hope to achieve is the successful implementation of a focus strategy in which innovation is undertaken to enhance the firm's current offerings – eventually, the incumbent firm will be selected out by new entrants (Lewin & Voberda, 1999). A slightly less extreme view is offered by institutional theorists. Here, the firm becomes embedded in its own institutional context, making it difficult to respond to a changing environment. Because the firm imitates the population to which it belongs, the best an incumbent firm can hope to achieve is quick adaptation (a fast follower approach) to change (Lewin & Voberda, 1999). At the other end of the continuum is the view that managers have complete control over the destiny of their firm. Managers either have a clear vision of what the firm is and where the firm is headed and adopt a cult-like commitment to make this happen (Hamel & Prahalad, 1989). Alternatively, managers engage in a process of effectuation in which they begin with an understanding of who they are, what they know, and whom they know (Sarasvathy & Dew, 2005b). Here, managers begin with a general idea for a product, imagine the product in use, develop a sense of the problem for which the product will solve, and set about creating demand for the new product. The view is, if you can control the future, you do not need to predict it (Dew & Sarasvathy, 2003).

> Producers are like explorers going into the woods. They are embarking on an expedition with the aim of transforming tacit knowledge into articulated knowledge. (Robertson & Yu, 2001, p. 191)

Our second counterpoint queries whether or not managers make the right decisions based on the marketing research they collect. Here, we suggest that if market creation occurs *ex ante*, managers are not sure what pieces of information to pay attention to when making decisions about the future of the firm (Sarasvathy & Dew, 2005b). Managers are also constrained by mental schema and bounded cognition in that they are only able to attend to a few pieces of information at a time (Sarasvathy & Dew, 2005a, 2005b; Shane & Venkataraman, 2000; Simon, 1957). Therefore, we question the ability of managers to make the optimum decision for the firm — perhaps ignorance is the dominant input into decision making (Kirzner, 1973; Sarasvathy & Dew, 2005b).

The preceding discussion presented and critiqued the value creation (i.e., the demand side) approach to market creation. This begins with managers undertaking a marketing research study in order to identify gaps in the market. As we have already discussed, the value creation approach to marketing assumes that markets exist and managers are able to "read" the market in order to accurately identify gaps or opportunities. Once gaps are identified, managers leverage or acquire resources to support the selected value creating strategy (Barney, 1991; Penrose, 1959; Wernerfelt, 1984). In addition, managers examine the way in which resources are utilized. For example, managers might question routines and long held assumptions of the market in order to facilitate quick adaptation to changing conditions (Teece et al., 1997), and leverage tacit knowledge and adjust routines in order to accommodate those changes (Nelson & Winter, 1982). Central to this approach, however, is the view that environmental changes are exogenous, perhaps caused by new firms launching new products, competitor firms introducing new technology, and consumers forming new tastes and preferences – all of which bring about potential opportunities for the firm to identify and exploit. What has been largely overlooked in the extant literature is whether or not new product ideas are derived endogenously and whether or not new products result in market creation, in particular, supply-side market creation. The following section seeks to expand these perspectives by offering a dynamic approach to market creation.

10.4. An Alternative Perspective — A Dynamic Approach to Market Creation

When we began this chapter we outlined supply-side and demand-side approaches to market creation. We concluded that both focus on the creation of homogeneous tastes and preferences. We believe that managers need to adopt a balanced approach to market creation, rather than choosing between demand-side or supply-side approaches.

As we have argued, demand-side market creation makes many appearances in different guises within the domain of marketing. Supply-side market creation, on the other hand, has made only sporadic appearances in marketing although it has always been at the center of entrepreneurship, a discipline concerned with how, in the absence of current markets for future goods and services, these goods and services manage to come into existence (Venkatraman, 1997, p. 120). We suggest that marketers need to be reminded of Coutant's (1936, p. 28) position that progress [in marketing] will come about by creating and satisfying new wants. Put another way, we believe that progress in marketing will come about by adopting a more entrepreneurial approach to marketing, and in the context of this chapter, by blending demand- and supply-side approaches to market creation and, therefore, working at the marketing/entrepreneurship interface.

In this section, we bring the demand- and supply-side perspectives together into one framework to allow for dynamic interactions between the two (Robertson & Yu, 2001). Our approach is outlined in Figure 10.2. We explain why the market is a dynamic process and always in a state of flux (Dickson, 1992). In addition, we allow for both exogenous and endogenous changes that result in opportunities for new product development. We also explain why some firms do not engage in market creation.

Identifies and exploits opportunities. Initially, the market is in disequilibrium and demand exceeds supply because consumers have needs that are not currently being met by existing products (Kotler, 1973, p. 44). Consumers might be able to articulate their unmet needs or they might be able to articulate problems they have with current product offerings. However, because products do not exist to satisfy those unmet needs, consumers are unlikely to articulate a solution. Therefore, managers must possess superior market sensing and opportunity recognition capabilities (Day, 1994; Hayek, 1948; Kirzner, 1997) because traditional marketing research methods might not successfully uncover latent demand. However, those within the firm are likely to be immersed in the market and very connected to the players within it. Thus, the task of marketing management is to actively exploit new opportunities by developing new products and creating demand for these products. Thus, the firm generates supply to satisfy latent demand and so moves the market back to equilibrium.

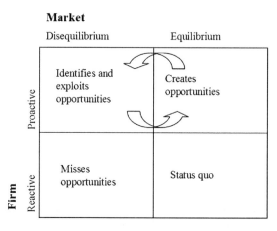

Figure 10.2: A dynamic model of market creation.

Creates opportunities. Here, the market starts out in equilibrium and managers actively seek to create new opportunities through innovation (Schumpeter, 1934), thereby generating supply that pushes the market out of equilibrium. In order to develop an innovation, managers make use of existing resources by, for example, leveraging R&D in order to produce technology push innovations. Using Kotler's (1973) demand framework, we suggest there is no demand for the innovation — consumers are either disinterested or indifferent to the innovation. Here, the task of marketing management is to create or stimulate demand by making consumers aware of the innovation and demonstrating the value the innovation has over current offerings. Once sufficient demand has been created the market moves back to equilibrium. However, as part of the process of creating demand, new consumer preferences are formed. We believe that firms operating within this quadrant are characterized as decisive and very much in control of their environment. Those within the firm will work quickly and will be highly competitive, wanting the esteem that comes with new product development.

Missing opportunities. The market is in disequilibrium because, as before, there are unmet consumer needs — that is, demand exceeds supply. However, those within the firm fail to identify market opportunities. Firms operating in this quadrant are in danger of losing ground to competitors because they are neither satisfying existing consumers (who have unmet needs) nor creating new consumer groups. Such a firm is very tied to the security that is offered by maintaining the status quo. The firm does not want to cause conflict in the market by confusing or alienating its consumers and so those within the firm listen to its customers, and will be slow to react.

Serve customers. The market is in equilibrium and supply equals demand. Because the firm is not proactive, it will not endeavor to alter the supply curve. It will stick to its knitting, preferring to serve current customers well. The task of marketing management is to maintain full demand or revitalize faltering demand (Kotler, 1973) and this might result in making incremental adjustments to existing products or revitalizing current offerings in response to feedback from customers to avoid a situation of faltering demand (Kotler, 1973). This strategy is highly effective in a market with preferences that are relatively stable. The danger however is that a competitor might engage in Schumpeterian-type innovation (Schumpeter, 1934) and upset the status quo by altering consumer preferences and creating demand where once again the firm runs the risk of losing ground and becoming uncompetitive. Firms that excel in serving customers are likely to be characterized as perfectionists, wanting to make improvements to products in order to completely satisfy existing customers. Those within the firm will strive to maintain relationships with customers for fear of alienating or providing inferior products or services to them.

So far, we have considered whether or not the market is in disequilibrium and whether or not the firm is passive or active in response to its market. We have identified a number of demand states — latent demand, no demand, faltering demand, and full demand. In this chapter, we are not only interested in whether or not firms innovate but also the impact the innovation has on the market. We suggest that an innovation that alters established patterns of behavior is creating a new market. What is important with our conceptualization is that the changes occur after the innovation has been launched. The following examples further serve to illustrate our perspective.

Sandberg's (2005) recent work on market creation provides an example that illustrates many of the motives behind market creation with her case on Nordic Walking as radical innovation and an example of market creation. Sandberg (2005) describes how a Finnish composite manufacturing corporation Exel dominated the ski pole market during the 1970s and 1980s and grew rapidly as cross-country skiing gained in popularity; but suffered terribly in the 1990s as the winter sports public's enthusiasm for cross-country skiing diminished. At the same time, there was various social dynamics creating pressures for a more efficient, low-cost, low-skill outdoor exercise which have only increased during the past decade. These include the epidemic of diabetes, obesity, and cardiovascular problems that much of the developed world is facing. However, as Sandberg (2005, p. 217) states:

> The development challenge was that it was not only the product, but also the sport that had to be created. At first, the market research did not seem to be appropriate in terms of anticipating demand because not even the sport existed.

Sandberg (2005, p. 219) quotes a Senior Vice President of Exel, the firm attempting to create the Nordic Walking market:

> In a way this was a special project for us, usually companies manufacture products to fulfill a certain demand and then market the product, talk about its technical properties. But in our case, we actually had to develop a sport, market it and invent a product for it.

Sandberg (2005, p. 216) illustrates how the sport of Nordic Walking was created quoting the head of physiological testing for the Finland's Central Association for Recreational Sports and Outdoors Activities:

> I was thinking about types of exercise you could offer ordinary people as a training method and then I came across a survey where walking was number one. Then I saw a group of cross-country skiers walk past me with ski poles ... In my line of work I can see that Finland is split 20/80 — 20% are those who were satisfied with the services the leisure-sports industry was offering: step aerobics, spinning, gyms ... but the so-called average Joes, those who don't like that kind of sport. There were two million of them and all of them were walking!

Nordic walking, or walking with modified ski poles, was found to offer a low-cost, low-impact, efficient low-skill outdoor solution to controlling weight, lowering blood sugar, and improving cardiovascular fitness deficiencies (Pereira, 2007). To create the market for their "Nordic walking" highly modified ski poles (exhibiting different grips, shafts, and tips for walking on tarmac), Exel and Finland's Central

Association for Recreational Sports and Outdoors Activities attempted to overcome the social stigma of walking with ski poles and lack of information on proper walking pole techniques by creating a "critical mass" of walking instructors. In 2002, while Scandinavians were very familiar with cross-country ski equipment, Nordic walking throughout the lakes and forested parks of Stockholm was still an oddity (the second author is an avid Nordic walking enthusiast and lived and Nordic walked in Stockholm in the spring of 2002).

To create a market in the United States, Leki GmbH, a German firm, selected less fit middle aged women with an interest in losing weight and gaining fitness to help create the Nordic Walking market by becoming their army of instructors, illustrating to their friends and family that really any one can benefit from this sport (Pereira, 2007). Although Nordic Walking as a sport was developed only in 1997 there were approximately 5 million Nordic Walkers internationally in 2005 (International Nordic Walking Association, 2007).

Concept2 (see www.concept2.com) is another example of a firm that created a new sport and a market for their product, an indoor rower to design better rowing oars taking advantage of new "space age" carbon fiber composites. Established in Vermont by the Dreissigacker brothers from California in 1976, Concept2 designed rowing oars that were used in the 1977 World Championships. However, the winters in Vermont kept them from rowing during the colder seasons of the year. They solved this problem by developing a low-cost, portable "indoor rowing machine" from bicycle components, first sold in the fall of 1981 (Dreissigacker, 2001). Although there were other "indoor" rowing machines, these were large, heavy, and very expensive and were generally not suitable for home or club use. By the spring of 1982 indoor ERG racing on Concept2s had become formal with Boston's C.R.A.S.H.-B (Dreissigacker, 2001). As Peter Dreissigacker (2001, p. 2) stated "it was as if the rowing community had just been waiting for the (Concept2) ERG to come along." This was the conception of the indoor rower market. The use of ERGs moved from competitive rowers looking for a way to maintain fitness during winter to the general public looking for a low impact, fun, full body fitness device to help with strength training, weight control, and cardio vascular fitness.

Concept2's founders "created" the indoor rower market by building this new market around their extensive rowing club background. They quickly sponsored indoor rowing races for rowers in the "off-season," ultimately creating a global community of Concept2 users first through a semiannual newsletter and contests designed to encourage people to use their Concept2 more often and more effectively. Later, Concept2 leveraged the internet creating online instructions, rowing logs, events, contests, and even now online rowing clubs (Golann, 2006).

10.5. Conclusion

The central thesis of this chapter is that both demand-side and supply-side market creation is important and yet traditional marketing has overemphasized demand-side market creation and been largely silent on supply-side market creation, while entrepreneurship has focused on supply-side market creation. We suggest that creating needs and wants is positioned as an intangible asset and therefore a source of competitive advantage. Thus, we encourage managers to adopt a blended approach to market creation — sometimes beginning with the product and sometimes beginning with the consumer. We also contend that marketing could benefit by borrowing more from entrepreneurship, a discipline in which supply-side market creation has been central.

In this chapter, we refer to demand-side market creation as an approach that originates from consumer needs, whereas supply-side market creation originates from suppliers and the product itself. Because our focus is on market creation, we further refine demand-side market creation as emanating from unmet needs, either explicit or latent, and supply-side market creation as often creating new needs. For a market to exist, however, there needs to be a homogeneous group of customers with the same needs and wants, that is, who demand the same combination of attributes in a product. So at some point, there needs to be a match between a product, which is a bundle of attributes, and the market, which is a group of customers who demand a certain combination of product attributes. That is, at some point equilibrium needs to be achieved.

We position market creation, that is, creating a market for a new combination of attributes, a source of competitive advantage in that the market creating firm manages to shift the market and encourage consumers to value a new combination of attributes that the firm itself offers but where no other competitor is yet to compete.

Even though marketing did once acknowledge market creation as a source of competitive advantage, we argue that marketing has become more silent in recent decades and has instead developed tools and techniques to identify explicit consumer needs and wants, many of which will not lead to market creation. We observe, however, that the entrepreneurship literature has continued to embrace and encourage market creation as a source of competitive advantage. Accordingly, we encourage a blended approach, one that draws from current practice in marketing and entrepreneurship and we present this in a model we call "A dynamic model of market creation" (Figure 10.2).

We encourage academics and practitioners alike to embrace entrepreneurial marketing as an appropriate way to balance the supply side with the demand side so as to create a sustainable competitive advantage.

References

Alsem, K. J. (2007). *Strategic marketing: An applied perspective.* Boston, MA: McGraw-Hill.
Ansoff, I. (1957). Strategies for diversification. *Harvard Business Review* (Sept-Oct).
Arndt, J. (1979a). The market is dying: Long live marketing. *MSU Business Topics, 27*(1), 5.
Arndt, J. (1979b). Towards a concept of domesticated markets. *Journal of Marketing, 43*(4), 69–76.
Arnould, E. J., & Wallendorf, M. (1994). Market-oriented ethnography: Interpretation building and marketing strategy formulation. *Journal of Marketing Research, 31*(4), 484–504.

Barney, J. (1991). Firm resources and sustained competitive advantage. *Journal of Management, 17*, 139–157.

Burgelman, R. A., & Doz, Y. L. (2001). The power of strategic integration. *Sloan Management Review, 42*(3), 28–38.

Campbell, A., & Park, R. (2004). Stop kissing frogs. *Harvard Business Review, 82*(7/8), 27–28.

Carpenter, G., & Nakamoto, K. (1989). Consumer preference formation and pioneering advantage. *Journal of Marketing Research, 26*(3), 285–298.

Carpenter, G., & Nakamoto, K. (1994). Reflections on Consumer preference formation and pioneering advantage. *Journal of Marketing Research, 31*(4), 570–573.

Coase, R. (1988). *The firm, the market and the law*. Chicago, IL: University of Chicago Press.

Coutant, F. R. (1936). Where are we bound in marketing research. *Journal of Marketing, 1*(1), 28–34.

Covin, J. G., & Slevin, D. P. (2002). The entrepreneurial imperatives of strategic leadership. In M. A. Hitt, R. D. Ireland, S. M. Camp & D. L. Sexton (Eds.), *Strategic entrepreneurship: Creating a new mindset* (pp. 309–327). Oxford: Blackwell Publishing.

Daniel, C. (1988). A critique of the controversy about the stability of consumers' tastes. *Journal of Economic Education, 19*(3), 245–253.

Daniel, C. (1970). *Mathematical models in microeconomics*. Boston, MA: Allyn & Bacon.

Danneels, E. (2004). Disruptive technology reconsidered: A critique and research agenda. *Journal of Product Innovation Management, 21*(4), 246–258.

Day, G. S., & Wensley, R. (1988). Assessing advantage: A framework for diagnosing competitive superiority. *Journal of Marketing, 52*(April), 1–20.

Day, G. (1994). The capabilities of market-driven organizations. *Journal of Marketing, 58*(October), 37–52.

Day, G. S., Shocker, A. D., & Srivastava, R. K. (1979). Customer-oriented approaches to identifying product-markets. *Journal of Marketing, 43*(Fall), 8–19.

Dew, N., & Sarasvathy, S. D. (2003). *Immortal firms in mortal markets? How entrepreneurs deal with "the innovator's dilemma"*. Charlottesville, VA: Darden School of Business Administration, University of Virginia.

Dickson, P. R. (1992). Toward a general theory of competitive rationality. *Journal of Marketing, 56*(January), 69–83.

Dickson, P. R., & Gintner, J. L. (1987). Market segmentation, product differentiation, and marketing strategy. *Journal of Marketing, 51*(April), 1–10.

Dreissigacker, P. (2001). *Reflections on 25 years at Concept2*. Morrisville, VT: Concept2 Inc.

Drucker, P. F. (1985). The discipline of innovation. *Harvard Business Review, May-June*, 67–73.

Eisenhardt, K. M. (1989). Making fast strategic decisions In high-velocity environments. *Academy of Management Journal, 32*(3), 543–577.

Eisenhardt, K. M. (1990). Speed and strategic choice: how managers accelerate decision making. *California Management Review, 32*(3), 39–55.

Friedman, M. (1962). *Capitalism and freedom*. Chicago, IL: University of Chicago Press.

Golann, B. (2006). Achieving growth and responsiveness: Process management and market orientation in small firms. *Journal of Small Business Management, 44*(3), 369–385.

Gort, M., & Keppler, S. (1982). Time paths to diffusion of product innovations. *Economic Journal, 92*, 630–653.

Hamel, G., & Prahalad, C. K. (1989). Strategic intent. *Harvard Business Review, 67*(3), 63–76.

Hayek, F. A. (1948). *Individualism and the economic order*. Chicago, IL: University of Chicago Press.

Hills, G. E., & LaForge, R. W. (1992). Research at the marketing interface to advance entrepreneurship theory. *Entrepreneurship Theory & Practice, 16*(3), 33–59.

Hirschman, A. O. (1984). Against parsimony: Three easy ways of complicating some categories of economic discourse. *American Economic Review, 74*(May), 89–96.

Houston, F. S. (1986). The marketing concept: What it is and what it is not. *Journal of Marketing, 50*(2), 81–87.

Kahneman, D., & Snell, J. (1988). Predicting utility. In R. Hogarth (Ed.), *Decision making*. Chicago, IL: University of Chicago.

Kaldor, A. G. (1971). Imbricative marketing. *Journal of Marketing, 35*(April), 19–25.

Kim, C. W., & Mauborgne, R. (2004). Blue ocean strategy. *Harvard Business Review, 82*(10), 76–84.

Kirzner, I. M. (1973). *Competition and entrepreneurship*. Chicago, IL: University of Chicago Press.

Kirzner, I. M. (1997). Entrepreneurial discover and the competitive market process: An Austrian approach. *Journal of Economic Literature, 35*(1), 60–85.

Kirzner, I. M. (1979). *Perception, opportunity and profit*. Chicago, IL: University of Chicago Press.

Kotler, P. (1973). The major tasks of marketing management. *Journal of Marketing, 37*(October), 42–49.

Kotler, P., & Levy, S. J. (1969). Broadening the concept of marketing. *Journal of Marketing, 33*(January), 10–15.

Kotler, P., & Keller, K. L. (2006). *Marketing management* (12th ed.). Englewood Cliffs, NJ: Prentice Hall.

Lancaster, K. (1971). *Consumer demand: A new approach*. New York, NY: Columbia University Press.

Levitt, T. (1960). Growth and profits through planned marketing innovation. *Journal of Marketing, 24*(1), 1–8.

Lewin, A. Y., & Voberda, H. W (1999). Prolegomena on coevolution: A framework for research on strategy and new organizational forms. *Organizational Science, 10*(5), 519–534.

Mason, C. H. (1990). New product entries and product class demand. *Marketing Science, 9*(1), 58–73.

Miles, M. P., & Darroch, J. (2006). Large firms, entrepreneurial marketing and the cycle of competitive advantage. *European Journal of Marketing, 40*(5/6), 485–501.

Mintzberg, H., & Waters, J. A. (1985). Of strategies, deliberate and emergent. *Strategic Management Journal, 6*(3), 257–273.

Mises, L. V. (1949). *Human action: A treatise on economics*. New Haven, CT: Yale University Press.

Morris, M. H., Schindehutte, M., & LaForge, R. W. (2002). Entrepreneurial marketing: A construct for integrating emerging entrepreneurship and marketing perspectives. *Journal of Marketing Theory and Practice, 10*(4), 1–19.

Morris, M. H., Kuratko, D. K., & Covin, J. G. (2008). *Corporate entrepreneurship and innovation*. Mason, OH: Thomson South-Western.

Nelson, R. R., & Winter, S. G. (1982). *An evolutionary theory of economic change*. Cambridge, MA: Belknap.

Penrose, E. T. (1959). *The theory of the growth of the firm*. New York, NY: Wiley.

Pereira, J. (2007). New exercise targets the less-than-fit. *The Wall Street Journal*, February 1, B1.

Persig, R. M. (1974). *Zen and the art of motorcycle maintenance: An inquiry into values*. New York, NY: Bantam Press.

Porter, M. (1979). How competitive forces shape strategy. *Harvard Business Review* (March/ April).

Robertson, P. L., & Yu, T. F. (2001). Firm strategy, innovation and consumer demand: a market process approach. *Managerial and Decision Economics, 22*(4,5), 183–199.

Sandberg, B. (2005). *The hidden market – Even for those who create it? Customer-related proactiveness in developing radical innovation.* Turku: Turku School of Economics and Business Administration.

Sarasvathy, S. D., & Dew, N. (2004). *When markets are grue.* Darden Business School Working Paper No. 04-06. University of Virginia.

Sarasvathy, S. D., & Dew, N. (2005a). New market creation through transformation. *Journal of Evolutionary Economics, 15,* 533–565.

Sarasvathy, S., & Dew, N. (2005b). New market creation through transformation. *Journal of Evolutionary Economics, 15,* 533–565.

Schindehutte, M., Morris, K., & Kocak, M. H. (2008). Understanding market-driving behavior: The role of entrepreneurship. *Journal of Small Business Management, 46*(1), 4–26.

Schoemaker, P. J. H. (1991). When and how to use scenario planning: A heuristic approach with illustration. *Journal of Forecasting, 10,* 549–561.

Schoemaker, P. J. H. (1995). Scenario planning: A tool for strategic thinking. *Sloan Management Review, Winter,* 25–40.

Schumpeter, J. A. (1934). *The theory of economic development.* Cambridge, MA: Harvard University Press.

Shane, S., & Venkataraman, S. (2000). The promise of entrepreneurship as a field of research. *Academy of Management Review, 25*(1), 217–226.

Simon, H. (1957). *Models of man.* New York, NY: Wiley.

Smith, W. R. (1956). Product differentiation and market segmentation as alternative marketing strategies. *Journal of Marketing, 21*(1), 3–8.

Teece, D., Pisano, G., & Shuen, A. (1997). Dynamic capabilities and strategic management. *Strategic Management Journal, 18*(7), 509–533.

Venkataraman, S. (1997). The distinctive domain of entrepreneurship research, Advances in Entrepreneurship. *Firm Emergence and Growth, 3,* 119–138.

Wernerfelt, B. (1984). A resource based view of the firm. *Strategic Management Journal, 5*(2).

Wiltbank, R., Dew, N., Read, S., & Sarasvathy, S. (2006). What to do next? The case for non-predictive strategy. *Strategic Management Journal, 27,* 981–998.

Chapter 11

Innovative Marketing in SMEs: An "APT" Conceptualization

Abstract

This chapter considers the concept of innovative marketing within the context of SMEs. It is based upon the recognition that SMEs may engage in a form of marketing which may not be readily recognized or understood and which is hindered by resource constraints such as finance and expertise. To overcome such barriers SMEs use more innovative forms of marketing. The chapter first explores literature with specific reference to the characteristics of SME marketing and the characteristics of innovation in business to help identify the nature of innovative marketing in SMEs. Following this exploration, innovative marketing literature is presented and the core variables suggested by literature are encapsulated in a theoretical framework that categorizes SME innovative marketing constructs (marketing variables, modification, integrated marketing, customer focus, market focus, and unique proposition) in accordance with their role in innovative marketing and practices in SMEs.

11.1. Introduction

Innovation is well recognized to be important for business and has been debated in both the entrepreneurship and marketing literatures. In the entrepreneurship literature, innovation has been described as being central to entrepreneurship, the means by which entrepreneurs can exploit change and to provide them with an opportunity to create a different business or service. In the marketing literature, innovation has been described as a marketing-oriented construct that creates an outward looking focus for all the company does and "an environment, a culture — an almost spiritual force — that exists in a company, and ultimately drive value creation" (Buckler, 1997, p. 43). Thus, innovation can be a critical component of

Entrepreneurial Marketing: Global Perspectives
Copyright © 2013 by Emerald Group Publishing Limited
ISBN: 978-1-78190-786-3

competitive advantage in contemporary marketplaces (Miles & Darroch, 2006; Otero-Niera, Tapio Lindman, and Fernandez, 2009).

In practice, marketing in SMEs (small- and medium-size enterprises) is driven by innovation. However, studies of innovative marketing to date have focused on firm-specific characteristics of innovation (Capon, Farley, Lehmann, & Hulbert, 1992; Wolfe, 1994); large firms (Damanpour, 1991, 1988; Kim, 1980); market-based paradigms (Cooper, 1973; Danneels & Kleinschmidt, 2001; Jaworski & Kohli, 1996); SME innovation challenges (Fritz, 1989; Sweeney, 1983); product innovativeness (Schmidt & Calantone, 1998; Zirger, 1997); product or business success (Henard & Szymanski, 2001; Zirger, 1997).

This chapter considers the concept of innovative marketing within the context of SMEs. It is based upon the recognition that SMEs may engage in a form of marketing which may not be readily recognized or understood; "Often, SMEs cannot afford or unable to carry out effective and efficient marketing as prescribed theoretically" (Harrigan, Ramsey, & Ibbotson, 2012, p. 1). The marketing function in SMEs is hindered by resource constraints such as finance, expertise, business size, and customer-related problems (Carson, 1985; Chaston, 1998; Doole, Grimes, & Demack, 2006; Harrigan et al., 2012; Gilmore, Carson, & Rocks, 2006). To overcome such barriers SMEs use more innovative forms of marketing. The chapter first explores literature with specific reference to the characteristics of SME marketing and the characteristics of innovation in business to help identify the nature of innovative marketing in SMEs. Then innovative marketing literature is explored and the core variables suggested by literature are encapsulated in a theoretical framework TAPE (transformation, assimilation, prediction, and exceptionality).

11.2. Characteristics of SME Marketing

For many SMEs the marketing function is peripheral, a perception that has grown from the ability of SMEs to sell without planning their marketing activities (Carson, 1990; Stokes, 2000). This results in a lack of formal and conventional marketing which can be misconstrued as a lack of marketing in some instances. However, SME marketing literature identifies the presence of a form of marketing which is unique to small firms (Carson, 1993; Stokes, 2000), subject to entrepreneurs adapting general marketing concepts and activities for their own purposes (Carson, 1993), while concentrating on incremental innovations (Miles & Darroch, 2006). Instead of focusing on the traditional marketing paradigm of the 4Ps (product, price, place, and promotion), or the 7Ps adopted by service marketing (product, price, place, promotion, people, process, and physical evidence), entrepreneurs stress the importance of the 4Is (information, identification, innovation, and interaction) (Stokes, 2000).

Given its dynamic environment (Murray, O'Driscoll, & Torres, 2002), SME marketing decisions are taken in a haphazard and unstructured manner, which leads to spontaneous, reactive, and dynamic marketing activities. These decisions are also shaped by the enterprise life cycle as SME marketing evolves in response to market demands, new product, and customer requirements, taking into consideration the inherent characteristics and behaviors of the owner/manager, and the size of the firm (Carson, 1993; Gilmore, Carson, & Grant, 2001). Central to all SME marketing, however, is the continual knowledge development of the entrepreneur gained with experience over time (Grant, Gilmore, Carson, Laney, & Pickett, 2001). Therefore, a distinctive managerial style, independence, ownership, having limited resources, and the scale and scope of operations (Carson & McCartan-Quinn, 1995; Gilmore et al., 2006) all combine to shape SME marketing; enabling them to focus on achieving competitive advantage through added value marketing initiatives (Grant et al., 2001).

Competitive advantage is critical for SMEs and emanates from innate SME communication activities and networking activities (Gilmore et al., 2001), limited resources, vulnerability within an uncertain turbulent environment which customers and suppliers have significant impact on, as regards SME competitive advantage (Kesizer, Dijkstra, & Halman, 2002; Keskin, 2006). Within the context of marketing decisions, there is an instinctive understanding that networking beyond the organization enables entrepreneurs to be successful; therefore, entrepreneurs use networking as an inherent marketing tool (Gilmore & Carson, 1999). Such networking provides entrepreneurs with a rich flow of accurate market and customer information, providing the basis for the development of innovative products or processes which improve competitive advantage (Forrest, 1990; Low & MacMillan, 1988). Based on close customer contact SMEs are more flexible, change orientated, and innovative (Moriarty, Jones, Rowley, & Kupiec-Teahan, 2008). This helps to counter the resource imbalance faced by smaller firms in competing with larger firms, encouraging them to adopt more innovative marketing practices, generating more creative, alternative, and instinctive marketing.

These contextual influences, such as adapting marketing activities to combat the challenges of a dynamic competitive environment, resource constraints, distinctive owner/manager decision-making, customer orientation, and networking, all combine to mould SME marketing to maximize SME performance as illustrated in Figure 11.1.

11.3. Characteristics of Innovation in Business

Cumming (1998, p. 22) examined a range of innovation definitions from that given by the Zuckerman Committee in 1968 — *a series of technical, industrial, and commercial steps* — to the 1996 definition given by the CBI/DTI Innovation Unit: "the process of taking new ideas effectively and profitably through to satisfied customers." Notably, in the 30-year span between both definitions the word "innovation" has morphed from being about the process or introduction of change, into a focus on creativity, success, profitability, and customer satisfaction, a change reflected in literature (Johannessen, Olsen, & Lumpkin, 2001; Knight, Omura, Hills, & Muzyka, 1995; McAdam, Stevenson, & Armstrong, 2000). This is echoed by Lee, Shin,

Figure 11.1: Characteristics of SME marketing.

and Park (2011) who note the movement from product and process innovation to a market-oriented strategic process. In an SME context innovation generally refers to the introduction of more competitive and profitable new products or processes which address customer needs more effectively than existing solutions (O'Regan & Ghobadian, 2005; Otero-Niera et al., 2009; Zahra, Nielsen, & Bognar, 1999).

As with SME marketing, the principal source of successful innovation is the knowledge and experience of people within an SME, in particular, the owner/ manager (Cummins, Gilmore, Carson, & O'Donnell, 2000; Knight, 1995). However, to be successful, innovation requires individuals who are able to manage the process from opportunity recognition to customer satisfaction (Kleindl, 1997). This process is enhanced by systems integration, SME flexibility, effective use of technology, and adaptation of solutions used elsewhere within the SME (Knight, 1995; Rothwell, 1994).

SME organizational structures are generally less formal than those within larger organizations and have been identified as being conducive to innovation by encouraging a corporate culture which enables participation, networking, inclusion, and experimentation (Carroll, 2002; Johne & Davies, 2000). Coupled with environmental uncertainties and challenges many SMEs generate an innovative response to establish competitive advantage (Ashford & Towers, 2001; McAdam et al., 2000). This response enables SMEs to exploit new products and markets while improving their cost base and pricing policies (Mole & Worrall, 2001). In addition, it generates new competencies based on current and future market trends and customer demands; all driven by a profit-seeking mission.

"Small firms have been found to have higher rates of innovation compared to their share of sales or number of employees" (Das & He, 2006, p. 114). However studies demonstrate that innovative behavior only occurs when there is a match between the external environment, organizational goals, and an individual's personal values (Kleindl, Mowen, & Chakraborty, 1996). In a more challenging SME environment, there will be a higher level of proactive innovative behavior (Cummins et al., 2000; Morris & Lewis, 1995), which is a finding echoed by Arias-Aranda, Minguela-Rata, and Rodríguez-Duarte (2001) who noted that firms innovate in response to two factors: limited growth conditions and an appropriate business environment.

In exploring innovation within SMEs it is evident that it is based on a unique concept pieced together from existing ideas and concepts (Cummins et al., 2000); its success is determined by its newness, the extent of its adoption (Johannessen et al., 2001), and its translation into an exploitable opportunity for the SME (Arias-Aranda et al., 2001). Thus, innovation in SMEs can be categorized in four terms; first, the nature of innovation; second, continuity of innovation; third, degrees of innovation; and fourth, attributes of innovation (Cooper, 1998; Ettlie & Subramaniam, 2004; Utterback, 1994).

First, addressing the nature of innovation within an SME is dependent on the extent of departure from existing practices. Radical innovations produce fundamental changes in the activities of an organization and large departures from existing practices, whereas incremental innovations are an improvement of an existing process, product, service, or market approach, and involve a lesser degree of departure from existing practices (Ettlie & Subramaniam, 2004; Johannessen et al., 2001). While a small number of SMEs may experience rapid growth as a result of an innovation, the majority successfully engage in a process of incremental innovation which escalates their business (Carroll, 2002; Stokes, 2000).

Second, continuity of innovation within SMEs is explored in the context of market conditions, where discontinuous innovation focuses on altering market conditions to gain competitive advantage (Ettlie & Subramaniam, 2004; Gardner, 1991), and continuous innovation does not require any changes in consumer behavior (Gardner, 1991; Zairi, 1995). This is because the "new" product is similar to its predecessor, thereby minimizing disruption to established behavior patterns, and reducing the risks associated with innovating.

The third categorization of innovation, degrees of innovation, is encapsulated by Johannessen, Olsen, & Olaisen (1999) continuum of the three degrees of innovation. The first degree of innovation focuses on changes within existing production methods and management philosophy. The second addresses changes from one production method and management philosophy to a new type, while third degree concentrates on changes within the new production and management philosophy model.

The final categorization focuses on Rogers' (1995) attributes of innovation model which includes five key elements: relative advantage, compatibility, complexity, trialability, and observability. These attributes reflect the response of customers to the proposed innovation based on the strength of the advantages posed by the innovation (relative advantage) and the extent to which the innovation complements existing experience and needs (compatibility). In addition, the degree of difficulty in

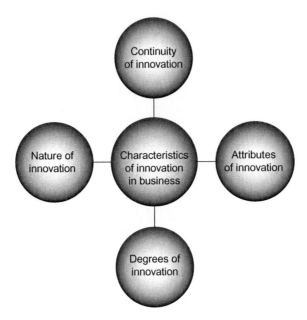

Figure 11.2: Characteristics of innovation in business.

using the innovation is examined (complexity) as is experimentation with the product or service (trialibility), and the visibility of results (observability) (Kautz & Larsen, 2000).

Thus, studies illustrate a change in perception of innovation from change centric to encompassing customer satisfaction, competitive advantage, creativity, and profit, all of which are influenced by an uncertain business environment, resources, the owner/manager, and key personnel. Within this environment, SMEs can successfully use innovation categorizations (see Figure 11.2) such as nature of innovation, continuity of innovation, degrees of innovation, and attributes of innovation to structure their innovative marketing.

11.4. Innovative Marketing in SMEs

Within the complex reality of an SME's environment, marketing is influenced by a number of critical factors such as customers, markets, trends, and competitors whose interaction helps SMEs develop a distinctive marketing style. SME marketing is restricted by resource limitations, including finance, personnel, perception of function, skills and attitudes (Carson & Cromie, 1989), which focuses on the creation and shaping of new markets (Morrish, Miles, & Deacon, 2010). However, these limitations serve to stimulate innovation to overcome the associated obstacles, thus resulting in innovative marketing. Innovative marketing in SMEs has been variously defined in terms of newness and opportunity, "creative, novel, or unusual solutions to problems and needs" including the "development of new products and services, and new processes for performing organisational functions" (Knight et al., 1995, p. 4).

A listing of key innovative marketing variables illustrates that there are six key constituents: marketing variables (product enhancement, alternative channels and methods of product distribution, and altering the marketing mix), modification (proaction and change management), integrated marketing (marketing integration and the permeation of marketing), customer focus, market focus (vision, profit, and market centered), and unique proposition (uniqueness, newness, and unconventionality) as illustrated in Table 11.1.

Table 11.1: Categorization of SME innovative marketing variables.

SME innovative marketing variables	Elements
Marketing variables	Product enhancement (Carson, Gilmore, Cummins, O'Donnell, & Grant, 1998; McEvily, Eisenhardt, & Prescott, 2004; Mostafa, 2005; Nieto, 2004)
	Alteration of the marketing mix (Cummins et al., 2000; Kleindl et al., 1996; Stokes, 1995)
	Alteration of the distribution channel (Carson et al., 1998; Johne, 1999)
Modification	Proaction (Cummins et al., 2000; Kleindl et al., 1996; Stokes, 1995)
	Change (Carroll, 2002; Johne, 1999; McAdam et al., 2000)
Customer focus	Customer focus (Martins & Terblanche, 2003; Morris & Lewis, 1995; Narver, Slater, & MacLachlan, 2004)
Integrated marketing	Marketing integration (Cummins et al., 2000; Knight et al., 1995)
	Permeation of marketing throughout SME (Cummins et al., 2000; Knight et al., 1995)
Market focus	Vision (Ahmed, 1998; Johne, 1999; Kuczmarski, 1996)
	Market centered (Cummins et al., 2000; Johannessen et al., 2001; Kleindl et al., 1996)
	Profit (Cummins et al., 2000; Day & Reynolds, 1997; Kleindl et al., 1996)
Unique proposition	New (Arias-Aranda et al., 2001; Johne, 1999; Kleindl et al., 1996)
	Unique (Johannessen et al., 2001; Martínez Lorente, Dewhurst, & Dale, 1999; McAdam et al., 2000)
	Unconventional (Kleindl et al., 1996; Knight et al., 1995)

Source: O'Dwyer, Gilmore, and Carson (2009).

While this listing of SME innovative marketing variables identifies and facilitates insight into the key constituents of innovative marketing, it does not increase understanding of possible hierarchies or inter-relationships between variables. In addition, the list does not increase comprehension of the role played by such variables in innovative marketing in SMEs. This chapter suggests a framework that categorizes these constructs (marketing variables, modification, integrated marketing, customer focus, market focus, and unique proposition) in accordance with their role in innovative marketing and practices in SMEs.

11.4.1.   Marketing and Modification Variables

In exploring marketing and modification variables, an underlying theme of change in SME innovative marketing activities and practices emerges. For example, product enhancement refers to SMEs engaging in identifying, designing, and implementing product improvements, which *transform* products and services making them more attractive to customers (McEvily et al., 2004; Mostafa, 2005). This is reflected in SMEs alteration of the marketing mix, which involves adapting marketing activities and practices to address aspects of their business (Cummins et al., 2000; Kleindl et al., 1996), including alteration of the distribution channel to gain competitive advantage (Carson et al., 1998; Johne, 1999).

In addition, elements such as proaction and change are also part of the transformation process which is integral to SMEs; in this context proaction refers to SMEs engaging in marketing activities that are based on prediction and anticipation, and that are acting rather than reacting (Cummins et al., 2000; Kleindl et al., 1996). Change refers to the SME actively exploring and embracing beneficial marketing transformations (Carroll, 2002). In this context transformation refers to change, or conversion, to better the nature, function, or condition of marketing activities and practices within SMEs. This process of transformation is one of the key elements of innovation within SMEs, enabling it to transform in anticipation of and in response to internal and external stimulus.

11.4.2.   Integrated Marketing

The incorporation and integration of SME marketing activities and practices into all organizational functions was found to be critical in enabling innovative marketing in SMEs to maximize resource usage (Cummins et al., 2000; Knight et al., 1995). In permeating throughout the organization marketing activities and practices become an integral part of the role of SME personnel in nonmarketing roles (Cummins et al., 2000). This *assimilation* of innovative marketing activities and practices illustrates the process by which marketing activities and practices are absorbed and incorporated into SMEs.

11.4.3. Customer and Market Focus

Customer and market orientation are two SME innovative marketing activities and practices founded on *predicting* and forecasting customer and market needs. Customer focus is a central element of prediction for SMEs, given its ability to maximize customer intelligence to predict and then satisfy customer needs profitably (Martins & Terblanche, 2003; Narver et al., 2004). The significance of prediction is reflected in SME vision, in the articulation of a future-oriented strategic vision for the business (Ahmed, 1998; Johne, 1999; Kuczmarski, 1996), which is market centered in anticipation of market conditions and marketing activities and practices that will maximize effectiveness and profitability (Cummins et al., 2000; Johannessen et al., 2001; Kleindl et al., 1996). This process of prediction in SME innovative marketing refers to the act of forecasting, anticipating, or calculating for the purposes of marketing activities and practices.

11.4.4. Unique Proposition

Explorations of the three variables which comprise unique proposition illustrate the significance of unusual or *exceptional* elements to SMEs innovative marketing activities and practices. In this context the variable "new" refers to SMEs introduction of new products, services, or processes as part of its marketing activities and practices (Arias-Aranda et al., 2001; Johne, 1999) while unique focuses on the uniqueness of each new element introduced (Johannessen et al., 2001; McAdam et al., 2000). In addition, the unconventional aspect of the SME strives for exceptionality by adapting or eschewing the industry norm in its approach to marketing activities and practices for at least some of its business (Kleindl et al., 1996; Knight et al., 1995). Therefore, literature illustrates that SMEs are driven by a need to develop marketing activities and practices that are in some way exceptional. In this context exceptionality denotes unusual skills and accomplishments; these skills and accomplishments contribute to elements of SME business that they deem to be rare or unique.

Based on this exploration of hierarchies and inter-relationships between innovative marketing variables, four key constructs emerge: transformation, assimilation, prediction, and exceptionality. These constructs are reconceptualized in a new innovative marketing framework, TAPE, which takes these constructs and categorizes them in accordance with their role within SMEs, that is, transforming marketing activities, assimilating marketing practices throughout the SME, predicting marketing requirements, and developing an exceptional product or service as depicted in Figure 11.3.

11.5. TAPE Conceptualization of Innovative Marketing: An exploration

In order to test the TAPE conceptualization of innovative marketing and to facilitate the theory building required for this study, eight interpretive case studies were

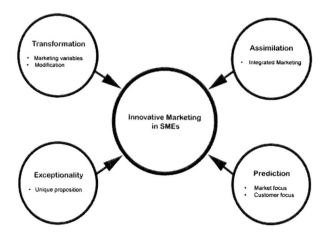

Figure 11.3: TAPE conceptualization of innovative marketing in SMEs.

undertaken with SMEs. This research approach facilitated achieving "substantive meaning and understanding of 'how' and 'why' questions in relation to the phenomena under investigation" (Carson, Gilmore, Perry, & Gronhaug, 2001, p. 64). Following Yin's (1994) suggestion regarding the use of multiple research techniques to build strong case studies, this research utilized converging lines of enquiry based on observation, interviews, participation in meetings, and access to documentation. Purposive sampling was utilized to select the eight participating case SMEs (see Table 11.2 for details) based on their relevance to the research issue, and their ability to highlight key insights regarding the phenomenon being researched (Ettlie & Subramaniam, 2004). In addition the selection of a heterogeneous sample of SMEs (two service, three manufacturing, three service and manufacturing) reflected the ability to extend the theory to a broad range of organizations (Eisenhardt, 1989).

The empirical findings are presented under the constituent elements of TAPE: transformation (marketing variables and modification), assimilation (integrated marketing), prediction (customer and market focus), and exceptionality (unique proposition).

11.5.1. Transformation

Transformation activities include marketing variables, modification, and SME image. Marketing variables contribute strongly to the innovative marketing activities and practices of most (five) of the case companies. This corroborates previous studies which suggest that marketing variables are an important constituent of innovative marketing (Cummins et al., 2000; McEvily et al., 2004; Mostafa, 2005; Nieto, 2004). However, the lack of prioritization of marketing variables by the other three SMEs studied is partially explained by the languid nature of some of the SMEs and the nature of the industry segments in which they operate.

Table 11.2: Case company profile.

Case company	Age	Customer profile
Case A — Systems development solutions company	25 years	International focus — Primarily major international semiconductor vendors
Case B — Software customization consultancy	11 years	National focus — Diverse assortment of world leaders ranging from blue-chip multinationals to smaller companies
Case C — PCB manufacturer	11 years	International focus — Varied, customer base ranging from small, one-man companies to the largest companies in Europe and the United States
Case D — Motor parts manufacturer	39 years	International focus — Agents, wholesalers, and those customers to whom it sells directly
Case E — Electronic display sign company	29 years	International focus — Blue-chip multinationals
Case F — Wood products manufacturer	28 years	International focus — Two main groups, large customers, and SMEs who purchase accordingly
Case G — Print media company	23 years	National focus — two distinct types of customers, its advertisers, and its readers
Case H — Heritage tourism company	46 years	National focus — Tour operators, accommodation providers, incentive houses, corporate, educational groups, individuals/families

In exploring the significance of modification to the innovative marketing activities and practices of the case SMEs, most (six) of the case companies identified modification as being very important in their marketing activities and practices, which supports the findings of previous studies (Carroll, 2002; Cummins et al., 2000). In addition to the variables identified in previous studies, all of the cases in this study demonstrated the significance of image to the transformation aspect of SME innovative marketing. Thus, this exploratory study illustrates that the two transformation elements identified from literature (marketing variables and modification) and one transformation element identified from the findings (image) are all core elements of SME innovative marketing.

11.5.2. Assimilation

Integrated marketing was found to be very important to the innovative marketing activities and practices of all of the case companies, which supports previous studies such as those by Cummins et al. (2000) and Knight et al. (1995). However, as well as exploring the variables identified in previous studies all of the case SMEs strongly emphasized the significance of strategic alliances to their innovative marketing activities and practices. In competing with larger organizations, strategic alliances are used by the case companies to enable them to act with the capacity of a larger firm with expanded resources, skills and abilities, and geographic spread. Thus, the study illustrates that the assimilation element identified from literature (integrated marketing) and one assimilation element identified from the findings (strategic alliances) are core elements of SME innovative marketing.

11.5.3. Prediction

One of the key findings of the study is the identification of market focus as being strongly significant to SMEs' innovative marketing activities and practices in all of the case companies. This supports the literature on innovative marketing where market focus is considered to be a significant constituent of innovative marketing (Cummins et al., 2000; Johannessen et al., 2001; Johne, 1999). In addition, customer focus was also found to be strongly significant to the innovative marketing activities and practices of most of the case SMEs, which corroborates previous studies by Narver et al. (2004) and Martins and Terblanche (2003). Thus, the study illustrates that the two prediction elements identified, customer and market focus, are core elements of SME innovative marketing.

11.5.4. Exceptionality

One of the key findings of the study is that unique proposition was found to be of less significance and demonstrated by fewer cases to be an integral element of SME innovative marketing activities and practices than anticipated, a finding which is in contrast with the predominant body of literature on innovative marketing. Previous studies suggest that the uniqueness of its selling proposition is a significant constituent of SME innovative marketing, a finding which is inconsistent with SME perspectives that incremental and continuous innovations, and the establishment of low levels of newness, uniqueness, and unconventionality, are more acceptable to SME customers (Arias-Aranda et al., 2001; Johannessen et al., 2001; McAdam et al., 2000). SMEs respond in kind, by producing less risk-laden innovations, with less emphasis on new products or services being unique and/or unconventional. Thus, the study illustrates that the exceptionality elements identified from literature (unique proposition, new, and unconventional) and one exceptionality element identified from the findings (product quality) are not core elements of SME innovative marketing.

This analysis illustrates that transformation, assimilation, and prediction are strongly relevant to the innovative marketing activities and practices of the SMEs who participated in this research, a finding which corroborates the extant literature.

However, surprisingly, since it is so strong in the body of literature, exceptionality was not found to be integral to innovative marketing in SMEs, and is, therefore, perceived as being of inconclusive relevance to SME innovative marketing. This empirical finding is remarkable for two reasons: first, it demonstrates the SME factor of variance, that is, the literature is inappropriate when set in the context of SMEs. Second, given that exceptionality and its components (newness, uniqueness, and unconventionality) are perceived to be of significance in the extant literature, however, based on the empirical findings, competitive advantage for SMEs does not appear to be intrinsically linked to exceptionality.

This finding is unexpected, given the consensus in the relevant literature with regard to the argument that the creation and sustenance of competitive advantage stem from engaging in innovative practices, a key factor in SME profitability, long-term growth, and survival (Doyle, 1998; Johannessen et al., 2001; Knight et al., 1995; Pelham & Wilson, 1995; Quinn, 2000; Salavou, 2004; Tower & Hartman, 1990; Zairi, 1995). Furthermore, from an SME perspective, innovation commonly refers to new products or processes which address customer needs more competitively and profitably than existing solutions (Mone, McKinley, & Barker, 1998; O'Regan & Ghobadian, 2005; Zahra et al., 1999).

Consequently, based on the findings from this study, the TAPE framework is condensed to TAP (transformation, assimilation, and prediction). In addition to the variables acknowledged by literature, innovative marketing was found to include the emergent variables: product quality, strategic alliances, and SME image (as illustrated in Figure 11.4). The implication of these additions to the perceived scope of innovative marketing has considerably widened the body of literature to include published sources which were previously loosely associated with marketing. For example, although product quality and SME image could previously have been considered areas related to innovative marketing (through its marketing heritage),

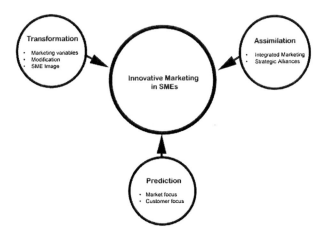

Figure 11.4: Findings: innovative marketing in SMEs — TAP.

strategic alliance literature is not generally incorporated into innovative marketing literature; this research suggests that it should be.

11.6. Innovative Marketing — APT

Based on the empirical findings, the TAPE conceptual model was revised to incorporate SME decision-makers' perspectives of innovative marketing, which includes the emergent issues of product quality, strategic alliances, and SME image. The significance attributed to each of the four elements in the theoretical framework TAPE (transformation, assimilation, prediction, and exceptionality) by the case SMEs contributed further to the revision of the conceptual model from TAPE to TAP. Further exploration of the significance attributed to the elements within TAPE model (see Table 11.3) suggests that the inter-relationships between TAP can be extrapolated to suggest that the most significant element is assimilation, followed by prediction, and then transformation, all of which are strongly significant to innovative marketing in SMEs. The conceptualization of innovative marketing in SMEs can therefore be reordered with the elements appearing in descending order of importance based on the empirical findings,

- assimilation,
- prediction, and
- transformation.

Thus, Innovative Marketing in SMEs is encapsulated in the conceptualization APT, assimilation, prediction, and transformation, based on constructs derived from the extant literature and categorized by a sample of SMEs in accordance with their role within SMEs. Therefore, innovative marketing in SMEs comprises assimilation, that is, the absorption of marketing activities and practices into SMEs incorporating the conceptual variables: marketing integration and permeation of marketing through all organizational functions. Prediction represents the act of forecasting, anticipating, or calculating for the purposes of marketing activities and practices, incorporating the conceptual variables: vision, customer centric, market centered, and profit. And finally, transformation denotes change, or conversion, to better the nature, function, or condition of marketing activities and practices within each case company, incorporating the conceptual variables: proaction, change, product enhancement, altered marketing mix, and altered distribution channels.

11.7. Conclusion

Innovative marketing research has been dominated by firm-specific characteristics of innovations, and/or the effect of the external environment, large firms, market-based constructs, product innovativeness, product, or business success with little research

Table 11.3: Cross-case analysis of innovative marketing.

	Significance of innovative marketing variables to SMEs' innovative marketing activities and practices		
	Strong	**Moderate**	**Weak**
SME1 — Systems development solutions company	Modification	Marketing variables	Unique proposition
	Integrated marketing		
	Market focus		
	Customer focus		
SME2 — Software customization consultancy	Marketing variables	Modification	
	Integrated marketing		
	Market focus		
	Customer focus		
	Unique proposition		
SME3 — PCB manufacturer	Marketing variables		
	Modification		
	Integrated marketing		
	Market focus		
	Customer focus		
	Unique proposition		
SME4 — Motor parts manufacturer	Modification	Customer focus	Marketing variables
	Integrated marketing		Unique proposition
	Market focus		
SME5 — Electronic display sign company	Marketing variables		Unique proposition
	Modification		
	Integrated marketing		
	Market focus		
	Customer focus		

Table 11.3: (*Continued*)

| | Significance of innovative marketing variables to SMEs' innovative marketing activities and practices | | |
	Strong	Moderate	Weak
SME6 — Wood products manufacturer	Marketing variables	Unique proposition	
	Modification		
	Integrated marketing		
	Market focus		
	Customer focus		
SME7 — Print media company	Marketing variables		
	Modification		
	Integrated marketing		
	Market focus		
	Customer focus		
	Unique proposition		
SME8 — Heritage tourism company	Integrated marketing	Marketing variables	Unique proposition
	Market focus	Modification	
	Customer focus		

undertaken into innovative marketing in the context of SMEs. It is evident from the literature that much of the research results in lists of components or attributes of innovative marketing.

This chapter sought to develop a framework that categorizes SME innovative marketing constructs (marketing variables, modification, integrated marketing, customer focus, market focus, and unique proposition) in accordance with their role in innovative marketing and practices in SMEs. Thus, the theoretical framework TAPE (transformation, assimilation, prediction, and exceptionality) was developed to encapsulate and explore elements of SME innovative marketing. Building on these elements the framework categorized these constructs in accordance with their role in transforming SME marketing activities and practices, assimilating marketing practices throughout the SME, predicting SME marketing requirements, and developing an exceptional product or service. The framework facilitates the identification of themes, and the exploration of the significance of such themes which contributed to the theory building required for this research.

Based on the results of this study, the TAPE framework should more appropriately be changed to APT, to reflect the finding that exceptionality is inconclusive in terms of its significance to innovative marketing in SMEs and to reflect the ranked significance of the assimilation, prediction, and transformation to SMEs. The exclusion of exceptionality from the framework is a surprising insight emanating from the research that contradicts previous studies. Traditionally these elements would have been considered to be the core of innovative marketing.

Implications for SMEs arising from this study focus on their need to formulate and maintain a profit-based vision for their business. This will involve focusing on a long-term depiction of a profitable business relating to strategic rather than tactical issues, and should form a major component of business efficiency programs targeted at SME owner/managers. Additionally, SMEs need to further emphasize customer and market focus in their marketing activities and practices, in addition to integrating marketing across all organizational functions. Such focus and integration can best be achieved by educating the heads of function and all employees in the rudiments of innovative marketing with a clear focus on how this function is an integral element of their job.

References

Ahmed, P. (1998). Culture and climate for innovation. *European Journal of Innovation Management, 1*(1), 30–43.

Arias-Aranda, D., Minguela-Rata, B., & Rodríguez-Duarte, A. (2001). Innovation and firm size: An empirical study for Spanish engineering consulting companies. *European Journal of Innovation Management, 4*(3), 133–142.

Ashford, R., & Towers, N. (2001). The impact of effective production activity control systems and the implications for customer relationships in SMEs. *AM conference proceedings*, July 2001.

Buckler, S. A. (1997). The spiritual nature of innovation. *Research-Technology Management, 3*(2), 43–47.

Capon, N., Farley, J. U., Lehmann, D. R., & Hulbert, J. M. (1992). Profiles of product innovators among large US manufacturers. *Management Science, 38*(February), 57–169.

Carroll, D. (2002). Releasing trapped thinking in colleges. Part 2: managing innovation and building innovation into ordinary work. *Quality Assurance in Education, 10*(1), 5–16.

Carson, D. (1985). The evolution of marketing in small firms. *European Journal of Marketing, 5*, 7–16.

Carson, D. (1990). Some exploratory models for assessing small firms' marketing performance (a qualitative approach). *European Journal of Marketing, 234*(11), 8–51.

Carson, D. (1993). A philosophy for marketing education in small firms. *Journal of Marketing Management, 9*, 189–204.

Carson, D. J., & Cromie, S. (1989). Marketing planning in small enterprises: A model and some empirical evidence. *Journal of Marketing Management, 5*(1), 33–51.

Carson, D., Gilmore, A., Cummins, D., O'Donnell, A., & Grant, K. (1998). Price setting in SMEs: Some empirical findings. *Journal of Product and Brand Management, 7*(1), 74–86.

Carson, D., Gilmore, A., Perry, C., & Gronhaug, K. (2001). *Qualitative marketing research.* London: Sage Publications.

Carson, D., & McCartan-Quinn, D. (1995). Non-practice of theoretically based marketing in small business — Issues arising and their implications. *Journal of Marketing Theory and Practice, 3*(4), 24–31.

Chaston, I. (1998). Evolving "new marketing" philosophies by merging existing concepts: Application of process within small high-technology firms. *Journal of Marketing Management, 14*(4), 273–291.

Cooper, A. C. (1973). Technical entrepreneurship: what do we know? *Research and Development Management, 3*(2), 59–64.

Cooper, J. R. (1998). A multidimensional approach to the adoption of innovation. *Management Science, 36*(8), 493–502.

Cumming, B. S. (1998). Innovation overview and future challenges. *European Journal of Innovation Management, 1*(1), 21–29.

Cummins, D., Gilmore, A., Carson, D., & O'Donnell, A. (2000). What is innovative marketing in SMEs? Towards a conceptual and descriptive framework. *AMA conference proceedings,* July 2000.

Damanpour, F. (1988). Innovation type, radicalness, and the adoption process. *Communication Research, 15,* 545–567.

Damanpour, F. (1991). Organisational innovation: A meta-analysis of effects of determinants and moderators. *Academy of Management Journal, 34*(3), 555–590.

Danneels, E., & Kleinschmidt, E. J. (2001). Product innovativeness from the firm's perspective: Its dimensions and their relations with project selection and performance. *Journal of Product Innovation Management, 18*(6), 357–373.

Das, T. K., & He, I. Y. (2006). Entrepreneurial firms in search of established partners: Review and recommendations. *International Journal of Entrepreneurial Behaviour and Research, 12*(3), 114–143.

Day, J., & Reynolds, P. L. (1997). Considering the marketing/entrepreneurship interface: Approaches and directions, 1987 to 1995. *Research at the marketing/entrepreneurship interface, Conference proceedings,* University of Illinois, Chicago, IL (pp. 97–112).

Doole, I., Grimes, T., & Demack, S. (2006). An exploration of the management practices and processes most closely associated with high levels of export capability in SMEs. *Marketing Intelligence and Planning, 24*(6), 632–647.

Doyle, P. (1998). Innovate or die. *Marketing Business, 20,* 3.

Eisenhardt, K. M. (1989). Building theories from case study research. *Academy of Management Review, 14*(4), 532–550.

Ettlie, J. E., & Subramaniam, M. (2004). Changing strategies and tactics for new-product development. *Journal of Product Innovation Management, 21,* 95–109.

Forrest, J. E. (1990). Strategic alliances and the small technology-based firm. *Journal of Small Business Management, 28*(3), 37–45.

Fritz, W. (1989). Determinants of product innovation activities. *European Journal of Marketing, 23*(10), 32–43.

Gardner, D. M. (1991). Exploring the marketing/entrepreneurship interface. Research at the marketing/entrepreneurship interface, *Conference proceedings,* University of Illinois at Chicago (pp. 3–21).

Gilmore, A., & Carson, D. (1999). Entrepreneurial marketing by networking. *New England Journal of Entrepreneurship, 12*(2), 31–38.

Gilmore, A., Carson, D., & Grant, K. (2001). SME marketing in practice. *Marketing Intelligence and Planning, 1,* 6–11.

Gilmore, A., Carson, D., & Rocks, S. (2006). Networking in SMEs: Evaluating its contribution to marketing activity. *International Business Review, 15,* 278–293.

Grant, K., Gilmore, A., Carson, D., Laney, R., & Pickett, B. (2001). Experiential research methodology: An integrated academic-practitioner "team" approach. *Qualitative Market Research: An International Journal, 4*(2), 66–75.

Harrigan, P., Ramsey, E., & Ibbotson, P. (2012). Exploring and explaining SME marketing: Investigating e-CRM using a mixed methods approach. *Journal of Strategic Marketing.* doi:10.1080/0965254x.2011.6060911

Henard, D. H., & Szymanski, D. M. (2001). Why some new products are more successful than others. *Journal of Marketing Research, 38*(3), 362–375.

Jaworski, B. J., & Kohli, A. K. (1996). Market orientation: review, refinement, and roadmaps. *Journal of Market Focused Management, 1*(2), 119–135.

Johannessen, J., Olsen, B., & Lumpkin, G. T. (2001). Innovation as newness: what is new, how new, and new to whom? *European Journal of Innovation Management, 4*(1), 20–31.

Johannessen, J.-A., Olsen, B., & Olaisen, J. (1999). Aspects of innovation theory based on knowledge management. *International Journal of Information Management, 19*(1), 121–139.

Johne, A. (1999). Successful market innovation. *European Journal of Innovation Management, 2*(1), 6–11.

Johne, A., & Davies, R. (2000). Innovation in medium-sized insurance companies: how marketing adds value. *The International Journal of Bank Marketing, 18*(1), 6–14.

Kautz, K., & Larsen, E. A. (2000). Disseminating quality management and software process improvement innovations. *Information Technology and People, 13*(1), 11–26.

Keskin, H. (2006). Market Orientation, learning orientation, and innovation capabilities in SMEs: An extended model. *European Journal of Innovation Management, 9*(4), 396–417.

Kesizer, J. A., Dijkstra, L., & Halman. (2002). Explaining innovative efforts of SMEs: An exploratory survey among SMEs in the mechanical and electrical engineering sector in The Netherlands. *Technovation, 22,* 1–13.

Kim, L. (1980). Organisational innovation and structure. *Journal of Business Research, 8*(2), 225–245.

Kleindl, B. (1997). Constituency group innovativeness: An empirical test of individual, firm and environmental innovativeness. *Research at the marketing/entrepreneurship interface, Conference proceedings,* University of Illinois at Chicago (pp. 583–596).

Kleindl, B., Mowen, J., & Chakraborty, G. (1996). Innovative market orientation an alternative strategic orientation in marketing. *Research at the marketing/entrepreneurship interface, Conference proceedings,* University of Illinois at Chicago (pp. 211–228).

Knight, G., Omura, G. S., Hills, G. E., & Muzyka, D. F. (1995). Research in marketing and entrepreneurship: An empirical analysis and comparison with historic trends. *Research at the marketing/entrepreneurship interface, Conference proceedings,* University of Illinois at Chicago (pp. 1–22).

Knight, R. M. (1995). Barriers to innovations: A cross-cultural comparison. *Research at the marketing/entrepreneurship interface, Conference proceedings,* University of Illinois at Chicago, pp. 453–480.

Kuczmarski, T. D. (1996). What is innovation? The art of welcoming risk. *Journal of Consumer Marketing, 13*(5), 7–11.

Lee, Y., Shin, J., & Park, Y. (2011). The changing pattern of SMEs innovativeness through business model globalisation. *Technological Forecasting and Social Change.* doi:10.1016/j.techfore.2011.10.008.

Low, M. B., & MacMillan, I. C. (1988). Entrepreneurship: Past research and future challenges. *Journal of Management, 14,* 139–161.

Martins, E., & Terblanche, F. (2003). Building organisational culture that stimulates creativity and innovation. *European Journal of Innovation Management, 6,* 64–74.

Martínez Lorente, A. R., Dewhurst, F., & Dale, B. G. (1999). TQM and business innovation. *European Journal of Innovation Management, 2*(1), 12–19.

McAdam, R., Stevenson, P., & Armstrong, G. (2000). Innovative change management in SMEs: Beyond continuous improvement. *Logistics Information Management, 13*(3), 138–149.

McEvily, S. K., Eisenhardt, K. M. M., & Prescott, J. E. (2004). The global acquisition, leverage, and protection of technological competencies. *Strategic Management Journal, 25*(8/9), 713–722.

Miles, M. P., & Darroch, J. (2006). Large firms, entrepreneurial marketing processes, and the cycle of competitive advantage. *European Journal of Marketing, 40*(5/6), 485–501.

Mole, K., & Worrall, L. (2001). Innovation, business performance and regional competitiveness in the West Midlands: Evidence from the West Midlands Business Survey. *European Business Review, 13*(6), 353–364.

Mone, M. A., McKinley, W., & Barker, V. L. (1998). Organisational decline and innovation: A contingency framework. *Academy of Management Review, 23*(1), 115–132.

Moriarty, J., Jones, R., Rowley, J., & Kupiec-Teahan, B. (2008). Marketing in small hotels: A qualitative study. *Marketing Intelligence and Planning, 26*(3), 293–315.

Morris, M., & Lewis, P. S. (1995). The determinants of entrepreneurial activity: Implications for marketing. *European Journal of Marketing, 29*(7), 31–48.

Morrish, S. C., Miles, M. P., & Deacon, J. H. (2010). Entrepreneurial marketing: Acknowledging the entrepreneur and customer-centric interrelationship. *Journal of Strategic Marketing, 18*(4), 303–316.

Mostafa, M. (2005). Factors affecting organisational creativity and innovativeness in Egyptian business organisations: An empirical investigation. *Journal of Management Development, 24*(1), 7–33.

Murray, J. A., O'Driscoll, A., & Torres, A. (2002). Discovering diversity in marketing practice. *European Journal of Marketing, 36*(3), 373–390.

Narver, J. C., Slater, S. F., & MacLachlan, D. L. (2004). Responsive and proactive market orientation and new-product success. *Journal of Product Innovation Management, 21*(5), 334–347.

Nieto, M. (2004). Basic propositions for the study of the technological innovation process in the firm. *European Journal of Innovation Management, 7*(4), 314–324.

O'Dwyer, M., Gilmore, A., & Carson, D. (2009). Innovative Marketing in SMEs: An empirical study. *Journal of Strategic Marketing, 17*(5), 383–396.

O'Regan, N., & Ghobadian, A. (2005). Innovation in SMEs: The impact of strategic orientation and environmental perceptions. *International Journal of Productivity and Performance Management, 54*(2), 81–97.

Otero-Niera, C., Tapio Lindman, M., & Fernandez, M. J. (2009). Innovation and performance in SME furniture industries: An international comparative case study. *Marketing Intelligence and Planning, 27*(2), 216–232.

Pelham, A., & Wilson, D. T. (1995). *Does market orientation matter for small firms?* Working Paper No. 95-102, April, pp. 1–35.

Quinn, J. B. (2000). Outsourcing innovation: the new engine of growth. *Sloan Management Review, 41*(4), 13–28.

Rogers, E. M. (1995). *Diffusion of innovation.* New York, NY: Free Press Publications.

Rothwell, R. (1994). Towards the fifth-generation innovation process. *International Marketing Review, 11*(1), 7–31.

Salavou, H. (2004). The concept of innovativeness: Should we need to focus? *European Journal of Innovation Management, 7*(1), 33–44.

Schmidt, J. B., & Calantone, R. J. (1998). Are really new-product development projects harder to shut down? *Journal of Product Innovation Management, 15*(2), 111–123.

Stokes, D. (1995). *Small business management* (2nd ed.). London: DP Publishing.

Stokes, D. (2000). Putting entrepreneurship into marketing: The processes of entrepreneurial marketing. *Journal of Research in Marketing and Entrepreneurship, 2*(1, Spring), 1–16.

Sweeney, G. P. (1983). *New entrepreneurship and the smaller firm,* Campus, Frankfurt. New York, NY.

Tower, C. B., & Hartman, E. A. (1990). Relationships between organisational variables and innovation in small businesses. *Research at the marketing/entrepreneurship interface, Conference proceedings,* University of Illinois at Chicago (pp. 200–211).

Utterback, J. M. (1994). *Mastering the dynamics of innovation.* Boston, MA: Harvard Business School Press.

Wolfe, R. A. (1994). Organisational innovation: Review, critique and suggested research directions. *Journal of Management Studies, 31*(3), 405–431.

Yin, R. K. (1994). *Case study research: Design and methods* (2nd ed.). Thousand Oaks, CA: Sage.

Zahra, S. A., Nielsen, A. P., & Bognar, W. C. (1999). Corporate entrepreneurship, knowledge and competence development. *Entrepreneurship: Theory and Practice, 23*(3), 169–189.

Zairi, M. (1995). Moving from continuous to discontinuous innovation in FMCG: A re-engineering perspective. *World Class Design to Manufacture, 2*(5), 32–37.

Zirger, B. J. (1997). The influence of development experience and product innovativeness on product outcome. *Technology analysis and Strategic Management, 9*(3), 287–297.

Chapter 12

Social Media, Customer Relationship Management, and SMEs

Abstract

This chapter will discuss how SMEs carry out customer relationship management (CRM). More than that, it will show how SMEs are utilizing new social media technologies as part of their "social CRM" activities. Findings from a comprehensive quantitative study of 159 SMEs are presented and shed significant light on the use of social media technologies in SMEs' customer relationships. Findings span a range of constructs including customer relationship orientation, social media technology use, customer engagement, customer information, and customer relationship performance. Marketing in SMEs is obviously different from marketing in larger organizations, but many of the strategies and subsequent terminologies that are often related to marketing in large organisations actually originate in small business. CRM is one such means of marketing. Thus we draw theoretical implications for the CRM and SME domains. This research has implications for SME marketers, where a clearer picture of the role of social media technologies in customer relationships is outlined. For social media marketing practitioners in general, framing social media within CRM may help to clarify aims, objectives, strategies, and tactics in the use of social media. Little research has made the link between CRM and SMEs, or linked social media and CRM. This chapter makes the link between all three domains, and illustrates the theoretical and practical implications of doing so.

This chapter will discuss how SMEs carry out customer relationship management (CRM). More than that, it will show how SMEs are utilising new social media technologies as part of their "social CRM" activities. Marketing in SMEs is obviously different from marketing in larger organisations, but many of the strategies and subsequent terminologies that are often related to marketing in large organisations actually originated in small business. CRM is one such means of marketing.

Entrepreneurial Marketing: Global Perspectives
Copyright © 2013 by Emerald Group Publishing Limited
All rights of reproduction in any form reserved
ISBN: 978-1-78190-786-3

12.1. SME Marketing

The importance of SMEs in the local, national, and global economies is clear. Thus, more research should focus on what they do well and not so well so as to provide them with the guidance and support that they require. SMEs struggle with a lack of resources, whether that is finance, time, expertise, influence, or people (Carson, Cromie, McGowan, & Hill, 1995; Harrigan, Ramsey, & Ibbotson, 2012). This is what sets them aside from larger organizations with marketing departments, budgets, plans, and reviews.

The type of marketing in SMEs is focused around customer relationships. This is where they draw on the advantages of being small, which are: closeness to customers, easy access to market information, flexibility, speed of response, opportunity-focused, and loyalty of employees (Carson et al., 1995; Harrigan et al., 2012). Specifically, SMEs do have a tendency to form closer relationships with customers than larger organizations, which exhibits many of the principles of relationship marketing and specifically CRM theory (Zontanos & Anderson, 2004). Of course, the terminology and large organization complexity of CRM are foreign to the vast majority of owner-managers (Zontanos & Anderson, 2004). However, that does not mean that it is not them that are actually *doing* CRM properly.

The approaches taken to marketing by SMEs are pragmatic adaptations of marketing theory in order to render relevance to the way they do business (Carson & Gilmore, 2000). Marketing in SMEs focuses on solutions that are simple and workable, affordable and efficient, and, most importantly, in line with their unique strategy and culture (Carson & Gilmore, 2000). For SMEs, their most valuable asset is their core customer base; thus, they devote resources to servicing this, which involves managing relationships with customers. In essence, this is CRM.

12.2. Social CRM

Previous research has asserted that truly effective relationship marketing cannot exist without the use of technology (Chen & Ching, 2007; Hamid & Kassim, 2004; Zineldin, 2000). With the advancement of information technology, marketing practitioners have developed new ways to interact with customers. These "CRM technologies" range from dedicated software package solutions provided by firms such as Oracle, Microsoft, or Sage right through to relatively simple websites, databases, and e-mail packages (Boulding, Staelin, Ehret, & Johnston, 2005; Harrigan, Ramsey, & Ibbotson, 2011). In any case, it is undeniable that technology is a key enabler of CRM, facilitating two key processes: engagement with customers, and the acquisition, management, and analysis of data on customers (Harrigan et al., 2011; Jayachandran, Sharma, Kaufman, & Raman, 2005). In turn these two processes can feed into numerous CRM performance outcomes. Previous research has found performance outcomes such as increased market awareness, reduced marketing costs, increased customer loyalty, increased competitiveness, and increased customer profitability (e.g., Harrigan et al., 2011).

Social Media Technologies is the "group of Internet-based applications that build on the ideological and technological foundations of Web 2.0 and that allow the creation and exchange of User-Generated Content" (Kaplan & Haenlein, 2010, p. 61). Social media has experienced exponential growth in recent years, among both consumers and marketers. The majority of marketers (58 percent) are using social media for 6 hours or more each week, and more than a third (34 percent) invest 11 or more hours weekly (Stelzner, 2011). The usage of social media among consumers generally has increased exponentially over recent years where 2.09 billion people now use the Internet.[1] More than 3 million English articles can be read on Wikipedia, and video of 20 hours is uploaded to YouTube every minute of a day (Shepherd, 2011). Even from these few statistics provided it is clear that social media technologies impact on consumers and therefore on business, whether marketers are actively engaging with the tools or not.

The latest trend in CRM technology use is to take advantage of these social media technologies, whose relational properties and characteristics are particularly suited to customer interactions. The use of these technologies in CRM in very different to previous, dedicated. or "off-the-shelf" CRM software packages that sought to collect, process, and manipulate customer data to feed into marketing decision-making (Jayachandran et al., 2005). Social media technologies are not designed for organisational CRM purposes, but nonetheless possess all the capabilities to facilitate customer relationships. This chapter is based on the premise that CRM technologies are not limited to dedicated software packages and that they have expanded to include social media technologies such as Facebook, Twitter, LinkedIn, YouTube, Google (+ and Analytics), and many more blogs and peer-to-peer websites. All of these tools are also experiencing exponential growth in the mobile arena, with consumer smartphone usage increasing rapidly. In short, social media is a platform where opinions, perspectives, insights, and media can be shared among consumers and is an area that marketing and CRM practitioners can ill-afford to ignore (Nair, 2011).

Greenberg (2010, p. 34) defines social CRM as:

> a philosophy and a business strategy, supported by a technology platform, business rules, workflow, processes and social characteristics, designed to engage the customer in a collaborative conversation in order to provide mutually beneficial value in a trusted and transparent business environment. It's the company's programmatic response to the customer's control of the conversation.

This definition includes the central principle of customer engagement, which has been missing from earlier CRM models.

---

1. Please see http://www.internetworldstats.com/stats.htm (accessed on September 17, 2011).

12.3. Social CRM in SMEs

SMEs, by using technologies such as social media, websites, e-mail, analytics tools, and databases to build on traditional CRM activations, can improve their inherent marketing orientation and customer focus (Harrigan, Ramsey, & Ibbotson, 2008; Simmons, Armstrong, & Durkin, 2008). Literature reports that CRM can produce a range of benefits to larger organisations, such as enhanced customer service, improved customer loyalty, increased personalisation (Harrigan et al., 2011) and market awareness (Boulding et al., 2005; Jayachandran et al., 2005), creation of costs savings in marketing, generation of sales (Payne & Frow, 2005), and improved overall profitability (Reichheld & Sasser, 1990; Reinartz, Krafft, & Hoyer, 2004; Storbacka, Strandvik, & Grönroos, 1994). CRM can also help SMEs compete more effectively in international markets (Harrigan et al., 2011).

There may be two main areas of CRM implementation in SMEs, customer engagement and customer information management (O'Cass & Weerawardena, 2009; O'Dwyer, Gilmore, & Carson, 2009).

12.3.1. *Customer Engagement*

Communication with customers in SMEs tends to be constant, informal, and open, with the purpose of creating mutual value (Gilmore, Gallagher, & Henry, 2007; Street & Cameron, 2007). There also tends to be a social aspect of these relationships, which takes the form of face-to-face contact (Gilmore et al., 2007). The notion of engagement with customers, which is a relatively recent area for academic research, is actually something that SMEs are particularly capable of. SMEs tend to involve their customers as active partners in the co-creation of products and services, due to the fact that they tend to have fewer customers and also place so much emphasis on customer satisfaction and retention (Harrigan et al., 2012; Zontanos & Anderson, 2004).

For larger organisations, social media technologies are enabling a level of customer engagement previously impossible due to the number of customers (Hennig-Thurau et al., 2010). Twitter and Facebook are tools that can be used to "crowd source" (i.e., gather views from a large number of customers), to provide customer service, to inform, educate and entertain customers, and to inspire viral marketing (Hennig-Thurau et al., 2010; Hoyer, Chandy, Dorotic, Krafft, & Singh, 2010; Krishnamurthy, 2009). Thus, engaging with customers through social media to create value through personal relationships can be seen as an extension of simply communicating with customers (Bijmolt et al., 2010; Kumar et al., 2010). The growth in importance of customer engagement has been recognized by the Advertising Research Foundation, the American Association of Advertising Agencies, and the Association of National Advertisers who have called for metrics to try to measure it (Dwyer, 2007).

For SMEs, the question exists if they can adopt these open source technologies to improve engagement with their own customers, getting even closer to them and letting them get closer to the business. Of course, face-to-face engagement is still vital, but online means could facilitate and improve overall engagement with customers particularly in growth-oriented and international businesses.

12.3.2. Customer Information Management

In order to meet the needs of customers effectively and efficiently SMEs must maintain a level of engagement with customers, but they must also be able to acquire and manage information on their customers (Hutchinson & Quintas, 2008; Payne & Frow, 2005). Such information is invaluable in marketing decision-making, specifically in recording customers' personal details, unique requirements, views, satisfaction level, purchase behavior, value to the firm, and projected future orders (Coltman, 2007; Keh, Nguyen, & Ng, 2007; Rai, Patnayakuni, & Seth, 2006). Where SMEs do not have the resources to engage in formal market research, the relationships they maintain with customers are key sources of valuable information (Hutchinson & Quintas, 2008; Keh et al., 2007).

The role of "back office" technologies such as web analytics tools, social CRM tools, and databases in customer information management lies in assisting the administration, storage, and processing of customer data. For SMEs, it may be possible to personalize product and service offerings to certain customers, treat their most valuable customers differently, and better predict customer behavior both online and offline (e.g. Hutchinson & Quintas, 2008; Parvatiyar & Sheth, 2001; Payne & Frow, 2005; Ryals & Knox, 2001).

CRM in SMEs should comprise information capture, information integration, information access, and information use. The notion of information capture is derived from market orientation literature (e.g., Kohli & Jaworski, 1990). Looking at social media, virtual communities collect a tremendous amount of data, most of which is both real-time and indefinite (Hennig-Thurau et al., 2010; Konus, Verhoef, & Neslin, 2008). However, the challenge for marketers is being able to filter usable information from such communities (Hennig-Thurau et al., 2010). Feedback on products and customer service can be gathered from social media sources, as well as general market related data.

Information integration requires the assimilation of customer information from all touch points, not just social media, to develop a single view of the customer (Jayachandran et al., 2005). Instead of customer information being stored in different systems, or not being stored at all, it needs to be stored in one place. Advances in CRM technology, at least prior to the social media revolution, have made it possible to facilitate such integration at least in large organisations. Integrating information from social media sources may be even more challenging than traditional sources of information, where information is not necessarily quantitative like accounting and sales data but is no less valuable with the customer and market insight it can provide (Bijmolt et al., 2010).

Information access means the marketer or owner-manager is actually having access to all the information on customers (Jayachandran et al., 2005). This means the data being in a simple and usable format that makes actionable sense. Does the information allow for any improvement to be made in existing face-to-face relationships?

Lastly and linked to information access, *information use* refers to the actual usage of customer information within the organisation. Really, customer information should be used to direct and inform customer engagement. Do SMEs know what customers or potential customers refer most, influence most, or possess most knowledge about their product or service (Kumar et al., 2010)? This is in addition to the more traditional measure of customer lifetime value; as in what customers have the highest purchase potential.

12.4. Customer Relationship Performance

Customer relationship performance is the outcome of implementing CRM successfully, bringing value and ultimately profits to the organisation and to the customers (Azila & Noor, 2011). The benefits include increased market awareness, increased customer loyalty, more effective and efficient marketing, better customer service and support, increased competitiveness, reduced costs, and increased profitability (Harrigan et al., 2011).

If organisations are utilising social CRM technologies to enable customer engagement initiatives and relational information processes, then there is potential for enhanced customer relationship performance, namely customer satisfaction and loyalty (Jayachandran et al., 2005).

However, there are certain challenges for SMEs trying to integrate technologies into existing customer relationship activities. First and foremost is the potential risk to carefully nurture personal relationships with customers (Gummesson, 2002; Jack, Moult, Anderson, & Dodd, 2010; Kumar & Reinartz, 2006; Piccoli & Ives, 2005). Another challenge is the level of strategic thought and direction required of the owner-manager. Previous research has shown similar initiatives to be short-term tactical projects, rather longer-term integrated strategies (Hills, Hultman, & Miles, 2008; Piercy, 2009; Quader, 2007). Another challenge is the obvious relative lack of financial resources and marketing and technological expertise among owner-managers of SMEs (Admiraal & Lockhorst, 2009; Blili & Raymond, 1993; Street & Meister, 2004). For SMEs and customers alike there may also be a lack of trust in electronic channels, where customers are wary of divulging personal and financial details electronically (Houghton & Winklhofer, 2004).

In summation, social CRM in SMEs is not a simple case of imposing technology on existing customer relationships. It requires a careful strategic approach where the technology is always seen as the enabler of customer-oriented approaches (Chen & Ching, 2007; Kumar & Reinartz, 2006). In larger organisations, benefits of social CRM have been reported as enhanced customer service, improved customer loyalty, reduced marketing costs, increased sales, and improved overall profitability. It is proposed that, for SMEs to reap similar benefits, they may only need to make relatively small technological investments to build an approach to marketing that enables real competitive advantage, even on a global scale. Previous and copious research has advocated the benefits of social CRM for larger organisation, but few studies have explored the benefits, challenges, and general issues of social CRM for SMEs and their owner-managers.

12.5. Research

We have carried out research in the London area to ascertain the level of social CRM in SMEs. We developed a survey based on a combination of previous CRM measures and new measures developed from relevant literature. The survey was pre-tested and then distributed via e-mail to the e-mail address provided by the business. These e-mail addresses were sourced from a dataset provided by CorpData. Out of a sample of 3000 we received 159 usable responses, which is a response rate of 5.3 percent.

12.6. The State of Play

Figure 12.1 shows that almost half of our respondents (48.1 percent) were businesses employing 10–49 people. There were also 17.3 percent of businesses employing less than 10 people. This has implications for the remaining findings, where a business employing up to 250 people will be very different from one employing less than 50, even though both may be classified as an SME.

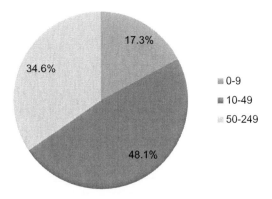

Figure 12.1: Number of employees.

12.6.1. Customer Relationship Orientation

Looking at the customer relationship orientation of SMEs, we report agreement on a range of issues. Most agreement is found with the statement that customer relationships are a valuable asset (mean = 4.71). Customer retention is also considered important and both management and staff are focused on relationships. The least agreement was reported with customising product/service offerings to individuals, but this agreement was still strong at 4.31. In summation, it is clear that the SMEs in this study possess a strong customer relationship orientation (Figure 12.2).

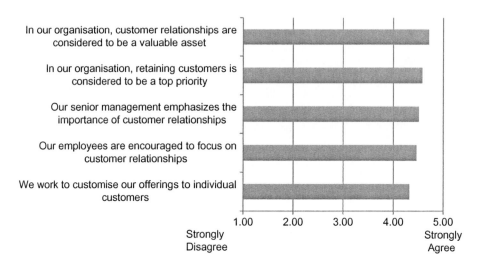

Figure 12.2: Customer relationship orientation.

12.6.2. CRM Technology Use

Looking at the social media or CRM technologies used, LinkedIn is rated the most popular with mean agreement of 3.56. Next are Twitter (3.33), the Company Blog (3.25), and Facebook (3.04). The other tools, including YouTube, were less popular. In fact, none of these mean levels of agreement are particularly high. Perhaps this reflects an uncertainty among SMEs about which social media to focus on for CRM, out of the ever increasing range available (Figure 12.3).

SMEs report that social media enables a range of CRM processes, most notably customized customer communications (3.37) and providing customers with information (3.15). It also provides the SME with information on customers, such as sales opportunities and responses to marketing efforts. It should also be noted that where agreement with the last item ("We don't see social media as useful for CRM") is low, this indicates positivity toward social CRM. However, there is a range of CRM processes not particularly affected by social media, notably the calculation of customer loyalty, retention rates, customer profitability, and even identification of customer preferences (Figure 12.4).

Focusing on the ability of social media technologies to collect forms of data, SMEs report that they collect general online customer data via social media (3.25).

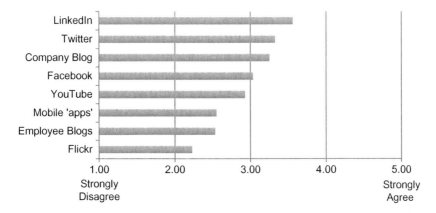

Figure 12.3: CRM technologies Used.

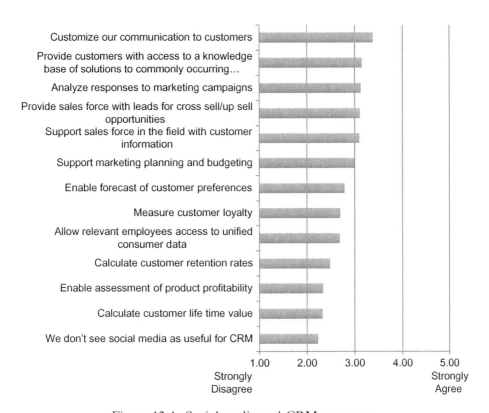

Figure 12.4: Social media and CRM processes.

There is less agreement with social media's ability to collect the other forms of data, such as customer interaction, service demographic, and lifestyle data (Figure 12.5).

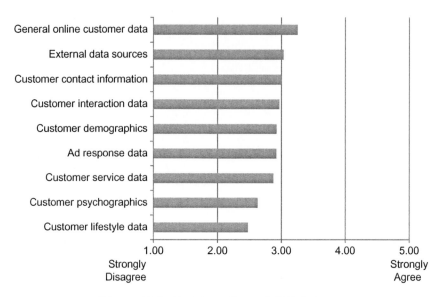

Figure 12.5: Social media and CRM data.

12.6.3.   Customer Engagement

Moving on to the customer engagement construct, Figure 12.6 illustrates that social media is facilitating communication with customers, notably in a two-way (3.92) and interactive (4.04) manner. However, social media is not reported as to bring customers into marketing decision-making, or co-creating.

Figure 12.7 focuses on online customer communities, which are viewed as a way of engaging with customers (3.65) and creating loyal customers (3.51). There is some agreement with the general statement that the range of social media is a positive thing for SMEs (3.21). As for the negatives, SMEs tend not to participate in customer-owned communities (2.95) and communities in general do not tend to be seen as central in marketing (2.77 and 2.67).

Figure 12.8 presents data on how SMEs are managing online communities, and the data shows that in general they are not. SMEs do agree that word-of-mouth is an important issue for them online (3.87) and they agree that transparency is a key issue in online communities (3.66). There is moderate agreement with issues around having conversations with customers (3.20), monitoring customers (3.14), and picking out important customers (3.15). However, there is less agreement with other areas such as the proactive (2.90) and strategic (2.75) use of these communities. It also appears that SMEs do not try to control conversations (2.58), nor do they find that customers use communities mainly to make negative comments (2.55).

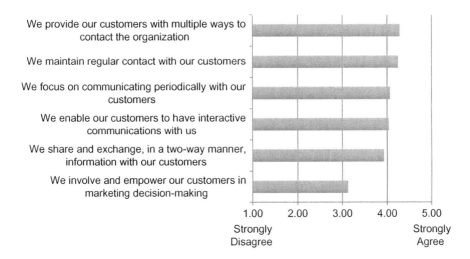

Figure 12.6: Communication with customers.

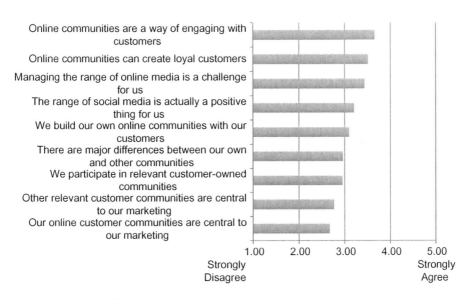

Figure 12.7: Online customer communities.

Figure 12.9 presents data around the use of mobile technologies for CRM. SMEs are reporting challenges in this area, where they find too many challenges in engaging with customer communities via mobile or smartphones (3.20). In general, they are not taking advantages of the extra communication or engagement potential that mobile technologies and apps offer for CRM.

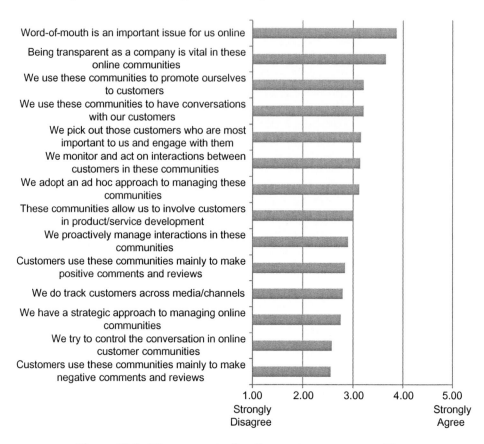

Figure 12.8: Management of online customer communities.

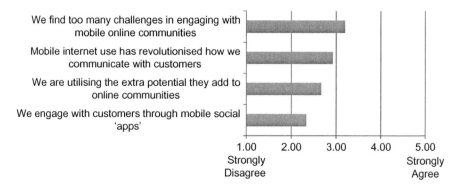

Figure 12.9: Mobile technologies.

12.6.4. Customer Information Management

Figure 12.10, on information capture, tells the story that SMEs do collect customer information, but generally not from newer social media sources. For example, low agreement is reported with the collection of customer information from online customer communities (2.96) and from clickstream data such as Google Analytics (2.22). In fact, low agreement is reported with the collection of information from external sources generally (2.79).

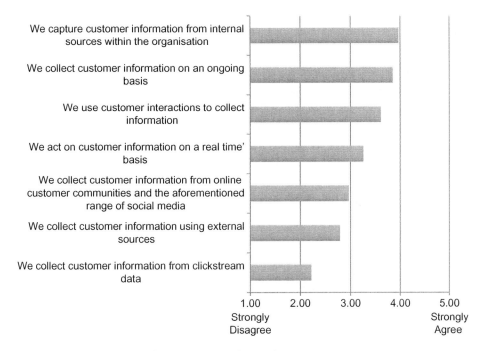

Figure 12.10: Information capture.

Looking at information integration, SMEs do report that they are integrating customer information from different communication channels and customer interactions (3.85 and 3.69). This information then does tend to be brought together (i.e., integrated) (3.49). There is slightly less agreement with the statement that social media information is integrated just like other information (3.00). Finally, SMEs report that the amount of information available online is not particularly overwhelming for them (2.91) (Figure 12.11).

Looking at information access, findings related to the first three items in Figure 12.12 show that employees within the business have access to customer information (3.80, 3.68, and 3.68). The other items around analytical skills,

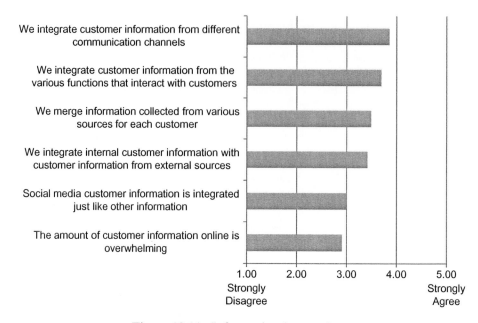

Figure 12.11: Information integration.

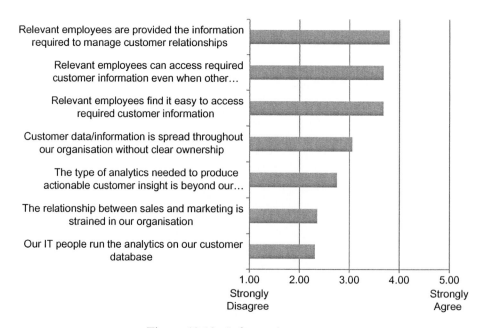

Figure 12.12: Information access.

information ownership, and the sales/marketing strain are negative and where low agreement is reported this infers generally positivity about accessing customer information in SMEs.

The final measure of customer information management relates to the use of information. Figure 12.13 presents a range of findings, starting with reporting that

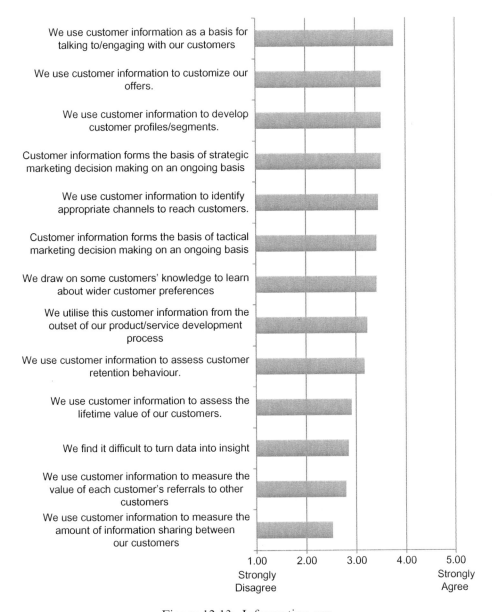

Figure 12.13: Information use.

information is used to drive engagements with customers (3.77). The reported agreement with the next set of items around the use of information for understanding customers, segmentation, retention, and general decision-making is an important trend. Less agreement is reported with the items on using information to calculate customer lifetime value (2.91) and to measure customer-to-customer (C2C) interactions such as referrals (2.80) and information sharing (2.52).

12.6.5. Customer Relationship Performance

Finally, customer relationship performance is measured through whether the SME is achieving customer satisfaction and retaining customers as a result of their social CRM activities. It is reported that they are in both cases with mean levels of agreement of 4.11 and 4.05, respectively (Figure 12.14).

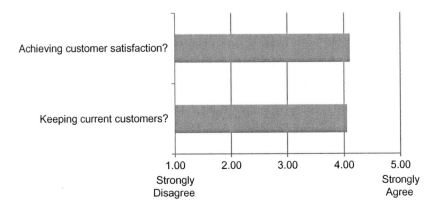

Figure 12.14: CRM performance benefits.

12.7. Discussion, Conclusions, and Implications

In general our comprehensive range findings enable us to succinctly conclude that SMEs are carrying out social CRM. However, there are some issues that can be derived from the findings.

First of all, the SMEs do possess a strong customer relationship orientation. This has been discussed by many previous researchers (e.g. Carson et al., 1995; Jack et al., 2010; O'Dwyer et al., 2009). In this study, we investigated how this is enabled or hindered by the use of social media technologies. Previous CRM research has underlined the importance of a customer orientation, rather than technology, driving CRM (Coltman, 2007; Payne & Frow, 2005).

As for the social media technologies in use by SMEs, we found that LinkedIn was by far the most popular, followed by Twitter, a business-ran blog, and Facebook. It is important to note here that these are all interactive, Web 2.0 technologies, and where new tools may replace them, the Web 2.0 principles of interaction and empowerment will endure. We found that these tools were enabling two-way communications with customers and providing customers with information. Previous research has outlined how communication with customers in SMEs tends to be constant, informal, and open, with the purpose of creating mutual value (Gilmore et al., 2007; Street & Cameron, 2007). In this way, social media technologies appear to be the ideal vehicle for SMEs to open up even more to their customers. Further, by providing more information to customers and being more transparent, SMEs are using social media technologies just to build on their underlying customer relationship orientation (Harrigan et al., 2008; Simmons et al., 2008). SMEs are also using social media as a source of information on customers, a property that has been well discussed in the social media marketing literature (Hennig-Thurau et al., 2010; Hoyer et al., 2010; Krishnamurthy, 2009). SMEs reported acquiring general information such as sales opportunities and responses to marketing efforts.

Looking in more depth at how SMEs are engaging with customers via social media technologies, we have found that two-way interaction is facilitated but that this does not go as far as co-creation of product/services or marketing efforts. Perhaps such an advanced level of interaction, where greater trust is required, is still reserved for face-to-face interaction (Gilmore et al., 2007). Another area where social media technologies offer value to businesses lies in the amount of C2C interactions that occur, often in open environments. These interactions offer opportunities for businesses to get involved and engage with customers on their own terms, and therefore learn much more about them (Bijmolt et al., 2010; Hoyer et al., 2010; Krishnamurthy, 2009). However, we find that SMEs stop short of seeking out C2C interactions, preferring to focus on the direct interactions between them and their customers. Perhaps this is due to a lack of resources or expertise to reach out to relevant communities (Harrigan et al., 2012; Zontanos & Anderson, 2004). We do find that SMEs are concerned about word-of-mouth and being transparent online, so it is most definitely not that they misunderstand the nature of social media (Greenberg, 2010; Kaplan & Haenlein, 2010). In fact, they report that they are creating more loyal customers through engaging with them, which is clearly using social media to build on existing CRM competencies (Harrigan et al., 2012; Peltier, Schibrowsky, & Zhao, 2009). A lack of strategy may be the underlying constraint, which is common in such initiatives in SMEs (Quader, 2007). Social media marketing certainly requires objectives and a strategy, otherwise the amount of engagement opportunities and information available will very quickly become overwhelming (Hennig-Thurau et al., 2010; Konus et al., 2008). To conclude, we also find that SMEs are not yet utilising mobile "apps" to engage with customers, where the potential for more location accuracy and real-time interaction exists (Hennig-Thurau et al., 2010; Nair, 2011). Again, a lack of resources combined with an unclear plan of action may be restraining SMEs from taking their CRM activities to this platform. Where SMEs are often driven by their customers, this will surely change quite quickly and it will be up to SMEs to understand the extra value that mobile can add to customer relationships.

Moving on to how SMEs are utilising social media technologies for customer information management purposes, we find that gathering information from social media is less common than from traditional information sources, such as website, e-mail, and offline (e.g. sales) data. Social media information is also not particularly well integrated with the above information. Where information integration is key (e.g. Coltman, 2007; Jayachandran et al., 2005; Keh et al., 2007; Rai et al., 2006), this may prevent SMEs from an advanced level of social CRM, where customer information can be used to calculate lifetime value, create detailed segments, and proactively engage with the most important customers (Bijmolt et al., 2010; Jayachandran et al., 2005; Kumar et al., 2010). The SMEs in this study do report some level of agreement with being able to do some of the above but it is perhaps telling that SMEs report that information overload from social media is not an issue for them. In reality it probably should be, due both to the sheer amount and to complex nature of market and customer information that is created on social media (Hoyer et al., 2010; Van Bruggen, Antia, Jap, Reinartz, & Pallas, 2010). This is not like sales data that can be easily collected and quantified; social media data is real-time, qualitative inputs from people and this can be difficult to monitor, collect, and turn into insight (Bijmolt et al., 2010). For SMEs, the time required to delve into social media and extract relevant information may be so daunting that they stick to only direct interactions, avoiding the C2C information that is further from their reach (Chen & Ching, 2007; Van Bruggen et al., 2010).

The final part of the research asked SMEs if they were achieving performance benefits as a result of their social media use. They positively reported increases in both customer satisfaction levels and customer retention rates. Thus, it may be that SMEs are currently doing enough by exploring ways to engage with customers via social media without necessarily focusing on information collection, analysis, and use. However, in order for SMEs to maintain their unique customer relationship advantage over the larger organisations investing more and more in social CRM year-on-year; they will have to advance their social CRM efforts beyond engagement and realize the value of social media as an information resource that can fuel more effective, efficient, and profitable customer relationships. There are more and more relatively simple software packages becoming available that, unlike more traditional CRM software, are actually scalable and adaptable to the smallest SME. Due to their head start in the nature of their relationships with customers, SMEs need not necessarily invest in advanced software packages or employ data mining experts; rather it is those firms who approach social media entrepreneurially that will succeed and for many SMEs that approach comes naturally.

References

Admiraal, W., & Lockhorst, D. (2009). E-Learning in small and medium-sized enterprises across Europe: Attitudes towards technology. Learning and training. *International Small Business Journal, 27*, 743–767.

Azila, N., & Noor, M. (2011). Electronic customer relationship management performance: Its impact on loyalty from customers perspective. *International Journal of e-Education, e-Business, e-Management and e-learning*, *1*(1), 1–6.

Bijmolt, T. H. A., Leeflang, P. S. H., Block, F., Eisenbeiss, M., Hardie, B. G. S., Lemmens, A., & Saffert, P. (2010). Analytics for customer engagement. *Journal of Service Research*, *13*(3), 341–356.

Blili, S., & Raymond, L. (1993). Information technology: threats and opportunities for SMEs. *International Journal of Information Management*, *13*(6), 439–448.

Boulding, W., Staelin, R., Ehret, M., & Johnston, W. J. (2005). A customer relationship management roadmap: What is known, potential pitfalls, and where to go. *Journal of Marketing*, *69*(4), 155–166.

Carson, D., Cromie, S., McGowan, P., & Hill, J. (1995). *Marketing and entrepreneurship in SMEs: An innovative approach*. London: Prentice Hall.

Carson, D., & Gilmore, A. (2000). SME marketing management competencies. *International Business Review*, *9*(3), 363–382.

Chen, J., & Ching, R. K. H. (2007). The effects of information and communication technology on customer relationship management and customer lock-in. *International Journal of Electronic Business*, *5*(5), 478–498.

Coltman, T. (2007). Why build a customer relationship management capability? *The Journal of Strategic Information Systems*, *16*(3), 301–320.

Dwyer, P. (2007). Measuring the value of electronic word of mouth and its impact in consumer communities. *Journal of Interactive Marketing*, *21*(2), 63–79.

Gilmore, A., Gallagher, D., & Henry, S. (2007). E-marketing and SMEs: Operational lessons for the future. *European Business Review*, *19*(3), 234–247.

Greenberg, P. (2010). *CRM at the speed of light: Social CRM 2.0 strategies, tools, and techniques for engaging your customers* (4th ed.). New York, NY: McGraw-Hill.

Gummesson, E. (2002). *Total relationship marketing: Marketing management, relationship strategy and CRM approaches to the network economy*. Oxford: Butterworth Heinemann.

Hamid, N. R. A., & Kassim, N. (2004). Internet technology as a tool in customer relationship management. *Journal of American Academy of Business*, *4*(1/2), 103–108.

Harrigan, P., Ramsey, E., & Ibbotson, P. (2008). e-CRM in SMEs: An exploratory study in Northern Ireland. *Marketing Intelligence and Planning*, *26*(4), 385–404.

Harrigan, P., Ramsey, E., & Ibbotson, P. (2011). Critical factors underpinning the e-CRM activities of SMEs. *Journal of Marketing Management*, *26*(13/14), 1–27.

Harrigan, P., Ramsey, E., & Ibbotson, P. (2012). Entrepreneurial marketing in SMEs: The key capabilities of e-CRM. *Journal of Research in Marketing and Entrepreneurship*, *14*(1), 40–64.

Hennig-Thurau, T., Malthouse, E. C., Friege, C., Gensler, S., Lobschat, L., Rangaswamy, A., & Skiera, B. (2010). The impact of new media on customer relationships. *Journal of Service Research*, *13*(3), 311–330.

Hills, G. E., Hultman, C. M., & Miles, M. P. (2008). The evolution and development of entrepreneurial marketing. *Journal of Small Business Management*, *46*(1), 99–112.

Houghton, K. A., & Winklhofer, H. (2004). The effect of website and e-commerce adoption on the relationship between SMEs and their export intermediaries. *International Small Business Journal*, *22*(4), 369–385.

Hoyer, W. D., Chandy, R., Dorotic, M., Krafft, M., & Singh, S. S. (2010). Consumer cocreation in new product development. *Journal of Service Research*, *13*(3), 283–296.

Hutchinson, V., & Quintas, P. (2008). Do SMEs do knowledge management? Or simply manage what they know? *International Small Business Journal*, *26*, 131–154.

Jack, S., Moult, S., Anderson, A. R., & Dodd, S. (2010). An entrepreneurial network evolving: Patterns of change. *International Small Business Journal, 28*(4), 315–337.

Jayachandran, S., Sharma, S., Kaufman, P., & Raman, P. (2005). The role of relational information processes and technology use in customer relationship management. *Journal of Marketing, 69*(4), 177–192.

Kaplan, A. M., & Haenlein, M. (2010). Users of the world, unite! The challenges and opportunities of social media. *Business Horizons, 53*(1), 59–68.

Keh, H. T., Nguyen, T. T. M., & Ng, H. P. (2007). The effects of entrepreneurial orientation and marketing information on the performance of SMEs. *Journal of Business Venturing, 22*(4), 592–611.

Kohli, A. K., & Jaworski, B. J. (1990). Market orientation: The construct, research propositions, and managerial implications. *Journal of Marketing, 54*(2), 1–18.

Konus, U, Verhoef, P. C., & Neslin, S. A. (2008). Multichannel shopper segments and their covariates. *Journal of Retailing, 84*(4), 398–413.

Krishnamurthy, S. (2009). Mozilla vs. Godzilla — The launch of the Mozilla Firefox Browser. *Journal of Interactive Marketing, 23*(3), 259–271.

Kumar, V., Aksoy, L., Donkers, B., Venkatesan, R., Wiesel, T., & Tillmanns, S. (2010). Undervalued or overvalued customers: Capturing total customer engagement value. *Journal of Service Research, 13*(3), 297–310.

Kumar, V., & Reinartz, W. (2006). *Customer relationship management: A data-based approach.* New York, NY: Wiley.

Nair, M. (2011). Understanding and measuring the value of social media. *The Journal of Corporate Accounting & Finance, 22*(3), 45–51.

O'Cass, A., & Weerawardena, J. (2009). Examining the role of international entrepreneurship, innovation and international market performance in SME internationalisation. *European Journal of Marketing, 43*(11/12), 1325–1348.

O'Dwyer, M., Gilmore, A., & Carson, D. (2009). Innovative marketing in SMEs. *European Journal of Marketing, 43*(1/2), 46–61.

Parvatiyar, A., & Sheth, J. N. (2001). Customer relationship management: Emerging practice process and discipline. *Journal of Economic and Social Research, 3*(2), 1–34.

Payne, A., & Frow, P. (2005). A strategic framework for customer relationship management. *Journal of Marketing, 69*(4), 167–176.

Peltier, J. W., Schibrowsky, J. A., & Zhao, Y. (2009). Understanding the antecedents to the adoption of CRM technology by small retailers: Entrepreneurs vs owner-managers. *International Small Business Journal, 27*, 307–336.

Piccoli, G., & Ives, B. (2005). IT-dependent strategic initiatives and sustained competitive advantage: A review and synthesis of the literature. *MIS Quarterly, 29*(4), 747–777.

Piercy, N. (2009). Positive management of marketing-operations relationships: The case of an internet retail SME. *Journal of Marketing Management, 25*(5/6), 551–570.

Quader, M. S. (2007). The strategic implication of electronic commerce for small and medium sized enterprises. *Journal of Services Research, 7*(1), 25–60.

Rai, A., Patnayakuni, R., & Seth, N. (2006). Firm performance impacts of digitally enabled supply chain integration capabilities. *MIS Quarterly, 30*(2), 225–246.

Reichheld, F. F., & Sasser, J. W. E. (1990). Zero defections: Quality comes to services. *Harvard Business Review, 68*(5), 105–111.

Reinartz, W., Krafft, M., & Hoyer, W. D. (2004). The customer relationship management process: Its measurement and impact on performance. *Journal of Marketing Research, 41*(3), 293–305.

Ryals, L., & Knox, S. (2001). Cross-functional issues in the implementation of relationship marketing through customer relationship management. *European Management Journal, 19*(5), 534–542.

Shepherd, C. (2011). Does social media have a place in workplace learning? *Journal of Strategic Direction, 27*(2), 3–4.

Simmons, G., Armstrong, G. A., & Durkin, M. G. (2008). A conceptualization of the determinants of small business website adoption: Setting the research agenda. *International Small Business Journal, 26*, 351–389.

Stelzner, M. A. (2011). *2011 Social media marketing industry report: How marketers are using social media to grow their businesses.* Retrieved from http://www.socialmediaexaminer.com/SocialMediaMarketingReport2011.pdf

Storbacka, K., Strandvik, T., & Grönroos, C. (1994). Managing customer relationships for profit: The dynamics of relationship quality. *International Journal of Service Industry Management, 5*(5), 21–38.

Street, C. T., & Cameron, A. F. (2007). External relationships and the small business: A review of small business alliance and network research. *Journal of Small Business Management, 45*(2), 239–266.

Street, C. T., & Meister, D. B. (2004). Small business growth and internal transparency: The role of information systems. *MIS Quarterly, 28*(3), 473–506.

Van Bruggen, G. H., Antia, K. D., Jap, S. D., Reinartz, W. J., & Pallas, F. (2010). Managing marketing channel multiplicity. *Journal of Service Research, 13*(3), 331–340.

Zineldin, M. (2000). Beyond relationship marketing: Technologicalship marketing. *Marketing Intelligence and Planning, 18*(1), 9–23.

Zontanos, G., & Anderson, A. R. (2004). Relationships, marketing and small business: An exploration of links in theory and practice. *Qualitative Market Research, 7*(3), 228–236.

Chapter 13

Word of Mouth to Word of Mouse: Social Media and the Entrepreneur

Abstract

Word of Mouth (WOM) has long been the communication method favored by entrepreneurs to attract customers, but it was largely ignored by corporates and marketing theorists. Today WOM through viral and buzz marketing has become a mainstream communication method for larger firms and marketing theory is belatedly catching up with entrepreneurial marketing practice. This is partly the consequence of a significant shift in the composition of the business population toward smaller enterprises. There has also been a shift in WOM to "word of mouse" as person-to-person oral communications have been augmented by various forms of social media.

This chapter investigates why WOM is still the most powerful way to communicate marketing messages and how it has been enhanced by social media such as Facebook and Twitter. A case study of small businesses in a market town is used to illustrate the emerging ways that social media is changing the marketing communications process. Recommendations are made on how entrepreneurs can benefit and make the transition from WOM to word of mouse marketing.

13.1. The Evolution of Entrepreneurial Marketing

Early research into entrepreneurial marketing found a mismatch between the marketing theories as expounded in the text books used in university business schools and the marketing practices of entrepreneurs. The overwhelming conclusion of this research was that a difference existed between the traditional marketing theory and practice of large corporations and the entrepreneurial marketing carried on in SMEs (see Hills, Hultman, & Miles, 2008 for a summary of the evolution of entrepreneurial

Entrepreneurial Marketing: Global Perspectives
Copyright © 2013 by Emerald Group Publishing Limited
All rights of reproduction in any form reserved
ISBN: 978-1-78190-786-3

marketing). Were these divergences sufficient to redefine marketing based on entrepreneurial rather than corporate principles? There was much debate over whether the differences existed at the strategic level of the marketing concept or at the tactical level of the marketing mix. Certainly disparity was found in the way that entrepreneurs developed strategies from the bottom up by trying new products out in the market place to see what worked and then doing more of the same, in contrast to the corporate marketing strategies of segmentation, targeting, and positioning (Stokes, 2000).

However, it was at the level of marketing tactics that the distinctions were most obvious. Entrepreneurs tended not to indulge in impersonal, mass marketing campaigns but preferred marketing that relied heavily on recommendations that involved direct customer contact and Word of Mouth (WOM) communications.

Some argued that this merely reflected the different level of resources available to the entrepreneur compared to the large corporation (e.g., Covin & Slevin, 1988). Others claimed it was much more fundamental than that: it stemmed from the entrepreneurial mindset that wanted to do things differently, that wanted to innovate in marketing as well as other business functions (e.g., Chaston, 2001).

More recently the opposite trend has developed: there has been a convergence between corporate marketing and entrepreneurial marketing. Budgets are still different of course but an examination of the elements of the marketing campaign of a large organization would have many common components with that of a small entrepreneurial business. How has this change come about? Why does entrepreneurial marketing now look more "mainstream" than ever before?

To some extent it is the consequence of the natural evolution of marketing.

Marketing is such an integral business activity that it probably originated with the beginnings of trade itself.[1] However, it was not until the beginning of the 20th century that it developed into a more formalized management concept. As marketing practitioners extended their reach into different areas of economic life, they adapted their practices to suit the new contexts. The early consumer goods marketing of leaders such as Unilever, Proctor, and Gamble, Hoover and Philips emphasised the development of strong brands through mass marketing techniques. As industrial products such as office equipment became more widely marketed, companies such as Xerox and 3Ms successfully sold branded products in business-to-business markets. But they added a new emphasis on selling and field marketing such as exhibitions and hospitality as their complex products needed direct presentation to the buyers. As economies became more reliant on services rather than manufactured products, so the emphasis of marketing underwent further change. Intangible services in sectors such as finance and communications focussed less on short term transactions and more on long term relations, so theories of relationship marketing took hold (Stokes & Lomax, 2008).

---

1. For example, there is evidence of branding among the potters of antiquity and of sales promotions among medieval market traders.

Over the last three decades, businesses have become significantly smaller and SMEs now account for more than 95% of enterprises by number and well over half of total employment and value of output (Stokes & Wilson, 2010b). The economic influence of the individual entrepreneurs who run these smaller businesses has significantly increased as their numbers have swelled. Marketing has had to adapt once more, this time to the context of SMEs and an entrepreneurial-style of marketing emerged to suit the environment of smaller business units.

13.2.   The Influence of the SME Environment on Marketing

SMEs tend to be managed by one or two key individuals that own and run the business. These individual entrepreneurs develop the marketing strategy, and implement most of the marketing activities. Their personal experience, skills and attitudes become a major factor in the way that marketing is perceived and carried out. Entrepreneurial marketing describes how these entrepreneurs practice marketing. Before we consider how entrepreneurs market their enterprises in more detail, a word of warning: one thing we have learned about entrepreneurs is that they are not a homogenous group. Sometimes the divergences between entrepreneurs' behavior are as great as the similarities. However research can indicate significant groups that behave in comparable ways — the "archetypal" entrepreneur — and compare them to the typical marketing manager in a large corporation (Stokes & Wilson, 2010a). Thus, the archetypal entrepreneur tends to act in an informal, unplanned way, relying on individual intuition and energy to make things happen. A typical corporate marketing manager, on the other hand, takes action based on a deliberate, planned process involving a careful identification of customer needs and manipulation of the marketing mix through formal market research. The archetypal entrepreneur tends to have a limited view of marketing. They tend to define marketing in terms of selling and promotions to attract new business, while ignoring other aspects such as product development, pricing and distribution. However this does not necessarily mean that they overlook these other areas of marketing, only that they are unaware of the terminology. The entrepreneur's narrow view of marketing is not always borne out by what they actually do. For example, entrepreneurs rate recommendations from customers as the number one way of attracting new customers. However, this does not mean that they put little effort into marketing; such recommendations are often hard won. To an outside observer, it is all too easy to accept an entrepreneurs comment that they "do not have the time or resources for marketing" at face value, when further investigation reveals that those same entrepreneurs devote many hours building relationships with satisfied customers who then recommend the business to others.

This environment tends to give marketing in new ventures and micro-enterprises a distinctive, informal style that evolves with the business. An initial phase of proactive marketing activity when the business is first set up may be followed by a more reactive approach in which marketing efforts respond to customer enquiries or competitive threats. More positive marketing approaches may be adopted again as the firm grows, leading eventually to the planned, integrated campaigns of larger companies. In particular entrepreneurial marketing communications tend to be personalized and interactive, relying on WOM recommendations and personal selling, rather than advertising and sales promotions. Entrepreneurs often have a high level of interactions with their customer base which managers in larger firms struggle to match, even with the latest technological advances. Entrepreneurs specialize in interactions with their target markets because they have strong preferences for personal contact with customers rather than impersonal marketing through mass promotions. They seek conversational relationships in which they can listen to, and respond to, the voice of the customer, rather than undertake formal market research to understand the market place. In many smaller firms, the ability of the owner-manager to have meaningful dialogues with customers is often the unique selling point of the business. Interactive marketing for small firms implies responsiveness — the ability to communicate and respond rapidly to individual customers. Entrepreneurs interact with individual customers through personal selling and relationship building approaches, which not only secure orders but most importantly generate recommendations to potential customers (Stokes, 2000).

13.3.   Word of Mouth Marketing

This preference for building relationships with customers has led entrepreneurs to rely heavily on WOM marketing to develop the customer base through recommendations. Research studies inevitably cite WOM recommendations as the number one source of new customers for small firms (e.g., Stokes & Lomax, 2002). Such recommendations may come from customers, suppliers or other referral groups. So what exactly does WOM mean?

Arndt's (1967) classic definition of WOM still stands — with one major modification:

> Oral person-to-person communication between a receiver and a communicator whom the person perceives as non-commercial, regarding brand, product or a service.

The key change we must make is that it no longer relies only on face-to-face, *oral* contact between a communicator and a receiver. The Internet and electronic communications changed all that and became new sources of recommending and complaining communications from the 1990s (Buttle, 1998). However, the key ingredient of this definition remains — and is overlooked at our peril: the communicator is *perceived* to be independent of the product or service under discussion. As the consumer becomes increasingly cynical about the true independence of third party advice, WOM can be more influential than well-researched sources of product information such as "Which" (Herr, Kardes, & Kim, 1991).

Psychologists have discovered we are more likely to believe communications that we overhear than those specifically directed at us because there is a higher probability that it has not been designed to influence us. It is this perceived impartiality that distinguishes WOM communications from all other marketing communications and gives them their power.

Key characteristics of WOM communications are important for entrepreneurs who wish to harness this power:

- The *volume* of WOM volume relates to the number of people to which the message is relayed. This is important to the concept of viral marketing (see later section of this chapter).
- Its *valence* can be positive or negative. Negative WOM appears to be capable of greater volume than positive WOM; consumers complain more than they praise. The problem of dissatisfaction is compounded by the fact that this may be concealed from the supplier so that the issue is not dealt with quickly. Reported complaints invariably underestimate real levels of consumer dissatisfaction and, therefore, the likelihood of negative WOM communications; we are often reluctant to complain but agree with the negative comments of others.
- The *direction* of WOM changes:
  - Input WOM — recommendations form an *input* into the buyer's decision-making process, that is, the buyer is influenced by recommendations or referrals;
  - Output WOM — they may also be an *output* of the purchase process, that is, the buyer makes a recommendation following their purchase.

This distinction is important. If a buyer perceives there to be a dissonance between the input and output WOM, it can affect the volume of their output WOM. For example, if a buyer makes a purchase based on positive WOM input but finds that the performance does not live up to the recommendation, their negative WOM output is likely to be at a higher volume. The reverse is also true: consumers who have bought despite negative WOM are more likely to praise the product/service publicly.

Entrepreneurs like using WOM as a source of new business because:

- Referrals incur few, if any, additional direct costs;
- Most entrepreneurs prefer the slow buildup of new business which WOM marketing brings because they would be unable to cope with large increases in demand for their services.

Some are aware of potential disadvantages:

- It is self-limiting: reliance on networks of informal communications restricts organizational growth to the limits of those networks. If an entrepreneur depends on the recommendations of existing customers for new clients, their business growth is limited to the market sector of those customers. It is difficult to develop new markets through recommendations from existing customers alone if buyers in the new market have neither geographic, nor demographic, nor interest linkages with that customer base.

- It is perceived to be noncontrollable: some entrepreneurs believe they cannot control WOM communications about their business except by providing the best possible service.

13.4. Marketing Theory Overlooks WOM

The perception that WOM is not controllable, and therefore not susceptible to planning and monitoring, may explain why marketing theorists turned their collective backs on WOM for some time. Given that small businesses form such an important and growing sector, and that WOM recommendations are the number one way that most of these small businesses obtain new customers, we would expect to see extensive, academic coverage of the subject. Yet WOM is not considered in any detail in the major text books on marketing. Stokes and Wilson (2010a) undertook a review of the contents of the frequently used US and UK undergraduate and postgraduate marketing text books (e.g., Brassington & Pettitt, 2006; Jobber, 2006; Kotler, 2003) and found that they have little to say about "WOM marketing," "referrals," or "recommendations." These terms are mentioned but not in the detail that such important marketing tools deserve. The role of recommendations is reported as part of buyer behavior models particularly in the importance of opinion leaders and the need for reassurance in the prepurchase phase. The importance of WOM communications is mentioned in the chapters on marketing communications with reference to the power of WOM as an uncontrollable, positive or negative communication. But the topic gets scant coverage, often less than one page in texts of 700 or 800 pages. The discussions on WOM total about 1 page of the 718 pages in Kotler (2003); Brassington and Pettitt (2006) run to a few paragraphs in over 1,000 pages, with no listing of WOM in the glossary or index.

Why is WOM overlooked by theorists but not by practitioners? The academic assumption that WOM is a by-product of marketing effort rather than an integral part of any campaign is fuelled by the lack of any real understanding by entrepreneurs of how WOM communications work in practice: entrepreneurs know many customers come to them through recommendations, but they know little of who referred what to whom and when. For example, when asked which of their customers are generating referrals, many entrepreneurs will answer that it is their long-serving, loyal customers who generate most recommendations. It is usually the opposite. A number of studies (e.g., East, Lomax, & Narain, 2000) have shown that it is the most *recent* customers that refer most frequently; they are enthused by positive recent experiences that they are keen to share with friends. Thus, it is "stories" that make recommendations and more recent experiences tend to be the stories that we pass on the most.

13.5. Influencing WOM

This brings us to the key question about the use of WOM in marketing strategies: how can it be influenced? How can entrepreneurs encourage their satisfied customers to make more referrals? Research among entrepreneurs who have carried out successful WOM marketing strategies suggests the following stages (Stokes & Lomax, 2002):

1. *Investigate WOM processes*: The entrepreneur needs to discover exactly *who* are the active groups that recommend the business, *what* is being said about it, and *when* are the recommendations triggered.
   a. *Who?* Theories of relationship marketing incorporating a "ladder of customer loyalty" suggest that as the relationship progresses over time, the potential for advocacy increases at each stage. However, as we have already discussed, *recent* customers are more likely to recommend than longer-term customers. The rate of recommendations often declines with the duration of customer tenure. This suggests that recently acquired customers may be a more appropriate target for WOM campaigns than long-standing customers. Nor are customers the only source of recommendations (or complaints): suppliers, local services and employees can be valuable referral sources. The key action is to identify clearly who they all are.
   b. *What?* — Exactly what is being talked about and what is being recommended. Even positive comments may not be in line with the expectations of the entrepreneur who may have overlooked areas of satisfaction as well as dissatisfaction. Which particular benefits stimulate customers to recommend? What negative comments are being made, directly and indirectly, about the business?
   c. *When?* At which point are recommendations triggered? This is probably the most important and most difficult question to answer — when is a customer likely to make a recommendation and what might stimulate them to make them more often?
2. *Intervene to stimulate referrals*: Informed by answers to the above questions, entrepreneurs can now devise a campaign to improve referral rates. This may take the form of explicit requests and incentives for referrals or more subtle information in newsletters that creates a discussion point. Often the key is to give customers a reason to talk about the business by doing something exceptional or different. Telling stories and giving news about an enterprise through newsletters and articles may stimulate customers to talk about an enterprise. Visual aids such as free gifts have also been found to act in a similar way.

One factor stands out above all. Research indicates that customers who have a sense of *involvement* with a business over and above normal commercial relationships, are more likely to recommend it: increased participation levels between lawyer and client were indicative of increased numbers of referrals in the legal profession

(File, Judd, & Prince, 1992); parents who were more involved with their primary school through raising money or helping in the classroom had a higher rate of recommending than other parents (Stokes, 2002).

3. *Defend against complaints*: A defensive WOM strategy is at least as important as a positive one. It is important to minimize negative communications and to deal with complaints in an effective and generous way. Often problems can be turned from potentially negative to positive WOM: complaint handling is not just about damage limitation; it also creates opportunities for stories that generate referrals through a positive experience. The context of conversations is important; consumers display a preference to pass on bad news in negative environments and good experiences in positive ones (Heath, 1996).

13.6. "Word of Mouse" Marketing

More recently a new force has pushed marketing in all contexts into a more entrepreneurial style: the use of the Internet and in particular the emergence of social media has created a new channel of communication — "word of mouse." The Internet has created new opportunities for marketing in all industries and market sectors. It has enabled all companies large and small to have more direct contact with consumers and to place more emphasis on the recommendations of others rather than direct promotions — two of the principle characteristics of entrepreneurial marketing. Entrepreneurs have been actively involved in using the Internet to enable new forms of WOM communications, such as viral and buzz marketing, to emerge. There was evidence at the turn of the century that traditional marketing campaigns based on mass media advertising were less effective than they used to be and the return on investment in them was diminishing (Zyman, 2002). This is now widely accepted and all businesses have tried to come to terms with new forms of entrepreneurial marketing using social media.

13.6.1. Social Media

> Social Media is a group of Internet-based applications that build on the ideological and technological foundations of Web 2.0, and that allow the creation and exchange of User Generated Content. (Kaplan & Haenlein, 2010, p. 61)

This definition is useful in that it seeks to differentiate between terms that are closely related and interdependent, but are not the same:

• The *Web 2.0* concept emerged when Internet users who, until that time had just been consumers of information, began to get involved in the creation of its content by interacting and collaborating with software developers (Clapperton, 2009);

Table 13.1: Classification of social media by social presence/media richness and self-presentation/self-disclosure.

		Social presence/media richness		
		Low	**Medium**	**High**
Self-presentation/ Self-disclosure	**High**	Blogs	Social networking sites (e.g., Facebook)	Virtual social worlds (e.g., Second Life)
	Low	Collaborative projects (e.g., Wikipedia)	Content communities (e.g., YouTube)	Virtual game worlds (e.g., World of Warcraft)

Source: Kaplan and Haenlein (2010).

- *User-generated content*, as its name suggests, refers to the openly published content of social media, which is created by an end user (Kaplan & Haenlein, 2010, p. 61).
- Social media can be used to describe to a wide variety of applications such as Facebook, YouTube, Twitter, and Second Life that use these concepts. As these applications have multiplied, classifications have been developed to distinguish between the different types. Kaplan and Haenlein (2010) categorized social media according to:
  - their measure of self-presentation or self-disclosure, and
  - social presence or "media richness" (Table 13.1).

13.6.1.1. Viral marketing The concept of *viral marketing* is closely bound up with social media. It is the use of social media to take WOM recommendations to a whole new level of speed and scope as opinions about product and services — negative or positive — are spread over the Internet with exponential growth (Stokes, Wilson, & Mador, 2010). An underlying principle of WOM marketing makes the use of social media in particular, and not the Internet more generally, essential to its effectiveness: WOM communications have to be perceived to be independent of the provider of the product/service to work. Only when Internet users began to generate their own content through social media, could this condition be fulfilled.

As a result, viral marketing developed as a powerful, new marketing tool. It has launched new Internet phenomena: early adopters of Hotmail included an invitation to join the service with every e-mail they sent. It has helped elect presidents: Barack Obama employed one of the founders of Facebook to launch a full-scale social media application called "My.BarackObama" (or "MyBo"), which raised $55 million as part of his first presidential campaign (Penenberg, 2009) and Twitter was an essential ingredient in his reelection in 2012.

13.6.2. *Social Media and Small Businesses*

SMEs, particularly in North America, appear to have adopted social media at a faster rate than their larger counterparts. Recent research in the United States found that although just over half of all businesses now use social media, it is the smaller companies that are taking it the most seriously — just 47% of large companies have a formal social media policy, compared with 57% of smaller ones (Robson, 2012). Another survey revealed that 40% of SMEs are using social media marketing, and of these, nearly eight out of ten expect to increase their usage over the next year (Robson, 2012).

Why are they dashing to the new media? Research is in its infancy in this realm but it seems that entrepreneurs believe it can help them to engage on a personal level with customers, thereby improving customer service as well as increasing sales through recommendations and referrals. By registering on Twitter for instance, a small company can instantly reach potential customers and develop their brand through regular tweets. Facebook and LinkedIn allow users to create a page or a group for their companies, and links to a YouTube video may be seen by thousands of people and many more.

13.6.2.1. The social media hype   A word of caution before we all rush into blogging and tweeting: some viral marketing campaigns have undoubtedly raised brand awareness by sparking "a firestorm of buzz" on the Internet, but there are few tracking studies that have quantified the real impact of using social rather than other media (Ferguson, 2008). It may be that social media is currently subject to the kind of hype that previously surrounded other technological developments to their detriment, such as the dot com bubble in the 1990s (Sherman, 2010). Social media is probably being used by many businesses because they are fearful of being left behind rather than because they are convinced of its intrinsic merits. Such motivation into social media campaigns is likely to lead to disappointment and discontent when a user's unrealistic expectations are not met. In this sense social media is the same as other channels of marketing communications: it needs to be carefully conceived, well-planned and evaluated for future lessons (Finkelstein, 2010). There are many "experts" out there, who claim to know "the secrets of social media," who are taking advantage of the naïveté of some owner-managers caught up in the social media hype (Sherman, 2010).

13.6.3. *Social Media in Action*

Perhaps the best way to understand how social media is being applied by entrepreneurs is to see it in action. The case study presented below does just that by describing in some detail how a group of independent retailers are using the new media (Box 13.1).

Box 13.1. *Market town tweets: A case study of the use of social media*

This case study is based on qualitative research carried out in 2011 among seven micro-businesses offering retail services in a small market town in Norfolk, UK by Chloë H. Nelson (2011). It offers a snapshot view of where these entrepreneurs are in relation to the use of social media.

Use of social media: *The seven owners of the independent business-to-consumer enterprises conformed to the norm of entrepreneurial marketing: they all stressed the importance of WOM in attracting new customers to their business. Four of the seven are currently using social media to market their business, with all four businesses using Twitter and two using Facebook in addition. Three said that Twitter was their main social media marketing platform, while one said they had found Facebook to be more effective overall. In all of these cases, the entrepreneur owning the business had sole responsibility for social media activities, including set-up, new posts, monitoring, and maintenance.*

Choice of social media: *A number of factors contributed to the entrepreneurs' selection of social media applications. The two respondents using only Twitter explained that they thought Facebook was better suited to personal social interactions, and had been put off using it in their businesses either because they preferred to reserve it for their own social communications or because they did not feel that a Facebook business page would appeal to their existing or potential customers. On the other hand, the café, deli and B&B found that Facebook was an excellent way of reaching their customers, and they thought it was more effective than their Twitter page. They had a larger following on Facebook, and enjoyed its media richness in comparison to the relative simplicity of Twitter.*

Social media marketing strategy: *All respondents using social media admitted to having no formal social media marketing plan or strategy. This could be attributed to the convenient and instantaneous nature of social media, since it can allow a business to pass a message on to their online following within moments of the idea being conceived. This idea is supported by the examples of how these businesses use social media. By far the most common use of Twitter was to make announcements regarding new stock or services, promotions and forthcoming events and other relevant information for customers. Two of the businesses also used Twitter to interact with other local businesses to establish relationships and also reach shared customer groups.*

Benefits of social media marketing: *The entrepreneurs who were using social media listed several of its advantages. Above all, the fact that Facebook and Twitter are free to use was seen as a major cost benefit, particularly in comparison to expensive local media advertising. Similarly, the respondents liked that they could have complete control over the content of their Twitter or Facebook pages, as opposed* *to giving the responsibility to someone else, and they felt that both sites were user-friendly enough that they could pick up the necessary skills and techniques as they went along. Another major benefit expressed by respondents was the ability to convey a message instantly via social media. This makes it possible for business owners to tell their followers about changes to opening hours, for example, without having to contact their web site manager in advance, or leave customers disappointed when they arrive at the shop and see the closed sign on the door. These respondents also saw social media as being the best way to announce the arrival of new products, events or forthcoming sales or promotions. Respondents who had taken up social media marketing appeared to be highly conscious of keeping up with new technologies, and seemed to have been inspired to start using social media because they had seen other, larger companies and brands using Facebook or Twitter to good effect. Overall, these businesses enjoyed the new opportunities that social media presents. Ultimately, it was considered to be an extremely useful way of raising brand awareness, and the business owners found it to be a good way of communicating with some of their customers, both in terms of transmitting information but also because they can receive and respond to feedback from customers via social media.*

Problems with social media marketing: *The users of social media mentioned a few problems. Firstly, the limited number of followers on Twitter, or fans on Facebook seemed to be a concern, with a few of the entrepreneurs realizing that the majority of their social media following is other local businesses. While this could suggest that Twitter is not the best channel for communicating with existing and potential customers, it is also possible that the owners and staff of other local businesses are potential customers themselves — or potential competitors trawling for information. One entrepreneur said that she knew of other local businesses using Twitter who post new tweets on a frequent, almost habitual basis. She thought that this could cause them to lose sight of their marketing aims and the reasons why they were engaging in social media in the first place. She also explained that in her own tweets, she is careful to ensure that the content and tone is in line with the nature of her business and likely social media audience. She explained that she has had some debate with other business owners who argue that Twitter should reflect the personality of their business. She feels that there is a fine line between business image and individual personality, and that some businesses could be damaging their reputation by posting an excessive amount of irrelevant personal information.*

Summary: *The entrepreneurs in this case study seem to conform to entrepreneurial norms that we have noted above: they have complete responsibility for marketing and therefore the success of marketing activities was entirely dependent on their skills and availability. They were keen to develop strong relationships with their customers through the personal service and WOM was the most effective and significant factor in attracting new customers. They make use of the two social media applications most widely used by entrepreneurs: Facebook and Twitter (*Stelzner, 2011*). Over half were using social media for marketing purposes. They acknowledged that it plays a small part in their marketing at the moment, but they all anticipated that its true* *value would become more apparent over time. Although they believed social media to be a valuable marketing channel, they had no real methods for measuring its success. Perhaps the most significant attribute of social media applications, particularly Twitter and Facebook, is their potential to serve as a communications channel, facilitating the spread of WOM and viral marketing messages.*

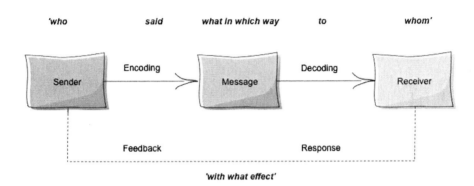

Figure 13.1: The Marketing Communications Process. *Source*: Stokes and Lomax (2008).

13.6.4. What is Different about Social Media?

Ferguson (2008) reminds us that "before the advent of the printing press, broadcast media and the Internet, WOM was the only way to market your goods." This suggests that WOM marketing has evolved as new communication technologies have emerged, and that the recent popularity of social media is part of this evolution: it is simply another channel for these indirect marketing messages. So what can the new channel learn from the older marketing method?

As a communication tool, social media can provide an ideal platform for the development of WOM and viral marketing since it is offers a personalized channel. It does have significant differences to what went before: it can reach larger numbers of people quicker because the communication process is different. Traditional WOM marketing communications passed from sender to receiver as shown in Figure 13.1. The message is communicated from sender to receiver directly with opportunities for different interpretations of the message though coding and direct feedback through responses.

The social media communication process works differently as shown in Figure 13.2. A business is able to send a message to their social media following, which may comprise of all the people who "like" their Facebook page or all the people who opt to "follow" their activities on Twitter. They are also able to send messages to individuals within the public sphere of Twitter and Facebook. The "follower," who is the recipient of this message, is able to respond to this message,

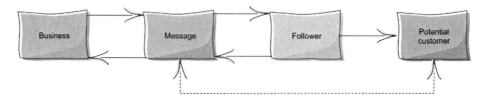

Figure 13.2: The Social Media Communications Process

perhaps by "liking" or commenting on a post on Facebook, or replying with a comment on Twitter. The follower can also spread this message to their entire following by "retweeting" the post on Twitter or opting to "share" the post with their friends on Facebook. They can also forward the message to specific individuals who they think will be interested in its contents.

What is different about social media in comparison with other communications channels is that the potential audience stretches beyond the original sender and receiver of a message. In fact, one message could be received by an unlimited number of people. This has implications for social media marketing because potential customers can view and participate in conversations between a business and their existing customers and social media following. This potential customer is then able to make judgments about the company based on these interactions. Essentially, they can learn a lot about a business by observing the way it maintains relationships with existing customers. Similarly, a business is also able to observe the spread of WOM via social media, and this presents an opportunity for the business to respond appropriately to positive *and* negative opinions expressed by their customers. It is important, therefore, that businesses convey their brand identity and values as effectively as possible, and pay sufficient attention to the monitoring and maintenance of their social media presence. Essentially, social media brings communication into the public sphere, and invites others to participate in conversations that would otherwise be conducted in a much less transparent context. WOM messages have been opened up for all to witness.

13.6.5. Recommendations for Entrepreneurs

The case study demonstrates that many entrepreneurs can benefit from social media marketing. The following recommendations are made with these entrepreneurs in mind:

- *Ensure that social media marketing is suitable* — there is little value in investing time and resources in SMM if the vast majority of customers are not social media uses.
- *Realistic integration* — SMM is not a standalone solution; it appears to be most effective when used in conjunction with other, established marketing methods.

Make sure that your business Twitter or Facebook profile is featured on your web site, and consider mentioning it in email and postal communications and even on your business card.

- *Monitor SMM very closely* — negative messages can spread just as quickly as accounts of positive experiences. Respond to criticism straight away — social media can draw your attention to problem areas and may enable you to resolve problems very quickly, so communicate directly with anyone who makes negative comments and you may well be able to regain their loyalty.
- *Maintain an appropriate tone* — there is a fine line between portraying the personality and values behind your business and being overly personal, too familiar or using inappropriate content in your tweets and Facebook posts. Keep it relevant and appealing to your following.

13.7. Conclusion

The evolution of marketing has now fully embraced the context of the entre-preneurial enterprise operated by entrepreneurs. WOM communications are still the favored way of attracting new customers, and it has been shown that this can be approached in a proactive way with deliberate marketing campaigns aimed at stimulating WOM. Such communications now have a powerful new tool in the form of social media — WOM has become "word of mouse." However, the old rules fundamental to WOM still apply: trust is still dependent on the perceived impartiality of the messages; involvement remains the key ingredient in generating recommen-dations; and negative as well as positive messages are significant and need to be addressed.

References

Arndt, J. (1967). Word-of-mouth advertising and informal communication. In D. Cox (Ed.), *Risk taking and information handling in consumer behaviour*. Boston, MA: Harvard University.

Brassington, F., & Pettitt, S. (2006). *Principles of marketing* (4th ed.). Harlow: Pearson Education.

Buttle, F. A. (1998). Word-of-mouth: Understanding and managing referral marketing. *Proceedings of the academy of marketing annual conference*. Sheffield Hallam University, UK (pp. 100–106).

Clapperton, G. (2009). *This is social media: Tweet, blog, link and post your way to business success*. Chichester, UK: Capstone.

Chaston, I. (2001). *Entrepreneurial marketing*. Basingstoke, UK: Macmillan Business.

Covin, J. G., & Slevin, D. P. (1988). The influence of organizational structure on the utility of an entrepreneurial top management style. *Journal of Management Studies, 25*, 217–237.

East, R., Lomax, W., & Narain, R., (2000). *Customer tenure, recommendation and switching*. Kingston Business School Occasional Papers, Kingston University, Kingston upon Thames.

Ferguson, R. (2008). Word of mouth and viral marketing: taking the temperature of the hottest trends in marketing. *Journal of Consumer Marketing, 25*(3), 179–182.

File, K. M., Judd, B. B., & Prince, R. A. (1992). Interactive marketing: The influence of participation on positive word-of-mouth and referrals. *Journal of Services Marketing, 6*(4), 5–14.

Finkelstein, B. (2010). Why is everyone using social media? Without a good reason for marketing in this fashion, strategies may not work. *Short Sales, 20*(2), 21.

Heath, C. (1996). Do people prefer to pass along good or bad news? Valence and relevance of news as predictors of transmission propensity. *Organizational Behaviour and Human Decision Processes, 68*(2), 79–94.

Herr, P. M., Kardes, F. R., & Kim, J. (1991). Effects of word-of-mouth and product attribute information on persuasion: An accessibility-diagnosticity perspective. *Journal of Consumer Research, 17*(March), 454–462.

Hills, G., Hultman, C., & Miles, M. (2008). The evolution and development of entrepreneurial marketing. *Journal of Small Business Management, 46*(1), 99–112.

Jobber, D. (2006). *Principles and practices of marketing* (4th ed.). Maidenhead: McGraw-Hill.

Kaplan, A., & Haenlein, M. (2010). Users of the world, unite! The challenges and opportunities of social media. *Business Horizons, 53*(1), 59–68.

Kotler, P. (2003). *Marketing management.* Upper Saddle River, NJ: Pearson Education.

Nelson, C. H. (2011). *Social media marketing for small businesses: A study of independent retailers in a market town.* Dissertation submitted in partial fulfilment of the requirements for the award of B.Sc. degree, Loughborough University, Loughborough.

Penenberg, A. (2009). *Viral loop: The power of pass-it-on.* London: Hodder & Stoughton.

Robson, S. (2012). Social media challenges traditional corporate structures. *The Daily Information.* Retrieved from http://www.theinformationdaily.com/2012/11/15/social-media-challenges-traditional-corporate-structures. Accessed on November 15, 2012.

Sherman, A. (2010). *You can stop the social media hype.* Retrieved from http://gigaom.com/collaboration/you-can-stop-the-social-media-hype/. Accessed on October 31, 2010.

Stelzner, M. (2011). *Social media marketing industry report.* Retrieved from http://marketing whitepapers.s3.amazonaws.com/SocialMediaMarketingReport2011.pdf. Accessed on April 10, 2011.

Stokes, D. (2000). Putting entrepreneurship into marketing: The process of entrepreneurial marketing. *Journal of Research in Marketing and Entrepreneurship, 2*(1), 1–16.

Stokes, D. (2002). Entrepreneurial marketing in the public sector: The lessons of headteachers as entrepreneurs. *Journal of Marketing Management, 18*(3–4), 397–414.

Stokes, D., & Lomax, W. (2002). Taking control of word of mouth marketing: the case of an entrepreneurial hotelier. *Journal of Small Business and Enterprise Development, 9*(4), 349–357.

Stokes, D., & Lomax, W. (2008). *Marketing: a brief introduction.* London: Thomson Learning.

Stokes, D., & Wilson, N. (2010a). Entrepreneurship and marketing education: Time for the road less travelled? *International Journal of Entrepreneurship & Innovation Management, 11*(1), 95–108. (Special Issue on Entrepreneurial Marketing).

Stokes, D., & Wilson, N. (2010b). *Small business management and entrepreneurship* (6th ed.). Andover: Cengage Learning.

Stokes, D., Wilson, N., & Mador, M. (2010). *Entrepreneurship.* Andover: Cengage Learning.

Zyman, S. (2002). *The end of advertising as we know it.* Hoboken, NJ: Wiley.

Chapter 14

Does Branding Matter to Start-Ups? Challenges and Opportunities

Abstract

In our view, a brand is the embodiment of the soul of the enterprise. Unfortunatly, entrepreneurs eschew branding because they equate it with sales gimmicks, expensive advertising, fancy logos, and the like. If, however, entrepreneurs understood branding for what it actually is, they would likely embrace it. To start-ups and small businesses, branding is typically the least of their worries. While this may be the reality, the concept and treatment of branding at this start-up stage is crucial. This chapter explains how a strong brand foundation can mould and shape a company, as it grows from a small business to becoming an established corporation through the creation of a sharply differentiated brand image. It argues that establishing a brand entails many of the same activities as building a business and ends by examining the importance of external branding for sustainable growth.

14.1. Introduction

Few small businesses take branding seriously. To start-ups and small businesses, branding is typically the least of their worries; making sales, managing inventory, making payments to suppliers, paying employees, and collecting accounts receivables occupy the entrepreneur's mind. Branding just does not seem to be a core or relevant function to a small business.

While this may be the reality, the concept and treatment of branding at this start-up stage is most crucial. With a clear and sharp brand identity, a start-up company can have a successful brand foundation that can mould and shape the company, as it grows from a small business to becoming an established corporation through the creation of a sharply differentiated brand image. Conversely, without a solid brand foundation, a start-up can get lost in its routine business functions and never fully evolve to become a significant player in its industry and target segment. Brand strategy, we argue, is therefore as important as business strategy.

14.2.   Brand Strategy is Business Strategy

In many way, a business is a brand and a brand a business. If one considers the task of building a business, all of the functions such as employee training, operations management, quality control, logistics, inventory planning, sales and marketing, and so on, that go to creating and delivering products and/or services that can better suit the target consumers' needs, are also manifestations of a brand's identity both internally and to the external stakeholders. Indeed, all the dealings with customers and suppliers are ways to share a brand's ideals and transfer internal brand values to external stakeholders. Therefore, each business activity communicates the values of the business and contributes to a brand's image.

Considering it the other way round, establishing a brand entails many of the same activities as building a business. Brands need to be built from the ground up and require both short and long term goals, they need to be periodically audited and evaluated to see whether the existing brand strategy is viable in the dynamic business market, so that what a brand offers is aligned with the needs of the internal and external stakeholders. Thus, a solid brand strategy is also a strong business strategy. When the two, that is, brand and business strategies are aligned, a strong and successful branded business emerges. Thus, brands need careful consideration from the get go.

14.2.1.   (Mis)perceptions of Branding

Notwithstanding the importance of having a clear brand strategy from the get go, there are several misconceptions about what branding is, that on the one hand make entrepreneurs not pay attention to branding from the start, and when they do, they make poor decisions that do not lead to effective brand building.

Many entrepreneurs and business managers equate branding to salesmanship (Balmer, 2001; Rust, Lemon, & Zeithaml, 2004). To many, the practice of branding is merely the act of putting a label on the product or service so consumers can differentiate it from its competitors. Branding, in this instance, is simply bringing a product or service to the market and selling it to target consumers. Indeed, many so-called corporate branding strategies are no more than short-term sales gimmicks that are bottom-line oriented and intended to boost short-term sales. This perspective leads businesses to pay little attention to the long-term consequences of their business activities on the overall perception of the offer and the relationship between the offer and consumers, which lies at the heart of branding. Overreliance on salesmanship and equating it to branding not only nurtures a short-term oriented, profit-driven culture within a business (internal brand culture) but also makes a business overly reactive to market changes and competitors' moves, instead of being more proactive, innovative, and sustainable.

Another equally severe misperception equates branding to advertising. Many entrepreneurs, business students, and even researchers confuse branding strategies with advertising. Advertising is only an outward communication channel from the brand to consumers. It is a push by the company to display what it has to offer that is unique and different that can attract the consumers' attention. With the advent of the Internet and social media, advertising or more generally marketing communications have evolved to adapt to the changes in media culture. However, communications continue to primarily remain a push by businesses to amuse, shock, or even snare consumers. By relying on advertisements as the main strategy, firms trap themselves in an infinite advertising loop of who can shout louder. In this game, the inevitable winners are the larger players with deeper pockets. Thus, the branding equals advertising perspective, not surprisingly makes entrepreneurs shy away from "branding" since given their smaller size and limited resources, this can only be a losing proposition for them.

Note, we are not saying that advertising is unimportant or unnecessary, but that relying entirely on advertisements as the strategy to build a brand is short-sighted. Advertisements are a great way to communicate a brand's values and ideals to consumers, as we shall see later, but it is limited to just that.

A somewhat less damaging and broader, but nevertheless problematic perspective, equates branding to marketing. Branding is more than marketing. As Gronroos (1989) noted, marketing is geared toward the relationship between consumers and goods or service providers. This is a relationship between the company and its consumers at the external boundary of the organization. As we will lay out, branding is more than just the external relationship with consumers. Branding involves the internal culture of the employees which reflects the views and values of the company, and acts as the back bone of the brand (Alsem and Kostelijk, 2008). Marketing, therefore, is an integral but only partial component of branding. Thus, leaving the task of brand building to the marketing department, as many businesses do, including established corporations, can be problematic.

14.2.2. Consequences of Branding (Mis)perceptions

These misperceptions of what branding is, are consequential, as they can lead to small businesses coming up with interventions like advertising or other marketing initiatives, whenever building the brand becomes an issue. When this happens, the outcome can be negative because these misconstruals of what branding is and the initiatives they spawn, overlook the core issues that the brand may be facing (Balmer, 2011). They only fix what is visible on the surface. Two great examples of this are Brita brand water filters in the United States (Chattopadhyay & Paavola, 2007) and Q94FM a Winnipeg, Canada based radio station.

14.2.2.1. Brita water filters Brita water filters were introduced in the United States in 1989 by the Clorox company. The brand rocketed to prominence and for the next decade sales grew dramatically with Brita holding a 70% market share. In 1999, Brita sales hit a wall, plateauing suddenly. The Brita brand team for the next 7 years tried a variety of advertising interventions to drive sales growth, but to no avail. The advertisements were individually clever in their execution but, on the one hand, they did not convey a clear, consistent, and differentiated message, and on the other, did not address the key problems with the Brita brand that had led to the sudden stalling of sales growth.

Growth had stalled as consumers were unsure as to when the filters needed changing and because alternative, more easy to use filter formats had become available in the market. The solution for Brita thus lay with targeted new product development which could embed an indicator in the filter to signal to consumers when the filter needed changing, and with the development and introduction of new filter formats under a common brand umbrella with a clear differentiated promise that was understood inside and out. Advertising was not the solution; it exacerbated the problem by bringing Brita's real shortcomings to the notice of consumers.

What Brita needed was a brand centric approach that articulated Brita brand's identity and positioning clearly and communicated that internally, to begin with. A clear brand identity would have helped Brita to understand what was needed to strengthen and align R&D, and product development capability, as only then would they be able to deliver against the brand identity with a stream of consistent innovations to build a clear and differentiated brand image, relative to the new competition that had emerged. Sadly, the Brita brand team never understood this and relied on advertising to dig themselves out. In 2007, fed up with their less than expected performance, Clorox (parent company of Brita) downgraded Brita's standing within its portfolio, withdrawing the financial support that it had enjoyed earlier.

14.2.2.2. Q94FM radio station Another example of the misperception of branding and its consequences is highlighted by Q94FM. Q94FM, a local radio station (Winnipeg, Canada) that had been owned by CHUM radio since 1965, was a successful station with a strong and loyal listener base. The station focused on "hot adult contemporary music" and played "Today's Lite Rock" and "Today's Best Music." The station lived by the slogans consistently for 30 years and, as a result, had built a clear brand image and a loyal following among Winnipeggers (Wan, 2008).

After the station was sold by CHUM to CTVGlobalMedia in 2007, the brand along with its DNA was changed by the new owner. The brand name changed from Q94FM to Curve 94.3. The morning radio hosts, the core personalities of the station, were moved to a sister station, and the "hot adult contemporary music" format that had been the core of the station for more than 30 years of its history, and the format that local listeners had come to know and love, was replaced by "Pop Alternative." The changes were drastic and proved fatal to the brand. Listeners were confused by the change and many left the radio station since its on-air personalities and music format no longer suited their tastes.

The rebranding fiasco turned from bad to worse as the new Curve 94.3 not only struggled to find listeners but also failed to truly establish an identity from the inside. With the key on-air personalities gone, the radio station lost its original identity, and during the transition period, no strong new voice came out that could lead this station in the new direction that it wanted to go. The new owners had not taken adequate steps to communicate the new direction to the employees and, as a result, most employees were lost and did not have the ability to step up to create the new voice that was so badly required. And, while advertising attracted consumers to try the new brand, they rarely stayed as the station lacked a clear and distinct voice that only key on-air personalities could give it.

Struggling to survive the new owners tried to change the format from its intended "Pop Alternative" to a "Christmas" song station during the Christmas holiday season of 2010, and to what is now "FAB 94.3," playing oldies and classic hits. FAB 94.3 remains a shadow of the Q94FM brand that CTVGlobalMedia acquired in 2007.

The rebranding of Q94FM provides a hard lesson for brand owners. First, it is essential to have a clear understanding of what the brand wishes to stand for in consumers' minds. This is what we call the brand identity. The brand identity has to be clearly articulated as a first step as without it there is no guidance for brand building. Trying to build a brand without articulating the brand identity is akin to trying to build a house without a building plan first being created.

In the example of Brita, the brand identity had not been articulated clearly and formally. This led the brand to try a variety of knee-jerk advertising responses that lacked a coherent message, ultimately leading to the brand being relegated to a relative backwater by Clorox, the corporate owner of the Brita brand.

For Q94FM, again, there was no formal brand identity beyond the slogans. The new owners did not take the time to try and understand and formally articulate the identity of the brand, perhaps by decoding the brand image in the minds of local listeners and understanding what had led to it being created, which would have been the implicit brand identity. The failure to understand Q94FM's identity led the new owners to taking the missteps that resulted in the decline of the business.

Second, both examples highlight the importance of communicating the brand identity internally. In the case of Brita, this would have helped the brand stewards to think about initiatives beyond advertising that were necessary to strengthen the brand in alignment with its desired identity. In the case of Q94FM, one could argue that Curve 94.3 could have been a success had a clear new identity for the latter been articulated and communicated internally. Had this happened, a set of strong new voices could have emerged, giving Curve 94.3 a distinct and authentic voice that may have helped it establish itself.

14.3. The Branding Opportunity for Entrepreneurs

As we have noted earlier, entrepreneurs eschew branding because they equate it with sales gimmicks, expensive advertising, fancy logos, and the like. If, however, entrepreneurs understood branding for what it actually is, they would likely embrace it.

In our view, a brand is the embodiment of the soul of the enterprise. Just as we as individuals, once in a while reflect and ask ourselves some of the most fundamental questions like who am I, what do I value, where did I come from, and where am I going(?), likewise to build a brand we need to ask the same questions.

If we do not define ourselves, we end up strolling through our lives from day to day enthralled by our mundane obligations, but going nowhere in a systematic goal directed way. Just as people who ask these difficult and often irksome questions of themselves and then live by the way they define themselves to reach their goal of becoming who they want to be, so too should brands evolve by the way they are defined. Thus, entrepreneurs and, more broadly, business leaders need to define the brand, that is, what should the brand stand for in the minds of all stakeholders. This is what we referred to earlier as the brand's identity. In the case of entrepreneurial and start-up businesses, the responsibility of articulating the identity lies with the founder. S/he needs to provide the brand with its initial vision in terms of the values the brand wishes to embody and become known for.

Defined in this way, the organization and its values and culture which are reflected in every activity the business undertakes play a part in building the brand. If entrepreneurs understood that their business, and the many activities that running it involves, leads to the creation of their brand, that is routine activities, such as hiring and training staff, product design and manufacturing, sales and after-sales customer care, go into building their brand, and one does not need to set aside a specific dollar amount for "branding," it is likely that they would embrace branding.

Indeed it is ironic that it is at the early entrepreneurial stage that it is easiest to sow the seeds of a successful branded business, since the entrepreneur through their direct contact with the members of the organization can communicate the core brand values through both word and deed, to build a business culture around the brand values, creating a seamless integration in values among management, employees, and external stakeholders like customers, suppliers or distribution channels. When brand identity truly guides small business firms, there is alignment between the brand and business strategy, enabling small entrepreneurial businesses to create strong branded businesses as the example of A&L Concrete Services below shows.

14.3.1. A&L Concrete Services

A&L Concrete Services is a small business-to-business supplier of goods and services to the home improvement sector. The company has been in business for around 15 years and employs fewer than 20 full-time workers. Its competitive advantage is quality of service and the company is respected by the business customers it serves, who see it as a preferred supplier. Most businesses who try the services of A&L Concrete Services typically continue to do business with them. Thus, A&L Concrete Services has all the hallmarks of a strong branded business with a loyal customer following (Wan, 2010).

How did this happen, particularly when (1) the owner-manager did not have any marketing experience, nor did any of his employees, and (2) A&L Concrete Services use only a minimal of promotional materials to target potential new customers? A&L Concrete Services' brand is built on the basis of the consistently high quality professional products and services it provides its customers. The proof of the pudding, as they say, is in the eating; there is no better signal of what a brand stands for than actual business practice.

A&L Concrete Services has acquired the ability to deliver consistently on the key values that the brand stands for, through the products and services, because these are the values of the owner — "doing the job right" — which he has conveyed to all the employees, ensuring that it is evident in each individual employee's work and the services the individual provides.

The opportunity to build the brand internally is far greater in small entrepreneur led firms (Walton & Huey, 1993). In such firms, even when there is no conscious effort and formalization in passing on a set of values that the business and the brand stand for, because good entrepreneurs lead by example and the employees respect and follow, the owner's ideals and values, enabling them to get transferred to the employees, creating a strong internal culture. In the case of A&L Concrete Services the values of quality workmanship and professionalism in dealings with customers transferred to the employees through the behaviors of the owner, which set an unambiguous example of what was expected. The key values were also communicated and strengthened during routine planning meetings through the discussions of how to ensure quality workmanship. The fact that employees were also stakeholders reinforced the acceptance of the core values of the A&L Concrete Services brand. Thus, without spending money specifically to build a brand, A&L Concrete Services has crafted a well-respected brand in the local community.

14.4. The Importance of External Branding for Sustainable Growth

All major corporations were once small businesses, and all small businesses are started by an individual or group of individuals. Thus, while most businesses start from the same point, a question to ask is why do some go further than others? Why do some evolve and grow to become multibillion dollar multinational corporations, while others continue to remain small and never break the boundaries of the locale where they started?

Even with the best products and/or services on the market, a business cannot achieve its full potential if it fails to inform the consumers of its superior quality. Thus, the external aspect of branding is also important in communicating the superiority of the product/service and the vision, ideals, and values for which the business stands. However, this should happen after the brand has already been communicated internally and a clear image established in the minds of all employees.

The challenge for start-ups and small businesses generally is twofold. First, it has to build brand awareness, and second it has to create a sufficiently distinct and strong set of beliefs to convince potential consumers to actually buy the product or service on offer. This is not a trivial challenge since consumers are risk averse. Thus, start-up and small businesses need to consider how they can communicate their values and the benefits they offer credibly. These challenges are made all the more severe because of budget constraints, constraints that make the resources available to small businesses typically being orders of magnitude less than their competitors. It is imperative, therefore, that small businesses think creatively about how to communicate effectively to their target consumers. With creativity and ingenuity, small businesses can and have built strong branded businesses going up against much larger competitors with infinitely higher resources, as the example of "Under Armour" below shows.

14.4.1. Under Armour

Under Armour today is a major American sports clothing and accessory company founded by Kevin Plank in 1996, just after he graduated from college at the age of 23 (Plank, 2012). The company specializes in sportswear and casual apparel. In particular, Under Armour focuses on hi-tech sportswear for professional athletes and thus has come to be known as a brand that specializes in professional sports (Under Armour, 2011).

The origins of the brand go back to the time when, as a high school and college level athlete, Plank got tired of the way his sport attire felt as sweat accumulated, as a result of his physical activities. To remedy this problem, he sets out to design and manufacture sportswear that would not be weighed down by sweat. He believed that this would be appealing to professional athletes. The vision was there, the product was there, and the quality was there. What were still missing were the awareness and the legitimacy of the brand.

Plank knew that he had limited resources and could not compete head on with the marketing power of the major players such as Nike, Adidas, and Reebok in the sportswear industry. Instead of advertising through mainstream channels such as TV, billboards, and magazines, as the major players did, Plank turned to his network: he took his brand to his friends in the locker room. By giving the clothing he had designed to his college friends who had now been drafted in to professional football, he was able to get his clothing line in to the locker rooms of a dozen or more professional football teams and, as some of his friends who really liked what Under Armour had to offer, started to use his line of clothing in practice sessions and after games.

Other sport celebrities who were introduced to the product by word-of-mouth in locker rooms also started to wear Under Armour clothing, becoming de facto free endorsers for the brand. As the Under Armour brand awareness and popularity grew among professional players, it also became visible to the broader consumer market for athletic apparel, establishing the brand firmly in this broader market, both in terms of awareness and credibility. Thus, aligning a good product with a well-thought-out brand communication strategy can transform a small business in to a successful branded business, even in a category dominated by global majors.

14.5.   The Ying and Yang of Internal and External Branding

As one can see, external and internal aspects of a brand go hand in hand; one cannot succeed without having both. Internal branding must exist in order for the brand to become imbued with the desired values through the aligned decisions and actions of each and every employee. External branding must exist in order to fully and successfully promote the ideals of the brand achieved through internal branding to suppliers, channel members, after sales service providers, and end consumers.

It is important that both internal and external branding should develop and evolve in sync. Where most small businesses fail is that they only pay attention to one aspect of branding. Some only sustain and maintain their internal branding (or ignore external branding), relying solely on their superior products and services to maintain existing customers and word-of-mouth to attract new customers (Aurand, Gorchels, & Bishop, 2005). Some only seek to develop external branding without the internal branding to back-up their brands, relying on advertisements, promotions, and marketing gimmicks to drive sales to increase bottom line in the short run.

With only internal branding and no external branding, the brand is simply a rock. Lacking proper promotion channels or consumer brand awareness, even the best products and services can only remain as a diamond in the rough, never to be discovered or appreciated. Yet, owners of small businesses we have interviewed tend to share the mindset that "We are good! Come and find us!" The complacency reflected in this mantra reduces small business's external branding efforts and impedes their potential to grow, by reaching out to broader consumer segments. With only external branding but no internal branding, the brand is simply a shell. Lacking proper product and service qualities, enticing promises and exquisite allures used in advertising and marketing only turn dreams into mirages as consumers realize their choice folly and abandon the brand altogether. Therefore, to sustainably grow the brand and the business, there needs to be a coevolution between internal branding and external branding.

14.6.   Summary and Conclusions

Start-ups and small businesses need to pay attention to branding from the get go because brand strategy is business strategy. Without a clear brand strategy, as we have defined brand strategy here, it is unlikely that a start-up or a small business will flourish and grow to someday become a major player in its industry.

Having a brand strategy begins with clearly articulating what the brand should stand for in the minds of all stakeholders both internally and externally. This we call the brand identity. The brand identity should be based on the entrepreneurs vision, the raison d'etre of the business, as this is what differentiates the new business from what exists.

Once articulated, the brand identity needs to be communicated internally through word and deed. This, on the one hand, aligns the employees to a common cause and, on the other, helps identify and rectify any potential shortcomings in terms of being able to deliver against the brand identity.

Finally, once the brand identity is clearly understood internally and the organization is made ready to deliver against the brand identity, it needs to be communicated externally to both business partners such as suppliers, logistic and other service providers, and channel members, and target consumers. In communicating externally, start-ups and small businesses need to constantly be in search for ways to multiply the impact of their limited budget, be that through attracting free publicity, through leveraging social networks, and the like.

References

Alsem, K. J., & Kostelijk, E. (2008). Identity based marketing: a new balanced marketing paradigm. *European Journal of Marketing, 42*(9/10), 907–914.

Aurand, T. W., Gorchels, L., & Bishop, T. R. (2005). Human resource management's role in internal branding: an opportunity for cross-functional brand message synergy. *The Journal of Product and Brand Management, 14*(2/3), 163–169.

Balmer, J. M. T. (2001). Corporate identity, corporate branding and corporate marketing – Seeing through the fog. *European Journal of Marketing, 35*(3), 248–291.

Balmer, J. M. T. (2011). Corporate marketing myopia and the inexorable rise of a corporate marketing logic: Perspectives from identity-based views of the firm. *European Journal of Marketing, 45*(9), 1329–1352.

Chattopadhyay, A., & Paavola, N. (2007). Brita: In search of a winning strategy. INSEAD Case Study No. 10/2007-5426.

Grönroos, C. (1989). Defining marketing: A market-oriented approach. *European Journal of Marketing, 23*(1), 52–60.

Plank, P. (2012). How I did it: Under Armour's founder on learning to leverage celebrity endorsements. *Harvard Business Review*, May, pp. 45–49.

Rust, R. T., Lemon, K. N., & Zeithaml, V. A. (2004). Return on marketing: Using customer equity to focus marketing strategy. *Journal of Marketing, 68*, 109–127.

Under Armour, Inc. (2011). *2011 Under Armour annual report.*

Walton, S., & Huey, J. (1993). *Sam Walton: Made in America.* Bantam

Wan, F. (2008). *Q94FM: Brand confusion.* Case study. Asper School of Business, University of Manitoba.

Wan, F. (2010). *A&L Concrete Services: Rightfully branding.* Case study. Asper School of Business, University of Manitoba.

Chapter 15

The Soloist in Entrepreneurial Marketing

Abstract

The extent to which many in the arts, crafts, trades, and professions earn their living working "on their own" is often overlooked. However, the local and the small scale efforts of the soloist can also be viewed collectively and globally. From this perspective, individual enterprise whether full time or part time, even on the smallest scale can be seen as significant in the context of identity, economic and personal development, and the creative potential emerging from these aspects.

The chapter opens by briefly considering the nature and status of the solo self-employed before exploring the special challenges of solo working and its relationship to the entrepreneurship process. Following this, the chapter addresses in more detail a number of themes including portfolio working, the role of formal and informal entrepreneurial groupings, and the value of diversity in providing opportunities for learning.

15.1. Introduction: The Context

During the last few decades there have been major shifts in the pattern of economic activity in the United Kingdom, similar to those that have occurred in the rest of Western Europe and North America. The 2008 global crisis and its aftermath have accelerated such shifts. Mergers, acquisitions, downsizing, and globalization, with its shift of employment to lower cost countries, have all reduced the numbers employed in large corporations. For the first time widespread redundancy affected managers, including very senior managers, just as much as it had previously other members of the labor force. This change is reflected in the increased proportion of people employed in small and medium enterprises (SMEs), now around 59% of private sector employment (BIS, 2012). The future of work, it is argued, seems to lie in small to medium sized businesses, outsourced workers and soloists (Cooper, 2005). Government policy-makers have recognized this change and responded to it in various ways. Academic research interest has also increased.

Another significant shift in the global pattern of economic activity has received far less attention. As the number of those surviving the changes in large corporations declines and the number surviving in small organizations increases, there has been a rapidly growing minority who find that they either must or want to survive on their own, outside any formal organization. Furthermore, both in the United Kingdom and elsewhere, there is a significant increase in the proportion of those over 50 and wanting to carry on working part time after retirement (Platman, 2003; Weber & Schaper, 2004). Such working appears critical not just to their financial position but to their sense of identity. Many of those surviving in this way, and working locally, may wish only to have lifestyle operations, and to avoid growing and facing the complications and responsibilities of employing others. In holding such apparently modest aims they have been neglected by policy makers and academic researchers alike (Devin, Johnson, Gold, & Holden, 2002). In this chapter I set out to review how that significant minority of all ages and backgrounds that I call the soloists, technically the solo self-employed, operate and survive in the United Kingdom today. Some of the key questions addressed throughout this chapter are: How do they obtain work? How do they carry out their work? What are the issues they confront? How do they learn to do what they do? Where do they look for advice and assistance? In doing so, what attitudes and behaviors do they encounter among others?

Before addressing the relevant issues in entrepreneurial and small business marketing theory and practice, the nature of the soloist must first be addressed.

15.2. Nature and Status

A related issue is, considering their aggregate contribution to the economy (BIS, 2012), just how little attention, from policy makers to business schools, soloists receive. Why is this? A range of issues seems to be involved. First, although there are glaring exceptions in the form of high profile talent — star actors, celebrity sports people and writers — each individual usually represents income that is low relative to the employment, income and taxation generated by large companies. Indeed, some soloists work only part time or, while struggling to become established, particularly in the arts, may work without any income at all. The contribution of the individual self-employed person can be disparaged as a lifestyle or hobby business and tends therefore not to be treated as significant.

Governments and political parties tend to be obsessed by the need to deal with the relatively short term (say the period running up to the next election) (Garri, 2010) and the easily quantified.

Government policies and the need for them have to be easily communicated and if national statistics can be attached in their support so much the better. However, global data collected largely for purposes of economic and taxation management has some well-known limitations. For example, the focus tends to be on the individual: the owner manager or entrepreneur and the firm (Blackburn & Kovalainen, 2008; Scott & Rosa, 1996). Policy making must suffer from the fact that in many surveys the micro-business of 0–9 employees, which incorporates solo workers, often gets lumped in with SMEs of up to 500 employees (Devin et al., 2002). There is relatively little specifically on soloists. Similarly, in addressing how to support older entrepreneurs, those over 50, not at all an homogenous group, tend to be treated as one (Kautonen, 2008; Kautonen, Down & South, 2008). In this extremely diverse sector some of the fine grained detail such as clusters of firms, or individuals being directors of a number of SMEs, is lost and emerges only in more detailed research (Blackburn & Kovalainen, 2008). Even individuals doing business as soloists may for tax and branding reasons run several distinct and separate local business activities which are easily overlooked in the global. Such richness suggests that to consider the activity of "lifestyle" soloists as simple relative to that of management in larger organization is misleading.

Many, perhaps most, of conventional concepts, frameworks and models in classical marketing theory seem impractical and unhelpful for the time-pressed soloist. References to the distinctive nature of marketing activity by the small business have become more prominent. There is a significant body of work world-wide relating to entrepreneurship and the small business and, indeed, the micro-business; and highlighting the significance of marketing and networking (Conway & Jones, 2012; Shaw, 2012; Shaw & Conway, 2000). However, there seems to have been little in the UK academic marketing and other literature specifically written about soloists, at least in most sectors. The term self-employed is normally used in a way that covers micro-businesses and those who are self-employed for tax purposes, but employing others — in other words, not true soloists working alone. Government policy and support has been increasingly focused away from the micro-business and the very small scale. The picture across the United Kingdom is patchy. Although business start-up programs and support workshops are still delivered in England through enterprise agencies and the like, take up rates of formal training courses by owner managers have always been low (Devin et al., 2002). Business Link was heavily restructured in 2011, largely in line with the Richard report recommendations (2008). With the loss of local advisory services and the move to a largely web-based information offering, it is significantly harder for the owner manager or solo operator in England to find formal sources of personal or face to face support. Whether, given low rates of take-up generally, Business Link offerings will be much missed by soloists is questionable.

Nevertheless, trends in the UK labor market and in recent academic work suggest that more significance now needs to be attached to the growth of the soloist. Statistics produced by the Department for Business, Innovation and Skills on UK employment makeup demonstrates that there is now in the United Kingdom a record number of "one man band" businesses (BIS, 2012). Of the total of 4.8 million private enterprises operating at the start of 2012, there were 3 million sole traders, 448,000 partnerships and 1.3 million limited companies. Across all business trading formats, over 3m are apparently soloists, those self-employed who do not have employees or fellow partner-directors. These figures represent an increase over the previous year of 4–5%

and demonstrate that, whatever the reasons, an increasing number of people appear to be "going it alone."

What are the implications? When the issue of self-employment is addressed, or when similar problems and issues are dealt with in the SME literature, the focus of attention remains on the firm or business unit. In the literatures generally, and especially in the dominant metaphors and frameworks, SMEs are treated as if they were miniature versions of large corporations. Even more important for the purpose of this chapter is the way in which the self-employed individual person is treated as a one-person business, as if he or she were a mini- or micro-organization. Immediately the reality of the person is lost. What really motivates people tends to be hidden or forgotten and it is assumed that they are seeking growth and profit. The heroic success stories of the individual entrepreneur are inappropriately taken as the prototype.

A major critique of this whole approach is that, despite its focus on the individual, the way of focusing loses the person. The way of thinking is simply transferred with minor adjustments from thinking about large corporations. The point of this chapter is to shift to a different way of thinking. A focus on the self-employed person as participant in an ongoing web of relationships enables one to understand how the very identity of the self-employed person emerges in these relationships. Self-employment is more than a form of economic survival. It is a form of participation in the living present in which the very identity of the participants arises. To make links between participation in this relating and the area of theory known as small business and entrepreneurial marketing is therefore challenging if the person is not to be obscured. The dominant position is to avoid taking a holistic perspective and to separate off different activities such as marketing for closer inspection.

As soon as one focuses on the self-employed as a person whose identity continues and is potentially transformed in the ongoing relationships of self-employment, important issues relating to community, support and living with anxiety arise.

15.3. Who Am I Now?

A soloist may devote considerable thought to self-presentation, perhaps even using one or more trading names. Perhaps just as important to their identity is how others refer to them, both as an individual and as representative of a grouping. In relation to descriptions or labels for the person who is working on their own, there is a wide range of terms in everyday use. Most of the people concerned are working as sole traders who for tax purposes are treated as "self-employed," undoubtedly a curious description, but one that is simply framed in contrast to what has become the conventional "employed" person.

Articles in *The Economist* were early in drawing attention to the phenomenon and opened by emphasising the range of images conjured up by this term: the self-actualizing entrepreneur; the freelancer; the single mother working from home; and the redundant manager turned consultant. These all helped underline the richness and resulting difficulty in generalizing about this field (Macrae, 1976, The Economist,

1992). Conventionally, in the literature the term "micro-business" applies to businesses of nine persons or fewer. Within this the soloist would be considered as a special category. But we have as other possible names, some apparently sector-specific: not just the "self-employed" or the "freelance," but the sole proprietor or the sole trader; the one-man band; the one-person firm or one-person business; the solo operator, the soloist; the solo practitioner. The term "Free Agents" seems recently to have had some currency in the United States, an expression that aligns the phenomenon with both the old theatrical agent and themes in the complexity sciences (Pink, 2001).

Entrepreneurial theory is fragmented (Anderson, Dodd, & Jack, 2012). The term entrepreneur, and how to represent he or she and what they do, is contested and much discussed (McAuley, 1998). Use of the word and its conventional definition is particularly challenging in relation to small scale activity. Nevertheless in America, there are those who call themselves "lone entrepreneurs" and the term "second job entrepreneur" has been applied to those moonlighting from their full time employment (Gruenert, 1999). Increasingly the term "portfolio worker" popularized by Handy is being used to indicate the fact that such people may be juggling a range of activities and may not be so easily categorized (Handy, 1994). All the above may be operating as sole traders or using other legal forms, but the essential difference, whether working full time or part time, from home, the car, or office premises, surely must lie in the fact that they are operating and surviving on their own. Clinton et al find that the characteristics of portfolio working include: the self-management of work; the independent generation of work and income; the development of a variety of work and clients; and a working environment situated outside any single organization (Clinton, Totterdell & Wood, 2006).

15.4. How Do they Carry their Work Out?

Handy, in popularizing the term "portfolio work," identified five categories: first, paid work divides into wage or salary work where payment is given in exchange for time; and fee work where the payment is for results delivered. Fee work is on the increase as more organizations contract out or outsource their activities. Unpaid work can be divided into his other three types: homework — done in the home; gift work such as charity or community work; and finally, study work such as the learning of a language, a skill or sport (Handy, 1992). This may seem somewhat superficial; it is hard to envisage anyone who is not to some degree a "portfolio worker," for example, in combining homework and paid work.

Soloists may therefore juggle a range of different activities. This cannot be efficient but as Hopson points out, this provides variety. "Also they don't have all their career eggs in one basket. If one job gets boring they can focus more on the other ones or indeed even ditch the boring one. If they lose one job, they have other revenue streams to rely on." Hopson, like Handy, takes a generally positive view, saying that a "portfolio career gives legitimacy to people who have diverse interests and talents and want to express them" (Hopson, 2009).

Cooper (2005) argues that the "new" working arrangements or increasing numbers of soloists have two things in common: "they involve little or no personal contact with coworkers and the communications and businesses are conducted by electronic technologies." This poses the question of how an independent can make the time not just to carry out fee earning work but to develop skills in say, new media. Particularly given that many are setting out on this path in their mature years, this seems a challenging "make or buy" decision.

With the aim of developing a strong set of survival skills in enterprise, any soloist might be expected to know everything, or at least be a "jack of all trades." There would have to be an adequate understanding of management issues across the board. On the other hand, to be expert in all areas seems improbable. Hopson, in his critical reflection on portfolio working, highlights the example of a portfolio worker who has eight diverse roles. He then quotes Bruce Lynn of Microsoft who believes the aim should be "jack of many trades and master of some" (Hopson, 2009).

15.5. What Kind of Business Activities Do They Represent?

Generally, soloists operate in areas such as agriculture and construction which have many operators, low barriers to entry and exit, and high competition. However, there is a wide range of such small scale activity. Other categories include the traditional (e.g., arts and crafts from blacksmith to illustrator); retail (e.g., shoe repairs, photography, beauty services); personal and domestic services (e.g., cleaning, catering, child-care, and personal services). Perhaps also considered traditional nowadays would be professional services (e.g. accountants, solicitors, dentists, GPs and consultants — management, computer software or hardware).

How far have these soloists been researched? There are several examples of a sectoral approach to making sense of what is going on. Labor process and employment themes are prominent but there seems little from a marketing perspective specifically on the soloist. Stanworth and Stanworth (1997) explored the role of freelancers in book publishing; Blair (2001) studied freelance workers in the film and media sector; and freelance translators were considered by Fraser and Gold (2001). The entrepreneurial role of freelancers in the construction industry was investigated by Burke (2011). In their research into craft workers in Orkney and elsewhere McAuley and Fillis (2005) addressed a range of craft business types and sizes down to the hobby or part time worker, categories that include many soloists. More recently, other perspectives adopted for groups for whom being a soloist seems particularly relevant include reviews of women (Huang, 2004; Hughes, Jennings, Brush, Carter, & Welter, 2012) and the mature or older worker (Platman, 2003; Weber & Schaper, 2004).

15.6. "It's Not What You Know, It's Who You Know": The Value of Networking

Networking is prominent in digests of the small business and entrepreneurial marketing literature (Conway & Jones, 2012; Halliday, 2011; Shaw, 2012). Gilmore, in summarizing entrepreneurial and small business marketing themes, points to how networking has been increasingly presented as the fundamental process in doing business. Information gathering as owner managers engage face to face with others may arise informally from simple conversation. Owner managers "may be proactive and passive, overt and covert." They are in "constant flux." Networking fits with an individual's way of working (Gilmore, 2011) and is something of an umbrella activity for everything else.

The preference of the entrepreneur for informal cost-effective activity shows up well in the development and use of their relating. The suggestion has been made that as the activity and sales income grows, what might be an unconscious or social process develops to serve more business-focused purposes, and finally a strategic network; and that only part of this may, for example, be used for what we might consider marketing processes (Carson, Cromie, McGowan, & Hill, 1995).

What is called "networking" is a critical process. Many analyses make it also seem a complicated and abstract phenomenon. However, contact with others and the cocreation of community will relieve a sense of isolation. Building a reputation is critical. Networking cannot be planned in any detail and any first encounter is essentially exploratory. New media aside, any one person can only interact locally and with a limited number of people. For the individual deciding what steps to take in relation to the many available groupings and formal organizations can seem baffling. Analyzing logically where to start and in which grouping to engage seems futile. Each first step has to be taken in the spirit of exploratory gesture. Response can be evaluated as part of the peculiar dance of getting to know someone else for the first time.

Furthermore, it is impossible to appreciate the importance of individual encounters, to distinguish between contacts for "business" and contacts for "pleasure." Such significance appears only with hindsight and perhaps after years. Learning can be seen as arising out of social and group processes (Stacey, 2003). Many soloists note the potential problems involved in combining business with friendship, one even quoting the old adage, "never do business with friends." Yet if they followed this as a strict rule, then a very high proportion of their commercial activity — perhaps in one case as much as 70% — might have to be foregone (Fraser, 2000). Nevertheless, some enriching relationships arise, providing a source of support and advice. In the relating, identities are created and reputations emerge.

15.7. How They Learn to Do What They Do

Just as business schools came to be included relatively late as part of UK universities, small business and entrepreneurship has been even more of a newcomer within business schools. Status or its lack rears its head in relation to other areas: I well recall a colleague on hearing about the marketing practice of a part time soloist asking "but is this a real business?"

Formal business school education in the United Kingdom and in its case studies has always tended to be focused on the practice of management and marketing in major corporations. Business plans and planning are prominent in the syllabus, arguably because they can be readily taught (Hills & Hultman, 2005, 2011) and not because they are used by successful entrepreneurs, let alone soloists. In my experience, owner managers who take business school courses and degrees have often expressed some disappointment about the syllabus and its perceived lack of relevance, not least the limited attention given to fundamental issues such as building relationships, sales and selling. Some practitioners and soloists therefore ignore such offerings and shun business schools as places not likely to help them develop insight into their day to day working. Several have made far-reaching observations on the narrow boundaries of management education in the United Kingdom (Blackburn & Kovalainen, 2008). For example, Charles Handy, who conducted a review of the subject, commented that it is "odd, to say the least, that the education which we devise for the best of our managers has so little in it about personality theory, what makes people what they are; or about learning theory, how people grow and develop and change; or political theory, how people seek power, resist power and organize themselves; or moral philosophy, how they decide between right and wrong" (1992). Historically, people have learned how to do business by learning from others, joining groups of "experts" and peers in apprenticeship schemes, as members of guilds, chambers of commerce, professional organizations and the like. Less formal and "local" bodies used by soloists would include business clubs, wealth clubs, religious, sport and hobby groupings and in fact any available forum that might offer friends, allies and role models. In addition to formal knowledge, they would also hold potential value for networking, building social relationships and perhaps even obtaining customers.

In addition to work written for the owner manager generally, there are many nonacademic or "how to" books offering description or guidance specifically for those in business on their own (Bird, 1996; Judson, 2005; Lonier, 1998; Rubin, 2000; Viney & Jones, 1992). Such how-to literature normally offers a limited number of models and guidelines to assist the practitioner. Such concepts seem to be basic and not taxing academically. One piece of guidance suggests some key skills are: be persistent; face facts; minimize risks; learn by doing; be good with numbers; be organized; read carefully (Whitmyer & Rasberry, 1994). Some how-to books aim to provide checklists on some common issues. Bird, for example, stresses how people need to be able to be flexible in adapting to circumstances; but image "is not just the way you dress. It is the perception people have of you and consists of the total picture you present to the world. Other people will form their opinion of you from a number of different facets of you as a whole person — your looks, speech, dress, actions, skills, attitudes, posture, body language, accessories, surroundings and even the company you keep"; and if you present the wrong image in any of these areas it could affect "how keen people are to do business with you" (Bird, 1996, p. 92). But around identity there is clearly a tension between someone meeting the expectations of customers and potential customers and "being yourself." Bird suggests that those who despite their best efforts still feel like a square peg in a round hole should try to find another sector or area in which to work.

In this context we might need to think not only of conventional tangible aids to branding such as documentation and promotional literature, but also of electronic means. How do soloists communicate? How do they set about gaining skills with new media? Cooper's comment about the significance of electronic technology is pertinent. Gilmore seemed optimistic, arguing in relation to SMEs that such technology can be used in conjunction with other business activities; can assist in expanding marketing activities in a cost-effective manner; and can reach a wider or more specific target market. Potentially the relatively low cost is also appealing. However it seems fair to assume that the soloist is even more limited in the resources available for this. It will be even harder to find new skills and resources to establish and maintain web sites complementing conventional marketing. Likewise, new media such as Facebook, Twitter, and LinkedIn require time but in return offer huge potential but Gilmore adds that the owner manager may need support from an e-marketing specialist if this area is to reach its potential. The significance of this is likely to differ from individual to individual. An obvious option is to outsource this activity. But some soloists lack the funds, knowledge, and perhaps even the interest, to ensure that this is implemented professionally.

The cost of training for the soloist may be beyond their budget. But little training appears to exist. One course offered in 2005 under the Business Link brand was presented as a "Painless Business Workshop." The promotional material promises that "You will define the many roles involved in making your small business a success — service delivery, sales, finance, administration, production — and then define the right team to fulfil those roles. This generic offering had no sectoral focus, sounded diffuse and does not seem to have been repeated."

15.8.   The Nature of Solo Working

The pattern of management problems which the small service operation encounters includes fluctuating demand; and therefore the need for extra help to be called in. Things can be extremely fluid. Some who are superficially solo workers will be prone to collaborating on some projects. One designer said that "essentially we're a one-two-three person business depending on what's really happening, what we're involved with."

What looks like a soloist often seems to dissolve and blur on closer exploration and inspection, regardless of the legal vehicle for any trading going on. Family, spouses and other soloists may cooperate from time to time to allow trading to develop or simply to survive a short term crisis; or soloists collaborate on projects which they could not otherwise cope with. Marketing may take up a "considerable amount of time and effort" (Hopson, 2009), others suggesting perhaps as much as one third of the working week. Life can seem a succession of short projects and managing relationships with multiple clients, with the soloist having to manage high degrees of anxiety.

What are the essential differences between the SME owner manager (even of the micro-business) and the soloist? Some of the more obvious distinctions might include the following:

- Differences arising from legal status, that is, between a sole trader and a partnership or limited company.
- A greater degree of informality. Though it might depend on the nature of the activity and the individual, the notion of many soloists producing formal business plan documents seems improbable. Operations are more likely to be carried out with support from diaries, notebooks and back-of-the-envelope stuff only.
- Potentially a greater difficulty in formal delegation; you can only avoid work; subcontract, or delegate informally to family members. However some practitioners carefully cultivate those in their networks with delegation in mind.
- Different level of risk, for example, the greater vulnerability in the case of illness or debility. Such assessments are relative, for example, when compared with a business in which several people were working
- Greater difficulty in, for example, taking holidays or other breaks; obtaining feedback, or appraisal of performance
- More internal or psychic conflict in dealing with offers of "undesirable work"; this is all the more acute if that work which is sought turns out to be in short supply and short term expediency takes over. Might turning down work, or demarketing, be of relatively greater importance to the soloist?
- Psychological pressures; for example of identification with the business; and anxiety and loneliness presumably are more intense; though on the other hand to compensate on the psychological side there may be less pressure resulting from the fact that there are no employees to observe behavior.

15.9.   How Do They Obtain Work? Promotional Activity

High failure rates are assumed, partly at least, to be due to a lack of insight into marketing. Many soloists include those in the arts and crafts who, even now, have little exposure during training to business and marketing theory and practice. What promotional activity does a soloist pursue? Even by the standards of the SME the soloist is likely to be lacking in resources, skills, and impact when it comes to marketing in general and promotion in particular. Marketing, with the exception perhaps of that by specialist marketers, is seen at best as a part time activity carried out by a generalist. But there is no reason in principle why many small scale marketing activities would be unsuitable. A wide range of advertising, PR and personal selling options are feasible. Many soloists have stories around their use of job titles and business cards. Personal appearance is fundamental in some professions. Even within the constraints of working solo, some have devised effective but small scale service enhancements that encouraged positive word of mouth. For example, one hairdresser who worked with clients in their homes would always present them with a high class chocolate on settlement of the bill. To support his exhibition, one artist self-published a glossy coffee-table book of a standard that would put some professional publishers to shame.

For the soloist, selling may present particular problems if they see their personality or disposition as being unsuited to some sales or promotional activity. Some soloists are able to outsource this by using agents. For those dealing in more tangible goods or services and working within a well-defined catchment area, as well as those in the performing arts, being seen to do the job and do it well was sufficiently effective promotion (Fraser, 2000).

15.10.   Where Do They Look for Advice and Assistance?

One of the challenges is to build up supportive relationships with those working the same patch. Such individuals may of course be less potential customers or suppliers than competitor or collaborator. Nevertheless, identifying or cocreating groupings and clubs is likely to be helpful. To take one example, music, whether classical or jazz, is well known as a profession in which there is a serious oversupply of talent, careers take time to build, and the performing life starts late and may be short. Hours of practising can be isolating. Combining the stresses of a freelance life with those of performing can make practitioners feel insecure. A strong sense of living with anxiety is common. Addictions and psychological problems are not unknown (Dobson, 2011). A conference held in London in 2012, the Singing Entrepreneur, provided a venue for young singers in opera and classical music to learn from one another, network and gain mutual support and advice on a whole range of career development issues. Evidence from presentations and discussion confirmed that many in this branch of the performing arts have much competition and little work.

One arts entrepreneur, reflecting on the relative lack of opportunities today compared with the time when she started out on her own performing career, commented: "It takes five years to build a business in this field so that you can eat. Think twice and think very hard before you turn down any work …" To paraphrase her other comments, she stressed that it was critical to build trust and to make yourself useful. There are lots and lots of people around who can sing. But is that all that companies look for? Most opera companies do a lot of education and outreach work but find it hard to get singers who want to do that. Why not do some? Throw yourself into it and get a reputation for helping (Flowers, 2012).

15.11.   What Attitudes and Behavior Do They Encounter among Others?

The image and reputation of a soloist are critical in their marketing. Adjusting the performance of appearance, dress and setting can be critical in influencing attitudes and inspiring trust (Goffman, 1959). Subsequently, there have been references in marketing literature to front stage, back stage, scripts, roles and settings in the context of service encounters (Pine & Gilmore, 1999). In the hospital environment, research has shown that patients have certain expectations of clinicians and many doctors are well aware of this. For example, some doctors have been known to wear white coats or surgical gowns in front of patients when there is absolutely no clinical need for this. In the commercial world, one soloist consultant favored what might be called the chameleon approach, taking on aspects of the culture of the client company as appropriate. If with a banker, you would need to "dress like a banker, walk like a banker ... talk like a banker as well" but simultaneously managing to be authentic to yourself. Success, he suggested, would come from holding both together and from the creative tension between the two sides (Fraser, 2000).

Just as the sector itself is diverse, so too the behaviors can be individualistic. Taking into account the expectations of others, in trading some soloists try to give the impression of having a larger presence than they really do. Some options for this include operating as a limited company rather than a sole trader; adding "and Associates" to the business card; or even in the case of B2B trading, registering for VAT. Others are more comfortable with the image of small scale operating and some by contrast do not want to be thought of as a business (Fraser, 2000). Potential clients are said by soloists to appreciate the constraints they face.

15.12. Conclusions

Qualitative research approaches, such as a contribution from narrative, critical and reflexive accounts by the soloists themselves, might offer some revealing insights into their working lives and how they do business (Blackburn & Kovalainen, 2008). There remains plenty of scope for exploration of multiple and serial ownership of businesses, according to Scott and Rosa, "a rich avenue for study." This is so even among soloists.

Portfolio working seems to have become the generally accepted term. Several of the other expressions applied to soloists, such as micro-business, seem unsatisfactory for other reasons, often implying a future growth and size which is very far from the intentions of the individual concerned. Indeed, some self-employed individuals, consultants, as well as creatives appear to take strong exception to the notion that they were "businesses" at all.

Reviewing the themes reflected in the literatures raises again questions about the dominant way of assessing organizational behavior. Thinking in terms of organizations and indeed SMEs disguises the individual. Focusing on the soloist may throw light on the small scale gesture and response between individuals outside the organization; underline the significance of travelling light, being flexible and not planning very far ahead; and the value of relating, developing social skills and building trust.

What needs does the soloist have? The implication of some of these findings is that the individual needs to develop resilience, greater social skills and the ability to deal with the anxiety of not knowing. Much of these can be enhanced through engaging in networking with others like themselves in informal and formal support groups and organizations.

The soloist tends to be overlooked for a wide range of reasons. Nevertheless the collective contribution of so many individuals to an economy is quite considerable. Furthermore it is a mistake to refer to trading on this scale as simple or insignificant. Even to the individual trading part time or irregularly such experience is likely to have a major impact on identity, confidence and behavior. It might be more appropriate to consider fractal patterning and self-similarity, where patterning is recognizable at all scales, but is never the same. Doing business on the smallest scale will therefore be no less complex and rich than elsewhere.

Acknowledgment

This chapter mainly presents a review of relevant literature. However, some supporting material was drawn from a wide range of research activity spread over almost 20 years. Thanks are due to the large number of people who engaged with me in interview and conversation, and generously "allowed me in," to watch what they were doing and to ask questions. And to Ross Brennan, Julie Gregory and those others who commented on previous versions of this chapter.

References

Anderson, A. R., Dodd, S. D., & Jack, S. L. (2012). Entrepreneurship as connecting: Some implications for theorising and practice. *Management Decision, 50*(5), 958–971.

Bird, P. (1996). *The working woman's handbook: The essential reference guide for every working woman.* London, Judy Piatkus.

BIS. (2012). *Business population estimates for the UK and regions.* The Department for Business, Innovation and Skills (BIS), London.

Blackburn, R., & Kovalainen, A. (2008). Researching small firms and entrepreneurship: Past, present and future. *International Journal of Management Reviews, 11*(2), 127–148.

Blair, H. (2001). You're only as good as your last job': The labour process and labour market in the British film industry. *Work, Employment & Society, 15*(1), 149–169.

Burke, A. (2011). International Review of Entrepreneurship, *9*(3), 1–28.

Carson, D., Cromie, S., McGowan, P., & Hill, J. (1995). *Marketing and entrepreneurship in SMEs: An innovative approach.* London: Prentice Hall.

Clinton, M., Totterdell, P., & Wood, S. (2006). A grounded theory of portfolio working experiencing the smallest of small businesses. *International Small Business Journal, 24*(2), 179–203.

Conway, S., & Jones, O. (2012). Entrepreneurial networks and the small business. In S. Carter & D. Jones-Evans (Eds.), *Enterprise and small business: Principles, practice and policy* (pp. 338–361). Harlow, UK: Pearson Education.

Cooper, C. L. (2005). The future of work: Careers, stress and well-being. *Career Development International, 10*(5), 396–399.

Devin, D., Johnson, S., Gold, J., & Holden, R. (2002). *Management development and learning in micro businesses: A 'missing link' in research and policy*. Leeds, Research and Evaluation Unit, Small Business Service, *51*.

Dobson, M. C. (2011). Insecurity, professional sociability, and alcohol: Young freelance musicians' perspectives on work and life in the music profession. *Psychology of Music, 39*(2), 240–260.

Flowers, K. (2012). It's All About You: Advice to opera singers on getting work. *Speech at the singing entrepreneur conference*, London.

Fraser, J., & Gold, M. (2001). Portfolio workers': Autonomy and control amongst freelance translators. *Work, Employment & Society, 15*(4), 679–697.

Fraser, P. J. (2000). *Surviving on your own: Making sense of the lived experience of self employment*, University of Hertfordshire Business School, Hertfordshire.

Garrì, I. (2010). Political short-termism: a possible explanation. *Public Choice, 145*(1), 197–211.

Gilmore, A. (2011). Entrepreneurial and SME marketing. *Journal of Research in Marketing and Entrepreneurship, 13*(2), 137–145.

Goffman, E. (1959). *The presentation of self in everyday life*. London: Penguin.

Gruenert, J. C. (1999). Second job entrepreneurs. *Occupational Outlook Quarterly, 43*(3), 18–26.

Halliday, S. (2011). Relationship marketing and networks in entrepreneurship. In S. Nwankwo & A. Gbadamosi (Eds.), *Entrepreneurship marketing: Principles and practice of sme marketing* (pp. 230–253). London: Routledge.

Handy, C. (1992). *Annual report & accounts*. The Association of MBAs, London.

Handy, C. (1994). *The empty raincoat*. London: Hutchinson.

Hills, G. E., & Hultman, C. (2011). Research in Marketing and Entrepreneurship: A retrospective viewpoint. *Journal of Research in Marketing and Entrepreneurship, 13*(1), 8–17.

Hills, G. E., and Hultman, C. M. (2005). *Marketing, Entrepreneurship and SMEs: knowledge and education revisited*. 10th Annual Research Symposium, University of Southampton, Academy of Marketing Special Interest Group on Entrepreneurial and Small Business Marketing, Southampton, UK.

Hopson, B. (2009). *From vocational guidance to portfolio careers: A critical reflection*. 12th Annual Lecture, University of Derby, December 10, Derby, UK.

Huang, Y. H., Hammer, L. B., Neal, M. B., & Perrin, N. A. (2004). The relationship between work-to-family conflict and family-to-work conflict: A longitudinal study. *Journal of Family and Economic Issues, 25*, 79–100.

Hughes, K. D., Jennings, J. E., Brush, C., Carter, S., & Welter, F. (2012). Extending women's entrepreneurship research in new directions. *Entrepreneurship Theory and Practice, 36*(3), 429–442.

Judson, B. (2005). *Go it alone!: The secret to building a successful business on your own*. London: HarperBusiness.

Kautonen, T. (2008). Understanding the older entrepreneur: Comparing third age and prime age entrepreneurs in Finland. *International Journal of Business Science and Applied Management, 3*(3), 3–13.

Kautonen, T., Down, S., & South, L. (2008). Enterprise support for older entrepreneurs: the case of PRIME in the UK. *International Journal of Entrepreneurial Behaviour & Research, 14*(2), 85–101.

Lonier, T. (1998). *Working solo*. London: Wiley.

Macrae, N. (1976). The coming entrepreneurial revolution. *The Economist*.

McAuley, A. (1998). The mirror and the lamp: Representing the entrepreneur. *Journal of Marketing Management, 14*(7), 721–731.

McAuley, A., & Fillis, I. (2005). The Orkney based craft entrepreneur: remote yet global? *Journal of Small Business and Enterprise Development, 12*(4), 498–509.

Pine, B. J., & Gilmore, J. H. (1999). *The experience economy: Work is theatre and every business a stage.* Boston MA: Harvard Business School Press.

Pink, D. H. (2001). *Free agent nation: How America's new independent workers are transforming the way we live.* New York, NY: Grand Central Publications.

Platman, K. (2003). The self-designed career in later life: A study of older portfolio workers in the United Kingdom. *Ageing and Society, 23*(3), 281–302.

Richard, D. (2008). *Small business & government: The Richard report.* London.

Rubin, H. (2000). *Soloing: Reaching life's everest.* London: Random House.

Scott, M., & Rosa, P. (1996). Has firm level analysis reached its limits? Time for a rethink. *International Small Business Journal, 14*(4), 81–89.

Shaw, E. (2012). Entrepreneurial marketing. In S. Carter & D. Jones-Evans (Eds.), *Enterprise and small business: Principles, practice and policy* (pp. 319–337). Harlow, UK: Pearson Education.

Shaw, E., & Conway, S. (2000). Networking and the small firm. In S. Carter & D. Jones-Evans (Eds.), *Enterprise and small business: Principles, practice and policy* (pp. 367–383). Harlow, UK: Pearson Education.

Stacey, R. (2003). Learning as an activity of interdependent people. *The Learning Organization, 10*, 325–331.

Stanworth, J., & Stanworth, C. (1997). Reluctant entrepreneurs and their clients: The case of self-employed freelance workers in the British book publishing industry. *International Small Business Journal, 16*(1), 58–73.

The Economist. (1992). Economics focus: Being your own boss. *The Economist,* p. 324.

Viney, J., & Jones, S. (1992). *One man band.* London: Thorsons.

Weber, P., & Schaper, M. (2004). Understanding the grey entrepreneur. *Journal of Enterprising Culture, 12*(02), 147–164.

Whitmyer, C., & Rasberry, S. (1994). *Running a one-person business.* Berkeley, CA: Ten Speed Press.

About the Authors

Pierre Berthon, Ph.D., is the Clifford F. Youse chair of marketing and strategy at Bentley University. He previously held academic positions at Columbia University, Henley Management College, Cardiff University and University of Bath, and has also taught at Rotterdam School of Management, Copenhagen Business School, Norwegian School of Economics and Management, University of Cape Town and Athens Laboratory of Business Administration. His research focuses on the interaction of technology, corporate strategy and consumer behavior, and has appeared in *Sloan Management Review*, *California Management Review*, *Information Systems Research*, *Technological Forecasting and Social Change*, *Journal of the Academy of Marketing Science*, *Journal of Business Research*, *Journal of International Marketing*, *Business Horizons*, and *Journal of Business Ethics*.

Björn Bjerke is a senior professor of entrepreneurship at Linnaeus University in Sweden. He has been involved in theory as well as in practice of this subject for more than 30 years and has published several internationally recognized books on the subject. His research during the past eight years or so has concentrated on social entrepreneurship.

David Carson is emeritus professor of marketing at the University of Ulster. His research interests lie in marketing for SMEs and service industries, particularly in travel and tourism. He has published in a variety of international journals and written three books on these themes. He has wide business experience both in consultancy and directorship roles. He is past president of the Academy of Marketing.

Amitava Chattopadhyay is the chaired professor in marketing and innovation at INSEAD. He is an expert on branding and innovation and has most recently published "The New Emerging Market Multinationals: Four Strategies for Disrupting Markets and Building Brands." He has published more than 60 articles, with the majority appearing in leading international journals such as the *Journal of Marketing Research, Journal of Consumer Research, Journal of Marketing*, and *Marketing Science*. He is an associate editor for the *Journal of Consumer Psychology* and the *International Journal of Research in Marketing*. He is on the board of the *Association for Consumer Research*. For his research, he has been the recipient of the Robert Ferber Award and Best Business Book of 2012 for strategy, from strategy + business. He is a fellow of the Institute on Asian Consumer Insights and the Ernst & Young Institute for emerging market studies. He has taught and consulted for MNCs in Europe, United States, Australia, Asia, and Africa.

Jenny Darroch is a professor of marketing & MBA academic director at the Peter F. Drucker and Masatoshi Ito Graduate School of Management. Prior to joining the Drucker School, she was the director of entrepreneurship and a senior lecturer (associate professor) in marketing at the University of Otago in New Zealand. Her research examines the interface between marketing, innovation and entrepreneurship. Her research currently focuses on how firms create new markets and transform existing markets through marketing and entrepreneurial activities (in fact, this inspired a new course she offered EMP students called "Transforming and Creating Markets to Generate Growth"). Her publications appear in leading journals such as the *European Journal of Marketing, Journal of Business Ethics*, and the *Journal of Small Business Management*. A career highlight was coediting (with George Day and Stan Slater) a Special Issue of the *Journal of the Academy of Marketing Science: A Tribute to Peter Drucker* in 2009.

Blakley Davis is a Ph.D. candidate in the School of Entrepreneurship at Oklahoma State University. He received both an MBA and a BBA in management from Texas Tech University. His research interests include examining the tactics undertaken by nascent entrepreneurs to attract financial capital — particularly within nontraditional funding contexts, and exploring the determinants of new venture emergence through the lens of complexity science.

Jonathan H. Deacon is a reader in marketing and entrepreneurship at the Newport Business School and is a graduate of the University of Wales and Ulster Business School. He is a trustee and fellow of the Chartered Institute of Marketing and editor of the *International Journal for Research in Marketing and Entrepreneurship* (JRME). At Newport Business School he is director of the Centre for Research in Entrepreneurship and Marketing (CREaM) where his research focuses on how small entrepreneurial firms "go to market" and he is a visiting academic at a number of universities in Europe and the United States. For relaxation he "enjoys" adventure sports.

Peter Fraser is a senior lecturer in marketing in the Hertfordshire Business School at the University of Hertfordshire. His teaching and research interests lie in micro and social enterprise, small business and entrepreneurial marketing; complexity; and arts marketing, particularly the marketing of opera. His doctoral thesis addressed the survival of the solo self-employed and his interest in this has continued ever since. He is active in the AM SIGs for entrepreneurial and small business marketing; and arts, heritage, nonprofit and social marketing. He is cofounder and consultant editor of Opera Scotland, the web site for listings and performance history.

Damian Gallagher is a lecturer and M.Sc./PGDip marketing course director in the Department of Marketing, Entrepreneurship and Strategy at the University of Ulster. His teaching and research interests are in the areas of relationship marketing, research methodologies, SME marketing and the marketing of small sports clubs. He has published widely in leading marketing journals including the *Journal of Research in Marketing and Entrepreneurship, Journal of Strategic Marketing, Journal of Small Business & Entrepreneurship, The Marketing Review, European Business Review, and Consumption Markets and Culture.* He currently serves on the editorial board for the *European Journal of Marketing*, as well as being an ad hoc reviewer for a range of marketing and small business journals including *Journal of Marketing Management, Journal of Small Business & Entrepreneurship, Asia Pacific Management Review, International Journal of Economic Sciences and Applied Research, International Entrepreneurship & Management Journal,* and *International Journal of Entrepreneurial Behaviour & Research.* He is a member of various organising committees, reviewing panels and track chair for number of academic conferences including the *Academy of Marketing, International Colloquium in Relationship Marketing* and the *Institute of Small Business & Entrepreneurship* and an active member and contributor to the UIC/AMA Marketing and Entrepreneurship Interface Group (USA).

Audrey Gilmore is a professor of services marketing in the Ulster Business School at the University of Ulster. Her teaching and research interests are in service marketing and management, SME marketing, competencies, networking, contemporary issues, and qualitative research methodologies. She has published in a variety of international journals and written three books on these themes. She was coeditor of the *European Journal of Marketing* for 14 years and is a member of editorial boards for a number of marketing and small business journals. Currently she is the Academy of Marketing's (UK) regional chair for Ireland; the Academy of Marketing's Special Interest Group (SIG) coordinator; and an active member and contributor to the UIC/AMA Marketing and Entrepreneurship Interface Group (USA).

Paul Harrigan is an assistant professor of marketing at the University of Western Australia. He received his Ph.D. on the topic of CRM from the University of Ulster, UK in 2008. His research interests span customer relationship management (CRM), social media marketing, and small business marketing. He has published in these areas in journals such as the *Journal of Marketing Management* and the *International Journal of Electronic Commerce*. He also teaches in these areas and broader marketing areas at his home institution in Australia and as a visiting professor at the University of Southampton, UK and IESEG School of Management, France. He is a member of a range of academic bodies, such as the Australian and New Zealand Marketing Association, the Institute of Direct and Digital Marketing, and the UK Academy of Marketing holding several committee positions that are responsible for conference management, and directions in research and education.

Jacqueline Harris is a senior lecturer in marketing and entrepreneurship in Newport Business, University of South Wales, UK. Her teaching and research interests are in the marketing entrepreneurship interface and in particular exploring how SMEs go to market, through their engagement with communities of interest and practice and contemporary issues such as their use of digital technology. She has presented at conferences in the United Kingdom, Europe, United States, Australia and China and published in a variety of peer-reviewed journals. She is a codirector of the Centre for Research in Entrepreneurship and Marketing (CREaM) and is a member of editorial review boards for a number of marketing and small business journals. Currently she is an active member of the Academy of Marketing's (UK) Special Interest Group (SIG) and an active member of the Institute of Small Business and Entrepreneurship (ISBE). She is a CIM Chartered Marketer and holds a fellowship from the National Council for Enterprise Education. She is currently completing her Ph.D. in the marketing/entrepreneurship interface focusing on small firms.

Gerald E. Hills holds the endowed Turner chair of Entrepreneurship at Bradley University. Dr. Hills earned his doctorate at Indiana University and was a pioneer in the development of the entrepreneurship discipline. Prior to joining Bradley, he developed an entrepreneurship program at another university that was consistently ranked in the top 10 nationally. Through his teaching he has spread entrepreneurship seeds among thousands of students. He has written and edited more than 100 entrepreneurship articles and 25 books, was the cofounder and first president of the U.S. Association for Small Business and Entrepreneurship (USASBE), and president of the International Council for Small Business (ICSB). He was also the cofounder and first president of the American Marketing Association Academic Council and a board director of the AMA. Finally, Dr. Hills is founder and president of the Collegiate Entrepreneurs' Organization (CEO), inspiring and supporting students who seek to become entrepreneurs. CEO clubs are on 180 university campuses nationally and the Annual CEO Conference attracts 1600 attendees.

He chaired an advisory board of the U.S. Small Business Administration under President Reagan, and, as Communism fell, he advanced entrepreneurship in Poland through a U.S. Congressional Commission and two other projects. He is currently expanding CEO and leading an effort to take entrepreneurship across all the colleges at Bradley as chair of the President's Committee on Entrepreneurship and Innovation.

Dr. Hills has received numerous awards including being named a Wilford L. White Fellow of ICSB; a Justin G. Longenecker Fellow of USASBE; the Advocate Award from the Academy of Management for "Outstanding Contributions to the Field of Entrepreneurship"; the Leavey Award for Excellence by the Freedoms Foundation at Valley Forge; the NASDAQ Center of Entrepreneurial Excellence Award; Entrepreneur of the Year Award, Ernst & Young; and the UIC Alumni Leadership Award.

Claes M. Hultman holds a Ph.D. in marketing and is a professor of business administration at Örebro University in Sweden. He is the author of many books and articles in marketing and entrepreneurship. He is currently on the editorial board of different scholarly US and UK journals and serves on the board of directors for several companies. Most of his research today is in the interface of marketing, entrepreneurship and innovation. He is also vice chair of the entrepreneurship SIG within the American Marketing Association.

Rosalind Jones is a Lecturer in Marketing at Birmingham University- as well as visiting lecturer at Singapore Institute of Management (SIM) for Birmingham University, and a fellow of the Higher Education Academy (FHEA). Previously she was a lecturer at Bangor Business School, Wales and a visiting professor at Jyvaskyla University, Finland. She teaches entrepreneurship at SIM, the Singapore Institute of Management. She is an active member of ISBE, the Institute of Small Business and Enterprise, a founder member of GIKA the Global Innovation and Knowledge Academy, and on the steering committee of the University of Illinois Chicago (UIC)/American Marketing Association (AMA) Marketing and Entrepreneurship Interface Group, USA. She is also a Member of the Academy of Marketing (AM), UK and she cochairs the Academy of Marketing Special Interest Group in small business and entrepreneurial marketing with Zubin Sethna. She is a member of the "Senior Levitt Group" at the Chartered Institute of Marketing (CIM), and a "Chartered Marketer." She is the CIM SME Ambassador for North Wales. Her research interests include entrepreneurship and small business, entrepreneurial marketing and more specifically, marketing in SMEs. Her current research focus is on technology and hospitality industries, innovation, e-marketing in SMEs, internationalisation strategies, and the strategic orientation of SMEs. She has published in leading marketing and small business journals including the *Journal of Research in Marketing and Entrepreneurship, International Journal of Marketing Research, Journal of Marketing Management, International Small Business Journal, Journal of Small Business and Enterprise Development, The Services Industries Journal,* and the *International Journal of Entrepreneurial Behaviour and Research.* She serves on the editorial advisory boards of *Management Decision* and the *Journal of Research in Marketing and Entrepreneurship.* She is a reviewer for several other international journals and conferences in this field. In 2012 she received the Emerald Outstanding Reviewer of the Year and her paper (Jones and Rowley) published in the International Small Business Journal was a top "most read" paper in 2012.

Chickery J. Kasouf is an associate professor of marketing in the Worcester Polytechnic Institute (USA) School of Business. His research interests are in opportunity recognition, family business, and interfirm relationships in the supply chain. His research has been published in several journals and has been funded by the Alfred P. Sloan Foundation, the Metal Powder Industries Federation, and the US Army Research Laboratory. He served as chair of the AMA Marketing and Entrepreneurship Special Interest Group, was a founding member of the Industry Studies Association, and is a member of the advisory board for the Research Symposium on Marketing and Entrepreneurship.

Olivia F. Lee is a marketing consultant and an adjunct professor of marketing at Northwest University, USA. She has worked as an operation manager at two university hospitals and as a senior e-business market analyst in a business-to-business company prior to her academic career. She is a two-time Target Corporation teaching award-winner for her capstone strategic management courses. As an active researcher with multiple streams of research interest, her work focuses on technology practices in business environment, health care and service organization, and business resilience strategy. She has published her work at *Psychology and Marketing, Healthcare Marketing Quarterly, Journal of Information Technology Management, International Journal of Organization Analysis, International Journal of Healthcare Information Systems and Informatics, International Journal of Information System Change Management, International Journal of Quality & Reliability Management, Review of Business Research*, and book chapters on marketing and technology.

Andrew McAuley joined Southern Cross University in December 2010 as pro vice chancellor (academic) having previously been a professor of marketing and head of the Department of Marketing at Griffith University. Prior to coming to Australia, in July 2009, he was head of the Department of Marketing at the University of Stirling in Scotland. His research interests have focused for some time on marketing management issues in the smaller enterprise, especially in relation to the marketing/entrepreneurship interface. He has published widely in leading marketing journals including the *European Journal of Marketing, Journal of Marketing Management, Journal of Strategic Marketing, Journal of*

Research in Marketing and Entrepreneurship, and the *Journal of Consumer Marketing*. He serves on the editorial advisory boards for *European Journal of Marketing*, *Journal of Research in Marketing and Entrepreneurship*, and *The International Journal of Management Education*. He is a founding coeditor of the *Journal of Social Marketing* launched in 2011. In addition he is the vice-president of the UK Academy of Marketing.

Morgan P. Miles is a professor of enterprise development at the University of Tasmania. Previously, he served as professor of marketing at Georgia Southern University. He has been a visiting scholar at Georgia Tech, Cambridge, University of Stockholm, the University of Otago, University of Auckland, and an Erskine Fellow at the University of Canterbury. He holds a DBA in marketing from Mississippi State University, an MS in agricultural economics from Virginia Tech, and a BS in agricultural economics from Mississippi State. His research interests include entrepreneurship, innovation, entrepreneurial marketing, and corporate social responsibility, resulting in more than 100 journal articles published.

Adam Mills is a doctoral student in marketing in the Beedie School of Business, Simon Fraser University, Vancouver, Canada. He holds a BA in sociology from the University of British Columbia, and an MBA from Simon Fraser University. An award-winning educator and case writer, he teaches classes in marketing strategy and business policy. His doctoral research focuses on the staging of experiences by the "famous," including celebrity chefs and rock stars. His work has been published in journals such as *Business Horizons*, *Journal of Public Affairs*, and the *Journal of Wine Business Research*.

Michael H. Morris, Ph.D., is the Ethridge professor entrepreneurship at the University of Florida. In addition to starting three ventures, he has built top-ranked entrepreneurship programs at three major universities. A pioneer in curricular innovation and experiential learning, his outreach efforts have facilitated the start-up and growth of hundreds of ventures. He has published ten books and over 130 articles in peer-reviewed academic journals. He is coeditor of the Prentice Hall Entrepreneurship Series and editor emeritus of the *Journal of Developmental Entrepreneurship*. In addition, he is a past president of the United States Association for Small Business and Entrepreneurship, and served as a chair of the American Marketing Association's Entrepreneurship and Marketing Taskforce. A former Fulbright Scholar, he has received the Appel Prize for contributions to the entrepreneurship and the Leavey Award for his impact on private enterprise education. He also received the AMA's Gerald E. Hills Best Paper Award for outstanding contributions to entrepreneurial marketing.

Sussie C. Morrish gained her Ph.D. from the University of Canterbury while simultaneously teaching at the University of Auckland Business School. She teaches strategic marketing from basic to advanced levels. Her main research interests revolve around the marketing and entrepreneurship disciplines including various strategic approaches to portfolio entrepreneurship, airline alliances, internationalisation, sustainability, and country of origin effects. Internationally recognised as a thought leader at the Marketing and Entrepreneurship Interface, she received the Outstanding Paper Award at the 2012 Literati Network Awards for Excellence. Her work is published in international journals including *the Journal of International Marketing, Journal of Strategic Marketing, Advances in Consumer Research*, and the *Journal of Research in Marketing and Entrepreneurship*. She is currently an associate head of the Department of Management, Marketing and Entrepreneurship at the University of Canterbury.

Chloë H. Nelson is the marketing and operations director at Nelson's Eye Patch based in Norfolk, UK, responsible for communications strategy, business development in growth markets, and supply chain management. She graduated in 2011 with a first-class honours B.Sc. degree in Publishing with E-business from Loughborough University. Her studies included knowledge and information management, social informatics, organisational theory and culture and change management. Her current research uses qualitative methods to focus on the use of social media by small businesses and entrepreneurial marketing strategy. In addition to providing consultancy to local SMEs on emerging digital communication channels, social media strategy and marketing trends, she serves as a committee member on the Holt Chamber of Trade and Commerce.

Michele O'Dwyer lectures entrepreneurship, innovation, and marketing in the Kemmy Business School at the University of Limerick. Through her close links with industry she contributes to research on innovation in SMEs, SME marketing, new product development and marketing communications. She has published in a variety of international journal such as *Journal of Product and Innovation Management, European Journal of Marketing, Journal of International Management,* and *Journal of Strategic Marketing.*

Leyland F. Pitt, Ph.D., is the Dennis Culver EMBA alumni chair of business, Beedie School of Business, Simon Fraser University, Vancouver, Canada, and also affiliate professor in industrial marketing at the Royal Institute of Technology, Stockholm, Sweden. He has also taught on executive and MBA programs at schools such as the Graham School of Continuing Studies (University of Chicago), Columbia University Graduate School of Business, Rotterdam School of Management, and London Business School. His work has been published in such journals, as *Information Systems Research, Journal of the Academy of Marketing Science, Sloan Management Review, California Management Review, Communications of the ACM,* and *MIS Quarterly* (which he also served as associate editor). In 2000 he was the recipient of the Tamer Cavusgil Award of the American Marketing Association for best article in the *Journal of International Marketing* and in 2010 he won the Elsevier Award for the best paper in *Business Horizons.*

Zubin Sethna's, Ph.D., thesis examines the entrepreneurial marketing activities within ethnic firms in the United Kingdom, and his research interests lie at the marketing and entrepreneurship interface. As a principal lecturer (associate professor) in marketing at the University of Bedfordshire's Business School, he oversees the postgraduate portfolio. He has successfully launched five businesses (one of which won a National Award) and in his capacity as managing consultant at Baresman Consulting (www.baresman.com), he has integrated marketing strategy/communications with management consultancy and training for numerous organizations both in the United Kingdom and internationally, and across a variety of industry sectors (including health care, professional services, music, travel, manufacturing, retail, it, education and "cottage" industries). These 22 years of industry experience allow him to take a practice-based approach to teaching whenever he is in the classroom. He previously taught innovation and entrepreneurship on the AMBA accredited MBA program at the University of Westminster, and prior to that ran an immensely popular and successful "Business Start-up" program for creative industry graduates from the University of the Arts London. He is currently cochair of the Academy of Marketing's Special Interest Group on "Entrepreneurial and Small Business Marketing" (with Rosalind Jones) and has been invited to conduct keynote lectures at HE institutions in the United Kingdom, European Union, and China and India, and regularly speaks at South East Asia's leading Business School, the Indian Institute of Management Ahmadabad (IIMA). He also serves as an editorial board member for two respected international journals: *Journal of Research in Marketing and Entrepreneurship* and *Journal of Urban Regeneration and Renewal*. In addition to this, he has also previously been instrumental in attracting funding in excess of £350k for academic projects from leading public and private bodies such as Department for Education and Skills (DfES), Learning and Skills Council UK, and Harrods!

Eleanor Shaw, MA, Ph.D., is a professor of entrepreneurship at the Hunter Centre for Entrepreneurship (HCE), University of Strathclyde Business School. She is currently Principal Investigator of an Economic and Social Research Council funded project which is exploring contemporary entrepreneurial philanthropy and is a lead researcher within the UK-wide Centre for Charitable Giving and Philanthropy (www.cgap.org.uk). Her work has been published in leading peer reviewed journal including *British Journal of Management, Business History, Entrepreneurship Theory and Practice, European Journal of Marketing*, and *International Small Business Journal*. She is regularly invited to speak on entrepreneurial networks and has presented research on this topic to audiences including academic researchers, entrepreneurs, policy makers and students both in the United Kingdom and abroad. She sits on an advisory board of Foundation Scotland is a board member of Impact Arts, director of Newcastle based consultancy firm Actif and a founding member of the AOM Special Interest Group in Entrepreneurial Marketing. Eleanor is passionate about engaging in research which can generate broader societal benefits and, as a researcher, is committed to providing evidence based research.

David Stokes is emeritus professor of entrepreneurship at Kingston University. Following education at Oriel College, Oxford and the City University Business School, he has combined a practical as well as an academic involvement with small and medium-sized enterprises and new ventures. He is the chairman of an LED technology company that he cofounded and a director of a well established electronics manufacturer. He held responsibility for the development of entrepreneurship education amongst students and staff of all disciplines at Kingston University and six other Universities collaborating in the WestFocus consortium until 2011. He was chair of the Higher Education Entrepreneurship Group (HEEG) that covers 23 universities in south east England from 2005 to 2011. His research interests include entrepreneurial marketing and business exits. As well as many academic journal and publications, he is author of popular text books including: *Entrepreneurship* (2010); *Small Business Management and Entrepreneurship* (6th ed., 2010); and *Marketing: A Brief Introduction* (2009), all published by Cengage Learning.

Daniel Sun received his undergraduate degree in finance and international business as well as his master's degree in marketing from the University of Manitoba. He is currently pursuing his Ph.D. in marketing in the field of consumer behaviour at the University of British Columbia. His research interests include brand consumer relationships and cross cultural consumer behavior.

Mari Suoranta is an assistant professor in marketing at the University of Jyvaskyla, Finland. Her current research interests include entrepreneurial start-up marketing, firm growth, and management & entrepreneurship education. In 2008 and 2010–2011 she was a senior Fulbright Scholar at the Center for Entrepreneurship & Technology and the Fung Institute for Engineering Leadership at the University of California Berkeley, USA. Her work has been published, for example, in the *Journal of Marketing Management, Service Industries Journal*, and *Journal of Financial Services Marketing*, and presented at various international conferences such as European Academy of Marketing Conference, AMA Educators' Conference, Academy of Marketing Science, Academy of Marketing, ICSB World Conference. She is a member of the Academy of Marketing Special Interest Group in Entrepreneurial & Small Business Marketing and European Council for Small Business and Entrepreneurship.

Can Uslay is an assistant professor of SCM and marketing sciences at Rutgers Business School, NJ. He earned his MBA and Ph.D. from the Georgia Institute of Technology. His research interests lie broadly within marketing strategy and theory construction. He is a recipient of the 2010 Valerie Scudder Award for outstanding scholarly activity. His research has been presented in over two dozen conferences and published in the leading academic journals such as the *Journal of Marketing, Journal of the Academy of Marketing Science, European Business Review, International Journal of*

Technology Management, International Journal of Quality & Reliability Management, Journal of Business-to-Business Marketing, Journal of Public Policy & Marketing, Journal of Research in Marketing & Entrepreneurship, Marketing Education Review, and the *Review of Marketing Research.* He currently serves as the vice-chair of research for the entrepreneurial marketing SIG of the American Marketing Association.

Fang Wan is an associate professor of marketing, Ross Johnson Research Fellow at the Asper School of Business of the University of Manitoba, Canada. Her research interests include brand management, cross-cultural consumer behavior, and media and advertising effects. She has published more than 30 articles some of which appeared in *Organization Behaviour and Human Decision Process, Journal of Personality and Social Psychology, Journal of Business Ethics, Journal of Advertising,* and *Journal of Interactive Marketing.* She has been actively teaching, researching brand management, and integrating them into her consulting work. With her Brand Consortium, a brand consulting platform she created for Canadian business communities, she and her team have provided brand consultation services to Canadian companies, ranging from small family business to industry conglomerates, representing a vast number of industries. Her brand workshops have won raving reviews from participants on both sides of the Pacific Ocean.

Sengun Yeniyurt is an associate professor of marketing and the vice-chair of the supply chain management and marketing sciences department at Rutgers Business School. He serves as the academic coordinator of the undergraduate and graduate marketing programs. He studied at Michigan State University, where he earned a Ph.D. in marketing and international business. He is an expert global marketing strategist who specializes in product and brand management as well as supplier relationship management. His work has appeared in journals such as the *Journal of Product Innovation Management, Journal of International Business Studies, Journal of International Marketing, International Marketing Review, International Business Review, Journal of Supply Chain Management,* and *Marketing Letters.* He has received numerous awards for his accomplishments in research and teaching. He frequently organizes and teaches in executive training and professional certificate programs. He has conducted research and provided expert consultation for projects regarding companies such as Bridgestone, BMW, Chrysler, General Motors, Lockheed Martin, and Toyota.